Owen Barfield

Philosophy, Poetry, and Theology

VERITAS
Series Introduction

"... the truth will set you free" (John 8:32)

In much contemporary discourse, Pilate's question has been taken to mark the absolute boundary of human thought. Beyond this boundary, it is often suggested, is an intellectual hinterland into which we must not venture. This terrain is an agnosticism of thought: because truth cannot be possessed, it must not be spoken. Thus, it is argued that the defenders of "truth" in our day are often traffickers in ideology, merchants of counterfeits, or anti-liberal. They are, because it is somewhat taken for granted that Nietzsche's word is final: truth is the domain of tyranny.

Is this indeed the case, or might another vision of truth offer itself? The ancient Greeks named the love of wisdom as *philia*, or friendship. The one who would become wise, they argued, would be a "friend of truth." For both philosophy and theology might be conceived as schools in the friendship of truth, as a kind of relation. For like friendship, truth is as much discovered as it is made. If truth is then so elusive, if its domain is *terra incognita*, perhaps this is because it arrives to us—unannounced—as gift, as a person, and not some thing.

The aim of the Veritas book series is to publish incisive and original current scholarly work that inhabits "the between" and "the beyond" of theology and philosophy. These volumes will all share a common aspiration to transcend the institutional divorce in which these two disciplines often find themselves, and to engage questions of pressing concern to both philosophers and theologians in such a way as to reinvigorate both disciplines with a kind of interdisciplinary desire, often so absent in contemporary academe. In a word, these volumes represent collective efforts in the befriending of truth, doing so beyond the simulacra of pretend tolerance, the violent, yet insipid reasoning of liberalism that asks with Pilate, "What is truth?"—expecting a consensus of non-commitment; one that encourages the commodification of the mind, now sedated by the civil service of career, ministered by the frightened patrons of position.

The series will therefore consist of two "wings": (1) original monographs; and (2) essay collections on a range of topics in theology and philosophy. The latter will principally be the products of the annual conferences of the Centre of Theology and Philosophy (www.theologyphilosophycentre .co.uk).

Conor Cunningham and Eric Austin Lee, *Series editors*

Owen Barfield

Philosophy, Poetry, and Theology

MICHAEL VINCENT DI FUCCIA
FOREWORD BY OWEN A. BARFIELD

CASCADE *Books* · Eugene, Oregon

OWEN BARFIELD
Philosophy, Poetry, and Theology

Veritas 20

Cascade Books
An Imprint of Wipf and Stock Publishers
199 W. 8th Ave., Suite 3
Eugene, OR 97401

www.wipfandstock.com

PAPERBACK ISBN: 978-1-4982-3872-4
HARDCOVER ISBN: 978-1-4982-3874-8
EBOOK ISBN: 978-1-4982-3873-1

Cataloguing-in-Publication data:

Names: Di Fuccia, Michael Vincent

Title: Owen Barfield : philosophy, poetry, and theology / Michael Vincent Di Fuccia.

Description: Eugene, OR: Cascade Books, 2016 | Series: Veritas | Includes bibliographical references and index.

Identifiers: ISBN 978-1-4982-3872-4 (paperback) | ISBN 978-1-4982-3874-8 (hardcover) | ISBN 978-1-4982-3873-1 (ebook)

Subjects: 1. Barfield, Owen, 1898–1997. 2. Philosophers—Great Britain—20th century. I. Barfield, Owen A. II. Series. III. Title.

Classification: B1618.B284 D392 2016 (print) | B1618.B284 (ebook)

Manufactured in the U.S.A.   OCTOBER 24, 2016

Contents

Foreword

ATTENTION TO GRANDFATHER'S WORK has ebbed and flowed over the century since he was first published, but in recent years the tide of admirers has been rising. Grandfather's work has a way of freeing us because it illuminates not just where we are, but why and how we got here. With this knowledge comes the joy of relief. That joy arises with the uncovering of a truth that is surprisingly simple, if we are shown in what direction to look. My gratitude goes to Michael Di Fuccia who has stood tall and pointed the way.

This essay is a milestone in Barfieldian studies. The contention is that Grandfather's thesis regarding the history of word meanings—that over time word meaning fades—is not merely about words and their meaning, but also about the recovery of a vision of ultimate reality in which the qualities of the world that transcend the realm of the sense perceptible are taken to be constitutively real in order that we might overcome our present idolatrous gaze (e.g., positivism) and its savage consequences. Di Fuccia shows that Grandfather's desire to envisage poetry as the perfecting of prose, and the imagination as the perfecting of reason, is no whimsical assertion. It is a thorough and coherent scheme that is intended to redirect us beyond our present gaze to a reality replete with meaning and significance. We are reminded that it is this "poetic philosophy" that lies at the heart of Grandfather's life work.

Grandfather's poetic philosophy is placed alongside early modern and contemporary trends in philosophy, the social and physical sciences, and theology, in order to show that it actually outwits early modern developments in secular thought that are still very much with us today. The argument goes that Grandfather's poetic philosophy is actually more philosophical than philosophies of immanence precisely because it admits to philosophy's real need of inspiration (via the imagination) or its "openness." Grandfather's attention to this openness is ahead of his time, because, as Di Fuccia stresses, the greatest and most promising achievement of Grandfather's poetic

philosophy is that it intimates a theological or middle realm that is denied
by philosophies of immanence. This is the impetus for the final portion of
the essay wherein he takes Grandfather's poetic philosophy to its theological
culmination, "theology as poetic metaphysics."

Grandfather's voice is like a distant drumbeat drawing us to the parade
where we find like-minded revelers enjoying the rhythm of the festivities.
This essay brings a heightened awareness of that voice which stirs inside us.
Following Di Fuccia's appraisal Grandfather's voice is noticeably resounding
louder and clearer, and we look forward to the gathering it heralds. Grandfather's has been the quiet voice, but we may still find it to be the most
persuasive.

Owen A. Barfield

Grandson & Trustee
Oxfordshire, England
www.owenbarfield.org

Acknowledgements

I WOULD FIRST LIKE to thank my doctoral supervisor John Milbank for his constant patience and encouragement. Before I met John I had no idea it was possible for one man to have the intellectual capacity and charm of twenty. More often than not, his grace and humor were a welcomed antidote for my incompetence. Additionally, I am grateful for the academic and pastoral guidance of Simon Oliver, who was kind enough to take me on as a teaching assistant and trust me with his theology students. From him, I have learned so much. His example is something all of us should strive to attain. Also, I owe a special thanks to Conor Cunningham for his many lectures and conversations on philosophy and theology, and for trusting me with his students in the philosophy of religion seminars. If in my lifetime I can obtain half of his wit (and good looks) I will certainly have succeeded. I am deeply indebted to Catherine Pickstock for her continued intellectual generosity and her painstaking reading and commentary on my initial draft. I am forever grateful for my friendship with Eric Austin Lee, who embraced me as a new doctoral student. His academic and spiritual generosity sustained me throughout this process. I could not have asked for a kinder spirit with whom to have shared in this journey. I would also like to thank Owen A. Barfield, grandson of Owen Barfield, for his continued friendship and permission to view the "Owen Barfield Papers" at the Bodleian Library, Oxford University.

I also want to thank my parents, Chip and Janet. Thank you for believing in me time and time again. As a child, there is nothing better than to know that your parents love and approve of you. Thank you for constantly telling me how proud you are of me. I would not be who I am without you. The same goes for my little sisters, Janelle and Carly. Thanks for loving me even though I am so far away. I am always amazed by your capacity to love unconditionally.

Lastly, and most importantly, a huge thanks to my beautiful wife Sara. I love you. Thank you for literally risking it all with me and for leaving everything behind to follow God on this crazy adventure. Thank you for teaching me day in and day out what faith looks like. I could not have asked for a more unique, funny, pretty, passionate, and loving person to spend my life with, and, come to think of it, now that I'm done we can finally get started!

Introduction

> We must, then, make our choice. The whole basis of epistemology from Aristotle to Aquinas assumed participation, and the problem was merely the precise manner in which that participation operated. We can either conclude that this persistent assumption was a piece of elaborate self-deception, which just happened to last, not only from Aristotle but from the beginnings of human thought down to the fifteenth or sixteenth century A.D., or we can assume that there really was participation. I should find the second hypothesis the less fantastic of the two
> . . . .
>
> —Barfield[1]

Owen Barfield: A Poetic Philosopher

ARTHUR OWEN BARFIELD (1898–1997), "the first and last Inkling," has yet to obtain the legendary status of his fellows, yet he has had a profound influence on their thought. Lewis thought him quite remarkable, referring to Barfield as "the wisest and best of my unofficial teachers," who "towers above us all."[2] Eminent Tolkien scholar Verlyn Flieger claims that it

---

1. Barfield, *Saving the Appearances*, 97.

2. Lewis, *All My Road Before Me*, 67. See also, Adey, *C. S. Lewis' Great War*, 122. Adey's work highlights the influence Barfield had on Lewis. He concludes his erudite philosophical exposition of the intellectual exchange between the two as follows: "I express the belief that though Barfield's books . . . will never attract so wide a readership as the far more numerous books by Lewis, they will be read longer and more to make a profound effect. . . . That Barfield's thought is more original and more profound I have come to believe while studying these controversies . . . ." Also regarding the "Great War" in relation to Lewis's subsequent conversion to theism see, Feinendegen and Smilde, "The Great War of Owen Barfield and C. S. Lewis," "Introduction." See also, De Lange, *Owen Barfield*, 158. De Lange shows how Adey is not alone in his assessment. See also, 242, wherein De Lange notes that Barfield's early work on the history of language gave

was Barfield's linguistic thesis that formed the basis of Tolkien's conception of "Middle-Earth,"[3] while Robert James Reilly has identified strong elements of Barfield's romanticism in the work of Lewis, Tolkien, and Charles Williams.[4] Although a variety of authors have chronicled the influence and originality of his wide-ranging thought,[5] hitherto the theological implications of the most prominent and promising feature undergirding the breadth of Barfield's corpus have gone largely unexamined; that is, his attempt to wed philosophy and poetry utilizing what he, following Samuel Taylor Coleridge, called "polar logic." Therefore, what follows is an investigation of this poetic (or polar) philosophy, its shortcomings, and some remarks on its theological implications. It will be argued that in his poetic philosophy Barfield's subject appears to inhabit a medial or middle realm that, aside from some noted lapses, presents a formidable challenge to any conceivable closed or immanentized philosophy. Although lacking, when this poetic philosophy is brought to its theological culmination it intimates that finite being (immanence) is a "gift" that always-already participates in its infinite divine (transcendent) source.

Barfield notes that as a young boy he was raised without religious beliefs and if anything a slight bias against them. Indeed, he thought such things were "humbug." But as he grew older he noted, "I began to abhor this vacuum in myself which did not at all fit with the promptings either of my emotional or of my moral nature . . . ."[6] This drove him to study poetry,

---

him a unique voice above Lewis and Tolkien.

3. For Barfield's influence upon Tolkien see, Flieger, *Splintered Light*. Flieger shows how Tolkien's entire conception of "Middle-Earth," found in *The Hobbit* and *The Lord of the Rings* and best depicted his earlier *The Silmarillion*, was deeply shaped by Barfield's language theory. See also, Kern, "Tolkien's 'Essay on Man,'" 221–39. Kern makes a strong case linking Tolkien's "mythopoeia" to Barfield's *Poetic Diction*. He writes, "It would not be stretching things too far to say that Mythopoeia is a poetic version of the argument for Poetic Diction." Kern then locates this Barfieldian influence in Tolkien's, "On Fairy Stories," which he says forms the basis of his *Lord of the Rings* as well as his other works. Indeed, in a 1928 letter from C. S. Lewis to Barfield (in "Owen Barfield Papers," C. S. Lewis 1926–63, Dep. C, 1072), Lewis reflects upon Tolkien's own private remarks on Barfield's writing stating, "your [Barfield's] conception of the ancient semantic unity had modified his [Tolkien's] whole outlook and that he was always just going to say something in a lecture when your conception stopped him in time. 'It's one of those things,' he said, 'that when you've once seen it there are all sorts of things you can never say again.'"

4. Reilly, *Romantic Religion*, 11. Reilly claims that the romantic elements in the work of Lewis, Tolkien, and Williams "exist in their most basic and radical form in his [Barfield's] work," and that Coleridge influenced all of the Inklings.

5. See, "Literature Review," below.

6. Barfield, *Romanticism Comes of Age*, 4–5.

which kindled that part of him that his earlier skepticism had denied.[7] What he discovered was that poetry (i.e., the subjective imagination) actually enhanced the "outer" or objective world, revealing a deeper meaning than he had hitherto envisaged. This is precisely the type of aesthetic encounter his poetic philosophy seeks to verify. It was these early experiences that marked the beginning a lifelong endeavor to rectify the division between rational and poetic discourse. Hence, Barfield's bookplate reads, "Zwie seelen wohnen ach! In Meiner Brust" ("Two souls dwell, alas! In my breast!")—a line borrowed from Goethe's *Faust*. The "two souls" are the rational and

7. Barfield, *Poetic Diction*, 14–15. In his second preface to *Poetic Diction*, Barfield critiques I. A. Richards for dividing scientific language (or real language) from that which is poetic or emotive (not real), arguing poetry was a way to knowledge.

In her 1985 interview with Barfield, Majorie Lamp Mead indicates that as a young boy growing up in the Barfield household, Owen learned that things like religion and poetry were forms of self-deception. But as years went on he began to feel that suppressing these feelings was not good. This fueled his ambition to reconcile the objective claims of science with the subjective feelings of poetry. One of his earliest short stories, *The Silver Trumpet*, is an attempt to balance the rational and feeling aspects of life. As he describes it, the silver trumpet is a symbol of the feeling element in life, once "hidden and then . . . discovered again." See, "Afterword" in Barfield, *The Silver Trumpet*, 120–21. *The Silver Trumpet* is a story of two princesses ("Violetta" and "Gambetta") upon whom, at their Christening, a spell is cast joining them together for as long as they both live. The princesses are outwardly indistinguishable, but inwardly Violetta (who represents the feeling side—depicted as good) and Gambetta (the rational side—depicted as bad) are very different indeed. They are, however, so inseparable that the good done by Violetta creates dimples on Gambetta, while the bad done by Gambetta creates wrinkles on Violetta. Soon a Prince, who plays the silver trumpet, arrives and marries Violetta (who is now called "Violet"). But Gambetta (now called "Gamboy") hides the trumpet and eventually plots the death of Violet. With the loss of the trumpet and of Violet there is much unrest and famine in the town and castle. The Prince, now King, is dejected by his loss and rarely sees his daughter, Lily, who is driven into solitude by her fears. All the while Gamboy rules and manipulates people within the castle and amidst the towns using "black magic." But a Prince arrives in search of Lily (who he has seen in a picture) and rescues her from her solitude. At the same time the trumpet is discovered by a "stable-boy." The Prince demands to have the trumpet at his wedding to Lily. The trumpet is blown and suddenly Gamboy turns into Violet (who was thought to be dead). Life abounds, the King is overcome with joy and everyone is rejoicing, singing, and dancing again. Life is restored. Lily and her Prince become the King and Queen. The narrator seems to suggest that no one knows who is now in Violet's grave and leaves the reader with an eerie feeling that although Gamboy's marks could be seen all around, her memory was all but forgotten. The narrator then mentions that he is getting ahead of himself, but it makes one wonder if what he is describing is the future of "final participation" (this regards "The Evolution of Consciousness" spelled out in chapter 1) where man once again apprehends his participatory relation to the world, and looks back upon the vestiges of a scientific age (in the forms of large, narrow castles, i.e., skyscrapers) and begins to ponder what life was like in "those days" from some future state of consciousness.

poetic, objective and subjective, that his participatory philosophy sought to bring into harmony.

At bottom this poetic philosophy is linguistic, based upon his earliest work in philology. In a time when words had become merely arbitrary,[8] Barfield discovered them to be of vital, ontological gravitas. According to Barfield, the language one uses directly coincides with one's philosophy or consciousness (i.e., a restricted language coincides with a restricted ontology).[9] He had an uncanny ability to draw upon language in order to highlight the inconsistencies or limits of such reductive philosophies (e.g., nominalism, atomism, positivism, empiricism, mechanism, reduction, individualism, scientism, etc.). He is most critical of Cartesian thought (the relegation the non-material or non-spatial to the mind) for arbitrarily creating a chasm between subject and object, which dominates the modern consciousness and forms the basis of the social and physical sciences.[10] His poetic philosophy sought to overcome this dualism so that man might apprehend those real forms of reality (what he generally refers to as "qualities") in the world that had been lost to such reductive philosophies. Barfield believed that the properly trained imagination could "rediscover" a world before this Cartesian division, where subjects and objects are not divided, but "intermingle" or participate in one another.

More to the point, Barfield linked the emergence of the Cartesian worldview with the division between objective and subjective language. Hence, nowadays the scientist works with material objective facts and the poet with the non-material subjective imagination. In such a scheme fact and meaning are divided. But, Barfield argued that this is not the case. In his studies of word meanings he found that all words were once poetic or metaphorical and over time words divide, pitting what one now speaks of as "literal" or "prosaic" (i.e., objective) meaning over-against poetic or metaphorical (i.e., subjective) meaning. This is evident in the present categorization of words as *either* metaphorical *or* literal. One can see this in the evolution of individual word meanings. To borrow his own example, today one thinks of "blood" either in scientific terms (e.g., a red liquid that carries oxygen through the body) or metaphorically (e.g., "bad blood"). But, in the past these meanings were one; there was no sundering of the spatial from the mental (as Charles Taylor says, "black bile" *was* melancholia).[11]

8. Adey, C. S. Lewis' Great War, 92.

9. For example, analytical certainty often comes at the expense of the qualitatively real. For this reason a majority of Barfield's major works, both fiction and non-fiction, address the dire implications of de-ontologized language.

10. Adey, C. S. Lewis' Great War, 92.

11. Taylor, A Secular Age, 37. Taylor uses the example of "black bile" to critique the

As Barfield saw it this evolutionary philological phenomenon correlates with a society's social imaginary and is embodied in its social practice.
He found that while primitives employ metaphors to describe objects, the
modern scientific use of language intentionally seeks to eliminate metaphor
in the name of objectivity. In the same way, modern individualism can be
seen as having evolved from the cooperative exchange of primitive cultures.
It is in this way that Barfield's philological thesis forms the basis from which
he derives his aesthetic and sociological critique. It appears that one's initial
aesthetic encounter with the world holds a more true meaning which fades
over time.

This philological thesis not only turned the prevailing conception of
the history of language on its head (which espoused that later poetic or
metaphorical language was the result of the combination of earlier roots),
but what was most significant about his discovery was that it revealed that
the true nature of reality lies not in a division of matter and mind (or "spirit"), but in the participation of mind and materiality. This essay argues that
this is the most profound and promising element in all of Barfield's thought
because of what it suggests about the real. For, as Barfield would have it, a
language consistent with our initial encounter with the true nature of being (i.e., one that accounts for quality as well as quantity)[12] must account
for *both* subjective *and* objective reality. For this reason Barfield insists that
the subject and object exist in "polar tension" (i.e., their ground is neither
in themselves, nor in their polar opposite). In such a scheme, subjective
knowledge is not solely immanent (i.e., not an active arbitrary ground in
oneself, nor a passive receipt of phenomena), but arises by participation
in the object (elsewhere Barfield refers to his philosophy as "objective
idealism").[13] The essay argues that Barfield's poetic philosophy implicitly
resituates the subject in a theological "middle" (i.e., neither purely active nor
purely passive), which suggests that meaning is not immanent, but comes
by participation in the transcendent source of all being.

It will in turn be argued that this is not arbitrary speculation, but actually rescues language, as well as being, from dissolving into meaninglessness
(and Barfield was well aware of this).[14] Barfield's poetic philosophy evokes
a middle realm that denies autonomy to both what one commonly takes
to be subjective, equivocal poetry (non-identity) and objective, univocal

---

mind/body dualism. In a similar way, he indicates that in the past people would believe
that "bile *is* melancholia," whereas today melancholia is simply reduced to a state of
mind.

12. Barfield is often critical of modern science for ignoring qualities. See, chapter 4.

13. Barfield, *Worlds Apart*, 211.

14. Barfield, *History in English Words*, 144.

philosophy (repetition), allowing meaning ("non-identical repetition")[15] to supervene. His subtle gesture presents a formidable alternative to modern and postmodern philosophies of immanence, whose failure to ground the subject is exposed in the dialectical opposition of active and passive, respectively, which ironically reveals a theological "opening" within immanence that renders philosophy wanting. As such, a poetic philosophy exposes at once the myth of a totalizable or secular philosophy and the inevitability that immanent philosophy is sustained and perfected in theological transcendence.

Literature Review

As previously alluded to, to date there has been no significant work done on the theological implications of Barfield's thought. This book is broadly intended to fill that gap. Nonetheless, it remains necessary to mention the former literary contributions indebted to the explication of Barfield's thought. The notable works that deal explicitly with Barfield are:

- Simon De Lange, *Owen Barfield: Romanticism Comes of Age*. De Lange's text is the most significant to date. He offers an in-depth biographical sketch of the development of Barfield's thought by drawing upon his entire corpus, letters, and personal interviews.
- Another detailed work on Barfield's thought is Lionel Adey, *C. S. Lewis' Great War with Owen Barfield*, which sketches Barfield's intellectual debate with Lewis. Adey accentuates the uniqueness of Barfield's philosophy and the fundamental disagreement between Barfield and Lewis over the truthfulness of the imagination.
- Astrid Diener's *The Role of Imagination in Culture and Society: Owen Barfield's Early Work* draws upon Lewis and other valuable interlocutors to detail Barfield's thought. Diener does well to outline the philosophical influences that shaped Barfield's philosophy and the bibliographical context in which his views were formed. However, her overall argument seeks to show a different Barfield, unknown to those who failed to read his earliest works (e.g., "Dope," "The Devastated Area," "Seven Letters," "The Silver Trumpet," "Some Elements of Decadence," "The Lesson of South Wales," and "Danger, Ugliness, and Waste"). Against the prevailing trend, which maintains that Barfield's entire corpus utters a consistent warning against technological advancement, Diener argues that

15. I am here invoking Kierkegaard's "non-identical repetition." See, Kierkegaard, *Fear and Trembling/Repetition*, 186. Barfield's poetic philosophy, as it relates to Kierkegaard's non-identical repetition, is addressed in chapter 5.

the earlier Barfield is rather an advocate for such scientific progress. Distinct from Diener's analysis, I take Barfield at his word (there is no "late" or "early" Barfield)[16] by presenting his fascination with contemporary issues (e.g., individualism, ecology, the rise of modern science, etc.) as concomitant and "analogous" to his philosophical thought; hence, "aesthetic" and "sociological" participation. So against Diener's thesis, but not intended as a response to her work, this essay suggests that Barfield's poetic philosophy is the consistent theme underlying all of his thought. In this way, the following analysis of the relationship between Barfield's philosophical and social or cultural concerns is of a piece with Lange's, which is based on his reading of a collection of Barfield's notes. These notes, he claims, intertwine the most prominent eighteenth-century German and English philosophers with Barfield's cultural, social, and ecological reflections. Explicitly against Diener, De Lange notes that,

> Whether or not the body of notes referred to was reserved by Barfield strictly in chronological order, the strong indication from the way that the sequence alternates between matters pertaining to language and socio-economic themes is that his interest in social affairs was present from the outset and was not the manifestation of the stricken moral conscious of a somewhat aloof, armchair philosopher. Her failure to recognize this is a major weakness in the otherwise valuable book by Astrid Diener on Barfield's early years. I can find no evidence either in his personal papers or otherwise for the impression that she gives of this interest having been tacked on subsequent to his more well-known preoccupations with language.[17]

- Shirley Sugerman's *Evolution of Consciousness: Studies in Polarity* is an informative *festschrift* written by friends and colleagues on the significance of Barfield's philosophical thought, which was occasioned in anticipation of his seventy-fifth birthday.
- Other mentionable projects that draw heavily, although not exclusively, upon Barfield's work are: Sharon Warner, *Experiencing the Knowing of Faith.* Warner critiques Cartesian epistemologies, using Polanyi and Whitehead as her main interlocutors. She draws readily on Barfield's participatory philosophy in her attempt to account for "wholeness";

16. Sugerman, "A Conversation with Owen Barfield," in Sugerman, *Evolution of Consciousness*, 9. In Sugerman's interview with Barfield he asserts that there is no "early" or "late" Barfield, "I have always been saying the same thing."

17. De Lange, *Owen Barfield*, 269. For more details on De Lange's position see his chapter 14, "Vision for a Future Social and Cultural Order."

that is, the subject's role in the knowing experience. For Warner, "deep knowing," that which actually shapes one's identity, does not occur in scientific or objective observation, but only in the "interpenetration" of subject and object.

- Morris Berman's *The Reenchantment of the World* draws upon Barfield's *Saving the Appearances* in an attempt to "re-enchant" a world lost to physical science. Like Warner, he avers that Barfield and Polanyi's argument for the role of the subject in scientific observation deconstructs modern science's Cartesian premises.

- Stephen Talbott's *The Future Does Not Compute*, devotes two lengthy appendices to summarizing Barfield's thought ("Appendix A" is at bottom a list of bullet points, which consist of a number of Barfield's quotations, while "Appendix B" indicates how Talbott utilizes Barfield's thought to critique the advance of computers and information technology), which he draws upon to suggest that information technology is a furthering of the modern scientific revolution that creates more distance between man and his context. De Lange notes that Barfield was pleased with the work when he received a copy from Talbot.[18]

- For an example of a text regarding Barfield's espousal of Anthroposophy see, Gary Lachman, *A Secret History of Consciousness*. Using Anthroposophic principles, Lachman tries to flip the predominant view that consciousness is a product of matter suggesting that the physical world is rather a product of the evolutionary history of consciousness.

- A few notable works dedicated to Barfield's literary contributions are: Barfield, Hunter, and Kranidas, *A Barfield Sampler Poetry and Fiction* and Barfield and Tennyson, *A Barfield Reader*.

  Some additional dissertations and theses are:

- James Clark, "The Sacred Word," which tries to show how Barfield's linguistic epistemology indicates that knowledge is "neither dualistic or arbitrary";

- Jason Peters, "Owen Barfield and the Heritage of Coleridge," which shows how Coleridge's theory of language, imagination, and philosophy influenced Barfield;

- Donna Potts, "Howard Nemerov and Objective Idealism," which examines Barfield's earlier works to show the influence of his philosophy of "objective idealism" on Nemerov;

- Tiffany Martin, "'For the Future," which details Barfield's fiction work and his emphasis on the imagination for overcoming social and ecological devolution by creating harmony with man and the natural world.

18. Ibid., 3–4.

For a thorough biographical sketch see again, De Lange, *Owen Barfield*. Otherwise, an exhaustive bibliography of Barfield's work compiled by Jane W. Hipolito can be found here: http://barfieldsociety.org/BarfieldBibliog.pdf.

Overview and Plan

To advance the argument, the essay is divided into three parts that are each introduced by a brief summary. Generally, Parts I and II deal exclusively with Barfield's poetic philosophy and provide the basis for the theological exposition and critique that is Part III. Because Barfield indicates that all of his thought can be broken down into what he calls "aesthetic" and "sociological" participation, Part I, "Aesthetic Participation," examines the aesthetic upon which Barfield's thought is based, while Part II, "Sociological Participation," shows how Barfield saw an analogous relation between the aesthetic gaze of particular societies and the way in which it is embodied in their practices and customs. Parts I and II supply the framework for Part III, "Theological Participation," which builds upon the implicit conclusions of Parts I and II, in order to construct a discourse that is faithful to Barfield's poetic philosophy, albeit more properly theological.

Before delving into specifics it is important to note that there is an overarching premise present throughout the essay that loosely coincides with the three linguistic voice phenomena: passive, active, and middle. This pattern constitutes Parts I, II, and III, respectively. Part I seeks to underscore the limits of the passive voice, while Part II, the active voice, which necessitates a rediscovery of the middle voice, pursued in the final subsection of Part III. Generally, the constitution of Parts I to III (the passive, active, and middle voice) are meant to represent the predominant themes of postmodern philosophy (passive voice), modern philosophy (active), and theology (middle voice), respectively. This pattern is meant to draw out the significance of Barfield's poetic philosophy, as his medial subject appears to resist these modern and postmodern tendencies. This should become increasingly clear as the essay unfolds.

Each chapter draws upon various interlocutors, both influences and antagonists. For the purpose of the present work the chosen influences represent primarily those figures whose work shaped Barfield's poetic philosophy and secondarily those best suited to underscore the predominant themes of the essay mentioned above.[19] The antagonists are those interlocu-

19. The main influences who best represent Barfield's poetic philosophy and coincide with the overarching premise of the essay are anthroposophist Rudolf Steiner,

tors who represent the predominant trends in modern and postmodern philosophy to which Barfield's poetic philosophy is here presented as an alternative.[20] The essay overview is, then, as follows.

Chapter 1 introduces one of Barfield's largest influences, Rudolf Steiner. Early on, Barfield found Steiner's theory of the "Evolution of Consciousness" startlingly similar to his discoveries regarding the evolutionary history of words. As Steiner saw consciousness evolving toward an increasingly

---

poet and philosopher Samuel Taylor Coleridge, anthropologist and philosopher Lucien Lévy-Bruhl, and quantum theorist David Bohm, each of whom are the subjects of chapters 1–4, respectively. Chapter 5 surveys Barfield's theological influences and then draws upon some contemporary Catholic theologians, with whom he was presumably unfamiliar.

A majority of Barfield's thought is taken directly from Steiner and Coleridge, and although he interacts less with Lévy-Bruhl and Bohm, it will be shown that their work is integral for understanding how Barfield developed his theory of sociological participation. Other fruitful influences, some of whom are only briefly mentioned, are those post-Kantian German philosophers who attempted to wed poetry and philosophy. To briefly cover this obvious German element in the work of Barfield, chapter 2 discusses the work of Manfred Frank. Therein, it is argued that the German romantic philosophers' reading of Kant is much aligned with Barfield's. To mention a few other fruitful interlocutors that are not explicitly engaged, Goethe would be the most significant figure, although Barfield seemed to always read him through Steiner and Coleridge. A great text on Goethe's thought is Bortoft, *The Wholeness of Nature*. Also, Friedrich Schiller's emphasis on wholeness, his attempt to reconcile inner and outer, ideal and real, spirit and matter, his emphasis on the imagination, his attempt to be a poet and philosopher, his critique of materialism, machinery, and the division into parts at the expense of the whole, are all elements in Barfield's work. Also Schelling's *Naturphilosophie*, a corrective to Cartesian dualism and the post-Kantian subjective idealism that followed, is a direct attack on mechanism that seeks to bring together subject and object. For Schelling, without subjects, objects are dead and lifeless. Thus, Schelling's philosophy juxtaposes the self-movement of nature to the dead mechanistic cosmos of physics. His emphasis on wholeness, his critique of the fragmentation of the sciences, and his charge for scientists and poets to work together are all elements from which Barfield draws. For an erudite work on the philosophies of Schiller and Schelling see, Schindler, *The Perfection of Freedom*, in this series.

20. Barfield either directly or indirectly mentions the central antagonists cited in the present work. In chapter 1 Heidegger is important because of his emphasis on poetry and because he represents a predominant voice in postmodern philosophy. For the purpose then of clarifying how unique Barfield's poetic philosophy is, chapter 2 examines various interpretations of Kant and places Barfield accordingly. While chapter 3 does not deal with a specific antagonist, it generally surveys those sociological theories that employ mechanism to shed light on the Barfieldian alternative. Finally, chapter 4 is mostly a critique of Cartesianism and mechanism, the division of subject and object, which Barfield's poetic philosophy explicitly sought to overturn. In light of the overarching theme mentioned above, Heidegger is used because his poetry represents the passive subject of postmodernity and Descartes is used because his autonomous subject represents the active subject of modernity. This is meant to prompt a theological alternative (the middle), which culminates in the final subsection of chapter 5.

self-conscious state, so Barfield's studies in philology traced an evolution in word meanings from poetic (a participation of subjective and objective) to an increasingly "literal" or "prosaic" form that pits the subjective over against the objective. Quite simply, Steiner's theory, which traced the rise of self-consciousness seen over-against an outer world, was consistent with the gradual division between subject and object that Barfield identified in his earlier studies of words. As previously alluded to, Barfield's thesis challenged the prevailing theories of his time, but what is most significant was his claim that *no* language is ever purely objective or literal in the modern sense; rather, language is always a participation of subject and object; that is, *always medial.* Although not explicit in his work, this gesture forms the overarching premise that Barfield's poetic philosophy represents an alternative to those philosophies of immanence whose attempts to account for subjectivity (specifically regarding its relation to the object) result in a dialectic that shuttles between active and passive yet never arrives. Therefore, the final section of chapter 1 draws upon Heidegger as an interlocutor, maintaining that his work on poetry (presented as a reaction to modernity's active subject—e.g., "The Will to Power") fails to ground subjectivity in terms of passivity precisely because it is predicated on a philosophy of immanence, which one might say always-already presupposes a division between poetry and philosophy. The result is that Heidegger can grant his passive poet no creativity of his or her own. Trapped in an immanentized vision that can only conceive of either equivocal non-identity or univocal repetition, Heidegger is left to render poetry (the best language) meaningless. In the close of chapter 1, it is argued that Barfield's poetic philosophy outwits such passivity by resituating the subject instead in a participatory middle, thereby endowing the subject with a creative, albeit co-operative, meaningful expression of the real.

Building upon this, chapter 2 introduces another of Barfield's influences, Samuel Taylor Coleridge, who, more than any other figure, shaped his poetic philosophy. A brief survey of the varying responses to the work of Coleridge does well to underscore the dovetailed trajectory of those post-Kantian philosophies as they either promote or assuage the division between poetry and philosophy. By following the latter course, it is argued that Barfield's poetic philosophy, which he gleans most emphatically from Coleridge, represents a formidable alternative to those post-Kantian philosophies of immanence that render the *a priori* as regulative (the subject as a ground in him- or herself). Coleridge, by following a Platonic scheme, instead resituates Kantian subjectivity by speaking of the *a priori* as "constitutive." Indeed the "Platonic" Coleridge's subject is not an immanentized ground in him- or herself, but a subject by participation. It is this reading of the "Platonic" Coleridge that Barfield adopts. Barfield indicates that Coleridge's poet is thus not a closed but a humbly open subject, an "Aeolian Harp" whose strings are blown by the winds of divine inspiration. Such participation is not to be understood as a passive receptivity, as with Heidegger, nor as crossing an untraversable boundary (the postmodern "sublime"), which would be to "flatten" language to an immanentized (univocal/equivocal) discourse that divides the poetic and philosophical, but as a gesturing towards an imaginative or speculative participation, a grasping of that which arrives from "beyond the threshold" or, in the words of the influential German romantic Schlegel, a "finite longing for the infinite." Here the poetic utterance draws upon the imagination by stretching philosophical reason to new heights. Hence, Barfield's oft-cited Wordsworthian phrase, the imagination is "reason in her most exalted mood."[21] This concludes the sketch of Barfield's aesthetic participation.

Taking off from here, Part II turns to Barfield's theory of sociological participation. As he saw it, the loss of the poetic aesthetic (the gradual division of subject and object he saw in the history of language and of philosophy) coincided with the rise of the individualism and atomism adopted by the social and physical sciences. Therefore, chapter 3 introduces another of Barfield's influences, anthropologist and philosopher Lucien Lévy-Bruhl. In his *Saving the Appearances* Barfield indicates how Lévy-Bruhl's analysis of primitive consciousness (or "collective representations") also qualified his philological thesis. As it turns out, primitive societies embody the poetic aesthetic in their social practices, whereas modern (or civilized) societies tend to be more individualistic. Just as words become increasingly literal or objective and objects distinct from their subjects, so too does man become distant from his fellow man. However both Lévy-Bruhl and Barfield argue that this supposed distance is merely a figment of modern consciousness. As such, if one looks closer one finds traces of this poetic past within modern society. This poetic aesthetic still lies behind the present epistemological gaze, awaiting rediscovery. According to Barfield, recognition of this aesthetic would involve overcoming the epistemological presuppositions of the physical sciences that dominate the modern consciousness.

Thus, chapter 4 examines Barfield's greatest foe, modern science. Barfield suggests that the division of man (as subject) and nature (as object) upon which modern science rests is a result of the gradual sundering of subjective and objective language, which one finds in the evolutionary history of words. Mechanism speaks of a cosmos full of dead objects, bereft of

---

21. Barfield often refers to the imagination as "reason in her most exalted mood," a phrase he borrows from Wordsworth's *The Prelude*.

quality, subject to the will of humanity, which, according to Barfield, threatens life, both literally and figuratively. The art of human making presupposes a devalued or objective natural order that becomes a means to one's subjective end. Against claims of scientific objectivity he asks if science has not always employed metaphor to advance its knowledge? In so doing, has it not always-already relied on a subjective element? To buttress his polemic he argued that the Cartesian division upon which modern mechanical physics is based was being overturned by recent discoveries within physics itself. As Barfield saw it, discoveries such as the "uncertainty principle" (which suggests that objects seem to know they are being observed) undermined the staunch division between subject and object upon which classical mechanics is based. Quantum physics revealed that there is indeed an underlying "relationality" between subjects and objects that had hitherto been ignored. Here another of Barfield's influences is introduced, quantum theorist David Bohm, whose theories also affirmed Barfield's poetic philosophy. The close of chapter 4 rehearses how this poetic philosophy serves as an alternative to both Heidegger's passive subject and the equally untenable active autonomous subject of modernity. It is reiterated that the failure of philosophy to ground the subject, as displayed in the active/passive dialectical scheme, intimates a theological opening within immanence, implicit in Barfield's poetic philosophy.

Therefore, chapter 5 re-examines and builds upon Barfield's poetic philosophy. Therein, it is argued that nominalism (the denial of constitutive universals), of which Barfield was so critical, actually hindered the development of those subsequent disciplines that presupposed it, whether philosophical or scientific. Yet, even so, such philosophies left ajar the theological opening, or middle, to which Barfield's poetic philosophy leads. But ultimately Barfield fails to bring his own philosophy to its implicit theological consummation. Here the essay moves beyond Barfield, suggesting its theological culmination. To assuage the division between poetry and philosophy is to offer an alternative that absorbs such feigned philosophies by affirming an open immanence that is at all times shot through by transcendence; that is, *poiēsis* proper: a theology as poetic metaphysics that both baptizes and exceeds philosophy. Here, it is argued that meaningful language is not possible outside of a theological metaphysic. Corresponding with the analogous nature of being, meaning is contingent upon a theological metaphysics of nonidentical repetition (this is similar to Barfield's insistence that all language is a blending of poetic and prosaic), which situates beings analogically, as a gift arriving from a transcendent source, thereby rescuing language from an immanent abyss—the meaningless dialectic of univocal repetition and nonidentical equivocity. It is not a transcendental discourse that somehow saves theology, but rather a theology of transcendence that redeems language. It is argued that meaningful discourse is indeed poetic and culminates in a speculative, albeit real worship of God whose truth is encountered, while it always infinitely exceeds human finitude; that is, *poiēsis* proper. The final subsection suggests that a fruitful takeoff point in constructing a language capable of articulating a finite creation's participation in God may lie in a rediscovery of the middle voice. This follows the overarching premise expounded by the essay: if modern philosophy represents broadly the active voice and postmodernity the passive voice, then perhaps a theology of transcendence is best articulated in the middle voice. In the conclusion it is suggested that if the path of immanence that philosophy took when it broke from theology resulted in the failure to ground the subject, then perhaps a recovery of the middle voice, as neither purely active nor purely passive, represents the way things have always been, even in the face of such feigned secularism. Further, a theological recovery of the middle voice is consistent with the New Testament consciousness of both Jesus and St. Paul and a rich tradition of Christian theology. A middle voice, poetic, inspired, worshipful language, stretches one beyond any conceivable totality of finite being. This ceaseless finite grasping is one's openness to, one's participation in, one's *epektasis* towards, one's true identity, which is found only in the infinitely exceeding Persons of God.

Terminology

Finally, it is important to define a few key terms that are below identified using italics. *Poetry* or *poetic* takes on a particular meaning in the Barfieldian corpus that eludes the casual reader. At bottom, *poetry* or *poetic* coincides with *participation* as a critique of various forms of dualism. As such, the terms are used interchangeably throughout the essay and should be understood simply as an alternative to those philosophies that divide, for example, subject and object, the sensible and the supersensible, spirit (or mind) and matter, quality and quantity, and prosaic (literal or objective) and poetic (merely subjective) language. In this way a participatory or poetic philosophy envisages the real as symbolic in nature, a participation of spirit and matter. Again, this follows Barfield's most fundamental philological thesis that such divisions come later in the evolutionary history of consciousness, but are not actual.

This scheme follows Coleridge's philosophy of *polarities*, or polar logic (and is comparable to the theological metaphysic of *polarity* proposed by the late twentieth-century Catholic theologian Erich Przywara—see chapter 5), in which the aforementioned poles (e.g., subject and object) are understood to be inseparable as they participate in one another, existing in *polar tension*; hence, they are *polarities* of one another. So, for example, and of crucial importance, when Barfield insists that all language is inherently *poetic*, he does *not* mean it is mere subjective idle fancy or metaphor, but rather, *poetry* for him is a combination of what is now commonly known as literal and metaphorical language (which elsewhere Barfield describes as *prosaic* and *poetic* language, respectively). So to say that language is neither purely literal nor purely metaphorical is to say that language is *poetic*, a combination of what one today tends to think of as literal (i.e., objective) and metaphorical (i.e., subjective). It is this conceptual scheme, derived from his studies in philology, that structures all of his thought, and it is for this reason he is here deemed a *poetic philosopher* and his philosophy a *poetic philosophy*.

As previously mentioned, the essay presents this *poetic* or *participatory* scheme as a genuine alternative to modern and postmodern accounts of reality. Hence, chapter 1, "*Poetic* Language," presents Barfield's theory of language as an alternative to Heidegger's immanentist (passive) construal of poetic subjectivity. Chapter 2, "*Poetic* Philosophy," presents Barfield's *poetic philosophy* as an alternative to those immanentist philosophies that presuppose a division between philosophical and poetic discourse. Chapter 3, "*Poetic* Living," presents Barfield's reading of the primitive collective consciousness as an alternative to individualism. Chapter 4, "*Poetic* Making," presents Barfield's participatory relation of subject and object as an alternative to those modern making practices (ubiquitous in modern science) that presuppose a division of man over-above nature. Finally, chapter 5, "*Poetic* Theology," builds upon the work of Barfield presenting the analogical relation of theology and philosophy ("transcendence in-and-beyond immanence")[22] as an alternative to those philosophies that presuppose their division (transcendence over-and-against immanence). This analogical relation is also indicated by the term *open* immanence ("in-*and*-beyond") as juxtaposed to a *closed* immanence ("in-*or*-beyond"). The former representing the *middle* or *medial* realm, to which Barfield's poetic philosophy ascends. In this vein, the Greek term *poiēsis* is used to express the explicitly theological culmination (between active and passive) of the Barfieldian alternative.

Finally, the essay regularly employs another Barfieldian term, *rediscover*. The simplest way to describe this is to say that Barfield's romanticism is not an attempt to enchant an otherwise meaningless cosmos, as

---

22. The "in-and-beyond" repeatedly referred to throughout and most readily in chapter 5 is a formulation of Erich Przywara. See, Przywara, *Analogia Entis*.

romanticism is sometimes understood,[23] but rather Barfield wants to use the imagination to *rediscover* a real enchanted world of which one is now unconscious. So, to *rediscover* something is to see that which at present simply eludes one's consciousness.

   With the plan and terminology in place, the essay begins with Part I, "Aesthetic Participation."

23. Barfield, "Romanticism and Anthroposophy," 111–24. Barfield notes that from the term "romance" eventually came the pejorative "romantic," which came to be thought of as the poetic fictions of authors.

PART I
"AESTHETIC" PARTICIPATION

Part I explores what Owen Barfield called aesthetic participation; that is, the poetic philosophy upon which his thought is based. Chapter 1 explicates the insights Barfield unveiled in his earliest studies in philology and etymology. In his first two works of non-fiction, *Poetic Diction* and *History in English Words*, and later in his *Speaker's Meaning*, he attempts to overturn the dominative conception regarding the developmental history of language (a progression from literal roots to later metaphorical utterance) by suggesting paradoxically against this that language has always been metaphorical, only recently has it been taken in its more literal or objective sense. This evolution yielded the modern bifurcation between poetic and philosophical language (which elsewhere he classifies as "poetic" and "prosaic" language, respectively) that one could argue undergirds the majority of modern and postmodern discourse. Against this, Barfield attempts to show that no language is ever purely literal or objective, but instead subject and object inevitably participate in one another; and it is this claim that is tarried with throughout the essay. Further, this poetic philosophy challenges modern and postmodern assumptions regarding the type of discourse that is most capable of accounting for the real.[1] To unfurl this contention, chapter 1 concludes by suggesting that Heidegger's poetry fails to account for the true nature of being, because it is ironically based upon a myth of his own founding ("onto-theology") that perpetuates the division that Barfield's poetic philosophy seeks to assuage and then proceeds on these false premises. It is argued that a philosophy that divorces itself from theology presupposes a rupture between poetic and philosophical discourse that Barfield's poetic philosophy does not

1. Hipolito, "Owen Barfield's Poetic Diction," 3–38. Hipolito indicates that for Barfield it is only through metaphor that one encounters the real.

presuppose. Heidegger's shortcoming is revealed in his untenable account of poetry that shuttles between univocity and equivocity. Further, by presupposing this immanent trajectory one is left to ground subjectivity as either active or passive. Heidegger, in choosing the latter, concludes that poetry, the best of language, is actually meaningless, and his view serves as the basis for subsequent postmodern accounts of subjectivity. The close of chapter 1 maintains that Heidegger's poetry is not poetry at all because it strips the subject of creativity, while Barfield's poetic philosophy evokes a middle realm that outwits such passivity endowing the subject with a real co-operative dignity.

In chapter 2 the essay then further traces the division between poetry and philosophy by reviewing the philosophical reception of one of Barfield's greatest influences, Samuel Taylor Coleridge. The essay suggests that Barfield's poetic philosophy also presents a formidable alternative to modern philosophical discourse. Instead of identifying the Kantian *a priori* as regulative, Coleridge, by envisaging the *a priori* as "constitutive," implicitly resituates Kantian subjectivity. Distinct from, and unbeknownst to his post-Kantian critics, the "Platonic" Coleridge's subject is not a ground in him- or herself but a subject by participation. For Coleridge, subjects and objects exist in a polar tension. So for him a language best capable of articulating the true nature of being is poetic. The subject is not one who is a closed ground in oneself, but one whose posture is open to the divine. This inspired poetic utterance allows the subject to exceed the strictures of a pure philosophy precisely because the subject is not a ground in him- or herself (not purely active or passive) but is situated in a medial realm through which he or she paradoxically receives from the divine in the act of speaking or naming. To be clear this is not to conceive of the poetic utterance as a crossing of an untraversable boundary into a Kantian sublime as postmodernity would have it, but such language is indicative of a participation in that which lies beyond the threshold; that is, "reason in her most exalted mood."[2] It is this particular reading of Coleridge, as a poet *and* philosopher, which Barfield develops in his *What Coleridge Thought*; one in which the subject is endowed with a real creative capacity when suspended in a medial realm. In the close of Part I, the essay suggests that this poetic vision of creativity accentuates a theological opening and thereby exposes the myth of closed (immanent or secular) philosophy presupposed by both post-Kantian philosophy and Heidegger. This opening within immanence, reiterated in Parts I and II and further expounded in Part III, reveals that being is at all times shot through by theological transcendence.

2. Wordsworth, *The Prelude*.

1

Poetic Language

Barfield's hallmark as a philosopher has been his use of grammar and semantics to support his metaphysic . . . in a period where philosophers usually employ linguistic analysis to discredit metaphysics.

—ADEY[1]

Few and unimportant would the errors of men be, if they did but know, first what they themselves mean: and secondly, what the words mean by which they attempt to convey their meaning.

—COLERIDGE[2]

The Evolution of Consciousness

ANY SERIOUS INVESTIGATION OF the thought of Owen Barfield must take seriously the influence of Anthroposophist Rudolph Steiner (1861–1925).[3] Outlandish elements aside (see subsection below, "Barfield's Reception of Steiner"), Barfield never disavowed Steiner's theory of the

---

1. Adey, *C. S. Lewis' Great War*, 92.

2. Coleridge, *Letter to Thomas Allsop*, December 2, 1818. See, epigraph to Barfield, *Speaker's Meaning*.

3. Adey, *C. S. Lewis' Great War*, 25. See also, De Lange, *Owen Barfield*, 79. De Lange notes that the evolution of consciousness "was utterly crucial to Barfield's entire mental and spiritual endeavour." It is important to begin with Steiner's work in order to understand Barfield's ubiquitous references to the evolution of consciousness.

19

"Evolution of Consciousness." Indeed, Barfield himself states that this theory is the main theme that underlies all of his literary achievements.[4] One can scarcely locate a Barfieldian text that is not imbued with the idea that human consciousness evolves. One sees this in his earliest works, *History in English Words* (1926) and *Poetic Diction* (1928), in his middle works, *Romanticism Comes of Age* (1944) and his most well-known work *Saving the Appearances: a Study in Idolatry* (1957), and in his later works, *Worlds Apart: A Dialogue of the 1960s* (1963), *Unancestral Voice* (1965), *Speaker's Meaning* (1967), *The Rediscovery of Meaning* (1977), and *History, Guilt, and Habit* (1979). This chapter opens with a general overview of Steiner's evolution of consciousness and serves as a context for explicating the particulars of Barfield's thought throughout the essay. After summarizing Barfield's reception of Steiner the study of Barfield's poetic philosophy commences with an investigation of his unique thesis regarding the evolutionary history of words. Finally, Heidegger is employed as an interlocutor in order to draw out the intricacies and contemporary relevance of Barfield's theory of language.

Rudolf Steiner: Anthroposophy[5]

A comparison of Steiner's main thesis and Barfield's philological thesis reveals how such an obscure figure as Steiner could so heavily influence

4. Barfield and Tennyson, *A Barfield Reader*, xxv. Tennyson notes, "Barfield has said that his entire literary endeavour has been based on the concept of the evolution of consciousness and the ideas that flow from it. Therefore, to understand this idea is essential to understanding the basis of Barfield's philosophy." In addition to his main works, throughout his literary career, Barfield wrote numerous articles and reviews espousing Steiner's teachings in anthroposophy journals such as *The Golden Blade, Anthroposophical Quarterly, Anthroposophy Today, Anthroposophy: A Quarterly Review of Spiritual Science, Journal for Anthroposophy*, and *Anthroposophical Movement*. He also translated and edited a number of Steiner's works. See, Hipolito's bibliography referenced in the "Literature Review," above.

5. Rudolf Steiner is known as the founder of Anthroposophy, which the Anthroposophical Society in Great Britain describes as follows:

"Anthroposophy is a modern spiritual path that cherishes and respects the freedom of each individual. It recognizes however, that real freedom is actually an inner capacity that can only be obtained by degrees according to the spiritual development of the individual. The striving for this capacity, and the corresponding spiritual development, can be greatly assisted through a scientific study of the spiritual nature of humanity and the universe. Such a study is available in the writings and lectures of Rudolf Steiner—an initiate of the twentieth century. Steiner called his study spiritual research or Anthroposophy.

Anthroposophy is thus not only the spiritual path to freedom, it is also a scientific study of the spiritual knowledge gained on this path. For Steiner, Anthroposophy was the path that could 'lead the spiritual in the human being to the spiritual in the

Barfield.[6] As previously mentioned, in his early studies of the evolution of word meanings Barfield believed that he had discovered evidence indicating that the way humanity perceives the world changes over time. It was during his earliest studies in philology that Barfield was introduced to Steiner's evolution of consciousness, which he claimed validated and further shaped these earlier conclusions.[7] Bearing an unmistakable likeness to his theory of the evolution of words, the young Barfield was fascinated by Steiner.[8] As it turned out, Steiner's study of consciousness assisted Barfield in weaving a metanarrative that began to take shape in his own philological thesis. Of his first encounter with Steiner's work, Barfield remarked fondly,

> Now at a fairly early stage in the process which I have attempted to record I came into contact with the writings of Rudolph Steiner. I began after some hesitation, to study his spiritual science, or anthroposophy . . . seriously and steadily . . . many of the statements and ideas which I found there produced an effect very similar to the combinations of words to which I have already alluded . . . [;] some of my most daring and (as I thought) original conclusions were *his* premises—just as when you meet a man for the first time, without knowing his background, it is not some long harangue, but the casual way in which he uses a particular word in a particular context, that reveals quite suddenly the extent of his knowledge of a subject with which you are yourself well-acquainted.[9]

Based on Barfield's own words, it appears that his allegiance to Anthroposophy was predicated on the similarities between his own theory of the

---

universe.' And he showed that it is a path that is capable of inspiring many cultural innovations—in education, agriculture, medicine, architecture, science and the arts—and much else." See, http://www.anthroposophy.org.uk/.

6. For an account of Steiner's intellectual influence upon Barfield see, Diener, *The Role of Imagination*, Part II, "The Anthroposophical Background," 61–100.

7. Barfield, *Romanticism Comes of Age*, 9. Barfield remarks, "anthroposophy included and transcended not only my own poor stammering theory of poetry as knowledge, but the whole Romantic philosophy. It was nothing less than Romanticism grown up." See also, Barfield and Tennyson, *A Barfield Reader*, xvii. In the introduction Tennyson, a long-time friend of Barfield, notes that it was Barfield's earliest studies of language at Oxford through which he "arrived independently at ideas about language, metaphor, and the imagination that turned out to be congruent with those he encountered in Rudolph Steiner." See also, Diener, *The Role of Imagination*, 94. Diener indicates that Barfield himself notes that he "was already very far advanced in developing his own approach when he discovered Steiner."

8. De Lange, *Owen Barfield*, 193.

9. Barfield, *Romanticism Comes of Age*, 8–9.

evolution of word meanings and Steiner's evolution of consciousness. From his earliest work to his last Barfield remained so indebted to Steiner's evolution of consciousness that, even as an eventual convert to the Church of England (1949), he never renounced his commitment to Anthroposophy.

Steiner is a complex and rather audacious figure whose "Occult Science"[10] or Anthroposophy presents an alternative (or, as some have suggested, a "parallel")[11] account to Darwinian natural science and empiricist logic[12] by tracing instead the history of the spiritual evolution of man for which the hard sciences had failed to account. In his work, *Occult Science: An Outline*, Steiner weaves his detailed evolutionary account of a pre-existent celestial cosmology that consists of spiritual beings that over successive phases "descend," and thereby, "incarnate" the material world. This pseudo-gnostic cosmology is framed by the "descent" of what Steiner calls "Consciousness" or "Spirit" into matter that culminates in the incarnate Christ, whose material death and spiritual ascent marks the decisive turning point in the history of consciousness.[13] In the process of this descent of conscious-

10. Steiner, *Occult Science*, 26. Steiner remarks that Occult Science is drawn from the work of Johann Wolfgang von Goethe, who Steiner says, "spoke of the 'manifest secrets' in the phenomena of Nature. Whatever remains 'secret,' that is to say unmanifest in these phenomena when we apprehend them only with the outer senses and with the intellect that is bound to the outer senses, will here be treated as the subject-matter of a supersensible way of knowledge." His usage of "occult" and his claim that his occult science was as equally tenable as physical science is a strong indication that he borrows the term directly from Newton (as Newton self-admittedly ignores "occult" qualities—see, the "General Scholium" of Newton, *The Principia*). Steiner was ultimately making the case that the study of material reality was no more "objective" than his occult studies of immaterial realities. The only difference is they are simply utilizing a different consciousness.

11. See, Waterman, "Evolution and the Image of Man," in Harwood, *The Faithful Thinker*, 40. Waterman notes that in a time when Darwin's *Origin of Species* had led to a choice between a natural or divine origin for man, between evolution and creation, between science and religion, "Steiner ascribes to man *both* a divine *and* an evolutionary history." In my limited reading of Steiner, I am generally in agreement with Waterman's analysis. I am not aware of any work of Steiner's that discredits natural explanations of evolution. He only seems to suggest that scientific accounts tell only a *part* of the evolutionary process.

12. Steiner described empiricism as knowledge by sense perception alone, which he links with the materialism of natural science.

13. I say "pseudo" because, on the one hand, I am unclear as to how Steiner believes the material world was formed. It seems to be pre-existent with the spiritual; however, the gnostic proclivity to denigrate materiality is evident throughout his work. In chapter 5 I argue that Christianity overcomes the idealisms of this sort of pagan thought and the residual idealisms lurking in Barfield's poetic philosophy that he gleans from Steiner. Although Steiner seeks to balance the spiritual and material through conscious awareness of that which lies beyond the sensory perceptions, he seems to conclude

ness into the material world man receives a material body and is awakened to a sense of autonomy, to the idea of the self as a subject of free choice.[14] Eventually an "ego" or an "I" is formed in terrestrial man's physical body.[15] As an "I," man experiences himself as a fully individualized being, independent from the spiritual world (this is central to understanding Barfield's work—on the one hand, the "I" unifies the self, but on the other, it eventually creates a cutting and distancing from the spiritual world). Early on in this process, man still feels united to the spiritual world from which he came.[16] As Steiner indicates man had an "immediate experience of the supersensible world."[17] In fact, man was so close to the spiritual that he was more aware of divine beings and/or gods than material objects presented to the physical senses.[18] But bound by materiality and an overemphasis on sense perception, the human consciousness slowly loses the ability to apprehend this spiritual world. Hence, at this point in the evolution of consciousness man becomes less and less conscious of his spiritual origins.[19] For Steiner, this is the "fall" of man described in the Christian narrative. He refers to this

---

that in a later epoch man will eventually overcome materiality. See, Steiner, *Occult Science*, 312. See also, Harwood's essay, "The Historical Process and the Individual," in Harwood, *The Faithful Thinker*, 77–78, 85. Harwood writes that during this evolution a "gradual realization, or incarnation, in the material world of spiritual form, the form of man, and the lower kingdoms of nature represent what was, so to speak, 'sloughed off' in the process."

14. Steiner, *Occult Science*, 147–55. See also, Harwood, "The Historical Process and the Individual," in Harwood, *The Faithful Thinker*, 79.

15. Steiner, *Occult Science*, 113.

16. Ibid., 180–81. Steiner writes, "before this moment in his evolution, man had no independence in relation to the spiritual world. He did not in that world feel himself as a separate, single being, but as membered into the sublime organism composed of higher Beings above him. Now, however, the 'I' experience on Earth began to work on into the spiritual world; there too, man began to feel himself as a single unit. Yet at the same time he also felt he was eternally united with that world." This is a strong theme in Barfield's work, which, as shall be seen in chapter 3, he associates with Lévi-Bruhl's studies of primitives.

17. Ibid., 201.

18. See, Harwood, "The Historical Process and the Individual," in Harwood, *The Faithful Thinker*, 78.

19. Steiner, *Occult Science*, 254. Steiner writes, "Man is, as a rule, unconscious of the connection, since he is accustomed to apply his thinking faculty to the sense-world alone; hence, when he hears of communications from the supersensible world, he sets them down as incomprehensible. They are however thoroughly comprehensible—and not alone to those whose thinking has been educated through spiritual training, but to every thinking person who is conscious of the full power of his thinking and ready to apply it." See also, Harwood, "The Historical Process and the Individual," in Harwood, *The Faithful Thinker*, 85.

as a "contraction of consciousness."[20] This period of contracted consciousness, where humanity loses the ability to apprehend the spiritual world due to an overemphasis on sense perception culminates in the methodologies of modern sciences (which Barfield pejoratively and repeatedly refers to as "scientism").[21] With the rise of logic and pure intellectual reflection man's ability to apprehend the supersensory fades.[22] It thus becomes increasingly difficult for man to bridge this gap between the material and the spiritual, the external and internal. Thus, Steiner writes, "what we know today as the antagonism between external science and spiritual knowledge is nothing but a consequence of this fact."[23]

But as the intellectual powers of man have rapidly accelerated, a latent supersensible "hidden knowledge" has been "seeping into men's thoughts."[24] This means that the spiritual faculties presently dormant can be reawakened using "imaginative cognition,"[25] a process designed to expand the contracted consciousness. From this will emerge a new epoch (an ascension) that will "bring to full development the harmony between the two [worlds]" (the spiritual and material).[26]

The great "Prototype" and "Example" of the union the spiritual and material is Christ.[27] Those who are trained in this spiritual science can recognize this truth.[28] It is in this way that history centers on the incarnation of "the Christ,"[29] whose incarnation (descent) marks the fall of the spiritual

20. See, Harwood, "The Historical Process and the Individual," in Harwood, *The Faithful Thinker*, 79.

21. Steiner, *Occult Science*, 105. See also, 301. Steiner locates the epoch of contracted consciousness beginning in the fourth or fifth century AD and culminating with the work of figures like Bacon and Newton. See also, Harwood, "The Historical Process and the Individual," in Harwood, *The Faithful Thinker*, 83. Harwood notes that as a result of Bacon's subordination of nature and Newton's "mechanism" man's consciousness finds itself entirely cut off from its divine origin.

22. Steiner, *Occult Science*, 302.

23. Ibid., 220.

24. Ibid., 305.

25. Ibid., 235. Steiner believes that training the mind to look beyond the mere sense perceptible external object to the internal spiritual symbol awakens the faculties belonging to the soul, freeing or detaching the soul from sense perception, to see what, with merely the physical senses, one cannot. He is here distinguishing between "objective" and "imaginative" cognition.

26. Ibid., 221.

27. Ibid., 296. See also, 216–18 and 302.

28. Ibid., 304.

29. Harwood, "The Historical Process and the Individual," in Harwood, *The Faithful Thinker*, 84.

into the material (the contraction of consciousness), and whose resurrection (ascent) marks the decisive turning point in the history of the evolution of consciousness hitherto described. Christ's incarnation inaugurates the expansion of man's consciousness and eventually brings harmony between the spiritual and material worlds. In this next epoch man will be as fully conscious of his supersensible intuitions as he once was, but now he is able to combine them with the logic and intelligence fostered in earlier epochs (those which birthed the hard sciences). In this new epoch, man experiences himself again as a member of the spiritual world. Steiner writes that "not only does [man] feel it thus; he knows it in full consciousness and bears himself accordingly."[30] Steiner concludes by suggesting that at this stage of man's development are seeds for a future spiritual world ushered in by love, as it is the very nature of spiritual knowledge (wisdom) to be transmuted into love.[31]

At first glance Steiner appears to be painting a satirical picture of the so-called natural sciences by developing his alternative occult science perhaps in order to expose the narrowed ontologies of natural science. It is important to reiterate that Steiner is not necessarily opposed to natural science, but rather he seeks to expose the limits of natural science.[32] What he does wholeheartedly contend is that his account of spiritual evolution is no less scientific than the empirical sciences, because the intellect is as equally capable of apprehending the supersensible (spiritual) realm as it is the sensible (material) realm of the natural science.[33] This narrative drives Steiner's emphasis on pedagogy, which today lives on in the initiatives of the "General Anthroposophical Society."[34] As more and more people become

30. Rudolf Steiner, *Occult Science*, 306–7.

31. Ibid., 312. See Steiner's gnostic tendencies in footnote 13, above.

32. Ibid., 27. In chapter 1, Steiner distinguishes between natural science and spiritual science. He suggests that spiritual science "can go beyond the self-imposed limitation" of sense data to the "real point, which is that a certain inner attitude of the human soul has been applied to the revelations of the senses." Steiner and Barfield want to suggest that it is untenable to presume that one merely passively receives sense data, but instead, the subject's particular way of looking, one's consciousness or presuppositions, play an integral role in the interpretation of sense data; hence, it is important for science to recognize its own limitations. See also, 103–4. Steiner urges scientists to apprehend the spiritual behind the merely physical.

33. Ibid., 26.

34. For a summary of Steiner's philosophy of education see, Howard's "Educating the Human Being" in Harwood, *The Faithful Thinker*, 192–204. Steiner's education initiatives continue today as the "General Anthroposophical Society," which at present, is "an association of people whose will it is to nurture the life of the soul, both in the individual and in human society, on the basis of a true knowledge of the spiritual world." More information on the history of Anthroposophy can be found here: http://

consciously aware of this spiritual realm the successive phases of the evolution of consciousness will dawn.[35] One can see how this general narrative
roughly accords with Barfield's philological thesis and his desire to bring
philosophy and poetry back together.

Barfield's Reception of Steiner

In order to briefly summarize Barfield's reception of Steiner this subsection underscores three salient parallels in their evolutionary theories: (1) in
Steiner's theory of the evolution of consciousness man becomes increasingly
unconscious of his connection to the spiritual world; (2) this culminates in
empiricism (the reduction of the real to the senses), wherein modern man,
enslaved by his sense perceptions, finds himself isolated from (or unconscious of) the spiritual world (the epoch of the "Consciousness Soul"); but
(3) with proper training (of the imagination—the faculty of the mind which
apprehends the supersensible) man can once again become conscious of
his connection to the spiritual world (the epoch of the "Imaginative Soul").
Although appearing in a slightly nuanced form, this general narrative underlies nearly the entire Barfieldian corpus.

For the most part Barfield excludes Steiner's fantastical elements
(celestial beings, planetary migrations, etc.), while he holds to the general theory that consciousness evolves.[36] As such, Barfield identifies three
successive phases in the evolution of consciousness that mirror the above
summary.[37] Numbered correspondingly they are: (1) "Original Participation"—the study of words and the observations of indigenous tribes reveal a
past where the supersensible world of participatory relations pervades one's

---

www.goetheanum.org/Anthroposophical-Society.336.0.html?andL=1.

35. Steiner, *Occult Science*, 305. Steiner writes of his reason for writing *Occult Science*, "We are now living at a time when the higher knowledge needs to be far more
widely received into the general consciousness of mankind than hitherto; it is with this
in view that the present work has been written."

36. Barfield, *Speaker's Meaning*, 100–1. Barfield's account is also not meant to be an
alternative to biological evolution, but rather, a complementary narrative that brings
together the "inner" of the evolution of consciousness with the "outer" of biological
evolution. See also, Barfield, *Saving the Appearances*, 184. Similar to Steiner, Barfield
states that biological evolution is only one half of the story. See also, Fulweiler, "The
Other Missing Link." Fulweiler indicates that Barfield is opposed to modern science
only because it does not account for "the other missing link"; that is, the evolutionary
history of consciousness. Indeed, for Barfield a robust evolutionary account should address both the physical and spiritual aspects of evolution.

37. This theory is most succinctly developed in *Romanticism Comes of Age* where
Barfield blend's Steiner's evolution of consciousness with Coleridge's romanticism.

consciousness. During this time, knowledge of one's self was less defined, because it is understood that the self is constituted by these supersensible or participatory relations to one another and to the natural world;[38] (2) "Alpha-Thinking"—this epoch emerges with the disappearance of (or lack of consciousness of) participation wherein the self is gradually separated from the spiritual world. Man, now unconscious of the supersensible, finds himself autonomous or individualistic.[39] This epoch culminates in what Barfield refers to as "idolatry," a scientific gaze that intentionally brackets out the supersensible;[40] and (3) "Final Participation"—a state of future consciousness, distinct from Original Participation, wherein the Alpha-Thinking self becomes a unique self now conscious of the supersensible.[41] As with Steiner, Barfield wanted to overcome the present phase in the evolution of consciousness (Alpha-Thinking) by articulating the reality of the supersensible world to the scientific consciousness.[42] Both felt this could be achieved through the proper training of the imagination.[43] This drives Barfield's study of Coleridge's theory of the imagination. In this vein, much of Barfield's work sought to expand the modern consciousness and rediscover the worldview it had nearly lost in Alpha-Thinking.

Notwithstanding their similarities, Barfield's philological bent placed him above Steiner and stands as a formidable corrective to modern and postmodern discourse.[44]

38. Barfield, *Saving the Appearances*, 122–23. Here the reader will remember Steiner's insistence that in the past man, although inhabiting a material body, was still conscious of his intimate connection to the spiritual world.

39. Charles Taylor, *A Secular Age*, 38 and 41. Barfield's description of the modern "self" as isolated from the spiritual world is similar to Charles Taylor's description of the "buffered self" that coincides with secularism.

40. Barfield, *Saving the Appearances*, 185. Barfield calls the scientific revolution the "last and greatest step in idolatry."

41. The reader is here reminded of Steiner's future epoch wherein man, while both fully rational and logical, becomes conscious of his extrasensory relations to the spiritual world. See also, ibid., 45. Barfield is clear that final participation is distinct from original participation, precisely because of the introduction of the scientific mind during the later Alpha-Thinking epoch. Consistent with Steiner, Barfield explicitly states that he is not advocating a return to original participation. Again, this is not meant to be a critique of scientific methodology *tout court*, but rather a critique of its ontological premises.

42. Barfield, *Romanticism Comes of Age*, 12.

43. Ibid., 11. He writes, "From Steiner too I learned for the first time that a serious attempt to obtain exact results with the help of a perceptive faculty developed through controlled imagination . . . ." See also, Barfield, *Saving the Appearances*, 137 and 146.

44. Hipolito, "Owen Barfield's Poetic Diction." Terry Hipolito, a close correspondent and admirer of Barfield, claims Barfield's *Poetic Diction* represents a more mature

Language: Owen Barfield's Philological Investigations

This section commences the examination of Barfield's poetic philosophy by introducing his critique of modern linguistic theories as they regard the evolutionary history of word meanings.

Philology: History in . . .Words[45]

Barfield notes that he first realized the beauty of metaphor as a young eleven-to twelve-year-old schoolboy alongside lifelong friend and fellow Anthroposophist Cecil Harwood.[46] But it was during his studies of poetry at Oxford between the years of 1919–23 that he first began his serious investigations.[47] He discovered that the evolution of word meanings reveals how the world was perceived in different epochs.[48] He contended that modern studies of past languages were deceived by myths of "progress" (what C. S. Lewis referred to as "chronological snobbery");[49] the idea that today civilization is

---

linguistic theory that already saw past the shortcomings of the New Criticism before it even began. He argues that *Poetic Diction* outwitted the theories of eminent linguists such as, Saussure, Heidegger, Derrida, and Lakoff and Johnson. The insightful correspondence between Barfield and Hipolito regarding this eventual essay are available here: "Owen Barfield Papers," Hipolito-Hunter, 1969–97, Dep. C, 1070. See also, footnote 165, below.

45. This is meant to play on the title of Barfield's earliest work, *History in English Words*, wherein he attempts to weave an account of English history with a philological investigation of English words. He writes that, "evoking history from words is like looking back at our own past through memory; we see it, as it were, from within." Barfield, *History in English Words*, 42. Barfield's central thesis is that by using words we can overcome "external" accounts of history that lend themselves to what he calls "logomorphism" (to impose modern categories upon the past). Philology helps one to understand the "internal" feelings and sentiments of past epochs, rather than simply projecting one's contemporary consciousness upon them. In the "Afterword" Barfield indicates that Archbishop Richard Trench, Max Müller (the German philologist [1823–1900], not Max Müller [1906–94], the Catholic phenomenologist influenced by Heidegger), and most notably Mr. Pearsall Smith's *The English Language*, all "led the way" for him. See also, Barfield, "A Giant in Those Days" for Barfield's appreciation and critique of Müller.

46. De Lange, *Owen Barfield*, 150. De Lange, quoting from a 21st June 1977 lecture titled, "Owen Barfield and the Origin of Language," indicates that Barfield notes that it was the young Cecil Harwood's reaction to the metaphor "Cato walked out of life" as opposed to "Cato died" that marks "the proper moment to identify, if you want to place the origin of the subject's interests in, and feeling for, the nature of language."

47. Ibid., 18.

48. Tennyson, "Etymology and Meaning," in Sugerman, *Evolution of Consciousness*, 178–79.

49. Lewis, *Surprised by Joy*, 207. Lewis remarks that it was Barfield who helped him

simply more advanced than in the past. This ideology shaped the philological thesis that purported that language begins with "roots" or sounds that
merely represent objects, while expressive or metaphorical language came
later. In *Speaker's Meaning* Barfield contends that the pre-modern conception of history as a descent from a past golden age is, in modernity, inverted
and begins instead to be thought of as an ascent to a future golden age.[50] Just
because this notion of progress has become "common sense" does not make
it correct.[51] Instead, what Barfield argued is that a study of the semantic
history of words identifies changes in "outlooks" within different epochs,
which does not necessarily indicate the aforementioned progress or development that linguists typically associate with the evolutionary history of
words.[52] Words simply provide a glimpse into a different consciousness than
one's own. Since it is evident that past civilizations did not apprehend reality
in the same way, one must not impose contemporary structures of thought
upon the past.[53] Barfield critiqued these earlier philological theses for taking
such notions of progress for granted.

Following this model (from roots to later metaphor),[54] modern linguists proceeded under the assumption that primitive language was less
complex and over time became more advanced.[55] Presumably, roots, which
consist of various sounds or expressions that were meant to represent objects, marked the origins of the earliest languages, while metaphors were
only later advances in language that were taken to represent one's inner or

---

overcome his own chronological snobbery. Throughout his career, Barfield's is rather
critical of this heralding of progress.

50. Barfield, *Speaker's Meaning*, 16.

51. Barfield, *History, Guilt, and Habit*, 47. See also, De Lange, *Owen Barfield*. See
the endorsement by Barfield's friend Saul Bellow: "We are well supplied with interesting
writers, but Owen Barfield is not content to be merely interesting. His ambition is to
set us free . . . from the prison we have made for ourselves by our ways of knowing, our
limited and false habits of thought, our 'common sense.'"

52. Barfield, *History in English Words*, 171. He writes, "In this direction all that a
knowledge of [words] can do is to equip us a little better for forming opinions of our
own."

53. Barfield, *Poetic Diction*, 90. Herein, Barfield similarly warns against what he
calls logomorphism; that is, the projection of post-logical thoughts into a pre-logical
age.

54. See, Tennyson, "Etymology and Meaning," in Sugerman, *Evolution of Consciousness*, 177. Tennyson notes that Barfield sought to overturn reductionist accounts
of language that assume all language can be broken down into roots.

55. Barfield, *Saving the Appearances*, 120–21. He indicates that these early etymologists assumed that "men had on their lips the roots and in their minds the meanings,
very much as we have words and their meanings to-day, and then proceed to 'apply'
them to a varied selection of phenomena."

subjective feelings.[56] Barfield argued that to make such a claim is to already impose upon the past a (Cartesian) division between literal (outer or objective) language and figurative (inner or subjective) language upon which the later representational model is based.[57] Again one must be careful not to project a later consciousness upon the past. In fact, if one actually attends to past words one finds that what actually occurred is precisely the opposite: language began as metaphor and only later became divided (subjective/objective).[58] Barfield found that past words do not have what he variously called an "objective," "representational," "contracted," or "lexical" meaning free from subjective bias, as one tends to think of today.[59] He remarks, "that the concept of an object without a subject is as abstract as the concept of a surface without a depth and as futile as that of a back without a front."[60]

In fact, one does not find roots in primitive language. Instead, "Words grow longer, not shorter, the nearer we get to the end of our backward journey towards the origin of speech."[61] The further back one traces language, the more poetic it appears.[62] "Poetic and apparently 'metaphorical' values were latent in meaning from the beginning."[63] Hence philology indicates that consciousness undergoes an "age-long metamorphosis from the kind of outlook which we loosely describe as 'mythological' to the kind which we

56. Barfield, *Speaker's Meaning*, 64–65.

57. A "representational" epistemology holds that the mind merely *represents* the outer world, analogous to the way in which a camera might represent that which it captures. The distance between the photograph and the reality it captures can be likened to the distance between the subject's appraisal of an object and the actual object apprehended. Adey, *C. S. Lewis' Great War*, 76. Adey rightly argues that for Barfield truth is not a "copy or representation." Since for Barfield all objects are actually symbols, truth arrives through the mind's actual participation in the reality in which the object (as symbol) participates. So, whereas the representational model denies the ontological reality of symbol and metaphor by relegating them to a mere representation in the mind, Barfield takes symbol and metaphor to be an ontological reality in which the mind participates.

58. See, Barfield, "Either: Or." Barfield argues that the origin of what would become the separation of the metaphorical and literal use of language, between the poet and the logician, the imaginative and the rational, began with Aristotle and culminated in the "scientism" of modern physical science that divides spirit and matter.

59. Barfield, *Speaker's Meaning*, 32. All are terms Barfield used to describe later accounts of language that divide between subject and object.

60. Ibid., 115.

61. Barfield, *Saving the Appearances*, 121. See also, G. B. Tennyson, "Etymology and Meaning," in Sugerman, *Evolution of Consciousness*, 176.

62. Barfield, *Poetic Diction*, 70 and 83–84. See also, 85. As he puts it, "once upon a time we were all poets."

63. Ibid., 85. See also, Barfield, "The Nature of Meaning." This is a much later essay wherein he summarizes his philological thesis.

may describe equally loosely as 'intellectual thought'";[64] that is, from Original Participation to Alpha Thinking or idolatry. In declaring that language
did not derive from roots, but rather that metaphor appears to be primary,
Barfield ostensibly overturned the aforementioned roots-based thesis.[65]

Based on his study of words it would be incorrect to assume that earlier languages divided between subject and object, inner and outer. Barfield
writes, "To every word that has an immaterial import, there belongs also, or
at least did belong, a material one; to every word that has a material import
there belongs also, or at least did belong, an immaterial one."[66] Today, "the
more common a word is and the simpler its meaning, the bolder very likely
is the original thought which it contains and the more intense the intellectual or poetic effort which went to its making."[67] In his *Saving the Appearances*
Barfield distinguishes between the past metaphorical and the present literal
usage (elsewhere he refers to these as "poetic" and "prosaic," respectively)
of the word, "blood." He notes that the modern consciousness parses the
literal and metaphorical use of "blood."[68] One may employ the term literally, as in the statement, "the average male body contains 5 liters of blood,"
or one may employ the word metaphorically, as in the saying, "blood runs
thicker than water." However, this division[69] into literal and metaphorical
meaning is only a recent phenomenon that occurred when the symbolic
meaning of a word was reduced to its literal.[70] In this scheme, words that
lack objectivity (e.g., "good") are taken to have only an immaterial, inner,
or subjective meaning, whereas at one time such words also contained a

64. Barfield, *History in English Words*, 84.

65. Barfield, *Poetic Diction*, 152. The inception of words is "poetic" and only later
"prosaic." See also, Adey, *C. S. Lewis' Great War*, 90. Referencing Barfield's *Poetic Diction*, Adey summarize well, "primal languages used in the earliest mythologies were
more poetic than modern languages just because their words directly expressed the
realities men experienced."

66. Barfield, *Speaker's Meaning*, 64.

67. Barfield, *History in English Words*, 14.

68. Barfield, *Saving the Appearances*, 82–83. For example, Barfield writes, "we still
participate 'originally' in our own blood up to the very moment which it becomes
phenomenal by being shed. From that moment on, we abandon it to the mechanomor-
phism which characterizes all our phenomena." Nowadays we are clear to distinguish
between the metaphorical use of "blood" and its literal mechanomorphized use now
common to science.

69. Barfield, *Poetic Diction*, 94. Barfield notes that this division leads to the modern antitheses between "truth and myth," "prose and poetry," and/or "objective and
subjective."

70. Barfield, *Saving the Appearances*, 86–87. Today's symbolic use of language is
more akin to the pre-modern understanding of literal. See also, 123–24, where he refers
to "literalness" as a "hardness of heart."

material meaning.[71] In the past, "The outer and material is always, and of its own accord, the expression or representation of an inward immaterial."[72] As elsewhere he writes, "Look far enough back into the history of almost any word of the inner, or immaterial, language, and you come to a period when it had an outer meaning as well."[73] Over time words "contract"; outer words lose their inner significance and inner words their outer significance.

All of this indicates that present "nonfigurative language . . . is a late arrival. What we call literal meanings, whether inner or outer, are never samples of meaning in its infancy; they are always meanings in their old age—end products of an historical process."[74] Thus, the further one "go[es] back in history, language becomes more picturesque, until its infancy, when it is all poetry; or all spiritual facts are represented by natural symbols."[75] De Lange summarizes Barfield's thesis well:

> an etymologically based study of language makes it apparent that, far from words having been originally coined by their human creators to refer to external objects and applied metaphorically to certain inner experiences or inward perceived realities, these two aspects of experience—the outer and the inner—would seem to have originally been a single, complex whole whence these distinct aspects subsequently diverged.[76]

As already implied Barfield correlated this philological thesis with Steiner's evolution of consciousness.[77] He describes the connection as follows: "the attention which I had been giving to the semantic aspect of language (that is the study of meaning and changes of meaning) had thrown a flood of light for me on the history and evolution of human consciousness

---

71. Barfield, *History, Guilt, and Habit*, 40–41. See also, Barfield, *Speaker's Meaning*, 51. See also, Barfield, *Worlds Apart*, 50.

72. Barfield, *History, Guilt, and Habit*, 46–47.

73. Barfield, *Speaker's Meaning*, 56. See also, 53. See also, De Lange, *Owen Barfield*, 113. Primitive man's words were a bridge between the inner and outer worlds. See also, 114.

74. Barfield, *Speaker's Meaning*, 58–59.

75. Barfield, *Poetic Diction*, 92.

76. De Lange, *Owen Barfield*, 244.

77. Barfield, *History, Guilt, and Habit*, 61. Barfield writes, "language contemplated is a mirror of my consciousness and its evolution." See also, 25 and 74. See also, Barfield and Tennyson, *A Barfield Reader*, xxv. Tennyson also confirms that Barfield's evolution of consciousness came from his earliest studies on the nature and development of language: "One could say [Anthroposophy] is the study of etymology raised to the level of philosophy."

. . . ."[78] Combing Steiner's theory with his own work, Barfield associated the move away from a participatory metaphysic (a symbolic gaze wherein one's mind shares or participates in the same supersensible reality in which the objective world participates) with an overemphasis on objectivity (a methodological gaze wherein supersensibles are said to exist only in one's mind and the real is reduced to that which one apprehends via sense impression). On the one hand, one is left with what Barfield called "idols";[79] mere objects that lost their inherent symbolic meaning due to scientific objectivity. On the other, the self or subject develops through a sort of distancing from an objective world.[80] In this space phenomena are now *subject* to man's own appraisal.[81] Barfield warned, "If therefore man succeeds in eliminating all orig-

78. Barfield, *Romanticism Comes of Age*, 7.

79. Barfield, *Saving the Appearances*, 75. For Barfield, when an appearance is taken literally it becomes an idol.

80. Barfield, *History in English Words*, 164–66. Barfield found that the rise of modern civilization is marked by an increased sense of individualism. He notes that during this time the English idea of a privatized conscience (i.e., "my *conscience*" or "his *conscience*") emerges. This, he said, is a rather recent and marked shift between the modern and pre-modern consciousness: "The consciousness of 'myself' and the distinction between 'my-self' and all other selves, the antithesis between 'my-self,' the observer, and the external world, the observed, is such an obvious and early fact of experience to every one of us, such a fundamental starting point of our life as conscious beings, that it really requires a sort of training of the imagination to be able to conceive of any different kind of consciousness. Yet we can see from the history of our words that this form of experience, so far from being eternal, is quite a recent achievement of the human spirit. It was absent from the old mythological outlook; absent in its fullness, from Plato and the Greek philosophers; and, though it was beginning to light up in the Middle Ages, as we see in the development of Scholastic words like *individual* and *person*, yet the Medieval soul was still felt to be joined by all sorts of occult ties both to the physical body and to the world. Self-consciousness, as we know it, seems to have first dawned faintly on Europe at about the time of the Reformation, and it was not till the seventeenth century that the new light really began to spread and brighten. . . . After the Reformation we notice growing up in our language a whole crop of words hyphened with *self*; such are *self-conceit*, *self-liking*, *self-love*, and others at the end of the sixteenth century, and *self-confidence*, *self-command*, *self-contempt*, *self-esteem*, *self-knowledge*, *self-pity* . . . .

Though these two developments—the birth of an historical sense and the birth of our modern self-consciousness—may seem at first sight to have little connection with one another, yet it is not difficult, on further consideration, to perceive that they are both connected with that other and larger process which has already been pointed to as the story told by the history of the Aryan languages as a whole. If we wished to find a name for it, we should have to coin some such ugly word as 'internalization.' It is the shifting of the centre of gravity of consciousness from the cosmos around him into the personal human being himself." See also, 140, he writes, "It is probable that . . . there came for the first time into the consciousness of man the possibility of seeing himself purely as a solid object situated among solid objects."

81. Ibid., 126–27.

inal participation, without substituting any other, he will have done nothing less than to eliminate all meaning and all coherence from the cosmos."[82] Barfield's poetic vision seeks to reverse this evolutionary tendency.

Against the prevailing language theories of his time Barfield contended that the evolutionary history of words evinces a gradual decline of poetic language—that can be loosely described as a transition from participation (in a world of symbols) to one of representation[83] (a division of subject and object)—that culminates in the modern dualisms of metaphorical and literal, subjective and objective, poetic and prosaic, and inner and outer meanings.[84] But for Barfield, this tendency towards idolatry does not entirely hold sway. For today when one speaks of "bad blood" or "hot blood" one still elicits this participatory vision.[85] After all, according to the evolution of consciousness and Barfield's study of the evolutionary history of words, modern humanity is simply less conscious of this reality than its ancestors. The imposition of representational epistemology has made it difficult to experience the world as it is. However, if one attends to language, particularly its prior poetic nature, one begins to rediscover the ontological reality of this participatory vision.[86]

Words: A Bridge to the Past

So past words represent not merely different ideas, but a different vision of reality.[87] While historical studies were concerned with the outer meanings of past people groups (e.g., the facts gathered by an archaeologist or an historian's narratival reconstruction of the past) a faithful study of words allows one to actually think and aesthetically feel the thoughts of those whose history one studies. The inner perspective of words acts as a necessary supplement to the outer meaning.[88] This, in fact, was the only way to

82. Ibid., 144.

83. Ibid., 84. Barfield notes that in pre-modernity there was a much closer connection between words and things than one finds in modernity. In pre-modernity words were not "regarded as mere words." See, footnote 57 on representation, above.

84. For a similar critique of the separation of inner and outer as it relates to language see, Pickstock, *After Writing*, 88–100. Pickstock uses the term "nominalization" to describe the "prioritization of the noun in modernist poetics and contemporary discourse . . ." (89). Such nominalization depersonalizes speech by removing the subject from any particularized usage (e.g., expression, etc.).

85. Barfield, *Saving the Appearances*, 83.

86. Barfield, *History, Guilt, and Habit*, 36.

87. Ibid., 37.

88. Barfield, *History in English Words*, 14. Barfield critiqued the limits of historical studies, such as archeology, because they give only what he calls an outward knowledge

understand a past distinct from one's own. Otherwise one runs the risk of simply reading one's own thought into the past. In essence, what Barfield discovered was that the way one perceives the world is integrally tied with the language one employed to articulate that reality.[89] Barfield referred to this as his "semantic approach to history," which he detailed in his *History in English Words*.[90] Indeed, by utilizing the very words of the past, one begins to the see the world not only as it once was but also as it actually is.[91] Because language still inevitably carries traces of original participation, and because language is never entirely literal, one can indeed recover the poetic past in the present by evoking this latent poetic element.[92] It is thus for the poet to rediscover a past consciousness that was figurative, analogous, and meta-phorical through and through.[93] The poet actualizes what Barfield (drawing on Steiner) referred to as "a felt change of consciousness"[94] or an expansion of consciousness whereby one rediscovers the participatory nature of the present world.[95] Utilizing the imagination the poet fights against the tendency of the prosaic consciousness.[96] The poetic imagination unearths the symbolic meaning hidden within the objects of representation.[97]

of history, whereas language preserves "the inner, living history of man's soul. It reveals the evolution of consciousness." See also, 19 and 21. Barfield writes, "it is now possible for us, by penetrating language with the knowledge thus accumulated, to feel the past." See also, Barfield, *History, Guilt, and Habit*, 6. See also, De Lange, *Owen Barfield*, 244.

89. *History in English Words*, 74. He writes, "The characteristics of nations, as of races, are fairly accurately reflected linguistically in the metaphors and idioms they choose, in their tricks of grammar, in their various ways of forming new words."

90. Barfield, *Speaker's Meaning*, 24–25.

91. Ibid., 22–24.

92. Barfield, *History in English Words*, 13. There are "many ways in which words may be made to disgorge the past that is bottled up inside them . . . ." See also, 23. Barfield writes that "the past does indeed live in the language we speak." See also, Tennyson, "Etymology and Meaning," in Sugerman, *Evolution of Consciousness*, 175, 180–81.

93. Barfield, *Poetic Diction*, 72. See also, Barfield, *Speaker's Meaning*, 66.

94. Barfield, *Poetic Diction*, 52.

95. Barfield, *Speaker's Meaning*, 64. See also, Barfield, *Poetic Diction*, 57.

96. Barfield, *Poetic Diction*, 41. See also, Adey, *C. S. Lewis' Great War*, 84.

97. Barfield, *Poetic Diction*, 152–67. See also, Barfield, *Night Operation*. In his only work of science fiction, *Night Operation*, Barfield weaves a futuristic narrative that embodies his want to overcome this objective gaze. In the future people live in sewers "Underground" entirely disconnected from the natural world, from their own history, and incapable of "feeling." A young man Jon (who represents Barfield) discovers a library. By studying the history of word meanings he begins to understand how the world was once "felt" and eventually finds the courage to ascend to "Aboveground" alongside his friends Jake (who represents Lewis) and Peet (Cecil Harwood), who he convinces to come along with him and experience the natural world for the first time. They ascend "Aboveground" where "people felt only what they saw—but also saw only

While the work of Steiner accords with Barfield's philological thesis, Barfield's unique ability to draw on words to explicate his poetic philosophy ultimately sets him apart from Steiner. In suggesting that past languages were poetic and only later prosaic Barfield challenged the dominative conception of the evolutionary history of language; but furthermore, it will be argued that his assertion that modern language still evinces a poetic or metaphorical structure, which better accounts for the real, presents an alternative to the trajectory of modern and postmodern philosophical discourse.[98] If correct his theory carries significant philosophical implications. As the essay intends to show, Barfield's want to recover the symbolically real[99] rethinks the late medieval division between immanence and transcendence and resists the philosophical tendency to construe the real in terms of a univocal/equivocal dialectic. Barfield's claim that the symbolic is the most real, and, therefore, poetic language the most meaningful, challenges this trajectory. The following section begins to underscore how his poetic philosophy may represent such an alternative, medial way.

Language and Being: Poetry in Owen Barfield and Martin Heidegger[100]

The significance of Barfield's poetic philosophy lies in his attempt to bring language and being together. In other words, the language one uses

---

what they felt." The story ends with the three returning to the sewers with the hope that perhaps they will lead others to see the world as it once was (the narrative thus shares similarities with Plato's "Allegory of the Cave"). The story closes indicating that only time will tell if they were successful in accomplishing this feat.

98. A similar theory is espoused in George Lakoff and Mark Johnson, *Metaphors We Live By*. In their seminal work Lakoff and Johnson suggest that the conceptual systems by which humans act and think are fundamentally metaphorical. As such, they remark that the presuppositions of Western philosophy all the way back to the Greeks would have to be revised if a linguistic theory was to account for what is truly meaningful to human beings. To do so would be to account for metaphor.

99. As already mentioned above, Barfield often distinguishes past consciousness from that of the present by pointing out the various relative dualisms present in modern linguistic theory, i.e., "subjective/objective," "subject/object," "inner/outer," "metaphorical/literal," "poetic/prosaic," "spirit/matter," "mental/physical," "concrete/abstract," "material/immaterial," etc., that he believes misrepresents the symbolically real. See, Barfield, *Speaker's Meaning*, 52.

100. I am indebted to my doctoral supervisor John Milbank for pointing out the connection between Barfield and Heidegger. Heidegger is a fitting interlocutor because he and Barfield began their work at the same time and drew similar conclusions regarding the nature of language. In his written work, the only mention I've found that Barfield makes of Heidegger is his reference to him as an "outstanding" "non-analytic"

coincides with one's ontology. Coincidently, if the language employed by a particular philosophy divides philosophical and poetic language, then such a philosophy will be limited to these linguistic parameters. So in denying the constitutive nature of universals, the language employed by certain philosophies will always already divide philosophical and poetic language, and thereby limit ontological speculation to a univocal/equivocal dialectic. In this scheme poetic language is ostensibly meaningless as it is jettisoned from philosophical truth. But if being, as Barfield implies, is inherently symbolic—a polarity of subject and object—it appears that not only does the denial of symbolism fail to accentuate the real, but also that which is most meaningful to human beings. In what follows it is argued that Barfield appears to offer an alternative trajectory by resituating the real in a polar middle, which concomitantly renders symbolic language the most meaningful form of expression.

To unfurl the overarching thesis, this section examines the originality of Barfield's poetic philosophy by juxtaposing it to the work of Martin Heidegger, who dedicated particularly the latter part of his career to establishing a connection between language and being. Heidegger's conception of poetry, it will be argued, represents the culmination of what one might call the immanentization of language; that is, the attempt to ground linguistic meaning without reference to proper transcendence. In reaction to modernity's failure to ground the active subject, which culminates in Nietzsche's Will to Power, Heidegger's passive subject ironically reaffirms the very onto-theology that he and his postmodern successors loathe. In order to guard against such apparent metaphysical assertions Heidegger's poet becomes entirely passive. This gesture simply reinforces the aforementioned univocal/equivocal dialectic and again renders poetic language meaningless. As such, Heidegger serves as a fitting interlocutor, who at once unveils the nihilistic implications of his own philosophy and underscores the significance of the Barfieldian alternative.

Barfield's first major work, *History in English Words*, was published in 1926, one year prior to Heidegger's *Being and Time*. In his earliest work

philosopher of language, wherein he implies that he is familiar with Heidegger's work (both his opponents and commentators). See, Barfield's 1973 essay "Language and Discovery." However in his later informal correspondence regarding Heidegger he does not seem so impressed. See, footnote 165, below. There are a few others who have made a connection between Barfield and Heidegger. See, Patterson, "Philosophical Hermeneutics and the Nightmare of History" and Deeny, "Consciousness Unto Itself."

An earlier and abbreviated version of this section was presented at the annual Postgraduate Theology Symposium to the students and faculties of the Universities of Cambridge, Oxford, and Nottingham, and King's College London (KCL) in May of 2012 at KCL.

Barfield articulated a theory of language that he maintained throughout his literary career. Heidegger's theory of language, however, begins in *Being and Time* and culminates in his later work (most notably more than thirty years later in his 1959 publication of *On the Way to Language*).[101] Developmental processes aside, both figures share similar derivations and conclusions. The present section begins with a brief summary of both Heidegger's and Barfield's linguistic theories, respectively, which is followed by a close examination of their similarities and of their fundamental divergences. While Heidegger and Barfield enlist poetic language to resituate the modern subject, Heidegger's phenomenology remains trapped within an immanentized or flattened vision, which can only conceive of poetry as a passive "nothingness," whereas Barfield's poet, while perhaps not entirely able to escape the immanence of modern discourse, does indeed overcome onto-theology, constituting a real theological turn.[102]

The "Historicality" of *Dasein* and the Evolution of Consciousness[103]

Early on in *Being and Time* Heidegger speaks of the "historicality" of *Dasein*. In his formidable critique of Western metaphysics he argues that by treating being as an object *Dasein* has fallen prey to a tradition that has rendered it incapable of going back to the past to make it its own (hence *Dasein*'s "temporality").[104] To overcome this, the age-old question of being must be reexamined by dismantling Western metaphysics (particularly the Greek Aristotelian trajectory,[105] which has taken being as an object willed

101. Both figures developed their language theories simultaneously. Barfield's most notable works on language are his *History in English Words* (1926), *Poetic Diction* (1928), *Romanticism Comes of Age* (1944), *Saving the Appearances* (1957), and *Speaker's Meaning* (1967). Heidegger's later works on language include his 1935 publication of *Introduction to Metaphysics* and most notably his 1959 publication of *On the Way to Language*.

102. Barfield's theory, as it relates to theology, will be further explicated in chapter 2 and then critiqued in chapter 5.

103. Only in the following analysis are "being" and "beings" used in typical Heideggerian fashion. For Heidegger there is an equivocal ontological difference between being and beings or *Dasein*. This equivocity is questioned in the sub-section below, "The Primacy of Poetry: Critiques and Conclusions," and again in chapter 5, wherein this essay suggests that Heidegger failed to envisage the ontological difference in terms of analogy.

104. Heidegger, *Being and Time*, 42–43.

105. Heidegger, *Being and Time*. See, 48, for Heidegger's issues with Aristotle. See also, 43 for his critique of Scholasticism. These themes are taken up in the critique of Heidegger below.

by human subjectivity),[106] in order that one might "arrive at those primordial experiences in which we achieved our first ways of determining the
nature of Being."[107] This idea forms the basis of his passive phenomenology.[108] Furthermore one can no longer treat being as an object because all
one knows of it is, in a sense, mediated by *Dasein* itself, through the *logos*.[109]
For *Dasein*, as "man's Being, is 'defined' as the *zoon logon echon*—as that
living thing whose Being is essentially determined by the potentiality for
discourse."[110] Thus, "in order to be who we are, we human beings remain
committed to and within the being of language, and can never step out of it
and look at it from somewhere else."[111] So humans do not utilize language
as a tool standing over and above being or beings,[112] but instead the *logos*
(which communicates being) speaks through *Dasein* and/or beings.[113] For
Heidegger, language, like being to which it so integrally relates, is much more
mysterious and fleeting than Western metaphysics had hitherto asserted.[114]

106. For Heidegger this ultimately culminates in Nietzsche's Will to Power. See Taylor, "Heidegger on Language," 444.

107. Heidegger, *Being and Time*, 44. See also, Martin Heidegger, *Introduction to
Metaphysics*, 218–19. Heidegger talks of experiencing being anew by overcoming powers that have kept *Dasein* in confusion regarding being.

108. The allowing of phenomenon to "say," or show them-selves, is for Heidegger
proper phenomenology.

109. Heidegger, *Being and Time*, 62. "Being, as the basic theme of philosophy, is no
class or genus of entities; yet it pertains to every entity. Its 'universality' is to be sought
higher up. Being and the structure of Being lie beyond every entity and every possible
character which an entity may possess. *Being is the transcendens pure and simple.*"

110. Heidegger, *Being and Time*, 47. See also, Heidegger, *On the Way to Language*,
112. Heidegger notes, "The ability to speak marks man as man. . . . Language, in granting all this to man, is the foundation of human being. . . . We are all, then, within
language and with language before all else."

111. Heidegger, *On the Way to Language*, 134.

112. See Taylor, "Heidegger on Language," 445. Taylor remarks, "This instrumental-
ization of the clearing is one of the furthest expressions of the Will to Power."

113. Heidegger, *On the Way to Language*, 85. He states, "We speak of language, but
constantly seem to be speaking merely *about* language, while, in fact, we are already letting language, *from within* language, speak to us, in language, of itself, saying its nature."
See also, Taylor, "Heidegger on Language," 443. Taylor indicates, "The late Heidegger's
doctrine of language is strongly anti-subjectivist. He even inverts the usual relation in
which language is seen as our tool, and speaks of language speaking, rather than human
beings . . . ." See also, 442. "Indeed, Heidegger repeatedly inveighs against those views of
language which reduce it to a mere instrument of thought or communication[;] . . . it is
not humans that speak, but language."

114. Betz, *After Enlightenment*, 330. Betz writes, "Heidegger's philosophy, beginning with his early lectures on Hölderlin, is largely an extended meditation on the
mysterious relationship between language and being." See also, Heidegger, *Being and
Time*, 49. He writes, "In any investigation in this field, where 'the thing itself is deeply

Close to Heidegger's notion of historicality is Barfield's theory of the evolution of consciousness. Barfield (although much more convivial to Platonic metaphysics than Heidegger)[115] also locates a marked shift in Greek philosophy, particularly with the advent of Aristotle's categories.[116] Barfield says that during this time human consciousness begins to disassociate from its external surroundings, inaugurating the turn to subjectivity.[117] As previously mentioned, by utilizing language to trace this shift Barfield discovered a direct correlation between the human consciousness and language. Language not only tells one how one thinks, but more importantly language tells one about one's being in relation to the world (à la Heidegger's *Dasein*), and how this relation has changed over time (à la *Dasein's* historicality). For both figures, rather than projecting the current consciousness into the past—a methodology that both Barfield[118] and Heidegger[119] argue has plagued modern thought—language is the key to understanding the past, because by attending to it, the modern consciousness can break free from bad mental habits and thereby resituate its present relation to the world.

Blending both Heideggerian and Barfieldian language their theories appear closely allied: when one discovers the intimate relation between being and language it follows that language reveals something about being. And while one still recognizes the temporality of *Dasein*, language uniquely reveals *Dasein's* past, allowing it to resituate the future of *Dasein's* otherwise-closed temporality. For Barfield, while the modern human consciousness finds itself cut off from the world, language reveals a time wherein this was not the case. By utilizing language the otherwise isolated self-consciousness can learn from the past,[120] thereby necessitating a unique future posture to the world.

To summarize, both Barfield and Heidegger agree that (1) the rise of subjectivity is a misappropriation of being whereby the subject comes to dominate its object. As a result the modern consciousness (or *Dasein*) finds itself dissociated from the real in its present context and also its past.

---

veiled' one must take pains not to overestimate the results. For in such an inquiry one is constantly compelled to face the possibility of disclosing an even more primordial and more universal horizon from which we may draw the answer to the question, 'What is "Being"?'"

115. See, chapter 5.

116. Barfield, *Poetic Diction*, 60–61. Barfield is often critical of Aristotle for trying to construct a metaphysic based upon logic. Here he calls any such project a "nuisance."

117. Barfield, *Romanticism Comes of Age*, 89 and 109.

118. Barfield, *Poetic Diction*, 90. See also, Barfield, *Worlds Apart*, 134.

119. Heidegger, *Being and Time*, 43.

120. Barfield, *Worlds Apart*, 194.

However, (2) because there is an integral link between language and being, (3) it is only by way of a turn to language, particularly poetry, that a primordial understanding of being can be envisaged, and for this reason (4) the poet, who resists the aforementioned domineering gaze, can best apprehend the true nature of being.

Speaking a Familiar Language[121]

Charles Taylor remarks that, "the late Heidegger's doctrine of language is strongly anti-subjectivist."[122] Heidegger was highly critical of etymologists who, by drawing upon what they believe to be a very definite understanding of being,[123] argued that language is something that only humans do. Heidegger refers to this use of language as "commanding" and "enframing," which he claims abandons the "natural aspect of language" in the name of "formalization."[124] As such, his theory of language as "speaking" or "Saying" represents a reaction against this sort of enframing, where the mind takes control and robs language of its "mysterious character."[125] Clearly, Heidegger is here reacting against a subjectivist view of language. One in which language is conceived as an instrument of domination. This is comparable to Barfield's wish to overturn the reductionist account of language, which assumes that all of today's language can be broken down into its roots.[126] Here the modern subject finds him- or herself cut off and isolated from a world of objects; that is, idols made in man's image.[127] This fuels both fig-

121. For more on the similarities and differences between Barfield's and Heidegger's theory of poetry see, Hipolito, "Owen Barfield's Poetic Diction."

122. Taylor, "Heidegger on Language," 433.

123. Heidegger, *Introduction to Metaphysics*, 62. See also, 73, wherein he suggests that this occurs when being is confused with an abstraction of the word, "to be there" (i.e., *Dasein*). Thus, being's essence escapes us.

124. Heidegger, *On the Way to Language*, 132.

125. Charles Taylor, "Heidegger on Language," 435.

126. Tennyson, "Etymology and Meaning," in Sugerman's, *Evolution of Consciousness*, 177.

127. Heidegger and Barfield utilize etymology to come to similar conclusions. In the attempt to "save the appearances" the real is misconstrued. One is left incapable of understanding the elusive essence of being (Heidegger, *Introduction to Metaphysics*, 73), which lies beyond the realm of "appearances." Idols are created (Barfield, *Saving the Appearances*, 142), which are the products of a willful domination. See, Heidegger, *Introduction to Metaphysics*, chapter 2, "On the Grammar and Etymology of the Word 'Being.'" Heidegger's linguistic analysis of the word "to be there" or *da sein* concludes that originally being meant "living," "emerging," and/or "abiding," although eventually these meanings died out and only the abstract meaning "to be" survived. Again, being remains elusive.

ures' fascination with the Eastern world, a world that seems to have avoided such strong subjectivity.[128] Also, for Heidegger and Barfield the recovery of this former apprehension of being was crucial to overcoming technological manipulation and the resultant ecological crisis.[129] In response to Western subjectivity both figures sought to establish an integral relation between language and being; for both, this meant that *Dasein* (the subject) is somehow inspired by language (*logos*), which is clearly intended to resituate modern accounts of subjectivity.[130]

This is why Charles Taylor writes that Heidegger's philosophy of language "places him within the context of the revolutionary change in the

128. See, Barfield, *Romanticism Comes of Age*, "From East to West," 15–33. See also, Heidegger, *On the Way to Language*, 1–56.

129. As previously mentioned, for Heidegger, the turn to the subject culminates in Nietzsche's Will to Power. This can be likened to Barfield's staunch warnings against "alpha-thinking"; the forming of idols that occurs when the modern self-conscious assumes the freedom to assert meaning into the cosmos (Barfield, *Saving the Appearances*, 62). "What then had alpha-thinking achieved at precisely this point in the history of the West? It had temporarily set up the appearances of the familiar world. . . . But a representation, which is collectively a mistake for an ultimate—ought not to be called a representation. It is an idol. Thus the phenomena *themselves* are idols, when they are imagined as enjoying that independence of human perception which can, in fact, only pertain to the unrepresented." This is further supported in that both figures agree that this turn inaugurates the rise of the technological manipulation of the environment, which both weave so critically throughout their work.

For Barfield's critique of modern technology see, chapter 4. For Heidegger's critique see, Heidegger, *The Question Concerning Technology*; Heidegger, *Introduction to Metaphysics*, 169; and Heidegger, *On the Way to Language*, 132. See also, Taylor, "Heidegger on Language," 452. Taylor summarizes Heidegger's account of subjectivist language as it relates to technology and ecology stating that when language is used as a tool it simply, "reflects our goals and purposes. At the end of this road is the reduction of everything to standing reserve in the service of a triumphant will to will. In the attempt to impose our light, we cover the sources of the clearing in darkness. We close ourselves off from them [and] . . . if we make this our dominant stance to the world, then we abolish things, in a more fundamental sense than just smashing them to pieces, though that may follow." Additionally, Taylor points out, it is Heidegger's "deep ecology" that is one of the more "positive insights in his vision of language." Taylor writes, "Take wilderness, for instance. This demands to be disclosed as 'earth,' as the other to 'world.' This is compatible with a stance of exploration, whereby we identify the species and geological forms it contains, for instance, as long as we retain the sense of the inexhaustibility of their wilderness surroundings. But a purely technological stance, whereby we see the rain forests as simply standing reserve for timber production, leaves no room for this meaning. Taking this stance is 'annihilating' the wilderness in its proper meaning, even before we step in and chain-saw all the trees . . . ."

130. Interestingly, Heidegger refers to language as "the house of Being," while Barfield refers to it as "a kind of storehouse." See, Heidegger, *On the Way to Language* and Barfield, *Poetic Diction*, 57, respectively.

understanding of language . . . ."[131] The "revolutionary change" to which Taylor refers is again that *Dasein* does not speak language, but language speaks (through *Dasein*). Heidegger asserts that when one reflects upon language *qua* language, one abandons the traditional procedure of language study. Language is not merely a tool to be utilized, nor something to be studied, nor is it something one does or can control. One must get away from this understanding if one is to overcome the domination and enframing of objects. To do so, instead of understanding language as speaking one must understand it as "Saying." The question of language is really a reflection upon what he calls the "nature of Saying," because for Heidegger, all beings "Say."[132] Thus, the showing of phenomena is the "Saying" of phenomena. Saying is not just a name for human speaking, but is the essence of being.[133] Hence, he avers, "the essential being of language is Saying as showing."[134] He articulates this theory in a powerful excerpt from *On the Way to Language*, which is worth fully quoting,

> Saying is showing. In everything that speaks to us, in everything that touches us by being spoken and spoken about, in everything that gives itself to us in speaking, or waits for us unspoken, but also in the speaking that we do *ourselves*, there prevails Showing which causes to appear what is present, and to fade from appearance what is absent. *Saying is in no way the linguistic expression added to the phenomena after they have appeared—rather, all radiant appearance and all fading away is grounded in the showing Saying.*[135]

Here, Heidegger makes the integral connection between being and language. The astute reader will have noticed a link between Heidegger's language theory and his phenomenology. In the late Heidegger, language and phenomena are conceptually interchangeable.

---

131. See, Taylor, "Heidegger on Language," 433.

132. Heidegger, *On the Way to Language*, 49.

133. Ibid., 47. See, also 123, wherein he suggests that the "saying" of language must not be reduced to simply human speaking because it is the mark of everything that is present.

134. Ibid., 63 and 93. Therein, Heidegger makes his bold claim that "the being of everything that is resides in the word . . . therefore . . . language is the house of Being."

135. Ibid., 126 (emphasis added). He continues, "Saying sets all present beings free into their absence. Saying pervades and structures the openness of that clearing which every appearance must seek out and every disappearance must leave behind, and in which every present or absent being must show, say, announce itself."

Similarly, Barfield states that objects explain themselves much like people do.[136] For him, one does not merely describe objects as if they have nothing to say, but they reveal themselves to their subject in the aesthetic encounter. Like Heidegger, he also dispels what he calls "etymological accidents" by integrally relating language and being:

> Speech did not arise as the attempt of man to imitate, to master or to explain "nature"; for speech and nature came into being along with one another. Strictly speaking, only idolators [sic] can raise the question of the "origin of language." For anyone else to do so is like asking for the origin of origin. Roots are the echo of nature herself sounding in man. Or rather, they are the echo of what once sounded and fashioned in both of them at the same time.[137]

It should now be apparent that Barfield too believed that there is an integral relation between being and language. It is for this reason there can be no origin of speech, because speech actually sounds and fashions being coextensively.[138] For both, when one understands being as "speaking" one no longer dominates, but listens to, and hence learns from the world.[139] According to Barfield, once subjectivity is abandoned, "we become for the first time able to observe the phenomena of nature in a really unprejudiced way."[140]

Both figures indicate that a turn to poetry marks the true turn to language. The properly postured poet is one through whom the *logos* speaks.[141] In his introduction to Heidegger's *Poetry, Language, Thought*, Albert Hof-

136. Barfield, *Worlds Apart*, 145. Barfield mentions that we do not think of people as objects so we should not do the same with the natural world.

137. Barfield, *Saving the Appearances*, 123. For further reading see, entire chapter XVII, "The Origin of Language."

138. Barfield, *Worlds Apart*, 50. Barfield ultimately avers that it was not man who created speech but speech that created man. See also, Barfield, *Speaker's Meaning*, 25. Herein, he refers to the, "veiled and problematic origin of language itself."

139. Barfield, *Saving the Appearances*, 143. "The devoted love which thousands of naturalists, for example have felt for some aspect of nature to which they have been drawn, is not in spite of, it is actually dependent on their experience of the 'appearances' as substantially independent of themselves. The whole joy of it depends on its being an 'I-it' relation—oblivious, or contemptuous, of the teleological approach which dominated Aristotle and the Middle-Ages. *The happy bird-watcher does not say: 'Let's go and see what we can learn about ourselves from nature.'* He says: 'Let's go and see what nature is doing, bless her!'" (emphasis added).

140. Barfield, *Worlds Apart*, 157.

141. Heidegger, *On the Way to Language*. For several references to the poet—who seemingly embodies Heidegger's "hermeneutical circle"—see, "A Dialogue on Language" and "The Nature of Language."

stadter says that for Heidegger there is a striking contrast between the present technological age "in which everything, including man himself, becomes material for a process of self-assertive productions, self-assertive imposition of human will on things regardless of their own essential natures—and a life in which we would genuinely dwell as human beings."[142] Heidegger himself warns that being must be wrestled from the "subjection to a commandeering order."[143] It is to this subjective Will to Power that Heidegger juxtaposes the creativity of the poet.[144] Heidegger avers that one must not speak about language but let language speak itself as language.[145] The "authenticity" of *Dasein* thus occurs through "the self's disclosive nature, namely, as oriented towards the other through the openness of dialogue."[146] The poet's "self-denial" and "renunciation" of his own subjectivity produces intimacy with the word.[147] He writes, "Renunciation commits itself to the higher rule of the word which first lets a thing be as thing . . . ."[148] It is, therefore, the task of the poet to illuminate the possibilities of a true world.[149] The speech of genuine thinking is by nature poetic. It is, "the saying of truth, the saying of the unconcealedness of beings."[150] To quote Heidegger,

> Both poetry and thinking are distinctive Saying in that they remain delivered over to the mystery of the word as that which is most worthy of their thinking, and thus ever structured in their kinship.
>
> In order that we may in our thinking fittingly follow and lead this element worthy of thought as it gives itself to poetry, we abandon everything which we have now said to oblivion. We listen to the poem. We grow still more thoughtful now regarding the possibility that the more simply the poem sings in the mode of song the more readily our hearing may err.[151]

142. Heidegger, *Poetry, Language, Thought*, xiv–xv.

143. Heidegger, *On the Way to Language*, 132–33. See also, Heidegger, *Poetry, Language, Thought*, xv.

144. Heidegger, *Poetry, Language, Thought*, xv. See also, Heidegger, *On the Way to Language*, 59 and 66.

145. Heidegger, *On the Way to Language*, 50 and 59.

146. Schalow, "Language and the Social Roots of Conscience," 142.

147. Heidegger, *On the Way to Language*, 69.

148. Ibid., 150–51.

149. Heidegger, *Poetry, Language, Thought*, xv.

150. Ibid., x. See also, 71.

151. Heidegger, *On the Way to Language*, 155–56.

Heidegger's poetic esteem shares similarities with Barfield's poetic philosophy.[152] Barfield too juxtaposes the poetic with the modern scientific mind.[153] Fixated on what he believed to be the ills of the Cartesian legacy (see chapter 4), Barfield called modern culture "anti-poetic."[154] Without the poetic imagination, "all objects (*as* objects) are fixed and dead."[155] Modernity, in general, and modern science, in particular, deny the validity of the imagination, which must be rescued by poetry in order once again to make true knowledge possible.[156] Barfield saw romantic poetry—and its faculty of the imagination—as a way of ascertaining truth against the dominant scientific and intellectual trends of seventeenth- and eighteenth-century Europe. According to Barfield, the West had lost its way and it is the poet who must now restore that which was lost to this reductive methodology.[157] For poetry, he argued, reorients humanity's relation to the world.[158] The poetic imagination could restore the division between humanity and nature, and between fellow humans.[159] The poet disturbs bad mental habits (e.g., subjectivity) by affecting a "felt change of consciousness."[160] This is what spurred Barfield's interest in Coleridge. He saw that Coleridge's use of imaginative or poetic words revealed otherwise unapprehended parts of reality.[161] Poetry is thus

152. Heidegger, *Poetry, Language, Thought*, 70–72. Much like Barfield, Heidegger avers, "Language itself is poetry in the essential sense."

153. Barfield, *Poetic Diction*, 62–63.

154. Ibid., 94.

155. Barfield, *History in English Words*, 211. Barfield is here quoting from Coleridge's *Biographia Literaria (BL)*. Barfield, *Poetic Diction*, 180–81. Barfield notes, that "without the continued existence of poetry, without a steady influx of new meaning into language, even the knowledge and wisdom which poetry herself has given in the past must wither away into a species of mechanical calculation."

156. Barfield, *Poetic Diction*, 34.

157. It is difficult to locate anywhere in Barfield's work where he explores how other branches of art might serve his purpose. Here one is reminded of the work of Henri Bergson. See, Ruth Lorand, "Bergson's Conception of Art."

158. Ibid., 87.

159. Barfield, *Saving the Appearances*, 130. He writes that "the Romantic response to nature is exemplified in the relationship between Coleridge and Wordsworth . . . ." See also, Barfield, *History in English Words*, 209. "That mystical conception which the word [Romanticism] embodies in these lines—a conception which would make imagination the interpreter and part creator of a whole unseen world—is not found again until the Romantic Movement had begun." See also, Barfield, *Romanticism Comes of Age*, 140. Therein, Barfield states that Coleridge's work is divided into the relation of the self to nature and the relation of the self to other selves.

160. Barfield, *Poetic Diction*, 32.

161. Barfield, *Romanticism Comes of Age*, 6. See also, Barfield, *History in English Words*, 213. See also, Barfield, *What Coleridge Thought*, 133–34. Barfield viewed

an inner experience that reawakens one's conscious allowing one to jettison one's reductive proclivities for a moment in order to see things as they are.[162]

The Primacy of Poetry: Critiques and Conclusions

A brief summary of the language theories of Heidegger and Barfield indicates that when language is taken as a tool it enframes the real, rendering it in the form of idols. Such subjectivity is renounced when one realizes the integral relation of being and language. One might say that to envisage all being as "Saying" dispels a propensity for what Heidegger calls "violent"[163] subjectivity and makes space for a passive "listening" or "letting speak" to commence. This ensures, at the very least, that the sort of manipulation and domination that concerned both figures cease. For both, proper language— that which overcomes such violent subjectivity (whether via Heidegger's "renunciation" or Barfield's "imagination")—is poetic. The similarities of their language theories thus assume a primacy afforded to poetic discourse. In their attempt to overturn the dominant philosophical trends of their time, both looked to poetic language to resituate the subject's relation to the real. However, upon closer examination it is here that one finds a subtle yet decisive break regarding the subject's posture and ultimately his or her relationship to the source of inspiration.[164]

Coleridge as a visionary whose philosophy of "polarities" forged beyond the external/ internal, subject/object, and observer/phenomena dualisms that haunt the modern consciousness. For the idea that poetry expands consciousness and brings more than simple recollection, see also, Barfield, *Poetic Diction*, 52 and 55.

162. Barfield, *Poetic Diction*, 49.

163. Heidegger, *Poetry, Language, Thought*, 24.

164. To summarize briefly with references: Heidegger's phenomenology lends a certain passivity of *Dasein*, "a letting speak" of being or *Logos*, that seemingly obliterates subjectivity in the poetic "experience" (for numerous references to the poetic experience see, "A Dialogue on Language" and "The Nature of Language" in Heidegger, *On the Way to Language*). Chapter 2 intimates that this "experience" does escape the Kantian "sublime," and coincides with a guised nihilism that is incapable of ascertaining good and evil (see, Taylor, "Heidegger on Language," 452). For a critique of Heidegger's "onto-theology" and the "theology of the sublime" see, Betz, "Beyond the Sublime." Barfield's "polarity," however, which he gleans from Coleridge (chapter 2), presumably suspends the onto-theological univocal/equivocal dialectic, thereby upholding the subject (Barfield, *Saving the Appearances*, 123). Elsewhere he refers to this philosophy as "objective idealism" (Barfield, *Worlds Apart*, 211). Distinct from Heidegger's utter passivity, Barfield endows the subject with an active, albeit co-operative participatory role (drawing on Coleridge's "active imagination" as opposed to passive "fancy"—see, Barfield, *What Coleridge Thought*, 87) in the identification or naming of phenomena (Barfield, *Worlds Apart*, 140. See also, Barfield, *Night Operation*, 55. Barfield notes that, "There are two kinds of seeing. There is just 'seeing'—and there is 'being shown.'" Then

The root of the distinction between Heidegger's phenomenology and Barfield's poetic philosophy is revealed in a close examination of their translations of the Greek word "phenomenon." Fascinatingly they both draw upon the term to develop their aesthetic. In fact, Heidegger's earliest formulations on language in *Being and Time*—those that would form the very basis of his phenomenology—sound nearly identical to Barfield's remarks in chapter VII of *Saving the Appearances*. Their analyses are so similar in their examination of the Greek middle voice translation of "phenomena" that one wonders if Barfield gleaned this from *Being and Time* before writing his *Saving the Appearances*. Although there is clear evidence that Barfield had read Heidegger much later, there does not seem to be any indication that Barfield had read *Being and Time* prior to writing *Saving the Appearances*, nor is there any indication as to which of Heidegger's work Barfield had read.[165]

Nonetheless, in their analyses of the term both figures distinguish between "phenomena" and "appearances,"[166] but it is in their definition of "phe-

later in the same story he says that humans can only do what the God's do in them). As will be evident in chapter 5, distinct from Heidegger, Barfield ultimately articulates this aesthetic as suspended between active and passive, viewing humans as co-creators with the divine.

165. Early on Barfield seemed, at the very least, fond of Heidegger (see, footnote 100 above), although later he has a change of heart. In letters dated from 18th July 1987 to 29th May 1988, Terry Hipolito writes to Barfield for clarification on Barfield's theory of poetic diction for an article he is writing. In the exchange Hipolito mentions that Barfield had read a great deal of Heidegger. These letters also imply that Barfield was familiar with the work of both Heidegger and Derrida. See, "Owen Barfield Papers," Hipolito-Hunter, 1969–97, Dep. C, 1070. For the actual article see, Hipolito, "Owen Barfield's Poetic Diction." In his later private exchange with Hipolito Barfield notes that he and Heidegger do not, "get on," and that in Heidegger's writings, "there is less than meets the eye." Also, in a 1989 publication Barfield takes issue with Heidegger's notion of "silence" for having "not yet caught up with Coleridge." Barfield, *Owen Barfield on C. S. Lewis*, 62. It is worth mentioning the Max Müller to whom Barfield credits his earliest work on language is the German philologist, not the later Max Müller, a student of Heidegger.

166. Barfield was critical of appearances. He alludes that appearances, too, are a reduction of the original Greek "phenomena" to "objects" and "events." Appearances result from the "more or less continuous progress from a vague but immediate awareness of the 'meaning' of phenomena towards an increasing preoccupation with the phenomena themselves." See, Barfield, *Saving the Appearances*, 142.

Similarly, Heidegger, in *Being and Time*, "A. The Concept of Phenomenon," argues that the term phenomenon "has proximally nothing at all to do with what is called an 'appearance' . . . because appearing is precisely a not-showing-itself." In this way, "phenomena are never appearances, though on the other hand every appearance is dependent on phenomena." Such "appearing is possible only by reason of a showing-itself of something." Appearing is "announcing-itself [*das Sich-melden*] through something that shows itself," but as not-showing-itself; in this showing-itself appearance indicates something that does not show itself. Thus, "appearance is tantamount to a 'bringing

nomena" that their subtle, yet crucial aesthetic differences emerge. Barfield avers that the word "phenomena" "has come to be practically synonymous with 'objects' and 'events'" (i.e., as objects or events distinct from their subjects), whereas in its original Greek middle voice the "verb suggests neither wholly 'what is perceived, from within themselves, by men' nor wholly 'what from without, forces itself on man's senses,' but something between the two."[167] In Heidegger, however, one finds a more complex and slightly nuanced version of Barfield's later analysis. Therein, Heidegger translates the Greek middle voice usage of "phenomenon" as "to show itself" or, in regard to being's deep connection with the *logos*, a "letting-something-be-seen,"[168] which again he later refers to as the "Saying" of being.[169]

To summarize, Barfield translates "phenomena" as "neither wholly 'what is perceived, from within themselves, by men' nor wholly 'what from without, forces itself on man's senses,' but something between the two," while Heidegger simply translates "phenomena" as "to show itself." The implications of these translations are crucial in that they pinpoint the fundamental point at which they diverge. Here, one may recall that for Heidegger poetry is a "renunciation" or "self-denial" that "commits itself to the higher rule of the word,"[170] and that Heidegger speaks of this posture of "listening" as an abandoning of everything, "which we have now said to oblivion."[171] This passive[172] "letting speak" denies the subject any active co-operation and

---

forth' . . . but something which does not make up the real Being of what brings it forth. . . . That which does the announcing and is brought forth does, of course, show itself, and in such a way that, as an emanation of what it announces, it keeps this very thing constantly veiled in itself. . . . But what thus shows itself (the 'phenomenon' in the genuine primordial sense) is at the same time an 'appearance' as an emanation of something which hides itself in that appearance—an emanation which announces." Barfield's and Heidegger's aesthetic seek to counteract a perceived subjectivity, which they believe yields mere appearances. Again, while their diagnoses are similar their solutions are not. This is further clarified below.

167. Barfield, *Saving the Appearances*, 51–55.

168. Ibid., "*B. The Concept of the Logos*," 56.

169. Heidegger, *On the Way to Language*, 155.

170. Ibid., 150–51.

171. Ibid., 155–56.

172. Such passivity seemingly culminates in Maurice Blanchot's concept of language. A fitting description of such passivity that also fits well with the trajectory of this chapter can be found in, Wall, *Radical Passivity*, 4–5. Wall writes, "That which poetry each time says will be nothing more than the empty totality of language itself. Before anything is communicated, communication itself is communicated. When someone gestures to me, for example, how do I know that there is an attempt to communicate even if the person speaks a foreign tongue? A mute communication precedes any *dit* (said). This communication is unspoken but irreducible. It is an image

thereby smacks of a sort of slavery to the mystery of being, which ultimately strips away all creativity from the poet who represents the properly postured subject.[173] This reaction against the domineering gaze goes too far.[174] While, Barfield, on the other hand, explicitly denies this form of passivity in his *Speaker's Meaning*, wherein he discusses of the nature of inspiration securing for the poet an active role.[175] He critiques the logic of such "extreme views" that suggest, "that all [the poet] has to do is to get out of the way, to surrender himself unreservedly to his genius or his imagination or his unconscious or whatever he calls it," because such passivity always-already necessitates a very real activity on the part of the subject. Thus, "we are left in no doubt that this surrender of the self is a *positive act*, and even a very difficult one to achieve."[176] Unlike Heidegger, Barfield does not altogether abandon subjectivity but affords the subject a real active creativity. Indeed, this may indicate why in Barfield's only reference to Heidegger he seems to suggest that Heidegger is incapable of explicating what language actually refers to. It seems Heidegger's phenomenology is akin to those, who "seem to oscillate between a somehow pregnant conviction that language does not 'refer' and the necessity, which arises as soon as they open their mouths, of assuring that it does."[177] As detailed in the following chapter, for Barfield, the imagination represents the active creative element in man, which cor-

---

of communication that precedes any message. Language that precedes itself, or that 'begins' in repetition, is poetry, and this preemptive 'speaking' belongs to no subjective intention to say anything. Older than the subject, it is a language spoken by no one, or by an anonymous 'someone' (Blanchot's *il*, 'he,' the Neuter), who cannot speak in the first person. Unable to communicate, this anonymity cannot cease 'his' saying just as it is unable to manifest 'himself' in any statement, for 'he' *is* only insofar as, and for as long as, 'he' speaks. Coinciding so perfectly with 'himself,' 'he' just as perfectly escapes 'himself' or is outside 'himself.' 'He' (or 'Someone,' for it is always another) is perfectly *in* language. Unable to turn around and grasp himself in a reflection without losing himself again, this 'Someone's' only being is that repetitive Levinasian *dire* (saying) that unsays itself. It is our thesis in this chapter that the Blanchotian writer is the one who is 'capable' of this inability to cease to speak. Refusing all self-presence, this anonymity nevertheless is a hollowing out that makes possible all presence, all work, and all thinking. 'Someone,' in short, is language itself. 'Someone's' being is so utterly absorbed in language without any residue that there is no longer anyone left to save or manifest."

173. Ibid., 29. For an example, Wall notes that with the "radical passivity" of Levinas and Blanchot "the artist neither creates nor reveals."

174. Milbank, "The Thing That Is Given," 505. Milbank suggests, "The question then arises of whether Heidegger does not, in rightly acknowledging the mediating role of the thing [object], in the end obliterate the role and significance of the living, creating and observing human person." See also, Schrag, *The Self after Postmodernity*.

175. Barfield, *Speaker's Meaning*, 83.

176. Ibid., 84 (emphasis added).

177. Barfield, "Language and Discovery," 133.

responds to the real. The poetic element in all meaningful language is of vital importance because it activates the imagination and its demand for unity (otherwise one is left with a theory of perception based solely on the passivity of the senses).[178] So, whereas Heidegger's phenomenological passivity tends to negate the subject's creativity,[179] Barfield's poetic imagination suspends the poet in a middle realm honoring him or her with an active, albeit co-operative role, an ostensible share in the creative source.

So it is the source, or inspiration, of the poet that ultimately separates Heidegger's phenomenology and Barfield's poetic philosophy. Recall, Heidegger uses *logos* as simultaneously the word for both being and Saying.[180] The word or *logos* gives being, and therefore phenomena abide in language.[181] But, Heidegger claims that one cannot know the origin of the poetic word.[182] In his later work he would go as far as to say that poetry and language, as with being, actually comes from nothing,[183] and in other instances he states that poetry is the advent of a truth that arrives out of "nothing."[184] Here, Heidegger's phenomenological gaze is not far from nihilism.[185] This analysis is supported by Taylor's claim that Heidegger's language

178. Barfield, *Poetic Diction*, 27.

179. Pickstock, *After Writing*, 22. Pickstock's critique of Derrida shares similarities with the present critique of Heidegger: "Derrida's written model suggests no people at all, only a word which comes from nowhere, an autonomous word which conceals or violently eradicates its origins and dictates to its 'author,' rendering him entirely passive before a disembodied and (spiritual?) power." Pickstock argues instead for a liturgical language where, a "genuine subjectivity is to be attained through the redemptive return of doxological dispossession, thus ensuring that the subject is neither autonomously self-present, nor passively controlled from without (the pendulum of 'choices' available to the citizen of the immanentist city)" (170).

180. Heidegger, *On the Way to Language*, 155. According to Heidegger, "The oldest word for the rule of the word thus thought, for Saying, is *logos*: Saying which, in showing, lets beings appear in their 'it is.' . . . The same word, however, the word for Saying, is also the word for *Being*, that is, for the presencing of beings. Saying and Being, word and thing, belong to each other in a veiled way, a way which has hardly been thought and is not to be thought out to the end."

181. Heidegger, *On the Way to Language*, 82.

182. Ibid., 140.

183. Heidegger, *Poetry, Language, Thought*, 73.

184. Ibid., 69–70.

185. Milbank, *The Word Made Strange*, 38. Milbank concurs, that in Heidegger "every finite 'presence' (of being) in its claim to a share of ultimate reality and of value is folded back into the flux of Being as time or non-present 'nothing' . . . ." Later on Milbank argues that Heidegger's critique of onto-theology is firstly a misreading of Plato (a misinterpretation of transcendence), which occurs by reading with "neo-scholastic spectacles"; that is, to appropriate beings by being as "nothing." According to Milbank, this is because the ontological difference—in terms of analogy and participation—was never seriously considered by Heidegger. See also, Wall, *Radical Passivity*, 11. Wall

theory, along with its positive uses (e.g., deep ecology), also has "terrifyingly dangerous" uses, because ultimately there is "no place for the retrieval of evil [or morals] in his system."[186] Likewise, Heidegger's pupil Hans Jonas remarks that the language of the later Heidegger "has become increasingly and obtrusively ontic, and however figurative or poetical such language is meant to be (and however poetic it is, even if bad poetry), its ontic meaning is inalienable from it on pain of it becoming empty sound."[187] Similarly, David Bentley Hart points out the irony of Heidegger's attempt to secure metaphor while his own ontology is itself equivocal (i.e., between being and beings),[188] while Milbank contends that there is no place for metaphor in

notes that in Levinas, poetic language loses its ability to refer. "Unable to reveal or aver, words are lost between meaning and showing, between saying and seeing, and they depart from the straightforwardness of intentionality as if lured by another destiny. Insofar as I cannot separate myself from these words that linger on my tongue—words that are no longer my own since they have defected from my meaning-to-say—they involve me in that other destiny of which they are already a part."

186. Taylor, "Heidegger On Language," 452. Therein, Taylor suggests that this tendency is "part of the reason why Hitler could blindside [Heidegger], and why he never thereafter could get a moral handle on the significance of what happened between 1933–1945." See also, Betz, *After Enlightenment*, 331. Betz argues that Heidegger's insistence upon the nothing of *Sein*, "becomes the source of ethics, revelation, and poetic inspiration. Such is the odd, uncompelling, and, in view of the horrors of the twentieth century, ethically chilling result of Heidegger's attempt to purify philosophy of theology . . . thereby bringing the history of philosophy (divorced from theology) to its explicitly nihilistic conclusion."
For Barfield's opposite view see, Barfield, *Romanticism Comes of Age*, 13. Barfield is vehemently against the "evil" "septic disease" of the political Reich. Barfield implies that the Holocaust represents a side of Germany that attempted to obliterate or drive out the spiritual side of figures like Steiner and Goethe. He seems to use these tragic events as a warning to his own country of the implications of the rejection of the romantic vision.

187. Jonas, *The Phenomenon of Life*, 252. See also, 247. Jonas reads this otherness of being as nihilistic (associating it with Gnosticism), because it denies the fundamental goodness of the cosmological order, and it places the self above any moral law freeing the individual to create values beyond good and evil. See also, 258. Like Taylor, Jonas makes explicit references to Heidegger's Nazism being a product of his moral-less philosophy that he describes as "pride," "neutrality," and "indifference." See also, 181–82, wherein Jonas critiques Heidegger's definition of truth (*alethia*) as "unconcealing." Jonas says this is not what "truth" means, but rather unlike Heidegger's definition, Jonas's maintains an ethical commitment, "to abstain from concealing and deceiving." For Jonas, "truth" carries with it moral implications that Heidegger ignores.

188. Hart, *The Beauty of the* Infinite, 215. Hart writes, "In truth, every attempt to talk of being is a metaphysical labor; the Heideggarian tendency to treat every philosophical discourse save Heidegger's as irredeemably metaphorical, as 'forgetful' of what Heidegger has recalled, is symptomatic of a dogmatism that never interrogates its own presuppositions regarding the trajectory a philosophical thought of being must take; the conviction that 'onto-theology' understands being simply in terms of 'causes' and 'grounds'—without any analogical latitude being granted such terms—is reductive, to

Heidegger's poetics.[189] One is left to ponder, is this at all poetry? Ironically, in his obsession to overcome modern subjectivity, Heidegger altogether annuls it.

What emerges from the above analysis is Heidegger's subtle commitment to the very metaphysics (onto-theology) he sought to overcome.[190] The language Heidegger used when he referred to poetry was ironically still trapped in immanence. As such, he was unable to articulate a theory of poetic utterance that was actually poetic. Instead, he is left in a dialectic shuttling to and fro from a prosaic language to a poetic language (to use Barfieldian terms), from a pure univocity to a pure equivocity, where any active univocal assertion of truth is seen as a Will to Power and whose only alternative is a passive equivocal surrender to the utter mystery or nothingness of being.[191] This is why Betz[192] and Milbank[193] can accuse Heidegger of a univocal ontology, while Hart is equally correct to accuse him of employing an equivocal ontology and its opposite (which he tellingly refers to as the "savage equivalence of univocity and equivocity"),[194] and Taylor, among others, accuses him of nihilism. The end game of Heidegger's immanentized subject is either one whose subjectivity can only be secured by the Will to Power or an equally diabolical passive surrender to meaninglessness, neither of which is poetic.

Barfield's poetic philosophy is, however, more ambiguous. He, unlike Heidegger, holds that meaning is not beyond metaphysical speculation. As Hipolito notes, "It is just where Heidegger thinks of himself as wandering in a mist 'beyond philosophy' that Barfield pitches base camp and plots

---

say the very least, and disingenuous insofar as it is a conviction oblivious to how easily deconstructable Heidegger's own metaphors are."

189. Milbank, "The Thing That Is Given," 531. Milbank suggests that Heidegger's poetry is instead a false *mathesis*, "which reduces it to a series of inert figures, either spatial or temporal, but never both at once." Further in denying the analogical or participatory element (the relationship between God and creature), "he simply cannot think poetry, or *poiēsis* at all" as in the end he fails to construct a poetic ontology.

190. See Hipolito, "Owen Barfield's Poetic Diction." Hipolito notes that one of the fundamental disagreements between the theories of Barfield and Heidegger was Heidegger's want to move beyond the history of philosophy and metaphysics, whereas Barfield is quite at home with traditional realist philosophy, viewing it as an undeniable necessity if history, words, and humanity are to be taken seriously.

191. See, Hart, "The Offering of Names," 281. Hart notes that Heidegger's univocity of being results in a poetic utterance that says nothing, "of being or of God."

192. Betz, "Beyond the Sublime (Part One)," 395.

193. Milbank, *The Word Made Strange*, 191. See note 19. See also, 108. Milbank notes that even metaphor, used univocally tends towards idolatry (i.e., pagan mythology).

194. Hart, *The Beauty of the Infinite*, 242.

his route to what he considers to be a clearly visible summit."[195] Distinct
from Heidegger, Barfield's ontology allows for an active participation in the
logos, the source of all creativity. Barfield quotes Coleridge's statement, "the
Primary Imagination I hold to be the living Power and prime Agent of all
human perception, and as a repetition in the finite mind of the eternal act
of creation in the infinite I AM."[196] For Barfield, the God-Man "polarity"
grounds all being.[197] This means that the *logos* is divine, but also human
(or the divine element of man), as the creative Son remains in each man,
endowing man with a real ability to create.[198] Thus he admirably maintains
that finite reason—its highest faculty being the imagination (see, chapter
2)—participates in the infinite *logos*, endowing the poet with a co-operative role in the creative poetic act.[199] For Barfield, this active creative co-
operative achievement of the imagination unifies the scattered members of
unrelated "percepts," thereby overcoming the passive scientific intellect.[200]
As such, one might here infer that for Barfield poetic language is not to
be understood as a leap from univocal to equivocal language (as with Heidegger), but his poetic philosophy is situated somewhere between the two.
Indeed, Barfield himself seems to be aware of this crucial difference in his
brief critique of what he calls Heidegger's "silence."[201] Indeed, for Barfield
the imagination overcomes this active/passive dialectic by suspending the
subject and object in a "polar tension."[202] By resituating the subject in the
middle, Barfield's poetic philosophy endows the poet with a moral obligation to hold to reason while drawing upon the imagination, which allows a
deeper metaphorical meaning of the real to supervene.

195. Hipolito, "Owen Barfield's Poetic Diction."

196. Barfield, *What Coleridge Thought*, 74. Barfield is here quoting from Coleridge's, *BL*, chapter 13.

197. Barfield, *What Coleridge Thought*, 113, 147, and 154.

198. Barfield, *Romanticism Comes of Age*, 52–53. See also, Barfield, *What Coleridge Thought*, 114.

199. Barfield, *Saving the Appearances*, 100–101. In *Saving the Appearances* he describes Aristotle's division of *nous patheticus* and *nous poieticus* in order to show the
passive and active elements in perceiving and in thinking.

200. Barfield, *Romanticism Comes of Age*, 27. See also, Barfield, *Poetic Diction*, 28.
See also, Barfield, *What Coleridge Thought*, 101. Idols are formed with mere passive
understanding that culminates in detachment, but "through imagination and the gift of
reason we realize, in polarity, that very culmination as the possibility of a different and
higher order of attachment."

201. Barfield, *Owen Barfield on C. S. Lewis*, 62.

202. Barfield, *What Coleridge Thought*, 78. The imagination consists of both active
and passive elements.

Here, Sugerman notes a move from the "horizontal" to the "vertical."
In Barfield, "we observe a move from the "I am," to the "thou art," from the
self to the world of objects, to the infinite 'I AM.'"[203] Is this implying that the
poet's participation in the infinite is univocal? At the moment, it would seem
this "vertical" move is premature. For, Barfield often exhibits a sort of collapse of the infinite into the finite, what Przywara called a "theo-pan-ism,"
or oppositely the finite into the infinite, which he called, "pan-the-ism."[204]
Indeed, further clarification is in order if one is to suggest that Barfield does,
in fact, overcome the immanence of modern discourse and offer a true
account of *poiēsis*.

Surely Barfield's symbolic worldview[205] is somewhat orthodox, but
when he articulates his concept of *logos* (particularly in *What Coleridge
Thought*) his philosophy of polarity appears similar to Hegel's "tri-unity,"
which ultimately collapses the subject in the "sublation" of "difference."[206]
For example, in his *Romanticism Comes of Age*, Barfield states the "creative
imagination means the subject somehow merges or resolves into the object," and hence disappears the "I" and the "not I."[207] In a much earlier work,
Poetic Diction (1928), he suggests that the real moment of knowing is when
one ceases to be a subject at all.[208] In such instances it appears that, like Heidegger's passive subject, Barfield's participatory poet altogether abandons
subjectivity. While further examination of the specifics of Barfield's poetic

203. Sugerman, *Evolution of Consciousness*, 197.

204. Przywara, *Analogia Entis*," 512. Chapter 5, suggests that this "holding in tension" of the subject/object dualism, which Barfield gleans from Coleridge, does not
entirely escape Hegel's "immanent trinitarianism," because the "holding in tension" to
which polarity refers is not far from Hegelian "sublation" (see, Barfield, *What Coleridge
Thought*, 31). Ultimately, Barfield's poetic philosophy does not account for theology's
"real distinction" between essence and existence, which constitutes the analogical difference between the Creator and creatures. But for the purposes of this chapter, one can
for now surmise that Heidegger's theory of poetry is based upon an immanent construal of being, which is the inevitable consequence of the very onto-theology he sought
to overcome. Chapter 5 argues that Barfield's poetic philosophy comes much closer to
realizing that transcendence (vertically) transects (horizontal) immanence precisely
because his philosophy is based loosely upon a participatory metaphysics, which envisages being in terms of transcendence. Chapter 5 underscores Przywara's "Polarities"
as it relates to Barfield's poetic philosophy. Although it is Przywara's theological vision
(*analogia entis*) that properly resituates the subject analogically in his or her horizontal
relation to the world and vertical relation to the Creator.

205. Hocks, "The 'Other' Postmodern Theorist."

206. This is further examined in chapter 5. This "sublation" is unable to account for
theology's "real distinction" between creature and creator, thus collapsing the economic
and immanent Trinity.

207. Barfield, *Romanticism Comes of Age*, 19.

208. Barfield, *Poetic Diction*, 209.

philosophy is still to come, it seems for now safe to say that integrity of the subject, although upheld, is somewhat compromised by his aesthetic. Nevertheless, one can here conclude that Barfield's poetic philosophy is more "on the way to language" than Heidegger's phenomenology. By resituating the subject in the middle, Barfield suspends, and thereby rescues, language from meaningless equivocal non-identity and univocal repetition. Further, in holding this tension, he affirms an opening within philosophical immanence that is traced throughout the essay.

Regardless of their shortcomings, the hallmark of both Heidegger's and Barfield's language theories—the turn from subjectivity, to poetry—marks a real turn to religion that should not be underestimated. For, as Milbank puts it, "the real achievement of a non-instrumental and metaphorical conception of language . . . is part of an ultimately theological and antimaterialist strategy," because "if metaphor is fundamental, then religion ceases to be a mystery *in addition to* the mystery of humanity itself."[209] Yet, for theology this is not enough, because a proper *poiēsis* upholds the integrity of the poet as subject by endowing the poet with an active, albeit co-operative, role via participation in the ultimate creative act achieved through the Word.[210]

This chapter examined how Barfield found Steiner's evolution of consciousness compatible with his philological thesis. But what exceeded Steiner's work was Barfield's insistence that language is inherently poetic or metaphorical. Heidegger was introduced as a formidable interlocutor to explicate the significance of Barfield's poetic philosophy. Both figures attempt to overcome modernity's domineering gaze through a repositioning of the subject. By envisaging language as mediated, Barfield at times gazes beyond the strictures of the immanent dialectic (i.e., univocal/equivocal) to the theological, whereas Heidegger's passivity falls short. Now, to further examine Barfield's poetic philosophy, chapter 2 draws upon a superior interlocutor, Samuel Taylor Coleridge, who, in the throes of modernity, weaves ancient Platonic and modern Kantian themes to bring poetry and philosophy together. An analysis of the contemporary reception of Coleridge sheds further light on the ambiguities of Barfield's poetic philosophy left unaddressed in the present chapter.

---

209. Milbank, *The Word Made Strange*. See, chapter 4, "The Linguistic Turn as a Theological Turn," 106. See also, 123, wherein Milbank argues that Christian theology must seek to locate a "poetic existence in Christ."

210. In chapter 5 it is argued that the theological use of analogy (centered upon the Christological formulation that the human and divine natures are united yet paradoxically "unmixed") solves the dilemma forged by its very rejection.

2

Poetic Philosophy

If the mind be not passive, if it be indeed made in God's image, the Image of the Creator, there is ground for the suspicion that any system built on the passiveness of mind must be false . . . .

—COLERIDGE[1]

Nothing could have been more distortive and reductive than the rigid separation that much modern philosophy imposed between imagination and perception.

—SALLIS[2]

I wish our clever young poets would remember my homely definitions of prose and poetry; that is, prose = words in their best order;—poetry = the best words in the best order.

—COLERIDGE[3]

Situating Samuel Taylor Coleridge

Coleridge: Poet . . . and Philosopher?

IN THE END, HEIDEGGER'S *Kehre*—if one could indeed call it that—does nothing to elude the bounds of immanence. His ontology restricts poetry

1. In a letter to Thomas Poole, March 1801, in Muirhead, *Coleridge As Philosopher*, 51.
2. Sallis, *Logic of Imagination*, 155.
3. Coleridge, *Specimens of the Table Talk*, 12 July 1827.

to a univocal/equivocal dialectic, which concomitantly divides philosophy and poetry, univocal truth and equivocal meaninglessness. His attempt to loose poetic language from metaphysical speculation, which for him bears the marks of a univocal ontology, ironically yields an equally untenable equivocal ontology, wherein the true subject, the poet as being, gives him- or herself over to the absolutely unknown or nothingness of being. In this way, Heidegger's poetics are ironically no less onto-theological than that to which his anti-metaphysical stance is opposed. In the end he falls prey to his own critique. Barfield's poetic philosophy, his realist or symbolic metaphysic, however, goes further to uphold the integrity of the subject in the creative act via an implicit rejection of the staunch separation of philosophical and poetic language that plagues Heidegger. Barfield's poetic philosophy, at the very least, intimates a viable alternative to such immanetized philosophies.

Long before Heidegger and Barfield developed their respective theories of poetry medieval nominalism began to shape the Western theological/philosophical mind.[4] By the sixteenth century objects were understood to be within an immanentized or flattened space (*res extensa*), while subjective qualities were relegated to the mind (*res cogitans*).[5] By the time of Kant this trajectory forged a staunch boundary between the realm of the transcendent and the immanent,[6] which it could be argued promulgates the division between philosophical and poetic language that Barfield traced in *Poetic Diction*.[7] In this late paradigm, when the philosopher traverses the bounds of immanence, he leaves philosophy behind and enters the sublime realm of myth and poetry. The subject thus, is *either* a philosopher *or* a poet, language is *either* philosophical *or* poetic; hence, the impossibility of a poetic philosophy. For this, Barfield implicitly blames Kant.[8] If a truly poetic

---

4. Funkenstein, *Theology and the Scientific Imagination.*

5. Lefebvre, *The Production of Space.*

6. Hoff, "The Rise and Fall of the Kantian Paradigm." For an excellent genealogy of the Kantian sublime and its effect on modern and postmodern discourse see, Betz, "Beyond the Sublime (Part One)," 395–96. Betz indicates that this Kantian sublime or difference, which purges the world of transcendence, is radicalized by the French postmodern philosophers (particularly Jean-Luc Nancy).

7. See, chapter V, "Language and Poetry," in Barfield, *Poetic Diction*, 93–101. Barfield traces the history of this division, which he says results in the division of truth and myth, prose and poetry, and subject and object.

8. Ibid., 184. Barfield notes that "it does not require a very active fancy to see the Königsberg ghost hovering above, and intertwining itself with the ideas of minds that never even knew Kant's name; and this direct reference may be just as strong over others which are directly acquainted with his books—and perhaps even despise them. In Croce's honest words, Kantian doctrine is '(so to say) immanent in all modern thought.'" See, also Adey, *C. S. Lewis' Great War*, 21–22.

philosophy can indeed be established, this presumed rupture between immanence and transcendence requires revision. With this in mind, and in order to understand better the significance of Barfield's poetic philosophy, one must turn to the work of Kant—whose noumenal/phenomenal distinction had limited the crossing of this immanent boundary—and to those whose questioning of Kant's boundaries assuaged the aforesaid division between philosophy and poetry that Kant had seemingly, or perhaps even intentionally, left unresolved.

The Romantic poet Samuel Taylor Coleridge is a particularly "polarizing" figure in post-Kantian philosophical discourse and is arguably Barfield's greatest influence.[9] As such, an examination of the reception of Coleridge's philosophical musings—as *both* a poet *and* a philosopher—provides a précis of post-Kantian philosophy and a lens through which to locate the particularities of Barfield's thought.

It goes without saying that Coleridge is among the greatest of the romantic poets, but as a philosopher[10] Coleridge is considered a novice at best.[11] His style invoked accusations of plagiarism—not without good reason—that would further deny him any consideration as a distinct contributor to modern philosophical discourse. Perhaps Coleridge was guilty of a negligent plagiarism, but is this an adequate reason to discredit his conclusions, or is there something more subtle at play? In theory, all proper philosophical discourse begins by reiterating prior conclusions in order to establish something that accurately gives account of the tradition while it is, in its own unique way, distinguishable from those prior conclusions.[12] In

9. Diener, *The Role of Imagination*, 94. Diener goes as far as to say that Coleridge had an earlier and more profound effect on Barfield than Steiner. It should be noted that Barfield's reception of Coleridge offers no critique. One cannot distinguish between Barfield's reception of Coleridge and Barfield's own philosophy. Barfield consistently employed Coleridge's thought throughout his writings at times directly quoting him in support of his own endeavors. See also, Barfield and Tennyson, *A Barfield Reader*, xv. Interestingly, Coleridge is buried at Highgate School in London which Barfield also attended.

10. Barfield, *Romanticism Comes of Age*, 148. At the time of his 1944 publication of *Romanticism Comes of Age*, Barfield notes that in England Coleridge the philosopher is "almost entirely unread and to a very large extent unpublished."

11. Bode, "Coleridge and Philosophy," 589. Bode details an exhaustive account of the various criticisms of Coleridge's philosophy to which Bode himself adheres. Some of the more harsh critiques mentioned are Rene Wellek's claim that Coleridge's philosophy was "futile" and "incoherent" and Mary Warnock's accusation of Coleridge's "unintellectual attitude to philosophy" as well as the oft-cited accusations of plagiarism.

12. Simons, "Coleridge Beyond Kant and Hegel," 465. Simons notes, "Addressing an imaginary, generalized reader in a planned 'preface' to his 'Meta[physical] Works' in a notebook entry from December 1804, Coleridge advises her/him to 'read Tetens, Kant,

fact, Coleridge himself suggests that the activity of genius is the relationship between tradition and the individual talent, which together produce
true "originality."[13] Barfield, who some take to be an authority on Coleridge
while others exclude him, was convinced that Coleridge's insights were
utterly unique.[14] Why then is he so easily dismissed as a philosopher?

Surely one may argue that the mainstream ignorance of Coleridge's
philosophical conclusions is simply the product of an intellectual naiveté.
But as Barfield saw it, the predominating philosophical climate propagated
by Cartesianism and British empiricism and its resultant materialism left
no room for such a thinker.[15] As such, Coleridge, the philosopher—if one is
willing to grant him the title—represents perhaps the antithesis of the philosophical climate of his time.[16] It was, in fact, the very heart of the romantics

_____

Fichte, and Schelling—and there you will trace or if you are on the hunt, track me.'
Some critics have accepted this challenge and traced him from Kant, through Fichte,
and then on to Schelling—at which point the trail appears to stop. To see this point as
the end of Coleridge's development is to charge him with tacit plagiarism and to deny
to him any originality. . . . Coleridge's philosophic soul is not only in the same spirit as
his predecessors but is indeed innovative and truly original in the Coleridgean sense of
the word . . . ." Simons argues that one of the significant distinctions is Coleridge's move
from Kant's transcendental to transcendence, which he says moves beyond Hegelian
aesthetics.

13. Hocks, "Novelty in Polarity to 'the Most Admitted Truths,'" 85.

14. Indeed, Barfield dedicated an entire text to espousing *What Coleridge Thought*.
See also, *Romanticism Comes of Age* for Barfield's defense of Coleridge. Regarding the
reception of Barfield's work on Coleridge see, De Lange, *Owen Barfield*, 72. De Lange
notes that in a 29th April, 1973 letter to Barfield, Prof Craig Miller of the University of
British Columbia, a leading Coleridge specialist, wrote that Barfield's *What Coleridge
Thought* is "the best book on Coleridge in existence." However, contemporary works
on Coleridge pay little heed to Barfield's work on Coleridge (e.g., Douglas Hedley, in
Coleridge, Philosophy and Religion, gives little attention to Barfield, citing his work as a
secondary source. In the more recently published collection of essays on the Coleridge's
Opus Maximum, *Coleridge's Assertion of Religion*, edited by Barbeau, Barfield does not
even make the index).

15. See Barfield, *What Coleridge Thought*, 30. See also, Vigus, *Platonic Coleridge*,
14–18. Similarly, Vigus notes an anti-Platonic sentiment in England.

16. Muirhead, *Coleridge As Philosopher*, 259. Muirhead too talks of a "certain un-
ripeness of the time for the acceptance by philosophers of these ideas." This may indeed
be what Coleridge is implying in his admittedly fictional letter in which he addresses
the reception of his "opinions and method of argument" regarding the "necessity" of his
"conclusions" on the imagination found in chapter 13 of the *BL*. The author of the ficti-
tious letter states that Coleridge's thought is, "directly the reverse of all I had ever had
been accustomed to consider as truth . . . ." See also, Barfield, *What Coleridge Thought*,
27. Regarding the final three paragraphs of chapter 13 of the *Biographia Literaria*
Barfield states that, "Coleridge had in contemplation a great book on the Constructive
Philosophy, which was likely to contain opinions and a method of argument not merely
different from, but 'directly the reverse' of all that his contemporaries were accustomed

to overcome the detachment of man from nature that remained in the wake of the rise of the scientific imagination. As Barfield saw it, Coleridge's "dynamic philosophy," his philosophy of "polarity," was the only true alternative to the malaise caused by the fashionable philosophy of his time.[17] A number of Barfield's texts employ Coleridge's philosophical insights as a corrective panacea to the various modern dualisms of which he was so critical, one of which was the division between philosophical and poetic language.

So in turning to Coleridge the question one must attempt to answer regards ultimately the relation (or lack thereof) between philosophical and poetic language. How this question is answered depends generally upon one's view of the limits of reason; that is, whether poetic language (or religious discourse) oversteps these limits (the Kantian "Sublime")[18] or paradoxically exceeds these limits, while still remaining within the limits of reason (as in Coleridge's mention of the poet saying the unsayable). This question formed the philosophical milieu from which Coleridge's philosophical writings emerged. As such, this chapter will analyze the various conclusions of critics and admirers of Coleridge alike who base the validity of his philosophical work upon their conception of the relation between philosophy and poetry. On the one side are those who disdain Coleridge for overstepping the limits of reason imposed by Kant. These critics often associate Coleridge's philosophy with the work of the German Idealists (particularly Fichte, Schelling, and Hegel), who they believe attempted to "absolutize" Kant's transcendentals. On the other side are those admirers of the "Platonic Coleridge"[19]

---

to think."

17. Barfield, "Either: Or," 27.

18. Kant, *Critique of Judgment*, 99. Here Kant explicitly relegates the sublime to the subjective experience: "An aesthetic judgment . . . refers the presentation, by which an object is given, solely to the subject; it brings to our notice no characteristic of the object . . . ." See also, Leask, *The Politics of Imagination*, 109–11. Leask notes that in the *Third Critique* Kant frees the imagination from understanding as an aesthetic judgment of beauty. It is in this way that poetry could provide a sense of apprehension not possible by philosophy. Leask, in favor of this reading of Kant, argues that, "the power of Kant's aesthetic judgment of the beautiful was contingent upon the fact that it was set aside from the realm of objective knowledge." He, thus, makes beauty (the abysmal sublime in which the imagination gazes) subjective. For Kant, there is a "radical discontinuity" between the sublime and the rational and empirical faculties of mind." See also, Schindler, "Surprised by Truth, " 594–96. Schindler notes that, "Kant remarks in the Third Critique, because the sublime is infinite, it cannot be encountered anywhere in the world, and turns out to be reason's 'encounter' with itself. . . . What looks like the inbreaking of the radically Other is, in fact, the moment of the purest introspection. . . . Kant represents an extreme form of the rationalism that necessarily excludes the possibility of an intelligible revelation . . . ."

19. See, Vigus, *Platonic Coleridge*.

who commend his attempt to "Platonize" the work of Kant, arguing that Coleridge's poetic philosophy offers a robust critique that issues forth from an apparent *aporia* in Kant's system. This unresolved tension in the Kantian corpus is that he locates the transcendental categories beyond pure reason, yet refers to them quite liberally. For these, Coleridge's Platonizing of Kant affirmed this *aporia* by accepting Kant's limits (against those German idealists), while at the same time admitting an immanent apprehension (albeit limited) of the transcendent, envisaging philosophy as a "finite longing for the infinite." Here, Manfred Frank's distinction between the early German romantics (who heavily influenced Barfield)[20] and the German idealists, along with the Platonic readings of Coleridge by J. H. Muirhead, Douglas Hedley, and James Vigus, prove invaluable in vindicating Coleridge from those Kantians all too eager to associate his philosophy with transcendental idealism (overstepping Kant's system). Instead, Frank's insight into the early German romantics, whose blending of philosophical and poetic language shares similarities with the Platonic Coleridge, reveals a strong continuity between the laudable attempts of both Coleridge and the early German romantics who, following a strong philosophical conviction to address the Kantian *aporia*, employed poetic discourse to both honor and exceed the genius of Kant. It will then be suggested that it is precisely this reading of the Platonic Coleridge, the poetic philosopher, which Barfield adopts.

Overstepping Kantian Limits: Critiques of Coleridge

Contemporary critiques of Coleridge's philosophy argue that Coleridge overstepped Kantian limits. These staunch Kantians are loyal to the divorce of philosophy and poetry, and want to reject the attempt to mitigate a divide that they believe safeguards the rationality of philosophy from the irrationality of poetic or religious discourse.

An apt example is Christoph Bode's article, "Coleridge and Philosophy," in the recently published, *The Oxford Handbook of Samuel Taylor*

20. For now, it is important to note the influence of the German idealists Fichte, Hegel, and Schelling. These post-Kantian German philosophers greatly influence Coleridge. As such, they shape Barfield's thought both directly and indirectly. Additionally, one of Barfield's earliest short stories, *The Rose on the Ash-Heap*, is written in the *märchen* genre, a favorite of the German romantics. There are several elements of this short story that indicate his indebtedness to their legacy (e.g., Barfield's "Lady" is a characterization of the "Eternal-Feminine" found in Goethe's *Faust*). A thorough description of Barfield's, *The Rose on the Ash-Heap*, can be found in chapter 4. See also, Barfield, *History in English Words*, 206–7. Barfield underscores the impact of the *Sturm und Drang* upon Coleridge and the birth of the romantic movement in England.

Coleridge.[21] The distinguishing mark of Bode's work[22] is his attempt to identify a coherent philosophy in Coleridge, even if in the end he is highly critical of Coleridge's lack of systemization,[23] which he dismisses as religiously motivated or, indeed, as no philosophy at all. Bode utilizes Kant as, "an instrument to locate Coleridge's philosophical positions and their trajectory. . . . [Kant] offers a *system* of philosophy to which Coleridge's varying positions can be related."[24] In order to locate Coleridge's "deviations" from Kant, he likens Coleridge's philosophy to the German idealists (particularly Schelling).[25]

Bode begins by asserting that Coleridge failed to recognize Kant's "Copernican Revolution," namely that, "it is inadmissible to speculate . . . about realms which are by definition beyond our knowing. There are large areas about which it is not possible to say anything, let alone to argue rationally, and philosophy must confine itself to the other ones, which are its proper and only realm."[26] For Bode, Kant's unresolvable antimonies between the *a posteriori* and the *a priori* are meant to accentuate the limits of philosophy. Pure reason, the *a priori*, must always be "judged" and/or limited by the *a posteriori*. This limiting "synthesis" becomes unsettled when the mind's faculties extend "beyond the sphere in which they are applicable."[27] This is the crucial limit that Bode is unwilling to surrender to Coleridge. As he writes, "Many followers of Kant were not willing to accept these radical consequences, and Samuel Taylor Coleridge, for all his admiration of Kant, was one of them."[28] Further, "it is surprising how few of Kant's key concepts and ideas he was willing to accept unaltered."[29] This is why Bode rejects any talk of "intellectual intuition" or "mysticism" and claims that Coleridge borrows it from the idealists, who represent a radical break from Kant.[30]

21. Bode, "Coleridge and Philosophy," 588–619.

22. Ibid., 589.

23. Ibid., 589–92. Herein, he cites various inconsistencies in Coleridge's work.

24. Ibid., 592.

25. Ibid.

26. Ibid., 593.

27. Ibid.

28. Ibid., 594.

29. Ibid.

30. Frank, *The Philosophical Foundations*. Frank argues that "intellectual intuition" is an adaptation of Jacobi's "faith" and a term employed by the early German romantics, who he distinguishes from the German idealists (i.e., Fichte, Schelling, and Hegel). Contrary to Bode, Frank notes that it was actually Hölderlin who coined the term "intellectual intuition" to replace Kant's synthetic judgments (see, 94, 100, and 125), while Novalis (see, 172–73) too employed the term, which distanced these early German

Bode is also critical of Coleridge for neglecting Kant's anti-realism. Bode notes that for Kant, the *Ding an sich* is beyond the grasp of reason. While Kant rendered the ideas regulative, the Platonic Coleridge held them to be constitutive of phenomena. Bode writes, "Coleridge held that ideas of Reason were somehow constitutive of knowledge—an option categorically denied by Kant."[31] Again, the suggestion made repeatedly is that Coleridge simply ignores, or "simply has no use for," Kant's key concepts.[32] Ultimately, Bode sees "a complete divergence of Coleridge from Kant, [because Coleridge] . . . ultimately sided with Plato against Kant."[33] He writes, "Samuel Taylor Coleridge either failed to grasp or refused to accept *any* of the key elements of Kant's *Critical Philosophy*."[34] Accordingly, "Coleridge is not a proper Kantian . . . ."[35] He asks rhetorically, "How can one praise all these qualities in a philosopher and yet refuse to accept a single one of his philosophical principles or concepts?"[36]

So why would Coleridge do such a thing? According to Bode, "What it boils down to is the difference between a philosophy that is not afraid of its own consequences and a philosophy that serves a religion. Some may call the latter bad philosophy or no philosophy at all . . . ."[37] In Coleridge one sees how, "Religiosity overrides philosophical consistency, and this leads to glaring contradictions and non-sequiturs, time and again: it is an inbuilt, irresistible force that leads to foreseeable fault lines in his arguments, as faith and logic pull in two different directions."[38] Indeed, "All his divergences from his greatest philosophical hero, Immanuel Kant, can be explained as divergences caused by Coleridge's religious needs and convictions."[39]

Pushing this further, Bode concludes by offering a new reading of the famous "gap" in Coleridge's *Biographia Literaria* (*BL*) showing where Coleridge both aligned and diverged from Schelling. He begins by claiming

romantics from Kant. According to Frank, "intellectual intuition" is precisely not a term that Fichte or Schelling used, nor would they accept it. As we shall see, Frank's work offers crucial insight for locating Coleridge in the nuanced world of post-Kantian German philosophy.

31. Bode, "Coleridge and Philosophy," 599.
32. Ibid., 597.
33. Ibid., 600.
34. Ibid.
35. Ibid., 597.
36. Ibid., 600. Of course, one might ask how this is any different than Kant's admiration of Hume?
37. Ibid., 603.
38. Ibid., 610.
39. Ibid., 604.

that by following Schelling, Coleridge is an absolute idealist, who disregards Kant's *Ding an sich* in declaring "that the object we behold is the real and very object."[40] Bode avers that here, Coleridge takes a "leap of faith,"[41] which he later calls "a leap the imagination,"[42] by substituting Schelling's absolute (or system of transcendental idealism) with the Christian God, but then quickly recants this position for fear of an infinite regress, since Schelling's identity is not transcendent, but absolute. Bode claims Coleridge eventually wrote off Schelling because he had no religious use for his philosophy,[43] and that his disagreement with Schelling was motivated by opportunism and religious zealotry.[44] Bode concludes, "At a time when Coleridge tried to prove time and again that reason and faith could be reconciled, if only one were willing to accept the ulterior superiority of faith, this was less and less seen as a helpful operation. Western civilization went down a different path and reserved for religion a more confined and a more specific cultural space."[45] Thus for Bode, the *BL* should simply be read as *fiction*, suggesting that Schlegel would have loved the irony of Coleridge's work. In the end, Coleridge is simply "a great poet and fiction writer, who happened to mistake himself for a profound philosopher. As a philosopher, he must, I think be regarded as a hopeless anachronism."[46]

Bode's staunch Kantianism relegates any relative overlap with philosophy as a crossing over into a realm of which one can say nothing. This is the sort of system that juxtaposes philosophy and poetry, wherein one is *either* a philosopher *or* poet. Coleridge, the latter, had mistaken himself for the former.

For similar reasons, Nigel Leask is also critical of Coleridge for exceeding Kant's limits. In a similar tone to Bode, Leask associates Coleridge's "ignorance" of Kant's limits with a quest for bourgeois political power. Like Bode, Leask draws upon Kant as an interlocutor remarking that, "Coleridge valued Kant's *Critique* more for the limits it imposed upon the scientific understanding, preventing its critical forays into the metaphysical sphere, than for its putative 'enlightened' aim of expelling the Ideas of Pure Reason from philosophy."[47] Accordingly, there are two ways Coleridge could have

---

40. Ibid., 606.
41. Ibid., 608.
42. Ibid., 617.
43. Ibid., 611.
44. Ibid., 612.
45. Ibid., 616.
46. Ibid., 617.
47. Leask, *The Politics of Imagination*, 97.

read Kant: "Kant could be seen either to have limited dogmatic knowledge and expelled metaphysics from the field of science, or to have freed the Ideas of Reason from the clutches of critical understanding. Coleridge's Kant was clearly the latter . . . ."[48]

Leask, like Bode, claims that Coleridge erred when he sought a direct knowledge of the *noumenal*, a knowledge not available to the Kantian faculties of analytic understanding.[49] Leask, too, is concerned because Coleridge ostensibly immanentizes the absolute,[50] and links what he believes to be Coleridge's absolutizing of the *noumenon* with the idealists Fichte and Schelling.[51] Thus, he reads Coleridge as replacing the unconditioned *noumenal* realm with self-consciousness against Kant who, "asserted the noumenal status of self-consciousness, denying it could be the basis of absolute or unconditioned knowledge: because it was limited to the same empirical procedures as knowledge of the phenomenal world . . . ."[52] According to Leask, Coleridge, in overstepping these limits, maintained that "the inspired mind was afforded an immediate insight into the transcendental powers which constituted the phenomenal product."[53] Such romantic attempts to possess the absolute here and now were the work of bourgeois academics who wanted to take a unified science and carry it into politics.[54]

These Kantian critics argue that as an idealist Coleridge (whether religiously or politically motivated) attempted to absolutize the *noumenal* and thereby overstepped the limits of reason. These critics—perhaps more Kantian than Kant himself—represent a rather contemporary avant-garde (i.e., analytic) indebtedness to establishing a pure philosophical discourse free from the realm of poetic discourse.

Now certainly Coleridge's philosophical indebtedness to the German idealists should not be underestimated. Coleridge draws upon the *Naturphilosophie* throughout his work. However, to suggest that Coleridge is attempting to absolutize the transcendental categories in order to exceed Kant's limits is an oversimplification that plagues those Kantians who are unable to recognize the very *aporia* in Kant's system alluded to by the German idealists and Coleridge himself. Upon closer examination it appears that there may be something subtler at play. What one finds implicit in the

48. Ibid., 99.
49. Ibid., 97.
50. Ibid., 132.
51. Ibid., 102.
52. Ibid., 103.
53. Ibid., 106.
54. Ibid., 101.

scholarship that follows is a general agreement that those who overstepped Kant (Coleridge included) did so in order to address an unresolved philosophical *aporia* that Goethe expressed in the following lines: "When I tried, if not to penetrate, then at least to make use of the Kantian doctrine, I often began to think that the dear man was dealing ironically, for he seemed intent on limiting the faculty of Knowledge, but then began to suggest, as it were with a sideways gesture, ways of crossing the boundaries he himself had set."[55] This is of a piece with Hegel's criticism that limits can only be defined by what lies beyond them. Indeed, as it turns out, Goethe and Hegel were not the only giants who Kant had left disquieted.

Honoring Kantian Limits: Coleridge the Poetic Philosopher

Surely if Coleridge had intended to absolutize the transcendentals then perhaps one could accuse him of being a religious zealot or crude libertarian whose philosophical language asserted truths that always-already exceeded the very philosophy he employed. However, what has often been ignored is that Coleridge was in agreement with the limits of philosophical discourse as Kant had envisaged them, but he also saw that the very *aporia* that Kant had established was proved implicitly by its very irresolution, and as such, his system required a supplement that he appears unwilling to concede (whether Kant himself had actually recognized this is debatable).

Manfred Frank's *The Philosophical Foundations of Early German Romanticism* offers another lens through which to approach Coleridge's philosophy. Frank's work provides a nuanced perspective into the multifarious thought world that Coleridge inhabited for nine months beginning in the autumn of 1798. Frank's analysis also sheds light on the German figures to whom Barfield was indebted. Frank's main thesis suggests that to lump all of those who broke from Kant in Germany into the category of "idealists" is not accurate. There were, in fact, a group of philosophers, whom Frank identifies as the early German romantics, who, in their attempt to "re-Kantianize" German idealism, sought both to honor Kant's genius and address his limitations by supplementing philosophy with poetry. In light of the prior critiques, Frank's work indicates that Coleridge's allegiance to German idealism may need to be re-examined.

To begin, Frank draws a clear distinction between the German idealists (i.e., Fichte, Schelling, and Hegel) and those he calls the early German romantics (i.e., Jacobi, Hölderlin, Novalis, and Schlegel). The former, he argues, sought to absolutize Kant's transcendental in self-consciousness, while

55. Ashton, *The German Idea*, 193–94.

the latter rejected idealism's absolute ground (whether in consciousness or in the world). This subtle, although crucial, move made by the early German romantics—what Frank refers to as a "re-Kantianizing" of the absolute—was to suggest that the absolute was "infinite." According to Frank, by declaring knowledge of the absolute to be infinite, the early German romantics, distinct from the idealists, sought to honor Kant by limiting finite knowledge of the infinite absolute. In this way, philosophy is never totalized, but rather, in the words of Schlegel, "a finite longing for the infinite." As Frank writes, like Kant, the early German romantics had a healthy "skepticism regarding the possibility that beliefs can be ultimately grounded through a deduction from a highest principle."[56] This means that against particularly Fichte, from whom the early German romantics "diverged radically,"[57] being cannot be grounded in self-consciousness (i.e., as a first principle).[58] Instead, for the early romantic "realists"[59] (Hölderlin, Novalis, and Schlegel), self-consciousness was contingent upon (or one among many principles of) being.[60] The explicit rejection of idealism's absolute knowledge is what distinguishes Frank's early German romantics from the idealists.[61] Instead, the early German romantics represent "a return to Kant even before absolute Idealism had time to spread its wings."[62]

In their explicit rejection of the absolute, the early German romantics paradoxically gestured beyond these limits, albeit subtly.[63] A fine example of this can be found in Frank's reading of Novalis who rejects Fichte's absolutization of self-consciousness. Distinct from Kant, Novalis preferred rather to approach the Kantian ideas in terms of an infinite progression.[64] So, following Kant, the early German romantics rejected any deduction of

56. Frank, *The Philosophical Foundations*, 32–33.

57. Ibid., 26.

58. Ibid., 167.

59. Ibid., 28.

60. Ibid., 154–55 and 172–73. Novalis was against the idea that consciousness could grasp phenomena in their totality. Instead, being precedes consciousness ontologically and exists independently of it. Self-consciousness is no longer a principle, but dependent upon being.

61. Ibid., 107.

62. Ibid., 171.

63. Ibid., 5. In her introduction to the work, Elizabeth Millán-Zaibert notes that what Frank attempts to show is how "the German romantics sought to constitute an alternative to both Kant and Fichte's transcendental idealism . . . ."

64. Ibid., 36. See also, 175. Novalis sides with Kant as a skeptic of philosophies based on first principles.

being to an "I" or any permanent foundation,[65] while distinct from Kant, they viewed the quest of philosophy as an open "longing for the infinite."[66] Frank expresses the distinction in this way: for the idealists being was absolute and thus one could have an absolute knowledge of it, but for the early German romantics being is transcendent.[67] Frank is clear, "In contrast [to idealism], early Romanticism is convinced, that self-being owes its existence to a transcendent foundation, which does not leave itself to be dissolved into the immanence of consciousness."[68] Frank writes, for these early German romantics, "transcendence of Being with respect to consciousness forces philosophy along the path of infinite progression, on which Being can never be given an adequate account through consciousness and so a path which can never offer a final interpretation of Being."[69] In this way, "Absolute Being" "is not grasped by logic or thought but by the senses, by intuition. The transcendence of Being with respect to thinking is founded precisely on the basis of this claim."[70]

Now what drove the early German romantics down this path was an *aporia* they recognized in Kant's philosophy, which a turn to idealism would collapse. On the one hand, to posit the transcendent beyond the limits of the knowable is contradictory and brings all philosophy to an end, but on the other hand, to claim absolute knowledge of the transcendentals is to do the same. Frank clarifies this stating, "It is impossible to determine

65. Ibid., 105. Being is not self-consciousness precisely because it objectifies. Whenever it calls itself "I" it does so based on a relation (the "I"-"non-I"). It is thus "conditioned" or "limited" in judgment, whereas absolute being is not relationally structured at all. Thus, being grounds even self-consciousness. Frank writes, "it is not consciousness that determines Being, but Being that determines consciousness." See also, 99. Frank notes that the early German romantics spoke, "of an infinite approximation of ('an infinite progress' toward) and idea that can never be realized.... The 'I' [of Fichte's 'Absolute Idealism'] is denied the status of a first principle because it stands in a relation of dependence upon a being that is neither the 'I' itself nor something merely sensibly given. The unattainability of this presupposition motivates an infinite striving toward its appropriation, and through this striving the Being that was originally lacking takes on the status of an equally unattainable final idea."

66. Ibid., 174. "For Novalis, the formula of philosophy as a 'longing for the infinite' is thus an indication of philosophy's intrinsic openness (or the non-final nature of its claims[;] . . . the search for foundations, so the argument goes, is necessarily infinite since an absolute foundation cannot be given to consciousness." See also, 184–87. For Schlegel's reference to philosophy as "longing for the infinite." See also, 72. Frank talks of an absolute dependence of the finite on the infinite.

67. Ibid., 24 and 28.

68. Ibid., 178. See also, Millán-Zaibert's intro, 19.

69. Ibid., 107. See also, 120.

70. Ibid., 94. For Hölderlin, being is apprehended by "intellectual intuition," not logic.

the limits of knowledge if we cannot, in some way . . . get beyond these same limits . . . ."[71] The *aporia* is necessary because it mediates such extremes. Philosophy neither begins nor ends with an absolute ground, but in a middle. True principles are not deduced but rather discovered as they are approached progressively, and as such they are "postulative" rather than "demonstrative."[72] Frank continues, "They are not derived from a principle, which had previously been established by 'more demonstrative evidence,' . . . but rather they make the existence of this principle only 'ever more probable' . . . ."[73] This is why for the early German romantics, "claims to truth can only be understood as an infinite approximation toward knowledge which is never complete . . . ."[74] Philosophy is rather a "feeling" of a lack of knowledge, a striving for what is lacking, what Novalis calls a "drive toward completion."[75]

By infinitizing the absolute these early German romantics both honored and exceeded Kant by replacing his "unconditioned" with a "search" for the unconditioned, or rather, an infinite search for a foundation.[76] Thus, for the finite to speak at all of the infinite is to envisage the transcendental as transcendent. In this way, the transcendent could thus be grasped by the finite, yet remain infinite, eluding idealist absolutization. The repositioning of the infinite indicates, that being, thus, cannot be fully comprehended by consciousness, and therefore must be delivered over in the aesthetic experience through beauty and art.[77] "The beauty of art enables us to experience something whose meaning cannot be exhausted by thought and hence helps us to comprehend or grasp Being (although never exhaustively)."[78] To be clear, this is not to be understood as an aesthetic sundered from the realm of philosophy. But rather, it is here that philosophy is brought up by poetry. In the same way the finite always already points beyond itself[79] so too poetry grasps the infinite in and through the *aporias* of philosophy.[80] Here the

71. Ibid., 181.

72. Ibid., 191–92.

73. Ibid., 202. See also, 203.

74. Ibid., 36. See also, 49–50. Frank labels this romantic "longing" that moves the finite toward the infinite a "coherence theory"; that is, "not as foundations that are given, but rather as foundations that appear in, "the connection of [all particular things] with the whole." Frank is here citing Novalis.

75. Ibid., 189.

76. Ibid., 50–51.

77. Ibid., 16–17, and 19.

78. Ibid., 19.

79. Ibid., 209.

80. Ibid., 219.

imagination mediates between the finite *aporias* and infinite, by drafting an image of that which is otherwise unrepresentable.

So while Kant was correct to claim that philosophical language is limited, he failed (at least explicitly) to account for its poetic complement. For the early German romantics, allegory properly expressed this complementarity. For according to Schlegel, allegory (i.e., a mode or specification of the imagination), like all poetic saying or art, alludes to that which it does not succeed in saying.[81] As Frank puts it, "Poetry is, namely, the collective expression for that which is inexpressible, the presentation of the unrepresentable: that which, as such, cannot be presented in any speculative concept."[82] According to Schlegel, allegory "satisfies itself in merely suggesting indefinitely the infinite, the divine, which cannot be described or explained philosophically[;] . . . the device of allegorical expression frees the finite from its material fixedness and refers it to the infinite."[83] Frank continues, "To say something determined in such a way that while expressing it this determinacy dissolves into some indeterminacy; to say something as if one were not saying anything at all, is something that only the poet can do. Here, too, philosophy finds its supplement, indeed, its completion, in and as poetry."[84] To quote Schlegel, "where philosophy ends, poetry must begin."[85]

Frank's erudite analysis unsettles familiar overgeneralizations of post-Kantian German idealism. Contrary to popular opinion, these German romantics were not in love with the Absolute.[86] What one finds in the early German romantics is not an ignorance of Kant's limits, but an attempt to address a philosophical *aporia* utilizing poetic language. By rendering idealism's absolute as infinite (in Frank's words, "transcendent"), the finite imagination could grasp the inexhaustibly infinite, albeit in a limited fashion. The poetic imagination intimates those things that exceed reason's grasp, allowing the poet to say a bit more than the philosopher. This is the romanticism Coleridge gleaned from Germany. For all of Coleridge's indebtedness to idealism he is not an idealist in the absolutist sense. If one wants to link Coleridge to the Germans, it is not with the idealists, but with Frank's early German romantics that one should situate his philosophy. To further this claim against absolutism the section now concludes with an examination of

81. Ibid., 207.

82. Ibid., 208.

83. Ibid., 209.

84. Ibid., 218–19.

85. Ibid., 219. See also, 21.

86. Ibid., 211–13.

Coleridge's Platonism. It is the Platonic Coleridge (who blends both Plato and Kant) who is, indeed, Barfield's Coleridge.

The following figures recognize the Platonic Coleridge, who like the early German romantics sought not to ignore Kant's limits, but rather, to address the *aporia* in Kantian philosophy in a way that both honored and exceeded Kant's limits. As with the early German romantics, and contrary to the popular Neo-Kantian hubris against Coleridge, the following analysis suggests that Coleridge's attempt to overcome the Kantian *aporia* was in fact philosophically motivated. Here, as with Frank's early German romantics, the poetic imagination takes on increasing relevance, acting as a sort of mediator between two worlds.

J. H. Muirhead's *Coleridge as Philosopher* tells the story of the early Coleridge, a natural philosopher who moves to Germany in 1798, and who in an 1801 letter to Thomas Polle writes that he has overthrown the passivity of mind as a lazy onlooker. If humans are truly made in the image of God they must bear a mark of creativity.[87] Of course, Coleridge is here indebted to Kant's "awakening," as Muirhead notes the heavy influence of Kant in the *BL*.[88] Regarding idealism, Muirhead states that Coleridge does not care much for Fichte, and even though he expresses his deep commitment to Schelling and wants to "bring" him to England,[89] he eventually renounces his treatment of Schelling in the *BL*.[90] In so doing, Coleridge moved away from the pantheism of Schelling (and Spinoza) and back to Kant (these remarks are consistent with Frank's assessment of the early German romantics' re-Kantianization of idealism).[91] Against empiricist logic, Coleridge saw that Kant's *a priori* was important for identifying objects as all judgments involved a synthesis.[92] Coleridge also sought to undermine the subject/object division in logic by invoking Kant's transcendental analysis.[93] But with Kant, he was limited. According to Coleridge, Kant's anti-realist strategy failed because his transcendental ideas were simply regulative principles; that is, because

---

87. Muirhead, *Coleridge As Philosopher*, 51.

88. Ibid., 52.

89. Ibid., 53.

90. Ibid., 56–57. Muirhead points out that within a month of his death Coleridge wrote, "The metaphysical disquisition at the end of the first volume of the *BL* is unformed and immature; it contains the fragments of the truth, but it is not fully thought out. It is wonderful to myself to think how infinitely more profound my views now are, and yet how much clearer they are withal."

91. Ibid., 58 and 118.

92. Ibid., 81.

93. Ibid., 71–73.

they do not correspond to reality they cannot be known.[94] Coleridge found help in a Platonic tradition that Kant had explicitly rejected (to rehearse, for Plato the ideas are not regulative, but rather, productive or constitutive of phenomena).[95] Had Kant not rejected this, he may have realized that the subject and object are complementary aspects of being.[96] Coleridge wants to say that the ideas "rise in the mind, as something which is neither merely given from without nor as something merely imposed from within, but as something in which outer and inner are united, deep calling to deep . . . ."[97] This led Coleridge to conclude that the speculative could transcend the limits of logical understanding, a Platonic door left open by Kant himself. Muirhead writes that for Coleridge, "there is a level of thought beyond the transcendental analysis, to which the genius of Plato had penetrated, but which all the talent of Kant had failed to reach."[98] It is in this vein that Coleridge saw himself completing what Kant had begun.[99]

So how did Coleridge complete this move? According to Muirhead he marries philosophy and poetry[100] by borrowing from Schelling's theory of poetry to construct his metaphysic.[101] Philosophy must be more than theory. It must involve the will and feeling, "it takes all experience: moral, aesthetic, intellectual . . . ."[102] Muirhead writes that Coleridge "knew so well on occasion how to assert the presence of the eternal in, as well as beyond, the temporal."[103] Muirhead indicates that Coleridge's philosophy is based on an infinite reality,[104] wherein Reason is responding to something beyond itself.[105] Ultimately for Coleridge, supreme reality is not something reached by the empirical senses nor by Kantian logic,[106] but by the imagination. According to Kant, "the imagination was continuous with that of the understanding . . . if the understanding in the end gives us no more than a world of appearance, a like limitation would have to be imposed on the deeper fac-

---

94. Ibid., 91.
95. Ibid., 95.
96. Ibid., 93–94.
97. Ibid., 101–2.
98. Ibid., 83.
99. Ibid., 89.
100. Ibid., 257–58.
101. Ibid., 203.
102. Ibid., 214.
103. Ibid., 234.
104. Ibid., 240.
105. Ibid., 252.
106. Ibid., 222.

ulty [the imagination]."[107] Yet, for Coleridge, "Unless the activity of the productive imagination were conceived of as in some way identical with that of
the Divine Imaging, it would be impossible to justify the claims of poet and
artist to be seers and revealers of essential reality."[108] Coleridge thought it
"possible to represent the work of the imagination as continuous not merely
with the understanding, as Kant did, but as continuous with the creative
work of the divine intelligence itself."[109] Analogous to God, Coleridge wants
to "explain the working of imagination as not merely a reproductive, but a
creative process; and secondly, a metaphysics that would account for the
appeal which its creations make to what is deepest in the soul of men."[110]

What one glimpses with the work of Muirhead is Coleridge's indebtedness to Kant, and his philosophical motivation to resolve the same *aporia*
that captivated the early German romantics by bringing together philosophy
and poetry. For Coleridge the imagination played a crucial function in the
creative process. This implies that Coleridge understood that poetry must
be an inherent complement of philosophy. While the imagination was the
means to overcoming Hume's passivity of the mind, the constitutive ideas
were the means to overcoming the active projection often associated with
romanticism (this should become more clear as the chapter progresses and
when it is explicitly examined in chapter 5). Poetry is not to be conceived of
as a meaningless repetition of sameness, nor in terms of an equally untenable difference, but a creative sojourning into the infinite depths of being.
Muirhead's rather Platonic reading of Coleridge is buttressed by the work
of James Vigus.

Vigus's *Platonic Coleridge* argues that Coleridge treats Kant and Plato
as "symbiotic";[111] in other words, Coleridge reads Plato through Kant.[112] As
Vigus sees it, Kant is both a "preparer and opponent" of Platonism.[113] On
the one hand, Kant issued a return to Platonism by reasserting the active
nature of the mind over against the passivity of empiricist logic,[114] but on
the other hand, Kant remained an opponent for limiting reason's access to
the transcendental realm. Vigus, too, points to the apparent *aporia* (what

107. Ibid., 201.
108. Ibid.
109. Ibid., 202.
110. Ibid., 199.
111. Vigus, *Platonic Coleridge*, 3.
112. Ibid., 35. See also, 24–27, and 100. In addition to calling Kant a "sage,"
Coleridge calls Plato a poetic genius.
113. Ibid., 35.
114. Ibid., 40–41.

he calls "antimonies") in Kant's philosophy. The "things-in-themselves" are said to be unknowable, yet Kant speaks of them. According to Vigus, this left a door open for Coleridge's Platonic reading of Kant.[115]

Vigus brilliantly remarks that there are really only two ways to read Coleridge; "Either he criticizes Kant's restrictions on our possible knowledge of the noumenal realm . . . invoking Plato in opposition; or he suggests that Kant was hinting at this Platonic knowledge all along."[116] The *aporia* seems too obvious to have been overlooked by the genius of Kant. As Vigus sees it, Coleridge employs the Platonic doctrine of the ideas in order to overcome the noumenal/phenomenal (intelligible/sensible) dualism in Kant.[117] Coleridge, he avers, "is correcting Kant through Plato. Whereas Kant argues that two logically correct yet mutually contradictory propositions demonstrate that we cannot know the solution, for Coleridge's Plato they demonstrate the need for a 'higher logic' . . . ."[118] For this reason, "Coleridge's Plato had long represented a path beyond the Kantian Antimonies"[119] via the poetic expression.[120]

How so? Coleridge "Platonizes" Kant's ideas.[121] Vigus continually avers, "Coleridge saw Kant and Plato as substantially aligned, but as differing on the 'highest problem' of philosophy, i.e., whether the Ideas were regulative or constitutive."[122] As Coleridge saw it, to assert the ideas as regulative not only ignored the *aporia* in Kantian philosophy, but it also made poetry an enemy of philosophy.[123] So to resolve this Coleridge borrows from the *Third Critique* wherein Kant introduces the imagination as a sort of mediator between two worlds. Coleridge wants to ask, what is it that is being mediated if one cannot actually know the things-in-themselves? To resolve this he maintains that the "primary imagination" actually apprehends the

115. Ibid., 45.

116. Ibid., 53. See also, 108. Vigus writes regarding Kant's regulative ideas that the "things-in-themselves remain radically unknowable, and the claim to intellectual intuition . . . is mystical in a meaningless sense. If Ideas are constitutive, as for Coleridge and Plato, the empirical model of the subject (mind) perceiving the object (Idea) actually dissolves, since the Ideas (so to speak) inform the mind."

117. Ibid., 42.

118. Ibid., 104.

119. Ibid., 152.

120. Ibid., 45–56.

121. Ibid., 167. See also, 30. Vigus notes that early on Coleridge was aware of Kant's *a priori* and aesthetic theories, which he well respected.

122. Ibid., 36. See also, 4 and 47.

123. Ibid., 6.

ideas in the object.[124] Instead of reducing the ideas to a regulative function (i.e., to the subjective realm of the mind), Coleridge identifies them as constitutive, thereby upholding their objective reality in the world.[125] For Plato, the idea is a symbol "consubstantial with the reality it represents."[126] In this way, "Coleridge deeply approved of Plato's detection of traces of the divine in the visible universe . . . ."[127] Coleridge's philosophy rests between materialism and idealism.[128] The imagination intuits the divine ideas as constitutive symbols.[129] It is for this reason that poetic language best represents the symbolic nature of reality.[130]

Vigus shows how Coleridge utilized Plato's doctrine of *anamnesis* to meddle with Kant's *a priori*.[131] His constitutive model challenges Kant's limiting of reason's access to the *noumenal* realm—that makes poetry an enemy of reason—by evoking "inspiration" as an "imitating," not a "copying," of the sense world.[132] Vigus clarifies this distinction, "Coleridge's 'dialectic' invokes Ideas not by exhaustive propositions, but by means of the sublime poetic discourse that takes over when propositional language is exhausted."[133] The imagination is the medium through which the divine ideas are intuited, wherein occurs an interpenetration between the ideas and the inspired mind.[134] The uninspired (so-called) poet simply copies the ideas of sense perception and denies divine inspiration, whereas the inspired poet and artist imitate (*mimesis*) the ideas via *anamnesis*.[135] This is true creativity, when the will aligns with God, which issues forth in a co-operative, not dictated, inspiration that at once honors the poet's creative capacity and exceeds it.[136] Vigus states, "the ambivalence of Coleridge's attitude to poetic inspiration—as divine, yet passive and requiring rational

124. Ibid., 51–52.
125. Ibid., 51.
126. Ibid., 112.
127. Ibid., 27.
128. Ibid., 96.
129. Ibid., 113–14.
130. Ibid., 148–49. For this same reason Coleridge is against Kant for separating the spiritual from the intellectual.
131. Ibid., 133.
132. Ibid., 4 and 7.
133. Ibid., 157.
134. Ibid., 113–14.
135. Ibid., 67–77.
136. Ibid., 80–81.

scrutiny—is strongly reminiscent of Plato."[137] By baptizing Kant's transcendentals in Platonic thought, Vigus's *Platonic Coleridge* honors Kant in his want to overcome the passivity of the mind. But further, by declaring the ideas to be constitutive, Coleridge's poetic philosophy resituates the subject and object relation wherein the subject is not a ground in oneself, but inspired. The poet's creativity *passively* reflects the ideas in each non-identical imitative *act*. Kant's antimonies revealed that philosophy always already remains open to its inspired poetic complement.

This section now concludes with some remarks on the work of Vigus's doctoral supervisor, Douglas Hedley. Hedley's work on Coleridge underscores the Platonic element in German philosophy that formed Coleridge's theology of divine transcendence, which is crucial to understanding his aesthetic. Hedley presents Coleridge's "ingenious"[138] thought as rather consistent with orthodox Christianity. What makes Hedley's work important here is that he sees German idealism as an attempt to revive Platonism.[139] As with Vigus, Hedley notes that Coleridge's decisive break from Kant is that Coleridge renders the ideas constitutive, i.e., transcendent not transcendental. Indeed, the German idealists provided a framework by which Coleridge might restore the Platonic metaphysic of transcendence. In his explication of Coleridge's theology, Hedley clearly associates Coleridge's thought with that of the "German Idealists"[140] (e.g., they fought "against the debilitating effects of empiricism and utilitarianism";[141] they conceived truth not as propositions but as the self-disclosure of the divine intellect;[142] they saw a vital connection between the Trinity and the spiritual nature of man;[143] they argued that thought [i.e., *logos*] is the structural principle of the universe;[144] they sought to renew the immanence of the divine;[145] and regarding Kant, the idealist position was to accept the strength of the enlightened critic, but also to criticize his narrow and abstract concept of rationality).[146] According

137. Ibid., 167.

138. Hedley, *Coleridge, Philosophy and Religion*, 19.

139. Ibid., 40–45. Herein Hedley indicates that Schelling and Hegel were deeply influenced by the readings of Plato (particularly Cudworth and Ficino) they encountered at the University of Tübingen.

140. Hedley, "Coleridge as a Theologian," 481. Hedley notes that Coleridge shares with Schelling the Neo-Platonic tradition.

141. Hedley, *Coleridge, Philosophy and Religion*, 290.

142. Ibid., 6.

143. Ibid., 240–43.

144. Ibid., 200.

145. Ibid., 10.

146. Ibid., 294.

to Hedley, it was in this last sense that Coleridge broke from Kant and the Enlightenment, which Hedley repeatedly interprets as an attempt to revive Cambridge Platonism.[147] Ultimately, in referring to Coleridge as a "Platonic Idealist,"[148] Hedley seems to suggest that Coleridge, although he adopts idealism's concept of divine immanence,[149] clearly aligns with the Platonic notion of the "One" or the "Good" as the transcendent principle of all being.[150] Hedley's analysis may explain why Coleridge would later distance himself from Spinoza's and Schelling's pantheistic proclivities.

Indeed, Coleridge's theology of transcendence escapes such immanentist deductions. Human knowledge does not arrive from the senses (i.e., empiricism), nor from the operations of the finite mind (as with Kant), but from God.[151] Thus for Coleridge, "the only way to hold together a vital religion and a reasonable apprehension of reality is the vision of the Logos as the pattern of the transcendent Godhead in the cosmos."[152] This theological move is philosophically motivated. The very fact that one can recognize knowledge as finite indicates that one does in a sense always-already transcend this finitude.[153] For Coleridge, the theory of ideas "is about the communion of the finite mind with God,"[154] as "the ideas within the divine word provide the instruments by which the finite mind can ascend to the divine."[155] Hedley writes, "The great weakness of eighteenth-century theology, whether Paley or Jacobi, was its inability to do justice to the profoundly Christian notion of a transcendent God who is also immanent, and most profoundly present in the striving of the soul, a God who is not just the goal of the good life but its sustaining power."[156] Coleridge's participatory

147. Ibid., 12. See also, 46, wherein Hedley refers to German idealism as a revived Platonism.

148. Ibid., 300.

149. Ibid., 70–73. See also, 85.

150. Hedley, "Coleridge as a Theologian," 483.

151. Hedley, Coleridge, Philosophy and Religion, 203. See also, 195. Coleridge thought that all finite knowledge is divinely disclosed.

152. Ibid., 194.

153. Ibid., 203. This concept is likely taken from Hegel's Science of Logic. See also, Sallis, Logic of Imagination, 58–59.

154. Hedley, Coleridge, Philosophy and Religion, 201. See also, 214. Hedley writes, "the capacity of the universe to generate organisms which are capable of understanding that universe suggests an affinity or communion between the mind of man and the divine mind."

155. Ibid., 115 and 223. See also, 196. Reason is both the realm of ideas transcending the finite mind and as those immanent in human thought.

156. Ibid., 189.

philosophy outwits this dichotomy mediating between natural theology and revealed theology.[157]

Hence, regarding creativity, the *logos* means, "that God cannot be thought of as a willful or arbitrary demiurge, but is at one with that creative pattern which is the source of the cosmos, and which is reflected in the beauty and order of nature, human culture, and society."[158] Because the *word* or *logos* belongs to God's essential being, creation reflects this rational nature.[159] God creates through the Word, which one's creative words mirror.[160] Words come to "reflect and partake in the communicative intelligence of the divine Logos";[161] thus, language is a participation in the eternal Word.[162] Elsewhere, Hedley writes that for Coleridge, "finite creativity is the image of that supreme perfection who is, in his essence, creative self-constitution."[163] It is in this way that the finite imagination reflects its transcendent divine source,[164] a "finite repetition in the infinite I AM." Reflecting on Hedley's analysis, in rendering the ideas as transcendent, Coleridge envisages the subject as inspired. This is not an immanent identical repetition of the passive mind, nor the subjective projection of Kantian ideas; rather, to be creative is to participate in the infinite mind of God.

By uniting poetry to philosophy Coleridge believed he had found an answer to that which Kant had (either intentionally or unintentionally) left unresolved. Whether one agrees with Coleridge or not, what cannot be denied is the strong *philosophical* motivation that drove his ambitions. Whether Coleridge succeeded in addressing these limits remains a matter of intense philosophical and theological debate, but what should not be doubted is the coherence of his philosophical system. Coleridge was not merely trying to wrest a particular political, poetic, or religious discourse from philosophical logic, but rather he had strong philosophical reasons to believe that philosophy and poetry are integrally related. For Coleridge, as with those like Goethe, it seemed even Kant was employing a latent poetic element when he imposed limits upon reason.

157. Ibid., 230.

158. Ibid., 285. See also, 141. Hedley's crucial point here is that the center of Coleridge's theology is incarnation, not atonement. See also, 288. Hedley mentions the tendency of Platonist theology to focus on incarnation.

159. Ibid., 86.

160. Ibid., 117–19.

161. Ibid., 136.

162. Ibid., 237.

163. Hedley, "Coleridge As A Theologian," 484.

164. Ibid. See also, 489. Hedley refers to Coleridge's description of the imagination as a "faint imitation" of the creative Godhead.

Coleridge's Platonization of the ideas (i.e., as constitutive) marked a decisive break from idealism, precisely because he sought to uphold the Kantian *aporia* that a pure totalized philosophy (i.e., absolute idealism) presumably had collapsed. This *aporia* exposes philosophy's openness, its incompleteness, and suggests that the type of discourse best suited to talk about the inherent symbolic nature of the real (a suspension of subject and object)[165] is poetic; that is, a blending of philosophy and poetry. It seems that when the mind becomes passive, mimetic, representational, unreflective, lazy and/or uncreative it devolves into a mere philosophy (e.g., formal logic). But since philosophy is inherently more than mimetic activity, it constantly appeals to poetic discourse. Drawing on poetry and metaphor philosophy is drawn forth in a "drive towards completion." Through participation in divine transcendence the poetic imagination crafts real symbols that overcome passive representation.

This brief précis of the reception of Coleridge's poetic philosophy provides a framework through which to locate Barfield's own reception of Coleridge. The following section examines Barfield's ubiquitous references to Coleridge in order to show that the Platonic Coleridge hitherto rehearsed is indeed Barfield's Coleridge.

Owen Barfield's Reception of Coleridge

Kant's Nominalism

Coleridge's influence appears in nearly every text Barfield wrote. In fact, Barfield argued that romanticism had not yet "come of age" because, outside of Coleridge, it lacked a robust metaphysic to buttress its poetic discourse.[166] As such, romanticism remained shrouded in the idea that the imagination was simply idle fancy, "a kind of conscious make-believe or personal masquerade," not a vehicle to truth or knowledge.[167] With this came charges of pantheism brought by those who, in the wake of Hume and Kant, saw the romantic penchant for re-enchantment as anthropomorphism, natural theology, and/or *Naturphilosophie*. Barfield's *What Coleridge Thought* stands

165. Sugerman, *Evolution of Consciousness*, 18. Sugerman summarizes that for Barfield life "consists in the polarity between the subjectivity and objectivity of the individual mind and the objective world it perceives."

166. Barfield does say that romanticism finally comes of age in Steiner's Anthroposophy. See also, Barfield, "Review of *Coleridge as Philosopher*." Barfield states that one of the strong points of Muirhead's work is that it dispels the myth that Coleridge's metaphysic was insincere.

167. Barfield, *Romanticism Comes of Age*, 15–19.

as an attempt to extract a romantic metaphysic from Coleridge's work. This was done to provide a philosophical rigor in support of the imagination that Barfield felt the romantics had failed to articulate. Additionally, this would further serve the larger Anthroposophic enterprise to which Barfield was indebted.

Barfield learned from his philological studies and from Steiner that consciousness evolves. He found in Coleridge's work on the imagination a way to reimagine (or re-enchant) the present objective world, which he believed would usher in a new stage of consciousness. In the coming epoch of final participation, the detached self-consciousness would once again become conscious of the vital connection to the world, which was nearly lost during the epoch of the consciousness soul. Following Steiner, he sought to train the modern mind to use the imagination to see the real elements in the world that had been relegated to the mind and/or altogether jettisoned by reductive philosophies. It is therefore no wonder why Barfield believed Coleridge's work on the imagination and his metaphysic of polarity to be of crucial significance in bringing awareness to the reality of the supersensible.

Like Coleridge, Barfield is keen to follow a Kantian trajectory in his ubiquitous criticisms of empiricism. Like Kant, Barfield argues that mere sense perception is passive (or "fancy"[168]—what Coleridge calls, "the despotism of the eye").[169] Against the Western worldview that assumes "the non-phenomenal is non-existent,"[170] Barfield indeed commends Kant for seeing beyond Hume's empiricism and "re-instating" what Barfield calls a "threshold" or "boundary"[171] between two worlds. Kant overcame empiricism by pointing out the active role of the mind in perception; the *a posteriori* is always conditioned by the *a priori*. For Barfield this meant there was no pure objectivity, nor mere passive sense impressions, because all perception is in some way regulated by the perceiving consciousness. So far, so good, but this is the point at which Barfield diverges from Kant. For Barfield, Kant is a nominalist who maintains that the ideas are "in men's minds" but not real, or in the world[172] (regulative and not constitutive).[173] For Barfield, when the universals or ideas are said to exist solely in the mind, and not in the world, the real is perceived as unreal. He warns that, "when

168. Ibid., 88.

169. Ibid., 89. He is here quoting Coleridge.

170. Ibid., 117.

171. Ibid., 118, 124, and 137.

172. Barfield, *Poetic Diction*, 94–95. Barfield is here not speaking of Kant, but he is critiquing nominalism (specifically for holding that universals are not real), which is precisely the issue Barfield has with Kant.

173. Barfield, *What Coleridge Thought*, 111.

the real is taken as unreal, and the unreal as real, the road is open to the madhouse."[174] Because it lacks the imagination necessary to apprehend the real qualities of the world, "understanding" or "judgmental" thought must divide or abstract qualities from phenomena."[175] So in the Kantian scheme reason apprehends the objectively real, while the imagination, the subjective fancy. This is the decisive break from Kant one sees in Coleridge that Barfield's poetic philosophy adopts.[176]

Like Coleridge, Barfield both honors and attempts to exceed Kant's limits. He, too, was philosophically motivated by a perceived "dilemma" in the role afforded to the imagination in the Kantian aesthetic.

> Either we strive to discuss metaphor, symbol, image, and meaning in the ordinary terms of logical discourse—in which case, because imagination almost by definition transcends logic, we become entangled in a more and more complicated mesh of thinner and thinner intellectual abstractions, or we cut through that Gordian snarl by proclaiming that meaning is something that cannot be talked about at all.[177]

Elsewhere he describes this dilemma as the "spell" of Kant, which leads people to believe that art is fancy and poetry unreality. Unless this Kantian conception is overturned poetry will continue to be understood as fancy (as a flight from reality),[178] or similarly, a "projected subjectivity"[179] into an otherwise empty cosmos.

In response to the Kantian paradigm, Barfield explicitly follows the Platonic Coleridge holding that the ideas are constitutive. For Coleridge, reason is "not, as with Kant, a merely regulative principle but constitutive in its speculative as well as its practical aspect."[180] Furthermore, Barfield claims

174. Barfield, *Poetic Diction*, 202.

175. Barfield, "Form in Art and Society," 226–27.

176. For Barfield's detailed critique of Kant see, "Appendix II" in Barfield, *Poetic Diction*, 183–96. He critiques Kant for subordinating the imagination to the understanding, for accepting the subjectivity of the individual, and for the categories having no real concrete unity by placing the *a priori* before the experience. He also takes issue with Kant for not relating the imagination to thinking and knowing. Barfield shows how Kant is errantly read into Plato and complains of the impact of Kant upon the modern consciousness. He writes, "So ubiquitous is the Konigsberg ghost that it is, in my opinion, wise to assume every modern writer on every subject to be guilty of logomorphism, until he has actually produced some evidence of his innocence."

177. Barfield, "Imagination and Inspiration," 124.

178. Barfield, Poetic Diction, "Appendix II."

179. Ibid., 204.

180. Barfield, "Coleridge Collected."

to have been much influenced by Gavin Ardley's, *Aquinas and Kant: The Foundations of the Modern Sciences*, which makes a strong case for metaphysical realism against the categorical (*a priori*) epistemology of Kant.[181] Barfield notes that in Coleridge, an "'idea' is at the same time both mind and nature; it is neither subjective nor objective; or it is both at the same time."[182] The "cardinal error," wrote Barfield, "of 'introducing a word or phrase which appears to stand for the thing itself' applies with at least as much force to the noumenal as to phenomenal 'things'."[183] Thus, the ideas are "the true link between the hither and the farther side of the threshold. For the Idea is neither subjective nor objective."[184] The point being, if the ideas are taken to be constitutive then the imagination could not be relegated to the subjective realm. This is precisely how, according to Barfield, Coleridge's poetic philosophy had re-envisaged the relationship between reason and the imagination,[185] one that has been a source of contention in the history of philosophy.[186]

In Barfield's scheme, the poetic imagination is not mere fancy, but rather, an inherent complement to philosophy. In the imagination subjective and objective realms merge, which is consistent with the symbolic nature of reality. Crucial to this understanding is Coleridge's distinction between "fancy" and the "active imagination." The idle or passive intellect is only engaged in mere fanciful abstract thinking that is privative of, or divorced from, reason, while the active imagination is "reason in her most exalted

181. Ardley, *Aquinas and Kant*. Barfield mentions the influence of Ardley in an interview. Ardley's work is a sort of apology for metaphysical realism. He employs metaphysical realism to critique what he calls a categorical science, which presumes that a representational stance is the only way to the real. He says that Kant wrongly employs this physicalist view to establish his *a priori* metaphysic. He is thus, unable to affirm the real. The interview wherein Barfield mentions Ardley's text can be found here: https://www.youtube.com/watch?v=oedVDN1xOWM.

182. Barfield, *Poetic Diction*, 179. See also, appendix IV, "Subjective and Objective."

183. Ibid., 19–20.

184. Barfield, "Imagination and Inspiration," 126.

185. Barfield, *The Rediscovery of Meaning, and Other Essays*, 107.

186. See, chapter 14, "The Creative Imagination," in Clarke, *The Creative Retrieval of Saint Thomas Aquinas*, 191–208. Clarke represents the imagination as a "handmaid" or "subordinate" to reason, but he does so to maintain a balance. As he states: "The history of the nature and roles of the imagination, especially the creative aspect of it, is a fascinating and conflicted story in Western thought, swinging from one extreme of suspicion of it as a threat to reason, to the other of exaltation of it as autonomous, opposed, even superior to reason" (208). Clarke is critical of "some of the Romantic thinkers" who argue that the imagination is autonomous from reason. Again, Coleridge's distinction between fancy and the active imagination guarded against such division. However, the difference being that Barfield and Coleridge do not explicitly remark on the active imagination being subordinate to reason, but rather, following Wordsworth they viewed the imagination as the highest expression of reason.

mood."[187] The imagination is not mere fancy, but rather a vehicle to truth,[188] a means of apprehending things as they actually are. In fact, Barfield notes that his "Great War" with Lewis was precisely about whether the imagination was a vehicle for truth (Barfield) or simply a pleasurable experience (Lewis).[189] "Lewis held that imagination has nothing to do with knowledge. We [Anthroposophists] hold that, although it is not knowledge, it is a step towards it and may develop into Inspiration and Intuition—with which he would have nothing to do."[190] Also, by distinguishing between fancy and the active imagination Coleridge introduced the concept of freedom of the will making space for the crucial moral dimension that empiricism lacked.[191]

Barfield's poetic philosophy affirms the active role of the subject granted by Kant's philosophy, but in challenging Kant's nominalism, Barfield's rather Platonic Coleridge held that the active imagination played a crucial role in the aesthetic encounter, unveiling the symbolic nature of the real, which indicates that philosophy and poetry, reason and the imagination, are not opposed, but inherent complements of one another.

Polarity: Keeping the Tension

Barfield cites Coleridge's "dynamic philosophy" of "polarity" as the central philosophical theme that permeates all of Coleridge's literary and philosophical work, and that which set him apart from all other philosophers.[192]

187. See, Wordsworth, *The Prelude*.

188. Barfield, *Romanticism Comes of Age*, 19. Barfield also depicts this relationship in his *The Rose on the Ash-Heap* wherein the "Poet" (who lacks discipline) and the "Philosopher" (who lacks determination and inspiration), once separate, come together forming a harmonious balance to war against a pervasive materialistic culture.

189. In Barfield's exchange with Lewis one glimpses the giant intellect of Barfield. In my own reading, his issue with Lewis is what Barfield describes as Lewis's separation of concept and percept. For Barfield this is, at bottom, a metaphysical debate regarding the real. In their lengthy and insightful exchange Lewis continually seeks a kind of analytic certainty at the expense of the real, while for Barfield the real simply exceeds the kind of analytic certainty Lewis is after, which for Barfield is only one weapon of cognition. He argues against Lewis, that polarity exceeds logic because it allows the aesthetic sensation to form a kind of deep knowing of that which is perceived; an intuition that logic precludes. See, "Owen Barfield Papers," C. S. Lewis, 1926–63, Dep. C, 1072. For the recently published manuscript see, Feinendegen and Smilde, "The 'Great War.'" See also, De Lange, *Owen Barfield*, 181.

190. Barfield, "On C. S. Lewis and Anthroposophy."

191. Barfield, *Saving the Appearances*, 145. It is here apparent that Barfield understood that the imagination could be used for "good" or "evil." See also, 161, for the morality of imagination.

192. Barfield, "Either: Or," 30. See also, Barfield, *What Coleridge Thought*, 145 and

Barfield argued that Coleridge's polarity offered a way out of the "either: or" philosophy that began with Aristotle, culminated in the Cartesian matter/mind dualism,[193] and continues to underlie all of modern science.[194] In his *Owen Barfield: Romanticism Come of Age*, Simon Blaxland De Lange argues that for Barfield, "unless the Coleridgean concept of polarity has been very clearly grasped the most insightful and noble of new ideas or impulses will be presented as an alternative (i.e., an either: or) to the existing state of affairs and will therefore fail to break the spell of this conundrum."[195] Barfield himself writes that,

> most of the much that has been written, in the last few decades, concerning the "reconciliation of opposites" in literature, and often with express reference to Coleridge as its putative father, betrays a lamentable failure to understand what "opposites" and their "reconciliation" actually signified in Coleridge's vocabulary. There is a world of difference between Coleridge's polarity and those "gorgeous ballets of dialectical opposition," to which

185. In his detailed work on Coleridge, Barfield notes that it is "difficult to find polarity *simpliciter;* that is to say, 'the law of polarity' as it is presented by Coleridge himself." This indeed renders it difficult to form a precise definition of Coleridge's polarity. Nonetheless, Barfield admits that Coleridge's claim to have taken polarity from Giordano Bruno is not entirely accurate. Bruno does not mention a "Law of Polarity." Barfield suggests that there is nothing to be found in the work of Bruno, "that is fairly recognizable as a law of polarity as Coleridge propounded it." The appendix of *What Coleridge Thought* is dedicated to finding the origin of Coleridge's idea of polarity. After reviewing Coleridge's predecessors, particularly Giordano Bruno, Cusa, and Lull, Barfield concludes that there is no direct relation to be found with any of them. However, in his concluding remarks he extracts a concept from Bruno's *De Progressu* that he believes may have provided Coleridge with his conception of polarity. Drawing on the work of Bruno and Cusa, Barfield then uses the example of a bisected line, divided into two lines that meet each other. The point at which these two lines meet is a "limit" that is the "essence" of both lines. Barfield writes, "the limit, though it belongs relatively to neither line, belongs absolutely to both; and in it the two lines coincide and are one line. This is taken to illustrate a universal principle; namely, that the infinite is present, or involved, in the simplest relation between finites" (190–91). Unfortunately, Barfield never read Coleridge's *Opus Maximum*, which was collected and finally published shortly after his death. In his private correspondence he seemed frustrated at the editor, Thomas McFarland, for keeping the manuscripts to himself. Had Barfield read the *Opus* he would have been surprised to discover that it was actually Aristotle's notion of potency and act that formed the basis of Coleridge's polarity (almost certainly to Barfield's chagrin, as he is often critical of Aristotle). He would have also been disappointed to see that the later Coleridge would come to focus far more on the will than on the imagination.

193. De Lange, *Owen Barfield*, 116. De Lange calls Coleridge "gifted," as a pioneer for bridging the mind/nature gap.

194. Barfield, "Either: Or," 35–36.

195. De Lange, *Owen Barfield*, 179.

we have been treated not only by literary critics theorizing about poetry, but also by psychologists, and more lately by theologians seeking to "reconcile" the sacred and the profane.[196]

Barfield describes this either/or philosophy as the "irreconcilable opposition,"[197] most fundamentally between the subject and object,[198] whose products are the various aforementioned dualisms that have plagued modern discourse. Barfield believed Coleridge's polarity could resituate these dualisms in a way at which Kant had only hinted. Any anti-realist endeavor falls prey to abstraction, yielding a division between subject and object. Instead objects are perceived as unified wholes, indicating that nothing is purely material or objective.[199] To apprehend a particular is, in fact, to apprehend the invisible in the visible. So paradoxically, while the whole is not bound materially, it is always present in the apprehension of anything material. Because polar opposites are constitutive of one another, they are never without their opposite (i.e., they cannot *actually* be abstracted or divided—although Barfield, admits that the mind is capable of distinguishing between the two; that is, one can *intellectually* abstract but never *actually* divide). This is precisely how Barfield saw that the Platonic Coleridge's philosophy of polarity corrected nominalism. What polarity means is that in the act of perception the mind encounters a real and irresolvable tension or an "interpenetration" (or participation) between spirit and matter, universal and particular, the invisible and visible, subjective and objective, not afforded by nominalism.

Furthermore polarity's metaphysical realism is evident in all of the processes of life.[200] Barfield refers to the "first polarity" of the organic world as seen in the continuity of the universal species present in each particular member.[201] He states, "For it has long been known from direct observation of nature that the individuals of every species, as they come to birth, recapitulate the history of the species itself."[202] In this way, "Nature must strive to reproduce itself and in the same act and moment it must strive

---

196. Barfield, *What Coleridge Thought*, 35–36.

197. Barfield, "Either: Or," 35.

198. Ibid., 32–33.

199. See, Barfield, "Either: Or."

200. See, Sugerman, "An Essay on Coleridge," 197. See also, Hocks, "Novelty in Polarity," 88. Hocks notes that polarity is not only a form of thought, but also a form of life.

201. Barfield, *What Coleridge Thought*, 36. Barfield begins by arguing for the presence of polarity in the inorganic world.

202. Barfield, *Romanticism Comes of Age*, 159. See also, Barfield, *What Coleridge Thought*, 53.

to *overcome* that detachment, to overcome that individuation, thus maintaining the unity."[203] The point here is that one cannot *actually* divide or
abstract the species from its particular instantiations. It is always inherently
there, as it were. The biological process consists in the unity of the poles
of reproduction and individuation as the species non-identically repeats
itself. In an even more telling description Barfield notes Coleridge's example
of polar opposition in chemistry (which he takes from Goethe), whereby
"water is neither oxygen nor hydrogen, nor is it a commixture of both; but
the synthesis or indifference of the two . . . "[204] This means that ultimately
these two forces (i.e., oxygen and hydrogen) are not abstract hypotheses (or
ideas) invented by the mind in order to give an account of phenomena,[205]
but they are actually constitutive of the very phenomena observed (i.e.,
water). Hence,

> The two forces, then, are not parts of phenomenal nature; they
> are not body, nor in any conventional sense the "causes" of what
> is bodily. They are not material in the sense that, for instance,
> the forces of electricity and magnetism are material. These "con-
> stituent powers," as Coleridge calls them . . . are acts or energies
> that are "suspended and, as it were quenched in the product."
> They are the "inside" of anything to which we can apply the
> noun *matter* or the adjective *material*.[206]

In the last line Barfield suggests that even that which is nowadays objectively identified as matter does not sit on one side of the threshold and its
properties on another, but rather, what is taken to be matter is actually the
product of the interpenetration of opposite energies.[207] As Barfield argues,
these energies do not cease to exist, but are hereby "suspended"[208] or held
in "polar tension" in the phenomena. It is only in the attempt to "save the
appearances," by forcing an epistemological framework upon phenomena,
that phenomena are rendered purely material, when, in fact, all phenomena
are a polarity of two realms.[209]

203. Barfield, *Romanticism Comes of Age*, 156.

204. Barfield is here citing from Coleridge's, *The Friend*.

205. Barfield, *What Coleridge Thought*, 33.

206. Ibid.

207. Ibid. Barfield is here citing Coleridge's, *Collected Letters*.

208. Ibid., 34. See also, 76. Barfield believed that the underlying reality or substance
of things is not matter but immaterial relationship.

209. Barfield's reading is here similar to Plato's matter/form distinction. Plato is
not a dualist who posits an immaterial realm over/against the material. Instead what
Plato indicates is that the ideas actualize matter. Matter, thus, is not set over/against the

It is for this reason that Barfield often criticized science for turning to "occult qualities"[210] after abstracting "laws of nature" from objects.[211] Newtonian physics, and particularly mechanistic accounts of the cosmos, tend to relegate all that is imperceptible to "laws" or "forces." These laws, known only in their effects, are no longer considered to be constitutive of objects. To the prevailing mechanistic cosmology that divides objects from the laws that act upon them, he juxtaposes Coleridge's polarity that simply distinguishes them so that the productive power is suspended and quenched in the product.[212] For, a "true system must be grounded neither in a *thing* nor an *abstraction* . . . ."[213] "Every thing or *phaenomenon* is the exponent of a synthesis *as long as* the opposite energies are retained in that synthesis."[214] For Barfield's Coleridge, in all phenomena the two sides of the Kantian threshold are held in polar tension.

Now, Barfield knew that polarity did not fit comfortably with philosophical logic. In fact, he felt it the only true way out of such a system. This is why he disavowed "paradox," which he took to be the acceptance of two mutually exclusive (equivocal) opposites. He felt paradox fell prey to the same either/or system.[215] Whether he was correct to distinguish polarity and paradox is not a cause for concern at this time. In fact, there are tenable similarities.[216] Nevertheless, this distinction between polarity and what

---

immaterial realm of the forms but rather particulars are the product of the participation of form and matter. For an excellent description of how Barfield conceives of the spirit/matter relationship see, Barfield, "Matter, Imagination, and Spirit." Barfield's critique of materialism is here similar to Clarke who, in his critique of non-reductive materialism, argues that "matter" is a term that was "made up," "precisely as a contrast term to indicate the inclusion in its meaning only those data subject in some way to spatial extension and quantitative measurement, at least indirectly, by us and our instruments . . . to erase or blur entirely the outside methodological limits that were the purpose of the creation of the term in the first place is only to introduce confusion." See, Clarke, *The Creative Retrieval of Saint Thomas Aquinas*, 187.

210. Barfield, *What Coleridge Thought*, 25. Occult qualities are anything "deemed to possess an exclusively objective existence, in spite of being imperceptible."

211. Ibid.

212. Ibid., 24. Barfield is citing Coleridge's, *On the Prometheus of Aeschylus*. See also, ibid., 30. Herein, he suggests that polar opposites are not themselves physical forces, although they give rise to physical forces.

213. Barfield, *What Coleridge Thought*, 31.

214. Barfield is here citing from Coleridge's, *The Friend*. He may be here distancing himself from Hegel.

215. Barfield, *Owen Barfield on C. S. Lewis*, 54.

216. One can assume that Barfield was somewhat acquainted with the work of Kierkegaard who is an obligatory interlocutor for any critique of paradox. Fellow Inkling Charles Williams was enthralled by Kierkegaard's work. See Hannay and Marino, *The*

Barfield took to be paradox assists in further clarifying his poetic philosophy. Ambiguities notwithstanding, Barfield's outright rejection of paradox was based on his belief that it involved abstraction. For this reason, he opposed what he called "logical" paradox to "dynamic" polarity. Barfield states that, "a logical contradiction is mere negation; contemplated as 'paradox' it becomes, in a sense, affirmative and positive; but it is still static," whereas "the essence of polarity is a dynamic conflict between coinciding opposites."[217] In *Speaker's Meaning* he further clarifies this distinction:

Cambridge Companion to Kierkegaard, 56–57. In chapter 2, in Roger Poole's, "The Unknown Kierkegaard: Twentieth-century Receptions," he writes, "Charles Williams had come to perceive some prophetic quality in the writings of the Danish master and set out on a one man crusade to get as much of it as possible into translation and into print as fast as he could." See also, Barfield, "The Nature of Meaning." Therein Barfield makes a brief mention of Kierkegaard. There are tenable similarities between Kierkegaard's "absolute paradox" and Coleridge's polarity as envisaged by Barfield. Coleridge's polarity and Kierkegaard's paradox are both derived from the incarnation. Barfield writes of Coleridge, that the God-Man is the basis of all polarity. God is at once the "ground of the unity between God and man, but also of the distinction between them" (Barfield, *What Coleridge Thought*, 113). In the *Philosophical Fragments* Kierkegaard's Climacus writes of the "absolute paradox" of the incarnation. Herein, God is at once absolutely different, while he is also "absolutely the equal of the lowliest of human beings" (Kierkegaard, *Philosophical Fragments*, 32–33). Much like Coleridge's active imagination, Kierkegaard's subject is moved by the paradoxical passion of understanding, the passion to understand that which it cannot understand (37). The paradox drives the subject to know the "unknown," "the god" (39). This is very similar to Coleridge's insistence that knowledge of polarity in the world requires a move beyond understanding by employing the imagination. Paradox ushers understanding to this moment (52). The understanding yields to the paradox, and in this moment the paradox concomitantly gives back to understanding. Lastly, Barfield and Kierkegaard reject Hegel for similar reasons. Against Barfield's claim, it would appear that at the very least Kierkegaard's vision of paradox is compatible with Coleridge's conception of polarity. It is suggested in chapter 5 that Kierkegaard's "non-identical repetition" is akin to Barfield's theory of language, while his metaphysic of theological transcendence outwits Barfield's poetic philosophy.

Nonetheless, Barfield wants to maintain that paradox and polarity are entirely different. Barfield may have been correct to distance polarity from other attempts at overcoming dualisms or abstraction, particularly those following a highly logical scheme (i.e., Hegel. See, Barfield, *What Coleridge Thought*, 31. Although Coleridge does use Hegelian language to describe polarity, Barfield discounts his logic stating that, "it has perhaps hindered rather than helped effective grasp of his meaning"), but not necessarily from paradox.

There has been one notable contribution to the difference between Coleridge's polarity and paradox that is here worth mentioning: Perez, "Coleridgean Polarity in the Poetry of Gerard Manley Hopkins. Perez, who draws on Barfield's *What Coleridge Thought*, states that a paradox is resolved in the compatibility of opposites, while polarity does not seek resolution but holds the tension.

217. Barfield, *What Coleridge Thought*, 187.

A polarity of contraries is not quite the same as the *coincidentia oppositorum*, which has been stressed by some philosophers, or as the "paradox" which (whether for the purposes of irony or for other reasons) is beloved by some contemporary writers and critics. A paradox is the violent union of two opposites that simply contradict each other, so that reason assures us we can have one *or* the other but not both at the same time. Whereas polar contraries (as is illustrated by the use of the term in electricity) exist by virtue of each other *as well as* at each other's expense.[218]

Although it is difficult to determine why precisely Barfield took Coleridge's vision to be different from Cusa's "coincidence of opposites,"[219] it seems that Barfield instead turns to the later Bruno due to his emphasis on the imagination.[220]

218. Barfield, *Speaker's Meaning*, 38–39 (emphasis added). The philosophy he here critiques seems Hegelian. See also, Barfield, "The Meaning of 'Literal,'" 38. Here he explicitly writes off Hegel for being an idealist.

219. Barfield's critique of the "coincidence of opposites" mentioned above lacks a thorough treatment of Cusa. It is difficult to know how much of Cusa Barfield actually read (all the literature in Barfield's notes are secondary). His notes appear as an attempt to distance Coleridge and Bruno from Cusa. It seems that Barfield's obsession with the imagination (and what he seems to intimate as Bruno's bringing the infinite to the world [via the imagination], as opposed to Cusa's keeping it in a realm beyond it—see, "Owen Barfield Papers," Research Notes and Correspondence, 1960–70, Dep. C, 1178) caused him to focus on the later work of Bruno and overlook the significance of the more thoroughgoing theological treatise of Cusa. Instead, he might have discovered that Cusa's metaphysic employs a logic similar to his poetic philosophy, but exceeds it, precisely because it does not collapse the infinite into the finite as Barfield seems to want to do with Bruno and Coleridge following him. Instead, for Cusa, the finite participates in the infinite. In his *On Learned Ignorance* Cusa develops his theology in a way that Barfield could only hint at in his poetic philosophy. Cusa tries to show that these opposites, as they appear in logic, nature, etc., are the essence of finitude, for only in the infinite (God) do such opposites coincide. This is to recognize a real distinction between finite and infinite (creation and God) that Barfield at times, seems to want to collapse. Crucially for Cusa (and something never fully clarified in Barfield's poetic philosophy), the "unity" of finitude is not God, but a borrowed unity that participates in God. This allows the finite mind to hold to logic while moving beyond it. For Cusa, this is how one learns ignorance. To unlearn what one thought possible is indeed to learn. This learning allows one to see truths otherwise inaccessible. This theological alternative is clarified further in chapter 5.

220. Barfield seems to want to link Coleridge's focus on Bruno to his [Bruno's] study of the imagination. See, Barfield, "Giordano Bruno and the Survival of Learning." Barfield spent a great deal of time studying Bruno and corresponding with special collections to discover the origin of Coleridge's "polarity," which he ultimately does not locate. These studies are well documented in his notes found at, "Owen Barfield Papers," Research Notes and Correspondence, 1960–70, Dep. C, 1178. Again, in his *Opus*, Coleridge is clear that it was Aristotle from whom he gleaned his polar logic. See

Nonetheless, polarity moves beyond the limits of logic in that it is not simply an attempt to affirm the theory of non-contradiction within the bounds of logic, but rather, polarity asserts the dependence and interpenetration of one polar opposite upon or in the other. On the one hand, polar opposites cannot be separated or abstracted from one another, but on the other hand, they cannot be dissolved into one another. There is no absolute synthesis, but a constant tension. It is precisely this irresoluteness, this tension that is crucial to understanding Barfield's poetic philosophy.

Here John Sallis's *Logic of Imagination: The Expanse of the Elemental*[221] provides a key insight. Sallis notes that since Aristotle, notions of logic have been ontologically, or rather ontically restrained. Logic, all the way up until Hegel, works within a sort of Kantian ontic of space-time (Catherine Pickstock refers to this as an "immanent spatialization").[222] Barfield refers to this sort of space as an idol.[223] In other words, a logical contradiction is typically thought of in ontic (i.e., spatialized) terms: two objects cannot occupy the same space at the same time without displacing each other. In seeking to uphold the limits of space-time, attempts to reconcile opposites remain within this paradigm. One can assume this is what Barfield means when he writes in the above passage, "reason assures us we can have one *or* the other but not both at the same time." However, by utilizing what Sallis refers to as the "exorbitant logic" of the imagination, polarity exceeds the Kantian strictures of space-time allowing two polar opposites to exist together (or "interpenetrate") in the same space and at the same time. In fact, Barfield refers to polar opposites as "dynamic," precisely because they do not exclude one another as objects in space, but rather "contain, and, in doing so, enhance one another."[224] Thus, pure reason or logic alone, so long as it remains committed to these space-time strictures, must either speak in

---

footnote 192, above.

221. Sallis, *Logic of Imagination*, 96–104. Sallis, like Barfield, suggests that the imagination may overcome the traditional ontic paradigm of logic. He states, "What is required, more precisely, is that the dismantling of traditional logic be carried through to the end and that the prospect of exorbitant logics be allowed to arise from this outcome" (101). "If there are fields other than that of things, fields that are differently ordered, then they could be expected to have another logic, a logic for which the principle of noncontradiction might not be fundamental, even a logic quite outside this principle, an exorbitant logic" (104).

222. Pickstock, *After Writing*. See, chapter 2, "Spatialization," 47–100, for Pickstock's critique of "immanent spatialization," which she claims denies transcendence.

223. Barfield, *Saving the Appearances*, 149.

224. Barfield, "Either: Or," 29–30. See also, Adey, *C. S. Lewis' Great War with Owen Barfield*, 101. Adey notes that for Barfield space and time have no influence on the relations between parts and whole. See also, Barfield, *Worlds Apart*, 126.

terms of a Cartesian and hence Kantian dualism (i.e., transcendentals existing *beyond* space and time) or in terms of an Hegelian identity (i.e., collapsing or absolutizing the transcendentals in space and time).[225] Yet, to talk of
transcendentals means that one must paradoxically immanently transcend
the strictures of space-time. This is to suggest that Kant's discourse about
transcendentals and thresholds inherently employed what Sallis calls an
exorbitant logic, the logic of the imagination, while at the same time rejecting it. In recognition of this, polar logic holds the two in tension, which
maintains that the transcendentals exist paradoxically in-and-beyond
space-time. This is similar to the previously rehearsed Platonic metaphysic,
which speaks of the transcendence of the forms or ideas as in-and-beyond
matter; the realism that informed Coleridge's critique of what one might call
Kant's nominalism. This is why for Barfield the ideas cannot be merely regulative and must instead be constitutive of phenomena. To clarify, Richard A.
Hocks's definition of Barfield's polarity is worth fully quoting. Polarity, thus,

> does *not* mean, "there is something to be said on both sides,"
> or, "each position contains a part of the truth"—and the like.
> Such locutions do not get at polarity, but express the thinking
> of dichotomy or, at best, dialectic. In either case they bespeak
> juxtaposition, far less likely interpenetration, and certainly not
> "seminal identity"—as opposed to the logical principle of iden-
> tity (opposed in dichotomy, not polarity!). Polar-concentration
> means that the predominating pole never ceases to require its
> opposite pole to *be* predominating; in fact, the very reason it
> is predominating in any given instance is that the energies of
> the nonpredominating poles are concentrated at their opposite!
> That is actually what polar concentration is, the energy of the
> nonpredominating pole concentrated at the predominating
> pole. Consequently it is, really, not too much to say that the es-
> sential test of whether we are grasping polarity in the first place,
> are resisting, that is, the many "look-alikes" of dichotomy, is
> whether we can grasp the relationship of polar-concentration.
> Polarity, after all, is the only relationship involving opposition in
> which the contraries can and do transform each other, back and
> forth, in predominance or polar-concentration[;] . . . they trans-
> form into each other, also transform each other more funda-
> mentally through their given polarity *to* each other. Otherwise
> there would simply be no way for the relationship in question

225. See, Barfield, "Review of *Coleridge as Philosopher*." Here one sees Barfield
distances Coleridge from the German tradition that "submerged in individual spirit
completely in the Whole."

not to be subsumed under the principles of contradiction and identity; otherwise it would indeed *be* a contradiction . . . .[226]

Again, Barfield maintains that polar opposites must be distinguished but never divided. He goes as far as to say that polar opposites are relative of one another, as each quality is present in the other.[227] The strictures of imma-nent spatialization present the *aporia* as a contradiction. Polarity, however, affirms the *aporia* by exceeding the logic of space-time allowing for the in-terpenetration of two polar opposites that mutually exist without contradic-tion. To put it as simply as possible, Barfield argued that attempts to resolve this *aporia* were untenable, because they tried to reconcile immiscible op-posites, whereas the success of polarity lies in the view that polar opposites are complementary or interpenetrate (they do not and cannot exist apart from one another). By employing an exorbitant logic, the poetic imagina-tion allows for qualities (that for the Cartesian subject exist beyond space and time) to transcend immanent space and time.[228] In this way the "imagi-nation uses the spatial to get to the non-spatial."[229] This emphasis on the imagination is pivotal for Barfield. Because polarity is "pre-phenomenal,"[230] it is not apprehended by the senses or even within the bounds of logic (out-side the imagination), but through them. Since all phenomena have their origin in a non-material and supersensible world[231] the real can only be truly known "by an understanding laced with imagination."[232] Therefore, "The apprehension of polarity is itself the basic act of imagination."[233]

Barfield's reception of Coleridge's polarity does indeed honor the Kan-tian *aporia*, not as a contradiction or non-contradiction as with logic, but by holding the two sides in polar tension and by declaring that polar opposites

226. Hocks, "Novelty in Polarity," 85–86.

227. Barfield, *What Coleridge Thought*, 36.

228. Barfield, *Romanticism Comes of Age*, 128–29. He notes that Dante's work is all about the relation between spatial and non-spatial world we inhabit. See also, Sallis, *Logic of Imagination*, 147. Indeed Sallis's remarks are here pertinent. He writes, philoso-phy must "forgo positing any 'beyond' that is not a 'beyond' *of the sensible*. Whatever might now be set beyond the sensible must also be such that it belongs to the sensible, even if it is not simply reducible to sensible things." Here and elsewhere Sallis frequently refers to this strategy as a "return to the elements" or "elementals."

229. Quote taken from and interview with *Towards: a Publication for Our Time*, found in "Owen Barfield Papers," *Lukacs-Neumeister*, 1956–95, Dep. C, 1074.

230. Barfield, *What Coleridge Thought*, 37. Barfield calls polarity pre-phenomenal in that polar forces, though they "are not directly perceptible . . . are nevertheless pres-ent in the phenomenal world."

231. Hocks, "Novelty in Polarity," 82.

232 Barfield, *What Coleridge Thought*, 37.

233. Ibid., 36.

simply cannot exist in and of themselves; they are, thus, constitutive of one another. Barfield believed Coleridge's polarity offered a way out of a modern philosophical dilemma by viewing the aforementioned dualisms not as contradictories, but as polar opposites. Distinct from dualisms or logical contradictions, these polar opposites are not abstract (or regulative) but constitutive of all phenomena.

Poetic Discourse: The Role of the Imagination

A summary of Barfield's poetic philosophy is now in order. In the initial aesthetic encounter the imagination is at work. Through the senses the mind initially perceives the unity of phenomena (Barfield calls this act "concrete thinking"—the basic act of perception).[234] But in an attempt to "save the appearances," the understanding or judgmental[235] thinking, through abstraction, sunders this unity. This creates, among others, a perceived division between understanding and imagination, which, if misunderstood, skews the real. When logic is correctly employed, distinguishing the pre-phenomenal (that which exists in and beyond space-time) from that which is immanent is *conceptual*, not actual (as with Platonism and nearly all philosophy up until the Middle Ages).[236] When wrongly employed, logic regards the pre-phenomenal, that which is only conceptually distinct, to be *actually* distinct and relegates it to a subjective realm (e.g., in the denial of universals or epistemologies of representation). As Barfield saw it, if one takes the ideas to be constitutive this allows the two sides to intermingle in a polar tension.[237] Bereft of the imagination, mere understanding or judg-

234. Barfield, *Poetic Diction*, 25. Barfield writes, "the demand for unity, is at all levels the proper activity of the imagination . . . or . . . concrete thinking."

235. Adey, *C. S. Lewis' Great War*, 105. Adey notes that judgmental thinking apprehends unity in multiplicity but sees universals as abstract of the parts, whereas for the "imaginal mind a polarity subsists as a dynamic participation in the process of actual life manifest in natures ordered multiplicity . . . a trained imagination could perceive subject and object to be the same essence."

236. Adey, *C. S. Lewis' Great War*, 21. As Barfield saw it, the Platonic forms began to erode with the development of Aristotelian categories and are finally ousted by the scholastic nominalists.

237. Barfield, "Participation and Isolation," 209. Barfield refers to the imagination as the "opposite" of abstraction. See also, Engell, *The Collected Works of Samuel Taylor Coleridge*, 299. For Barfield, following Coleridge, the imagination apprehends qualities in the natural order. See note 1. Engell defines Coleridge's definition of the imagination as, "Two forces or concepts in dynamic tension both find themselves in the imagination, which reconciles and unifies them: the self or mind ('I am') with nature or the cosmos, the subjective with the objective. . . . The imagination finally resolves all contradictions of real and ideal, nature and mind. The imagination is, sparely put, an act of

mental thinking fails to hold the two sides in proper tension, resulting in a closed system, a subject/object dualism or an identity of opposites (e.g., idealisms such as Hegel's,[238] which Barfield, like Manfred Frank, implicitly distinguishes from the "Romantic School" of Schlegel),[239] whereas the imagination was the "best-known" means of preserving the two sides of the threshold.[240] For this reason Barfield insisted that the creative and/or poetic imagination[241] could heal those various dualisms he fought so relentlessly to overturn (e.g., subject/object, mind/matter, and/or spirit/matter).[242] This poetic gaze could reverse those idolatrous ways of thinking by once again envisaging qualities in the material world. It should be stressed that Barfield was not at all interested in a sort of subjective enchantment of an otherwise banal world, but rather he sought to provide a poetic philosophy (i.e., a realist metaphysic) to rediscover an *already enchanted* natural order that was nearly lost to the modern consciousness.[243] By utilizing the imagination the poet's verse recounts the real, unearthing the phenomenon's hitherto unseen depths. Rather than a reductive abstraction or judgmental thinking that increasingly abstracts in the name of objectivity, proper poetic diction reverses this, allowing one to see the phenomenon in a fresh light. It is not a reductive objective gaze that gets to the bare bones of truth, but rather an imaginative encounter that admits the inexhaustibility of objects and the

---

ultimate synthesis in the dialectic of mind and nature."

238. Barfield, "The Rediscovery of Meaning," 20.

239. Barfield, "Where Is Fancy Bread?" 79–83. He calls Schlegel the, "real founder of the Romantic School."

240. Barfield, "Imagination and Inspiration," 125.

241. Barfield, "Where Is Fancy Bread?" 89–90. See also, Barfield, "Science and Quality," 176–86.

242. Barfield, "Matter, Imagination, and Spirit," 149.

243. Barfield, *History in English Words*, 175–77. Barfield is clear that the romantics were not subjects external to nature projecting meaning into the material, but rather, they received from it. Barfield, *Poetic Diction*, 35. He warns that if poets remain trapped in thinking in terms of science's detachment of the mind, then they will not change anything by merely projecting their subjective emotions into an otherwise objective nothingness. This is precisely why he wants to utilize poetry to alter the scientific outlook. Similarly, Bronislaw Szerszynski warns against this conception of romanticism as an interjection of the sublime into the empirical realm, where nature as a whole is taken to be immanentized and desacralised. See, Szerszynski, *Nature, Technology and the Sacred*, 169. See also, 87. Szerszynski refers to this as the romantics' monistic ontology. See also, 123–24. Therein, he states that simply "re-enchanting" nature won't be enough. See also, Northcott, *The Environment and Christian Ethics*, 85 and 89. Northcott argues a simple romantic view does not work, because nature simply becomes the new god. Such critiques are of the conception of a particular kind of romanticism that Barfield rejects.

truth they mediate. The intellect and the creative imagination are not immiscible.[244] The poet, who has a "simultaneous" awareness of both sides of the threshold, uses imaginative language, as "it could be that it is only in some such language that effective and badly needed inspirations from beyond the threshold that is fixed between the subjective potency of humanity and its objective perceptions can ever be either altered or apprehended."[245] Therefore, "when the two are held separate, yet united, in the tension which is polarity, . . . when the idea, which is neither objective nor subjective, is intuited or realized by the philosophical imagination, . . . the threshold . . . yield[s] new meaning for old and giv[es] birth to a future that has originated in present creativity instead of being a helpless copy of the outwardly observed forms of the past."[246] Indeed, the poet must strive to reject univocal language, because nothing can be revealed afresh otherwise.[247] In this way, for Barfield, Coleridge pointed towards inspiration as a "successor" to Kant's placement of the imagination beyond the threshold. Instead, inspiration mediates that which arrives from beyond the threshold.[248] In the creative act, the imagination apprehends that which transcends the Kantian threshold making the unknown known.

Barfield was certainly charmed by how well Coleridge's polarity aligned with both Steiner's evolution of consciousness and his own philological thesis.[249] Coleridge's emphasis on the polar relationship between subject and object not only coincides with Barfield's theory of language, but it also indicates that the modern isolated self was not, nor could ever be, entirely isolated.[250] Barfield believed that the properly trained imagination

244. Ibid., 178.

245. Barfield, "Imagination and Inspiration," 129.

246. Ibid., 127. See also, Adey, *C. S. Lewis' Great War*, 123. My analysis here is consistent with Adey's description of Barfield's thought as distinct from Lewis the logician: "What Barfield does seem to have in common with Einstein, Popper, Bonhoeffer, and for that matter De Chardin is a certain tentativeness, a sense that truth lies not in 'facts' that once discovered remain as certainties, but in a continuous reaching into the unknown or re-consideration of experience. They would all see the process of discovery as an exercise of imagination. . . ."

247. Barfield, *Poetic Diction*, 131.

248. Barfield, "Imagination and Inspiration," 129.

249. Polarity maintained an integral connection between the conscious and unconscious articulated by Steiner. It also serves to uphold Barfield's ubiquitous claim that the mind cannot be wholly divided from matter. For his essay devoted to this, see Barfield, "Matter, Imagination, and Spirit."

250. Talbott, *The Future Does Not Compute*, 279. Talbott's work draws readily on Barfield's theory of the evolution of consciousness. Talbott writes, "Our own hard-won separation, as Barfield points out, has proven a valuable gift—one never to be discarded. But insofar as it has metamorphosed into an experience of ourselves as wholly and

could once again apprehend these supersensible relations and usher in that future stage of consciousness he referred to as final participation; when, for the first time in the history of the evolution of consciousness the self-conscious individual becomes conscious of his or her intimate relation to the world. Or, as Stephen L. Talbott describes it, "It is the point where man is sufficiently detached from 'things' to appreciate their independent life, but not so detached that he has lost all consciousness of his inner connection to them. His separation from the world only allows him to savor all the more his union with it."[251]

Chapter 1 examined how Steiner's evolution of consciousness was of a piece with Barfield's earlier studies regarding the evolutionary history of words. Barfield affirmed that all language, as a participation of subject and object, corresponds to a symbolic world. This meant that the language most capable of accounting for the robust nature of being was indeed poetic. Chapter 1 then introduced Heidegger as an interlocutor and indicated that Barfield's theory of poetry outwits such immanentized (i.e., univocal/equivocal) visions regarding the posture of the poetic subject, because his poet is neither purely passive (as with Heidegger), nor purely active (as will be detailed in Part II), but a subject in the "middle." This intimates that the subject and object are not immanent but are instead vertically transected by a higher ordering principle. Therefore, a language that accords with reality is an inspired language that exceeds such immanentized or totalized philosophies. This required further clarification. Chapter 2 then sought to examine the relationship between philosophy and poetry arguing that Barfield's poetic philosophy represents an alternative to those immanentist paradigms that divide between philosophical and poetic language. A review of the contemporary reception of Coleridge revealed against such post-Kantian prejudices that Coleridge's attempt to unite poetry and philosophy was in response to an inherent *aporia* in Kant that could only be accounted for using poetic language. This rejects the idolatrous want for objective truth by instead suggesting that poetry plays an inherent role in the quest for truth, as philosophy's complement. Regarding the conclusion of chapter 1, this inexhaustible quest, this "finite longing for the infinite," indicates that language, like being, is never closed or totalized, but rather remains open to an inspiration that is mediated through immanence and apprehended via the imagination. As such, philosophy and poetry should not be understood as distinct (e.g., truth vs. myth), but rather poetry is a

absolutely cut off from the world, it is a lie. Furthermore, it is an unnecessary lie, for it is possible to enjoy the antithesis of subjective 'south pole' and objective 'north pole' without proceeding to act as if the antithesis were a clean severance."

251. Ibid., 254–55.

necessary complement to philosophy.[252] This directs the immanentist gaze to the openness of being, which is vertically transected by a transcendent theological ground that is examined in Part III. For now, this concludes the examination of Barfield's aesthetic participation. But, Barfield was not content with limiting his thought to the realm of language and philosophy, for the very nature of his philosophy challenged such limits. Indeed, as he saw it there is an "analogous" relation between aesthetic participation and what he called sociological participation, which is examined in Part II.

252. Barfield, "Philosophy, Poetry, and Transcendence." Similar to my analysis, Raymond Barfield, using Owen Barfield as an interlocutor, does well in his attempt to trace what he calls the "ancient quarrel" between philosophy and poetry to show how they are necessary complements of one another; as such, both form an integral whole that governs the speculative search for certainty.

PART II

SOCIOLOGICAL PARTICIPATION

With Barfield's theory of aesthetic participation in place, the essay will now show how he both critiqued and engaged the sciences to qualify his poetic philosophy. Barfield saw an analogous relation between aesthetic participation and what he called sociological participation; that is, that the language and/or philosophy that constitutes a "collective consciousness" is embodied in what one might call the "living" and "making" practices of particular cultures. Barfield argued that the gradual diminution of the poetic aesthetic coincided with the rise of the social and physical atomism that came to dominate the modern social and physical sciences.

So chapter 3 examines the influence of French philosopher and anthropologist Lucien Lévy-Bruhl, whose unique assessment of primitive consciousness Barfield discovered to be deeply akin to his study of words. Barfield identifies a connection between past languages and the way primitive societies live poetically with one another and with the natural world. In his *Saving the Appearances*, he indicates there is anthropological evidence that suggests primitive societies embody the very poetic consciousness he had discovered in his study of past words. Because supersensible relations were inherently part of the primitive consciousness, the primitive subject is not cut off from the world, but sees herself as both part of her kin and of the natural world. But over time, in the same way that words became increasingly literal and objective, man eventually finds himself as an autonomous subject cut off from a world of objects. Man, his kin, and nature grow apart. In the social sciences such progress culminates in the liberal construal of a negative freedom from social, ethical, and moral responsibility, while it is this same premise that justifies modern science's endeavor to overcome the limits of nature.

Chapter 4 examines Barfield's critique of modern science beginning with the pre-modern conception of poetic making that is lost in the rise of the active subject who exceeds the limits of nature. Here, it is suggested that the separation of man (subject) and nature (object) mirrors Barfield's thesis regarding the evolution of words. In modernity, the world becomes disenchanted; all quality, once in the world, becomes merely subjective (in the mind). The modern mechanistic cosmos becomes full of dead objects subject to the active human will. With norms, and hence, natural limitations now removed, man rises above nature; he no longer participates in the creative process by imitating nature, but dominates nature, creating it in his own image. For Barfield, this sort of "scientism" threatens life both literally and figuratively, and it is against such scientism that he launches his strongest polemic. He questions science's language of objectivity, asking if it has not all along employed a latent poetic element in its ephemeral processes, theorizing, hypothesizing, and causal explanations, remarking that there is, in fact, a participation of subject and object that cannot, and must not be ignored if the history of civilization is to survive the uninhibited advance of science. He challenged scientists to become artists. Ironically, he discovered that his critique of the presumed subject/object division, upon which modern physics had secured its autonomy, was being undermined by recent developments in the physical sciences themselves. These findings not only overturned the staunch objectivity and mechanistic cosmology upon which modern physics had rested its laurels, but more importantly, quantum theory suggested there exists an underlying "relationality" or "entanglement" beyond the efficient causality of space/time. Most importantly, quantum phenomena indicate that modern physics had overlooked a crucial hermeneutical element when it discovered the subject does indeed affect the observed object. In sum, for Barfield, these discoveries not only questioned many of the same presumptions of the social and physical sciences that he sought to undermine, but concomitantly they affirmed his own poetic philosophy.

To bring together Parts I and II, it is suggested in closing that Barfield's poetic philosophy serves as an alternative to both Heidegger's passive subject and the equally untenable active subject of the modern sciences. In their failure to ground the subject (in active or passive terms), the modern social and physical sciences, and the philosophy upon which they are built, intimate a theological opening within an otherwise immanentized cosmos that Barfield's poetic philosophy affirms. This theological opening will then be examined in Part III.

3

Poetic Living

Hobbits are an unobtrusive but very ancient people . . . for they love peace and quiet and good tilled earth; a well-ordered and well-farmed countryside was their favorite haunt. They do not and did not understand or like machines more complicated than forge-bellows, a water-mill, or a hand-loom, though they were skillful with tools. . . . [T]hey were, as a rule, shy of "the Big Folk," as they call us, and now they avoid us with dismay and are becoming hard to find. . . . They possessed from the first the art of disappearing swiftly and silently, when large folk whom they do not wish to meet come blundering by; and this art they have developed until to Men it may seem magical. But Hobbits have never, in fact, studied magic of any kind, and their elusiveness is due solely to a professional skill that heredity and practice, and a close friendship with the earth, have rendered inimitable by bigger and clumsier race.

—TOLKIEN[1]

Now a man attains perfection in the corporeal life in two ways: first, in regard to his own person; secondly, in regard to the whole community of the society in which he lives, for man is by nature a social animal.

—AQUINAS[2]

1. Tolkien, *The Fellowship of the Ring*, 1–2.
2. Aquinas, *Summa Theologica*, IIIa. q. 65, a. 1.

The Influence of Lucien Lévy-Bruhl

Participation Embodied

THIS CHAPTER COMMENCES THE examination of what Barfield referred to as sociological participation; that is, the idea that the general consciousness (or the "collective representation")[3] of a particular society is embodied in its social practices. Indeed, Barfield himself indicates that in his own work one finds an analogous relation between aesthetic participation (i.e., one's metaphysic) and sociological participation (i.e., how it is embodied in man's relation to his fellow man and to nature).[4] Barfield found strong evidence for this in the work of French philosopher and anthropologist Lucien Lévy-Bruhl, whose thought and influence upon Barfield are the subjects of this chapter.

According to Barfield, Lévy-Bruhl's analyses affirm the aforesaid analogical relation between aesthetic and sociological participation. In his most popular work,[5] *Saving the Appearances*, Barfield utilizes Lévy-Bruhl's findings to develop his evolutionary anthropology whereby he locates a marked difference between the collective representations of primitive and civilized man. Barfield found that a comparative study of primitive and modern humanity's collective representations indicates an evolutionary pattern consistent with his theory of language.[6] Simply put, whereas modern societies tend towards individualism, primitive societies tend towards collectivism. This collectivism, it should be noted, is not merely political, but accords with a primitive notion of the self that stretches beyond the physical body to one's kin and to nature. Thus, evolutionary history evinces a steady decline of this sort of collectivism (what shall be referred to as "poetic living") that coincides with a steady increase in individualism. Barfield wants to reverse this trend. As he states, the purpose of *Saving the Appearances* is to show that the spiritual wealth of this lost world, "can be, and indeed, if incalculable disaster is to be avoided, must be regained."[7] Barfield attempts to assuage the loss of poetic living by making modern man once again conscious of his

3. This is a term often used by Lévy-Bruhl that Barfield employs throughout his *Saving the Appearances*. Collective representations are univocal to Barfield's use of "consciousness" (i.e., to say that collective representations evolve is to say, generally, that consciousness evolves).

4. Barfield, "Participation and Isolation," 206.

5. Barfield and Tennyson, *A Barfield Reader*, xx.

6. Barfield, *Saving the Appearances*, 34–35.

7. Ibid., 85. See also, De Lange, *Owen Barfield*, 249. Similarly, De Lange notes that *Saving the Appearances* had a dual prophetic meaning of a "dire warning and visionary hope."

intimate connection to his fellow man and to nature, of which he is nowadays more or less unconscious.[8] To heal this distance man should imagine a time in which he did not feel alienated and cut off from his immaterial source.[9] He saw this poetic way of life embodied in primitive social practice and believed that there remain traces of this participatory consciousness latent in humanity's basic interactions and affectations. As far as Barfield was concerned, these studies pinpointed a poetic philosophy embodied in primitive social practices and a slide towards individualism in modern societies that directly coincided with the aforementioned developments of language and philosophy. In the same way that language became increasing prosaic, representing a division between subject and object, man (subject) became increasingly distant from his fellow man and nature (object).[10] However, as with his study of words and his philosophy of polarity, Barfield found that this past consciousness was not entirely lost. In the same way that modern language still bears traces of its poetic past, humanity is still inherently collectivist.

Akin to Barfield's critique of nineteenth-century philology is Lévy-Bruhl's polemic against contemporaneous sociology. According to Lévy-Bruhl one should avoid applying modern prejudices to the primitive mentality, but rather one should set aside one's presuppositions in order truly to understand the primitive mentality. In the same way that Barfield's study of words afforded relevance to poetic discourse that had been largely written off as fancy, Lévy-Bruhl's work brought prominence to a primitive mentality that had been largely jettisoned as illogical. Against common trends in twentieth-century anthropology that deemed primitives as illogical, mystical, occult, or magical, Lévy-Bruhl believed that serious attention should be given to the primitive mentality. Also akin to Barfield's study of words is that Lévy-Bruhl identified a marked shift in consciousness, which indicates that unlike the modern "civilized" consciousness, primitive collective representations are dominated by what he called a "law of participation."

8. Barfield, *Worlds Apart*, 153. See also, Barfield, *Eager Spring*, 22 and 33–34. This is the premise of his fictive narrative *Eager Spring*, wherein his protagonist, Virginia, speaks of the primitive who did not project onto nature, but received from, or was affected by, nature. Virginia, who represents Barfield's perspective, is against those anthropologists who read modern representation into the primitive mentality. The primitive does not project, but feels, because to him nature is alive.

9. Barfield, *History, Guilt, and Habit*, 60. See also, Martin, "For the Future." Martin has shown that nearly all of Barfield's fiction work was indebted to this endeavor.

10. Barfield, "Goethe and Evolution." Therein Barfield draws upon Goethe's *Urphänomen*. Barfield argues that if these "changing forms" in nature are understood not simply as subjective, but also as objective (constituting the real of nature) then this will overcome the modern division between man (subject) and nature (object).

This meant that for primitives, subjects and objects were not divided, but participated in one another through invisible yet real immaterial relations.[11] This is because, unlike the civilized mentality, primitives do not divide between the natural and supernatural, or matter and spirit.[12] Thus, Lévy-Bruhl finds that the distinguishing feature of primitive and modern collective representations is their contrasting views of participation. Indeed, the connections with Barfield's poetic philosophy are rather obvious.[13]

This chapter begins with a review of the subsequent scholarship for and against Lévy-Bruhl. It argues that, similar to the philologists against whom Barfield juxtaposed his theory of language, Lévy-Bruhl's critics always-already assumed that the enlightened, logical, civilized, and/or scientific mentality of the modern is superior to the magical, illogical, uncivilized, and/or unscientific mind of the primitive. But, in light of more recent scholarship, it turns out that such modern philosophical assumptions (e.g., mechanism) may have hindered these social scientists' understanding of primitive mentalities, causing them to overlook Lévy-Bruhl's significance. It will be shown that the primitive practice of poetic living has become increasingly relevant in more recent reflections upon Western notions of individualism.

Participation in Primitive and Modern Collective Representations

Lucien Lévy-Bruhl was a philosopher-turned-anthropologist and ethnographer who endeavored to make the study of humanity an objective science. What he meant by this was that human sentiments and attitudes ought to

11. Lévy-Bruhl, *The "Soul" of the Primitive*, 127. See also, De Laguna, "Lévy-Bruhl's Contributions to the Study of Primitive Mentality," 556.

12. Lévy-Bruhl, *The "Soul" of the Primitive*, 113.

13. For example, if modern philosophy was trapped in a particular linguistic paradigm it would inevitably render the division between poetic and philosophical language as given. But if this division is a product of a later consciousness, then perhaps an earlier consciousness can be examined and assessed alongside of the modern consciousness instead of taking a whiggish stance and writing off the past in the name of progress. Indeed, in his studies of primitives Lévy-Bruhl challenged the prejudices of his contemporaries who were quick to write off the primitive consciousness as illogical or merely mythical. To stretch this one might say that Barfield's connection between philosophical and poetic language is similar to Lévy-Bruhl's reading of primitives; comparing the civilized and primitive mentality is not so much a discussion about logic vs. illogic (philosophical vs. poetic), but about what these unique collective representations take to be real. The strength of Lévy-Bruhl's work is that he viewed the primitive from a neutral perspective through which he was able to make hitherto overlooked connections between primitive and modern consciousness.

be considered as objective facts.[14] His objects of study were the collective representations of societies. These "patterns of thought, are the lens through which different civilizations apprehend the world."[15] Once ascertained, the collective representations could be compared with and contrasted to the present consciousness. Like many sociologists and anthropologists of his time he noticed commonalities between primitive cultures and how they differed from those of modern civilizations.[16] His discoveries and stratagem were nothing new, but his approach was rather unique. He believed his predecessors and contemporaries had prematurely written off the primitive mentality. As he saw it, their narrow mechanistic conceptions of reality left them incapable of fully appreciating the alternative logic of the primitive. One should not project one's own world upon the primitive, but to properly understand the primitive one should try to consciously enter into the world that they inhabit. De Laguna summarizes this as follows: "The data should be collected in the native's own language, interpreted according to his ways of thought, not by concepts belonging to the ethnologist's culture. The test of an objective and accurate report will be that in it nothing the native does will seem absurd, for it will have enabled us to enter his way of thinking."[17] This is possible because one can still discover intimations of primitive participation in modern cultures. In this way, his thesis aligned with Barfield's theory of the evolutionary history of words and of consciousness: although the primitive mentality had waned over time, its traces are still clearly evident in civilized life.

E. E. Evans-Pritchard, a self-proclaimed admirer[18] of Lévy-Bruhl, argued that Lévy-Bruhl had drawn too strong a distinction between the primitive and civilized mentality.[19] In his 1934 letter of response[20] to Evans-Pritchard's "Lévy-Bruhl's theory of Primitive Mentality,"[21] Lévy-Bruhl

14. This idea of studying immaterial or consciousness objectively is similar to Steiner's claim that occult science, the study of immaterial, is equally as objective as physical science.

15. Lévy-Bruhl, "A Letter to E. E. Evans-Pritchard," 121.

16. Cazeneuve, *Lucien Lévy-Bruhl*, 2–3.

17. De Laguna, "Lévy-Bruhl's Contributions to the Study of Primitive Mentality," 553. De Laguna is here summarizing from *Le Mentalité primitive*, 504–10.

18. Lévy-Bruhl, "A Letter to E. E. Evans-Pritchard," 117. Evans-Pritchard notes that Lévy-Bruhl's letter of response "shows Lévy-Bruhl to have been as great a man as he was a scholar—tolerant, open-minded, and courteous."

19. For a critique of Evans-Pritchard see, H. O. Mounce, "Understanding a Primitive Society."

20. Lévy-Bruhl, "A Letter to E. E. Evans-Pritchard."

21. Printed in the *Bulletin of the Faculty of Arts* of the Egyptian University.

addressed the "hostility" and the "prejudice" again him "which exists in England."[22] To correct this misconception Lévy-Bruhl agreed that he renders the primitive more mystical and the modern more logical. However, he says that he does so "on purpose" in order to point out that there is a real distinction. He writes, "I ought to insist on the rational character of this [modern] mentality in order that its differences from the primitive might emerge clearly."[23] Furthermore, "I have not claimed to give a complete analysis and description of primitive mentality—above all I was trying to bring further into the light what distinguishes it from our own."[24]

This exchange reveals Lévy-Bruhl's overarching thesis that while there are tenable differences[25] between the way primitives and civilized cultures view the world, they are not utterly distinct from one another.[26] This clarification is insightful. What Lévy-Bruhl maintains is that his exaggerations should not be understood as dialectical (i.e., between the two extremes of the mystic primitive and the logical modern), but rather that both mentalities exhibit traces of one another, albeit in "varying degrees."[27] Indeed, there are both similarities and differences between the primitive and modern

22. Lévy-Bruhl, "A Letter to E. E. Evans-Pritchard," 117–18.

23. Ibid., 119.

24. Ibid., 120. See also, 121. For example, by distinguishing the tenable similarities between primitives and civilized societies one can understand that a primitive's "perception of, in the sense of noticing, or paying attention to, or being interested in, a plant is due to its mystical properties."

25. Cazeneuve, *Lucien Lévy-Bruhl*, 5. "The difference between the mentality of primitive people and our own derives not only from the mystical character of their collective representations, but also from the way in which these representations are interconnected. This does not mean that they obey a logic other than our own, because the two mentalities are not totally unintelligible to each other. Lévy-Bruhl is quite precise on this point, as certain of his detractors who have wrongly attributed to him a theory based on two different logics to have forgotten. From his first works on primitive mentality, Lévy-Bruhl clearly shows that it is not guided by a logic different from ours, but that he thinks that it does not exclusively obey the laws of our logic. It is in this sense that he calls it *prelogical*."

26. De Laguna, "Lévy-Bruhl's Contributions to the Study of Primitive Mentality," 554. De Laguna writes, "The criticism that Lévy-Bruhl has drawn too sharp a line between civilized man and the savage is largely unjustified and irrelevant." See also, Spurr, "Myths of Anthropology," 269. Similarly, Spurr shows how through the influence of Claude Levi-Strauss, "Lévy-Bruhl gradually adopted the position that the two mentalities were universal: both could be found in all societies, but in differing proportions."

27. Cazeneuve, *Lucien Lévy-Bruhl*, 4. "If Lévy-Bruhl schematizes and even seems at times to caricature the thought of preliterate peoples, he does it intentionally and knowingly." See also, 22. Cazeneuve remarks that, "in affirming that primitive mentality, on the one hand, and rational mentality, on the other, are both in varying degrees present in every human mind, Lévy-Bruhl confirms the structuralist interpretations put upon his doctrine . . . ."

mentality. As Cazeneuve puts it, Lévy-Bruhl simply "does not prescribe to a doctrine of two mutually exclusive mentalities . . . just as among the most primitive peoples the logic of non-contradiction has its place at the centre [*sic*] of a mentality which is sometimes indifferent to it, so, inversely, the advance of civilization will never be able to make the mystical mentality disappear completely."[28] For modern and primitive man, there exists both logical and pre-logical thought. As such:

> Lévy-Bruhl looked for intermediaries between these two terms [pre-logical and logical], and although he rejected the idea of a rectilinear evolution proceeding from the prelogical to the logical, he envisaged, at the heart of the primitive world, a succession of stages which make the transition from one type of civilization to another more conceivable . . . at the end of these transformations . . . can be found a transition from truly primitive mentality to conceptual thought.[29]

In response to subsequent critiques of his earlier works, Lévy-Bruhl wrote *Le surnaturel et la nature, La mythologie primitive,* and *L'expérience mystique et les symbols chez les primitifs* with the intent to both refine and vindicate his thought.[30] In these later works, Lévy-Bruhl described the primitive's mystical experience more in terms of "affective" emotions shaping one's reality as opposed to the rational mind of civilized man.[31] Some argued that in these later works Lévy-Bruhl had moved away from his earlier thesis regarding the complementarity of primitive and civilized mentalities. In response to these criticisms, de Laguna argues that Lévy-Bruhl's later work is simply clarifying his earlier work, not contradicting it.[32] It is worth fully quoting Lévy-Bruhl's posthumous response that vindicates his theory of the primitive collective representation and clarifies his overarching premise that the primitive participatory consciousness remains latent in modern consciousness. To his later critics Lévy-Bruhl wrote in his 1949 *Les carnets,*

> There is no doubt that for some time I have not spoken of a logic other than our own, nor used the term "prelogical," and have given up speaking of the law of participation. But the very

28. Cazeneuve, *Lucien Lévy-Bruhl,* 10. See also, 5. Lévy-Bruhl's use of "prelogical" does not "mean that it constitutes in the evolution of thought a stage prior to the appearance of logical thought."

29. Ibid., 9.

30. Ibid., 12.

31. Ibid., 14. See also, 68.

32. De Laguna, "Lévy-Bruhl's Contributions to the Study of Primitive Mentality," 552.

essence of this idea exists without this form; participation still seemed to me to be something essential to the primitive mentality, and probably to the human mind, making a complement and perhaps a counterweight to the regulating principles of logical thought. But if this is so, where does participation's field of action begin and end? How can one understand that it might be something essential to the structure of the human mind, which necessarily intervenes in the representation which the mind forms of objects and beings, and whose function has had to wait until the 20th century to be recorded? That neither psychologists, nor logicians, nor even metaphysicians such as Plato and Malebranche, who have spoken, and excellently, on certain participations, have attributed to it the function of the mind which was recognized in *Les Fonctions mentales*? And, since it seems that participation involves something deeply rebellious to intelligibility, how is one to understand that the human mind could be at one and the same time the mainspring of the rational and irrational?

From this it follows that, even allowing for the numerous and characteristic cases of participation of which my six volumes are full, there still exists doubts about the explanation— even as modestly reduced in Volumes 5 and 6—I have given of them in invoking the presence of mental habits different from ours among "primitive peoples." But, even with these conclusions, I still want to account for participation, if not from the logical point of view, at least from the viewpoint of the knowledge of objects, and of their understanding—while recognizing that this understanding, when it concerns participations, entails an important part of affective, not cognitive, elements.

... [L]et us expressly rectify what I believed correct in 1910: there is not a primitive mentality distinguishable from the other by *two* characteristics which are peculiar to it (mystical and prelogical). *There is a mystical mentality which is more marked and more easily observable among "primitive peoples" than in our societies, but when it is no longer set up as something which is opposed to a different mentality, all the above problems disappear.*[33]

In sum, elements of logical and pre-logical thought exist within the primitive and civilized man, even if a particular collective representation render them more or less apparent.[34] Ultimately, Lévy-Bruhl makes no ontologi-

33. Cazeneuve, *Lucien Lévy-Bruhl*, 85–86. Excerpt and translation from Lévy-Bruhl, *Les carnets de Lévy-Bruhl*, 129–30 (emphasis added in final sentence).

34. Cazeneuve, *Lucien Lévy-Bruhl*, 10. Cazeneuve indicates that Lévy-Bruhl's, "analysis of collective representations among primitive peoples allowed him to analyze

cal distinction between primitive and civilized humanity. The distinction maintained by Lévy-Bruhl is simply epistemological. Thus, he does not contend that reality actually changes. What changes are the collective representations. In other words, just because man views his relation to the world differently, this does not actually reconstitute his relation to the world. The only thing that changes or evolves are the perceptions or collective representations.

Ostensibly aware of the aforementioned criticisms, Barfield found evidence in Lévy-Bruhl that directly coincided with, and further buttressed, his earlier speculations.[35] Lévy-Bruhl's study of primitives revealed that although modern humans are understood to be individuals, a collectivist element still holds sway. This is what Barfield means when he says that although modern man is perceived as a physically distinguished self, on all other levels it seems he has maintained a primeval connection to the world.[36] The anthropological task ahead would lie in unveiling this latent connection in the midst of a mechanistic worldview.

Assessing the Primitive

Anthropological Mechanism

A narrative of the mechanization of the cosmos espoused by Barfield is detailed in the succeeding chapter 4, but for now the narrative often evoked by its critics can briefly be described as follows: Modernity is marked by the demise of the Aristotelian worldview. Aristotle's four categories of causation (material, formal, efficient, and final) are reduced to efficient causation and the material cause is taken as a given. Once the formal cause is jettisoned, qualities are no longer understood to be *in* objects, but abstract. In

a mode of thought which exists among us but which, among us, would be more difficult to observe." See also, 22. What Lévy-Bruhl means by "primitive mentality is undoubtedly a permanent structure of the human mind, but in our society this structure is blurred by the supremacy of scientific thought, whereas it remains in the foreground among preliterate peoples."

35. Barfield, *Saving the Appearances*, 33. One can assume that Barfield was generally familiar with these critiques. He lends a sentence to them in his remarks on Lévy-Bruhl: "I cannot pause to consider the adverse criticism which Lévy-Bruhl in particular has aroused. (I doubt if it was his case that all primitives *invariably* think in the prelogical way. It is certainly not mine)."

36. Barfield, *Romanticism Comes of Age*, 69. See also, Barfield, *Saving the Appearances*, 40. Barfield writes, "actual participation is therefore as much a fact in our case as in that of primitive man. But . . . we are unaware, whereas the primitive mind is aware of it."

championing the subjective gaze the object is stripped of any real qualities. All immaterial phenomena are simply the products of mind. The spiritual becomes something extra, in addition to the real material world. Once the world is desacralized and stripped of its inherent qualities, the supersensible is handed over to a mythical unreal dimension. In this picture man invents gods and projects his thoughts into an otherwise meaningless cosmos.[37] A once animated world succumbs to a mechanical vision: inanimate objects in space, which having no *telos* (i.e., purpose) of their own, are linked only by causal relations. Before long this mechanistic cosmology would subtly become the dominant collective representation of modernity. Indeed, it dominated anthropological and sociological theories regarding relationality.[38] When the only real things to be measured were external objective quantities, not internal subjective qualities, it became increasingly difficult for anthropologists and sociologist to talk about that which is most proper to humanity, relationality. For this reason Lévy-Bruhl indicates Cartesian thought is the antithesis of primitive participation, which envisages not a division between but an intermingling of subjects and objects, matter and spirit, etc.[39] As such, it is this form of mechanism to which the primitive law of participation was distinguished.

This mechanistic philosophy overshadowed early anthropologists' predispositions towards primitive cultures. It propagated the cave-man fallacy, which pits modern logic (i.e., efficient causality) against primitive illogic (i.e., affective or occult causality), evident in the above dialogue between Lévy-Bruhl and his contemporaries. Adjectives used to describe primitive mentalities (i.e., mystical or supersensible) were pejoratives, whereas terms such as "logic" or "civilized" indicated the superiority of modern mentalities. And this is still common parlance today.[40] However, unlike so many

37. Ibid., 20. See also, Sugerman, *Evolution of Consciousness*, 79. Barfield argues that over time spiritual things moved toward the subjective side of the Cartesian experience.

38. See, Freudenthal, *Atom and Individual*. Freudenthal argues that the application of "Newtonian" mechanism to social theory was an errant theoretical assumption.

39. Cazeneuve, *Lucien Lévy-Bruhl*, 5. See also, 8. For Lévy-Bruhl "the spiritual is not distinct from the material."

40. For instance, nowadays when one hears the word "primitive" one tends to associate with it words like stupid, dumb, naïve, immature, or stubborn. When a mother finds her two boys fighting she yells, "Stop acting like cavemen!" In so doing, she implies they should be more "civilized," like their older sister (who is on the sofa reading a book). Indeed, today one would be hard pressed to find someone who does not think that modern humanity is superior to the primitive. Perhaps one is reminded here of the GEICO insurance company slogan, "so easy a caveman could do it." One is also reminded of the opening chapter of G. K. Chesterton's *Everlasting Man*, wherein he identifies a prevalent unjustified bias against the "cave-man." Chesterton remarks that, "the whole

of his contemporaries, when Lévy-Bruhl distinguished between primitive and civilized mentalities, he did not presuppose that the primitive mentality was inferior to that of the civilized human.[41] Indeed, what their collective representations indicate is that primitives do not reason in the wrong way, they just do so differently.[42] Like Barfield, Lévy-Bruhl challenged this predisposition by seriously considering the primitive consciousness, asking if today one does not still see traces of it in the modern mentality.

According to Lévy-Bruhl, Barfield, and others, mechanism had deeply impaired conceptions of the primitive mentality.[43] In projecting a modern mentality upon the primitive, early twentieth-century anthropologists unduly dismissed the primitive. Lévy-Bruhl, however, proceeded on different grounds arguing instead that one must rid oneself of such biases if one is to genuinely understand primitive cultures.[44] By laying aside mechanistic assumptions, Lévy-Bruhl provided unique insight into the primitive mentality that would allow subsequent theorists the freedom to take seriously the thought of primitives. Without prejudice Lévy-Bruhl placed these distinct collective representations on a level playing field and assessed their efficacy. He found that the distinction was not between logic and illogic or pre-logic,

---

of the current way of talking is simply a confusion and a misunderstanding, founded on no sort of scientific evidence and valued only as an excuse for a very modern mood of anarchy" (Chesterton, *The Everlasting Man*, 31). In light of this, one must bear in mind that when Lévy-Bruhl distinguished between primitives and civilized these adjectives were loaded with presuppositions that he did not accept.

41. In fact, what is most obvious about Lévy-Bruhl's work is that it stood against those theories that viewed the primitive collective representations as inferior to those of civilized man. Lévy-Bruhl is well known for his critique of those anthropologists (e.g., E. B. Tylor and Sir James Frazer) who argued primitive mentalities to be inferior to Western logic. By imposing a modern social consciousness upon primitive man these theorists are incapable of properly assessing the primitive consciousness. See, for example, Evens, "On the Social Anthropology of Religion," 377. Regarding these criticisms, Evens remarks, "in the case of the first, the anthropologist may be accused of prejudicially impugning primitive man's mental capacity. In the case of the second, he may be charged with imposing on primitive man a social structure of modernity, one in which institutional separation is a sociological diagnosis." See also, Mauss and Brain, *A General Theory of Magic*, 6–7. Mauss argues against the supposition that one should impose contemporary categories on other cultures.

42. Cazeneuve, *Lucien Lévy-Bruhl*, 4. See also, 3.

43. Lotz, "From Nature to Culture? Diogenes and Philosophical Anthropology," 41–42. Regarding this Anglo-American anthropological tendency, Lotz argues that philosophical anthropology is only present in the Continental tradition and it never enters the Anglo-American philosophical discourse, "because it was never structured by any broader, non-scientific and cultural issues within philosophy itself, or by the epistemological difference between transcendental and empirical knowledge, nor, finally, by the ontological difference between man and nature."

44. Cazeneuve, *Lucien Lévy-Bruhl*, 3.

but between the primitive collectivist self that is undergirded by a participatory metaphysic and the individualism of the modern that is influenced by a Cartesian epistemology and mechanical vision of the cosmos.

The importance of Lévy-Bruhl's work is that it exposed the prejudices and presupposition of social scientists, thus paving a way forward for subsequent anthropologists like Marcel Mauss[45] and Marshall Sahlins[46] to suggest that it is perhaps modern humans who have something to learn from primitives.[47]

Sociology and Participation

Early attempts to break from the mechanistic consciousness are evident in the French tradition from which Lévy-Bruhl emerged. In an article critical of mechanistic sociology, Gibson Winter summarizes the attempt to move away from mechanistic philosophy. Winter indicates that the founder of sociology, French positivist Auguste Comte, treated humans like an object of the empirical sciences conceiving the individual as a part of a larger social mechanism (e.g., Locke's "atomism"). Yet, it soon became apparent that the attempt to apply methods of modern science to the study of humans could not account for those things that most fundamentally distinguished

45 Mauss and Brain, *A General Theory of Magic*. Mauss criticizes the analyses of figures such as E. B. Tylor and Sir James Frazer for too quickly writing off primitive thought as irrational or illogical.

46. Sahlins, "What Is Anthropological Enlightenment?" xi. Sahlins talks of the prejudice of these modern theorists who intend to supplant the irrational superstitions of indigenous peoples with progressive reason. See also, Sahlins, "Other Times, Other Customs," 522. Sahlins pushes the discussion beyond the individual/society distinction, whether "mechanical" or "organic" (participatory). Instead, he wants to supplement the "mechanical" and "organic" models with what he calls "hierarchical solidarity." He writes that, "in the heroic societies, the coherence of the members or subgroups is not so much due to their similarity (mechanical solidarity) or their complementarity (organic solidarity, as, e.g., Durkheim) as to their common submission to the ruling power."

47. Those who took Lévy-Bruhl's work seriously shared the belief that modern collective representations were not as enlightened as once thought. See, Winch, "Understanding a Primitive Society," 316–17. Winch wants to speak of "differences in *criteria of rationality*." For Winch this is because there are two different senses of the word "intelligible." He argues that, "something can appear rational to someone only in terms of *his* understanding of what is and is not rational. If *our* concept of rationality is a different one from his, then it makes no sense to say that anything either does or does not appear rational to *him* in *our* sense." Winch sees Alistair MacIntyre and Evans-Pritchard guilty of the same errors of Tylor and Frazor with the exception that MacIntyre and Evans-Pritchard concede that at least to the primitive their thought processes seem intelligible, when, in fact, they are not.

humans from lower animals (namely the social and/or culture element).[48] As Winter notes, it was quickly realized that, "Humanity could not be an object of an empirical science of society, since humanity was an ideal and not an actuality."[49] If man is considered merely as a part of a larger social mechanism, then the social or cultural is set over against individual men and women. As such, to be social or cultural is only accidental and not inherently part of what it means to be a human. Winter shows that it was Durkheim who would ultimately discard Comte's mechanistic conception. By maintaining that "society is no longer conceived as a set of externally related elements but is transcendent to the individual parts and yet immanent in the parts . . . Durkheim had shifted from external constraint (e.g., Hobbes's *Leviathan*) to participation of the parts and the whole."[50] What was discovered is that society is in man and man in society. Man is not simply a part governed by a larger social mechanism, but man is inherently social (i.e., relational).

This is actually more akin to primitive collectivism, wherein the self is established through a network of supersensible relations. In this scheme, the individual is not isolated (as with mechanism), but indeed extends beyond the body. To put it simply, *mechanism is incapable of accounting for any form of relationality beyond efficient causality*. In this way, it fails to account for the most fundamental aspects of what it means to be human. Once everything is reduced to extended space a third principle such as a social contract or some other means of efficient force (Machiavelli's *The Prince*) is often introduced as a means of mediating relationships, which forcibly supersedes the innate human desire to be in direct relation. To put it another way, because there are no natural social bonds or reciprocity (because again mechanism can only admit the immaterial if it is couched in terms of efficient causality as, e.g., forces), relations must be secured by an external force such as a state in the form of a contract. This assumes that humans are otherwise naturally selfish and hence individuality is more fundamental, while relationality is accidental.[51] But for sociologists, the ineptitude of the mechanical world-

48. Winter, "Society and Morality," 19. Winter argues that when the mechanistic cosmology was adopted, the human dimension is thus removed from the human sciences, denying the actual subject of social science, which is the interpersonal world of moral responsibility.

49. Ibid., 14.

50. Ibid., 15.

51. For an excellent critique of the effects of atomism upon social thought and its inability to account for relationality see, Pabst, *Metaphysics*, chapter 9, section 5, "Being Atomized (Hobbes and Locke)," 406–14. Pabst's work is an erudite analysis of the history of the participation metaphysic. He locates the loss of this worldview beginning with Aristotle's prioritization of substance over relationality and ultimately argues that

view had become increasingly obvious. It was soon realized that in order to account for relationality, anthropologists would have to look beyond the mechanistic worldview to more robust metaphysical explanations. The irony here is that the more robust the accounts of causality to which anthropologists turned, the closer they came to the primitive consciousness they had hitherto rejected.

Perhaps this is why Lévy-Bruhl claims that he is often misunderstood.[52] By applying philosophical principles, he discovered that primitives display a different understanding of causation than modern people. This unique perspective[53] enabled him to look without prejudice upon the primitive mentality, and in so doing, his work revealed a rather admirable quality of the primitive mentality that was largely overlooked.

Distinct from the modern mechanistic cosmology, primitives admit causal forces that lay beyond merely perceptible properties.[54] According to Lévy-Bruhl, for the primitive the real cause of anything lies "beyond what we call nature, in the 'metaphysical' in the true sense of the word."[55] For the primitive, "although the natural and supernatural are felt as qualitatively distinct, they yet form part of the same reality and constantly interpenetrate each other."[56] For the primitive, "things and beings which participate in one another form totalities which are perceived in a more qualitative than quantitative fashion, and the qualities themselves cannot easily be isolated from

only a theological vision as a participation in a prior relationality outwits immanentized attempts to construe relations in terms of substance.

52. Lévy-Bruhl, "A Letter to E. E. Evans-Pritchard," 123. Lévy-Bruhl writes, "PS.— What can explain to a certain extent the evident misunderstandings among many anthropologists of my theory is the difference between the points of view in which they and I place ourselves. They relate what I say to the particular point of view of their science (which has its tradition, its methods, its achieved results, etc.). What has led me to write my books is not the desire to add, if I could, a stone to the edifice of this special science (anthropology, ethnology). I had the ambition to add something to the scientific knowledge of human nature, using the findings of ethnology for this purpose. My training was philosophical not anthropological. I proceed from Spinoza and Hume rather than from Bastian and Tylor, if I dare evoke such great names here."

53. Spurr, "Myths of Anthropology," 267. Spurr writes, "Lévy-Bruhl was one of a generation of French intellectuals in the first decade of the century, including Emile Durkheim and Henri Bergson, who sought to apply philosophical principles to the new sciences of the human mind and society."

54. Cazeneuve, Lucien Lévy-Bruhl, 6. "Thus, primitive people, even if they are capable of actions comparable with ours, have a picture of the world which is very different from that which our science gives us."

55. Lévy-Bruhl and Clare, Primitive Mentality, 448.

56. De Laguna, "Lévy-Bruhl's Contributions to the Study of Primitive Mentality," 558. De Laguna is here citing Lévy-Bruhl's L'Expérience mystic, 12 and 79. See also, Cazeneuve, Lucien Lévy-Bruhl, 8.

the beings to which they are attached."[57] Lévy-Bruhl juxtaposes this view with the mechanistic collective representation. He writes,

> the antithesis of matter and spirit, so familiar to us as to appear almost natural, does not exist in primitive mentality—or, at any rate, it interprets it differently from ourselves. The primitive has no conception of matter, or of a body, whence some mystic force, which we should term spiritual, does not emanate. To him, too, there is no spiritual reality which is not a complete being, that is, a concrete thing, with a bodily form, even if this be invisible, intangible, without consistency or density.[58]

Lévy-Bruhl writes of the primitive experience that, "Primitive men also feel themselves in immediate and constant touch with an invisible world which is no less real than the other . . . ."[59] He refers to this worldview as mystical,[60] meaning that unlike the mind of the civilized man, the primitive mind is not constrained by logical contradictions.[61] As such, primitive thought (for which the base principle is the "law of participation")[62] is simply indifferent to non-contradiction. Lévy-Bruhl found evidence for this in that primitive man's individuality does not stop at the physical body, but is extended in what he called "appurtenances."[63] Constituted by these appurtenances, which include footprints, hair follicles, nails, clothing, personal property, social relations, such as past and present kin etc.,[64] the primitive individual is not limited to the body, but constituted by these non-spatial relations. As such, "The individual is only himself by virtue of being at the same time something other than himself. Viewed in this fresh aspect, far from being one unit, as we conceive him to be, he is one and yet several, at the same time. Thus he is, so to speak, a veritable 'centre [sic] of participation."[65]

57. Cazeneuve, *Lucien Lévy-Bruhl*, 6.

58. Lévy-Bruhl, *The "Soul" of the Primitive*, 113.

59. Lévy-Bruhl, *L'expérience mystique et les symboles chez les primitifs*, 8. Excerpt and translation in Cazeneuve, *Lucien Lévy-Bruhl*, 67.

60. Spurr, "Myths of Anthropology," 268.

61. Ibid.

62. Cazeneuve, *Lucien Lévy-Bruhl*, 5.

63. Ibid., 8. "Appurtenances" are real extensions of the body, although they lie beyond the physical body. As such, one's individualism is constituted paradoxically by one's social relations. This is a term Lévy-Bruhl frequently employs, particularly in his discussion regarding the exchange of goods or totemic customs and those regarding spirits of the dead.

64. Lévy-Bruhl, *The "Soul" of the Primitive*, 114–21.

65. Ibid., 202. See also, Adey, *C. S. Lewis' Great War*, 101. Barfield himself drew

John Milbank's work traces this philosophical shift (away from the collectivist or participatory mentality) in a variety of ways.[66] Milbank's work on gift exchange and reciprocity[67]—buttressed by anthropological and sociological evidence—aids the present discussion. Milbank's critique of modern social theory is replete with metaphysical undertones. Milbank does not have to look for an anthropological analysis as far back as the primitives to critique modern theorists.[68] Instead, he locates a metaphysic of participation in the civilized thought of Plato, Aristotle, and Aquinas, who thought of ideas not just in the mind, but as migrating from objects to subjects. He too finds this participatory metaphysic consistent with the thought and practices of primitive cultures. Familiar with the work of Owen Barfield, Milbank contends that what is most unique about Barfield's reading of Lévy-Bruhl is that he correctly[69] correlates Lévy-Bruhl's analysis of primitive participation with Platonic metaphysics.[70] Milbank asserts that Lévy-Bruhl's primitive actually embodies the Platonic and Neo-Platonic metaphysic of participation (and it should be noted that there are slight gestures toward this by Lévy-Bruhl himself).[71] Milbank avers that the difficultly in understanding the mind of the primitive results from the "enormous transition from participa-

---

upon this "regard[ing] the individual as both a part of and a subsidiary whole within the cosmic whole."

66. Milbank's general critique of modern social theory argues that these theories lack a participatory philosophy and, as such, can only offer an ontology of difference or of violence (subject vs. object, individual vs. state, state vs. state, finite vs. infinite, immanent vs. transcendent, God vs. Creation, etc.). See, Milbank, *Theology and Social Theory* and Milbank, *Being Reconciled*.

67. Milbank, "The Ungiveable." See also, Milbank, "Can a Gift Be Given?" Milbank argument is based on a Trinitarian theology. His critique of modernity and postmodernity asserts that the created world participates in the divine economy of harmonious gift exchange. This means that the created order is primarily relational. So against modern social thought that attempts to secure relationality by social contract or a symmetrical economic exchange, or postmodern attempts to reduce all exchange to some form of calculated unilateral altruism (e.g., Derrida), Milbank argues that true exchange is asymmetrical.

68. Milbank, "The Ungiveable." Milbank notes that this move away from participation occurs during the Arabic and Western Middle Ages.

69. Ibid. Milbank does however deny what he calls Lévy-Bruhl and Barfield's "evolutionism."

70. Ibid.

71. Lévy-Bruhl, *The "Soul" of the Primitive*, 324–25. However, Lévy-Bruhl seems to suggest that even Plato saw participation as a "metaphysical problem." In other words, Lévy-Bruhl implies that whereas primitives just accept participation and have no problem with the one and the many, Plato, in an attempt to make a metaphysical doctrine, complicates matters. See also, 156. See also, De Laguna, "Lévy-Bruhl's Contributions to the Study of Primitive Mentality," 558.

tion to representation" that begins to unfold in the Middle Ages. Milbank concurs that anthropologists tend to read representation into the primitive mentality, thereby misconstruing it. These anthropologists assume a Cartesian stance that takes subjects and objects as entirely external to one another. Instead of a participatory sharing in the object, in representation the subject is distant from the object. The subject then becomes the sole arbiter of knowledge of the object as, "material things are dissolved into our notions of them."[72] With representation the mind simply mirrors external objects, it abstracts facts and determines objects, whereas with participation the mind actually shares in the object, there is an interpenetration that affects one's knowledge that is contingent upon the object. While in modernity, "objects are seen as inert items to be manipulated and subjects as the possessors of free rationalities . . . ,"[73] for primitive thought, as with Platonism, the subject participates in the idea recognized within the material object.[74] Milbank talks of this primitive horizontal relation between the "subjectified-object" and the "objectivized-subject" in a language that attempts to overcome modern Cartesian categories.[75] Milbank suggests that as evident in primitive exchange, the object has "a life of its own," which "fascinates" the subject.[76] Objects are very much like the primitive subject, and subjects, very complex objects.[77] There is, thus, a sharing that takes place between subject and object, where no ontic priority is given to the subject.

Milbank's description of the metaphysics of participation is analogous to Lévy-Bruhl's analyses of primitive mentality. Lévy-Bruhl shows that primitive social structures embodied the same poetic philosophy that Barfield found in his studies in philology. This also coincides with Barfield's polemic against the subject/object dualism or, as he puts it, of phenomena being "neither objective nor subjective."[78] It seems that the observer and the observed are indeed part of one world and therefore both sides of the

---

72. Milbank, "The Ungiveable."

73. Ibid.

74. Ibid.

75. Ibid. Milbank's analysis finds similarities with Mauss, *The Gift*, 61. Therein Mauss speaks of primitive reciprocity where "persons and things merge."

76. Milbank, "The Ungiveable."

77. Ibid.

78. Barfield, *Romanticism Comes of Age*, 25 and 27. See also, Lionel Adey, *C. S. Lewis' Great War*, 20. Adey notes for Barfield subjects and objects are of the same essence. See also, 77. Adey notes that, "both subject and object, what we enjoy, and what we contemplate, are grounded in a primal reality that includes them both."

Cartesian divide are brought together in the union of objective measurable quantities with subjective qualities.[79]

Lévy-Bruhl's philosophical purview provided a fresh lens through which social scientists could assess the primitive mentality. In seeking to overcome mechanistic biases subsequent sociologists turned to metaphysical explanations.[80] The primitive more fully embodied the metaphysical principles required to articulate a robust account of human relationality. This, of course, is precisely what Barfield argued in *Saving the Appearances*, wherein he suggests that the Platonic and early Christian metaphysic of participation, which more thoroughly accounts for the relationships between subjects and objects and humans and society, is embodied in the primitive mentality. Primitive poetic living, thus, intimates a poetic philosophy. This is still the case in modern times, although the ubiquity of Cartesian epistemology and theories of social atomism have rendered human relationality less apparent. The final section examines the inescapable nature of this scheme, as some recent anthropologists have revealed traces of poetic living latent in the modern world.

Lucien Lévy-Bruhl's Successors: The Inherent Nature of Participation

Intimations of a Poetic Past

One of the remarkable achievements of Lévy-Bruhl's work, and certainly one that attracted Barfield, is that he maintained that the common traits present in primitive cultures also exist in civilized societies, albeit to a lesser extent. Theorists who have built upon the work of Lévy-Bruhl have sought to identify the various ways in which contemporary societies embody the primitive mentality.[81] Like Lévy-Bruhl and Barfield, theorists such as H. O. Mounce, Marcel Mauss, and Peter Winch have argued that the Western scientific conception of the physical world significantly impaired modern understandings of the primitive mentality. Instead, they suggest if one examines contemporary collective representations more closely, one finds that

---

79. Sugerman, *Evolution of Consciousness*, 81.

80. Pabst, *Metaphysics*, 430. In his theological critique of modern social and political theory, Pabst avers that, "By adopting the same positivistic approach as the natural sciences, the humanities and social sciences reject any import from metaphysics, and are therefore unable to describe or conceptualize the integral nature of being."

81. See, Winch, "Understanding a Primitive Society," 317.

intimations of a participatory vision are still latent in the most basic acts of perception.[82]

For example, Mounce maintains that in all societies, phenomena are always initially apprehended in their "affect." Only when logic is applied are they apprehended in their "effect." Because the "reaction" is fundamental and the "belief" secondary (based on the logic employed), one way to identify a basic commonality is to focus on the initial natural reactions to phenomena. As he states, "Indeed it is not the belief which gives rise to the reaction but rather the reactions which gives rise to the belief . . . ."[83] Mounce maintains, reactions are not logical, and as such, they are a derivative of the beliefs that constitute the more fundamental traits of societies. It is, thus, the reaction by which one discovers a shared belief structure.[84] Using this methodology, Mounce identifies similarities between the beliefs of primitives and those of the modern based upon their common reactions to stimuli. He cites numerous modern-day examples of the way these reactions manifest in everyday life.[85] By analyzing one's initial reaction to a stimulus, instead of the subsequent logical explanations, one discovers similarities between present and past consciousness. This conclusion is of a piece with Lévy-Bruhl's assessment of the affective qualities of phenomena: today, "the affective category of the supernatural survives, and the emotional basis of these representations is never entirely eliminated. Hidden, encapsulated, changed, it always remains recognizable."[86]

82. Lévy-Bruhl, Mounce, Mauss, and Winch share similar sentiments. See, Lévy-Bruhl's similar remark in *L'expérience mystique et les symboles chez les primitifs*, 9–10. Excerpt and translation from Cazeneuve, *Lucien Lévy-Bruhl*, 68.

83. Mounce, "Understanding a Primitive Society," 355.

84. Ibid., 354.

85. Ibid., 355. If, for example, a man is asked to mutilate a picture of his mother, he will be reluctant to do so, or if he is asked to stick a needle in a drawing of his mother and subsequently finds that her eye is afflicted, "the idea that he has actually injured her comes irresistibly to mind."

86. Cazeneuve, *Lucien Lévy-Bruhl*, 71. Excerpt and translation from Lévy-Bruhl, *Le surnaturel et la nature dans la mentalité primitive*. For Mounce see, Mounce, "Understanding a Primitive Society," 359. Mounce argues that it is mechanism that inaugurates what he sees as the transition from affective to effective causality. There is a loss of fascination when a modern philosopher gives an explanation for primitive practices. Thus, only after the affective reaction is contemplated does it become illogical or irrational. The difference lies in the logic employed in the subsequent explanation. He argues that in light of the belief of Western science one's reaction can be discounted as crazy or irrational, but, however absurd, they do still affect us deeply. Ultimately for Mounce, the primitive simply lacks "the spirit of inquiry" that is nowadays essential to philosophy. To be clear, this is not an argument against philosophical reason. On the contrary, Mounce finds the practices of primitives to be analogous to certain metaphysical beliefs: "The reactions will suggest this belief to one's mind, the belief will be

Similarly, in his *A General Theory of Magic* Marcel Mauss avers that the scientific worldview and the primitive are not that different after all, but are simply two ways of describing phenomena based on their effects. He distinguishes between the affects found in primitive magical practices and what he calls the "mechanical effectiveness" of modern science.[87] The only difference being, for primitives causation is not merely efficient. Beyond reductive accounts of physical causality the primitive consciousness also includes the affective or qualitative dimension of perception. Mauss writes,

> the idea of a magical force is moreover, from this point of view, quite comparable to our notion of mechanical force. In the same way we call force the cause of apparent movements so magic force is properly the cause of magical effects . . . .
>
> Distance does not prevent contact . . . everything is spiritual . . . we shall find—at the basis of magic—a representation which is singularly ambiguous and quite outside our adult European understanding.[88]

Mauss then uses the example of *mana* to further elaborate on this point. To the primitive, *mana*, is both natural and supernatural. Because *mana* is concrete it may act mechanically, but it may also produce effects from a distance because it is also a quality.[89] Mauss states,

> that a concept, encompassing the idea of magical power, was once found everywhere. It involves the notion of automatic efficacy. At the same time as being a material substance which can be localized, it is also spiritual. It works at a distance and also through a direct connexion [*sic*], if not by contact. . . . It is divisible yet whole. Our own ideas about luck and quintessence are but weak survivals of this much richer concept. As we have seen, as well as being a force, it is also a milieu, a world separated from—but still in touch with—the other.[90]

---

the result of the reactions, only to the extent that one is not reflecting on them. As with a metaphysical belief, in arriving at some understanding of how this belief arises, one is already beginning to free oneself from it."

87. Mauss and Brain, *A General Theory of Magic*, 25.

88. Ibid., 132.

89. Ibid., 36–37. In the following chapter it will be shown how the primitive allowance of action at a distance, over against mere efficient causality, is actually championed by quantum theorists in exploring the shortcomings of mechanical physics.

90. Ibid., 144–45.

According to Mauss magic has a concrete element it is not simply abstract.[91] Although located in space and individualized, primitive objects are related and can act upon one another because they share in qualities.[92] Mauss argues that the primitive's collective belief in magic practice is evidence of a "unanimous will and sentiment" found in the community,[93] and asks if one can simply write off these collective representations based on scientific advancement. He concludes, suggesting that today's talk of forces may be connected to past magical outlooks: "we are not being too daring, I think, if we suggest that a good part of all those non-positive mystical and poetical elements in our notion of force, causation, effect, and substance could be traced back to the old habits of mind in which magic was born and which the human mind is slow to throw off."[94] Herein Mauss also finds that for the primitive there is an integral relation between the part and whole. This means that a whole person can be represented in one of their parts and that, "each object contains, in its entirety, the essential principle of the species of which it forms a part."[95] "Each one is in the whole and the whole is in each one."[96]

To cite just one more example, Peter Winch, who draws upon the work of Giambattista Vico, recommends that anthropologists should look for connections, not in logic, but in those forms that all people groups have in common, such as marriage (or the man/woman relationship), birth (and the given relationships it implies), death (which is common to all and begs the question of the meaning of life), and those things that are perceive as good and evil. In so doing, civilized people can better understand the lives of primitives.[97]

> Forms of these limiting concepts will necessarily be an important feature of any human society and conceptions of good and evil in human life will necessarily be connected with such concepts. In any attempt to understand the life of another

91. Ibid., 92.

92. Ibid., 97–98.

93. Ibid., 120.

94. Ibid., 178. Mauss concludes his work on magic by suggesting that nowadays magic is similar to technology. But, what was once a collective experience believed and practiced by all, is now only practiced by individuals. Like technology, contemporary magic has become more individualistic and specialized in the pursuit of its goals.

95. Ibid., 79–80.

96. Ibid., 90. Mauss quotes a general principle from early alchemists, "each one is the whole and it is through it that the whole is formed. One is the whole and if each one did not contain the whole the whole could not be formed."

97. Winch, "Understanding a Primitive Society," 315.

society, therefore, an investigation of the forms taken by such concepts—their role in the life of the society—must always take a central place and provide a basis on which understanding may be built.[98]

Winch argues concepts and beliefs are embodied in the forms of life taken up by a culture. The culture of a people shares an integral relationship with the beliefs, and it is these forms taken by such concepts that bridge understanding between particular cultures. Winch reveals that such cultural forms (language and customs), which structure or limit society allowing it to function properly, simply cannot be described in terms of logic. Yet, it is these cultural customs that are so often shared by primitive and modern societies.

The aforementioned theorists suggest that the poetic consciousness is still latent in the basic acts of perception and in shared societal practices. Aesthetically, objects are not merely inert, but bear qualities that have a way of affecting the subject. Similarly, the relations that bind a particular society are not mere social contracts or a quantitative economic exchange, but a qualitative exchange of those things that have an inherent value, which transcends mechanistic logic.[99] It appears that there is an inherent poetic way of life that still undergirds the Western individualistic culture.

Nature vs. Culture or Gift?[100]

Barfield related the rise of subjectivity found in his study of the history of language and philosophy to the rise of individualism in modern societies.

98. Ibid., 324.

99. Pabst, *Metaphysics*, 435. This echoes Pabst's critique of modern social theory, as he writes, "With this nominalist space, the primary real relations among persons—who cooperate for both self-interest and the common, public good—are superseded by abstract, formal links consisting of either constitutional-legal rights or economic-contractual ties. Those links favor activities for either commercial-market or state-administrative purposes and therefore are to the detriment of practices that are not purely instrumental but might pursue wider, social purposes."

100. Two noteworthy texts on the division between nature and culture here addressed are Dupré, *Passage to Modernity* and Latour, *We Have Never Been Modern*. See also, Cunningham, *Darwin's Pious Idea*, 181. Cunningham, in his critique of Darwinian fundamentalism, argues that, "The modernist division between nature and culture must be closed . . . if we do not suspend this dualism, a static picture will set in, making us unable to speak properly of evolution. . . . [I]t is important to keep in mind that the idea of a pure, primitive nature is highly contentious." See also, 251. Cunningham argues that the modern division of nature and culture is based upon a Zwinglian metaphysic (i.e., philosophically, this is the Cartesian mind/matter dualism; theologically, it ends

In the same way objects are evacuated of qualities and increasingly relegated to the subjective realm, so too are relations. In the modern-world relations—because they lack a certain objectivity—must be mediated by a governing body (e.g., Hobbes's "social contract").[101] Relations are arbitrarily recognized by an external authority (e.g., a state that serves a bureaucratic function). Relationship is not fundamental, but accidental or external to the individual.[102] Barfield saw that primitive collectivism was decisively different, precisely because primitive peoples conceived relationality to be *real*, not accidental. Primitives recognize these relations as the "extra-sensory link between the percipient and the representations,"[103] a link which constitutes a real "relation between man and the phenomena."[104] Thus, if one is to live poetically, one assumes that relationality or sociality is inherently part of what it means to be human and that the qualitative dimensions of relationality supersede any accidental market exchange or any fixed notion of arbitrary "rights" and/or "privileges." However, the modern world often forgets this. In a world dominated by rationalism and empiricism, these extra-sensory links become increasingly difficult for people to apprehend.[105]

If mechanism is true and the world is indeed full of inert objects, then change (i.e. becoming or flux) can only be effected from the outside. In this scheme man is taken to be a naturally selfish individual. Therefore, culture or civility, so to speak, must be forced upon him in order to ensure more

---

up arguing that the "real presence" of God cannot inhabit matter; as this debate centers upon the Eucharist). For Cunningham, there is no such thing as pure biology or pure Darwinism, nor is there pure culture. Cunningham rightly critiques ultra-Darwinism for being too reductive. He implies that to simply reduce humanity to an animal nature (as real as it may be) is ironically "antievolutionary." Such "Darwinisms" deny the very evolution they propagate, because for anything to evolve (e.g., from organism to consciousness in man) there must be an obvious distinction between species that cannot be identified using reductive logic. This is why Cunningham says ultra-Darwinists are afraid of the word "progress," because it ironically denies their own reductive materialist account of biological phenomena. What Cunningham wants is a proper view of evolution that is somewhere between the presumption of creationists that man is utterly different from animals and that of the ultra-Darwinists who espouse that man is purely animal. Both extremes adopt one side of the Cartesian dualism, while ignoring the other. See also, chapter 5, "Matter over Mind," an obvious credit to the work of Latour.

101. Pabst, *Metaphysics*, 435.

102. See, Freudenthal, *Atom and Individual in the Age of Newton*, 161. According to Freudenthal all modern social theories have one thing in common; that is, "civil society is composed of independent individuals who enter into relations in contract form and only for their own advantage."

103. Barfield, *Saving the Appearances*, 34.

104. Ibid., 40.

105. Ibid., 81.

humane relations.[106] But this theory proved to be increasingly troublesome for anthropologists who recognized a glaring *aporia* in the division of nature and culture.[107] If humanity is not understood to be naturally cultural (or social), it becomes extremely difficult to account for the very cultures or social structures that sociologists examine, for without man (nature) there is no culture. The division of nature and culture drives the myth of progress of the naturally selfish man who becomes increasingly civilized through a mysterious birth of culture. But, ironically, in the modern world man actually becomes increasingly individualistic and defined in natural terms at the expense of the cultural. Peace is taken to be unnatural and must be secured by force. As presupposed from the outset man remains naturally unsocial. In order to resolve this glaring *aporia* and account for the natural emergence of culture in evolutionary history, anthropologists would indeed have to assert that humanity was and remains naturally cultural and/or naturally social and that humanity is inherently relational. Once this dualism is corrected, it appears that the primitive poetic living practice embodies what is most natural and therefore most human.

In his work, *The Western Illusion of Human Nature*, American Anthropologist Marshall Sahlins argues that Western thought has misconstrued the relationship of nature and culture in presupposing a division between nature and culture.[108] He couches this division in terms of the "Western Folklore" of the "savage" ("them") and the "civilized" ("us").[109] He contends that this "fairly cynical"[110] view of humanity posits human nature as bad (which he believes is propagated by the Christian doctrine of original sin),[111] which

106. Analogously, this pits the instinctive primitive man against the rational civilized man (no one is more indebted to this modern myth than the new-atheists).

107. Furthermore the nature/culture division presupposes the very division between sociology and anthropology, which should otherwise be complementary. Just as one cannot undertake the study of sociology without already presupposing a relational element in humanity, one cannot undertake the study of anthropology by ignoring that humanity is inherently social. Anthropology *qua* anthropology (i.e., distinct from sociology) only persists under the assumption that humanity is naturally selfish. Once this move is made anthropology becomes its own discourse, distinct from sociology. To put it simply, because humanity is instead naturally social anthropology always implies sociology and vice versa. See, Pabst, *Metaphysics*, 433–42.

108. Sahlins, *The Western Illusion of Human Nature*, 5.

109. Ibid., 103.

110. Ibid., 38.

111. Ibid., 107. Throughout his work Sahlins is critical of the doctrine of original sin, particularly in the work of Saint Augustine. He states that this philosophical presupposition must be overcome if the nature/culture gap is to be closed. However, his reading of Saint Augustine and the patristics is errant. It is based on Sahlins's own misunderstanding of original sin; one that appears to posit an inherently bad human

must be quelled by the good (i.e., culture). This division is based on an assumption that human nature is inherently self-interested and antisocial, and therefore must be redirected by the varied manifestations of culture (e.g., social contracts that found relationships),[112] a view which borrows from the modern mechanistic tendency to render individuals as autonomous creatures who must be coerced into relations externally. For Sahlins, Western political theory propagates this nature/culture divide under the assumption of an autonomous human nature. For Neo-Liberalism the more free the individual the less he or she is socially obliged.[113] Sahlins argues this is far from the way the primitive cultures behave. Rather, it is the primitive individual's real participation in the community that forms his very being, his individuality.[114] A human is not an autonomous individual whose nature needs to be restrained by a cultural artifice, but rather, is naturally social, as evident in the cultural practice of reciprocity. For the primitive, self-interest

---

nature against the spiritual good. Sahlins is here following a common misinterpretation of Saint Augustine in his work against the Pelagians. To be clear, Saint Augustine does argue that all people inherit original sin, but this does not mean that humans are bad, or rather, that it is unnatural to be good or in communion with others and God. On the contrary, human nature is brought to its *fullness*, not eradicated, by divine grace. Thus, for Saint Augustine, it is most *natural* to be in communion with God and with others. This is to say that Sahlins's critique of original sin is aimed at an errant theological anthropology of his own making. Pabst, too, remarks that this sort of critique is a misrepresentation of the fall narrative. See, Pabst, *Metaphysics*, 406. In chapter 4 this theological misreading is more thoroughly examined.

112. Sahlins, *The Western Illusion of Human Nature*, 14. See also, Milbank, *Theology and Social Theory*. Milbank's critique against secular social theory as founded on a "myth of violence"—that humans are inherently bad and need to be reined in by a secular state—aligns with Sahlins's argument, with the exception that Milbank's solution is theological.

113. Sahlins, *The Western Illusion of Human Nature*, 42. For Sahlins this ultimately culminates in capitalism, which turns the assumed natural desire of individualism and self-interest into the greatest good, which the state secures in all its legal and bureaucratic functions. Here, self-concern is masked as individual freedom. See also, Hart, *In the Aftermath*. In chapter 1, "Christ and Nothing (No Other God)," Hart argues that, according to the narrative of modern liberalism, the freedom of the individual will comes to take the place of the good. This nihilistic culture de-centers morality (the good) by placing it in individual competing wills whose end game is Nietzsche's Will to Power. The new good is individual freedom at the cost of the common good, never mind the implications this may have on others (to cite one example of Hart's—one's freedom to have an abortion).

114. Sahlins, *The Western Illusion of Human Nature*, 49–50. Sahlins's description of the primitive is strikingly similar to Lévy-Bruhl's. Sahlins talks of the primitive, "in sum and in general, in kin relationships, others become predicates of one's own existence and vice versa . . . [and] the participation of certain others in his own being."

is quite unnatural.[115] Thus, Sahlins asserts nature is culture, and culture is human nature.[116] When one looks back upon the primitive one finds that the human is naturally a social creature; thus, culture is the original state of human existence.[117] In fact, contrary to myths of civilized progress, one cannot locate a time in history that humanity is without a culture or society.

What's more, in his "What Is Anthropological Enlightenment?," Sahlins argues that recent studies have confirmed that primitive societies have adapted to modern market economies without sacrificing their culture. For example, he finds that surviving indigenous groups—like the Eskimos, the Maya of Guatemala, and the Tukanoans of Columbia—are evidence that, "contrary to the evolutionary destiny the West had foreseen for them, the so-called savages will neither be all alike nor just like us."[118] These indigenous tribes have adapted to modern technological advances employing them for Paleolithic purposes.[119] Even with all the engagement with the white man's civilized society and capitalist economy, these people groups have not succumbed to modern economic practices. How did they do it? They did not see the developments of modern technology as a death to their culture, but rather, the success of such tribes "express their confidence in a living tradition, a tradition that serves as a means and measure of innovation."[120] For these, money brought tribes together as it simply replaced other exchange valuables. Modern gifts are still given in the same initiatory way, although a modern vehicle may replace a pig. Contrary to earlier suspicions and myths of progress these indigenous people groups adapted the influx of modern civilization to coincide with their cultural traditions.[121] These people groups show that

> where there is no structural opposition between the relation-
> ships of economy and sociability, where material transactions
> are ordered by social relations rather than vice versa, then
> the amorality we attribute to money need not obtain. . . . So
> in general, one of the Big Surprises of "late capitalism" is that

115. Ibid., 51.

116. Ibid., 105. See also, 110.

117. Ibid., 104. See also, 109.

118. Sahlins, "What Is Anthropological Enlightenment?," iv.

119. Ibid., vi–vii. Sahlins is here referring to the, "vast arctic and subarctic stretches of Europe, Siberia, and North America . . . ."

120. Ibid., ix. See also, x. Sahlins refers to the primitive adaptation of the modern market as, "the indigenization of modernity."

121. Ibid., xii.

"traditional" cultures are not inevitably incompatible with it nor vulnerable to it.[122]

Sahlins also found such adaptation in the structures of indigenous peoples who migrated to cities.[123] In all, what he discovered is that primitive culture is not affected by the modern market economy, namely because their inherent social structure is based on a different culture. Crucially for Sahlins, the collectivist culture of the primitive remains because they do not conceive themselves as autonomous individuals, but rather, as individuals constituted by their reciprocal relations within their society, thus eluding modernist notions of individualism, even while living amidst such cultures. In so doing, these indigenous tribes have disproved the postmodern fallacy of an end to culture.[124] Sahlin's writes, "certain illusions born of the Western self-consciousness of civilization have thus proved not too enlightening."[125] It is for this reason that Sahlins and others advocate a return to such cultures that have not been overtaken by modernity, but rather adapted to them.[126] These cultural structures, practices, and politics present an opportunity for anthropology to renew itself. For him, real enlightenment is not to be found in the "universal march of reason proclaimed by the eighteenth century," but in culture, an inexhaustible reservoir of responses to the world's challenges.[127] As such, primitive practices provide several new points of inquiry that may help to contextualize one's own historical understandings.[128] But to do so, anthropology must break from the modern "intellectual bondage"

122. Ibid., xvii.
123. Ibid., xix.
124. Ibid., xx.
125. Ibid., ii.
126. Sclove, *Democracy and Technology*, 6–9. Sclove notes that the Amish are a great example of a community aware of the context in which they are immersed. They are willing to make adaptations to technological innovations, while their culture provides clear limitations. He refers to this as a pattern of "exclusions and adoptions" of those things that might otherwise subsume the Amish culture. "Each local Amish community—acting collectively rather than as a set of discrete individuals—asks itself how the adoption of a technology would affect the community as a whole. Innovations that would tend, on balance, to preserve the community, its religion, and its harmonious relation with nature are permitted; those that appear to threaten the community and its values are rejected. In either case, the decision is reached through a process of public discussion and democratic ratification."
127. Sahlins, "What Is Anthropological Enlightenment?" xxi. He is here partially quoting Abdou Touré.
128. Sahlins, "Other Times, Other Customs," 534.

that has hindered its ability to understand humanity's proper place in the world.[129]

To further articulate his thesis Sahlins compares the different modes of gift exchange, a practice which he finds evident in all societies. He argues that while, "different cultural orders have their own modes of historical action, consciousness, and determination"[130] that position particular societies, one can identify some common characteristic "types" of reciprocity. These are the (1) "general," (2) "balanced," and (3) "negative" types of reciprocity.[131] A general reciprocity is seen as mere gift exchange of intimate relations with no expectation for return. A balanced exchange seeks an equal sharing among friends but also among less-familiar relations. Here, the self-interest and material gains begin to take priority over the actual human bond itself. Lastly, a negative reciprocity seeks the self-gain of an individual at the exploitation of another.[132] Like Lévy-Bruhl and Barfield, Sahlins tends to favor the primitive structure of reciprocal relations, which he sees as a combination of his general and balanced types of reciprocity over against the typically modern negative aspects of reciprocity, which reduce qualitative real relations to quantitative monetary gains.[133]

Mauss, in his The Gift, agrees. He notes that modern forms of reciprocity are the result of the reduction of primitive exchange to bare economics.[134] Only when these relations are reduced to something like a calculated self-interested exchange does culture become set over against nature.[135] As for the primitive the circulation of gifts was the giving of one's self. It is thus the circulation of rights and persons, which is so distinct from contracts and the circulation of money,[136] which Mauss refers to as a "cold calculat-

129. Sahlins, "What Is Anthropological Enlightenment?" ii. Sahlins writes, "But from what intellectual bondage would anthropology need to liberate itself in our times? No doubt from a lot of inherited ideas, including sexism, positivism, geneticism, utilitarianism, and many other such dogmas of the average native Western folklore posing as universal understandings of the human condition."

130. Sahlins, "Other Times, Other Customs," 518.

131. Sahlins, Stone Age Economics.

132. These generalizations are drawn from Kirk, "Karl Polanyi, Marshall Sahlins, and the Study of Ancient Social Relations," 182.

133. Sahlins, "Other Times, Other Customs," 519. See also, 525, where he notes the contrast between primitives and the capitalist idea, "that social outcomes are the cumulative expressions of individual actions" based on their "material sufferings."

134. Mauss and Brain, A General Theory of Magic, 6–7.

135. Pabst, Metaphysics, 407. Pabst argues that when individuality is more fundamental than community nature becomes increasingly conceived in terms of a competition between all that must be reined in by the state.

136. Mauss, The Gift, 59.

ing mentality."[137] He warns that, "the brutish pursuit of individual ends is harmful to the ends and the peace of all, to the rhythm of their work and joys—and rebounds on the individual himself."[138] Primitive exchange is "far from being materialistic. It is far less prosaic than our buying and selling, our renting of services, or the games we play on the Stock Exchange."[139] Indeed, the primitive can help shed light on one's morals and direct one's ideals as well as one's economic practices and societies.[140] Mauss implores, "we can and must return to archaic society and to elements within it."[141] Similar to Sahlins's response, Mauss draws upon primitive notions commending a return to what he calls the "group morality," and suggests interplay between individuality and the group, which constitutes the individual. The individual "must have a keen sense of awareness of himself, but also of others, and of social reality. . . . He must act by taking into account his own interest, and those of society and its subgroups."[142] It is this moral obligation that is eternally present in all societies.[143]

It appears that a culture of reciprocity and gift exchange subsists in all cultures because it is human nature. However, in civilized societies (ostensibly comprised of autonomous individuals) the robust form of reciprocity is reduced to negative exchanges, which pit individuals, states, and markets against one another. These negative exchanges are predicated on the nature/culture divide. However, in the prior analysis of primitives one discovers a more robust version of human nature that outwits this dualism revealing that humanity is naturally social. Indeed, to be most fully human, to be free to be oneself, is not to exist in isolation, but to be in relation. Even if while at present it is skewed by the presupposed autonomous individual, benevolent reciprocity is evident in all cultures. While notions of negative freedom leave modern man cut off from his social responsibilities (e.g., moral obligations on the left and social responsibilities on the right), the primitive individual, constituted in his participatory relation to others, may, in fact, represent the more free and humane culture, as well as a way forward in a Western world now dominated by notions of negative freedom.[144] The

137. Ibid., 61.

138. Ibid., 98.

139. Ibid., 93.

140. Ibid., 91. See also, 100. Mauss notes that primitives shed light on "the path our own notions must follow, both in their morality and economy."

141. Ibid., 87–88.

142. Ibid., 89.

143. Ibid.

144. Pabst, *Metaphysics*, 430–37.

anthropological and sociological critiques of the nature/culture relationship suggest that a human is not an autonomous subject, but is instead—as seen clearly in primitive cultures and more subtly in modernity—fundamentally relational. These relations, although not reducible to quantitative analyses, resituate modernity's autonomous subject in relation to others and to the natural world. To be most fully human, to be most free, is to live poetically with one another and with the surrounding world.

Lévy-Bruhl and Barfield

As with the work of Steiner and Coleridge, Barfield discovered that his theory regarding the evolutionary history of words coincided with Lucien Lévy-Bruhl's studies of primitive people groups, which he believed provided tangible evidence to buttress his poetic philosophy. The evolution of consciousness is marked by the loss of a poetic consciousness that is embodied in primitive societies and the later slide towards individualism. As consciousness evolves, man experiences a gradual withdrawal from his participatory relation to others and to the natural world, becoming a self-conscious, detached individual.[145] This is the modern self-consciousness that is isolated from others and from nature.[146] Barfield warned that humanity must overcome "the universally prevalent assumption that human beings can only ultimately be governed by egocentric motives."[147] He believed that this poetic picture could be rediscovered if one was willing to step outside of one's current consciousness.[148] It was, perhaps, this rare quality of Lévy-Bruhl's anthropology that struck a chord with Barfield. As he saw it, Lévy-Bruhl's scholarship furthered his ongoing endeavor to inform the modern consciousness that the contemporary plight was not definitive, but only an epoch that would soon be overcome.[149] In fact, in Barfield's science fiction *Night Operation*, when the characters Jon, Jak, and Peet, who have been living "Underground" entirely cut off from nature (as Barfield writes, in a time

145. Sugerman, *Evolution of Consciousness*, 78.

146. Barfield, *History, Guilt, and Habit*, 72.

147. De Lange, *Owen Barfield*, 288.

148. De Laguna, "Lévy-Bruhl's Contributions to the Study of Primitive Mentality," 554. See also, Barfield, *Saving the Appearances*, 73.

149. It is important to note that particularly in *Saving the Appearances*, and generally throughout his larger body of work, Barfield pushes Lévy-Bruhl's thesis further by suggesting that primitive mentality is actually superior to the modern reductive worldview. This is a claim that Lévy-Bruhl does not make, although his unbiased consideration of the primitive mentality certainly opened a door for Barfield's critique of modern consciousness.

when "nature itself had now withdrawn from humanity"), venture "Aboveg-round," the narrative indicates that if they, "had time to travel, and some account must have been included of the scattered people groups of men and women they would have encountered, who had continued a physically primitive existence above ground even after civilization had disappeared beneath it."[150] This indicates that for Barfield it is indeed the primitive who truly embodies the participatory reality.

This chapter introduced the work of Lucien Lévy-Bruhl in order to weave an analogous relation between the ineradicable poetic nature of the real and the inherently collectivist nature of humans. What Barfield dis-covered in the work of Lévy-Bruhl was that primitives embodied what he found in his study of words. But, in time, as subjects and objects became increasingly divided (symbols shattered), the modern subject became sepa-rate from the world around him. However, this participatory relation had not entirely receded, as the truly autonomous self was found wanting. For a glimpse back to primitive societies indicates that humans are inherently social, living poetically, and this is more or less latent today, guised behind a division of nature and culture. In learning from primitive cultures, moderns can learn to counteract this assumption. However, according to Barfield, if the epoch of "final participation" is to dawn then the great "prison wall"[151] in the epoch of the "consciousness soul" must be dismantled. For, as civi-lization advanced, humans became increasingly *un*natural, driven by a scientism that had misconstrued the human relation to the world, thereby producing a creature set over against nature.

150. Barfield, *Night Operation*, 43–44.
151. Barfield, *History, Guilt, and Habit*, 82.

4

Poetic Making

To docket living things past any doubt, you cancel first the living spirit out: The parts lie in the hollow of your hand, you only lack the living link you banned.

—Goethe[1]

The atoms of Democritus, and Newton's particles of light, Are sands upon the Red Seashore, where Israel's tents do shine so bright.

—Blake[2]

Today we can illuminate our cities so brightly that the stars of the sky are no longer visible. Is this not an image of the problems caused by our version of enlightenment? With regard to material things, our knowledge and our technical accomplishments are legion, but what reaches beyond, the things of God and the question of good, we can no longer identify. Faith, then, which reveals God's light to us, is the true enlightenment, enabling God's light to break into our world, opening our eyes to the true light.

—Benedict XVI[3]

1. Goethe, *Faust*, 95.

2. "Mock on, Mock on, Voltaire, Rousseau," in William Blake, *The Complete Poems*.

3. A homily delivered on Easter Eve (Holy Saturday) 7th April, 2012 at Vatican City, Rome. The Vatican's translation can be viewed here: http://www.zenit.org/

The Rise of Modern Science[4]

The previous chapter outlined the gradual decline of the primitive collectivist self (i.e., the self that lives poetically wherein one's flourishing depends on the flourishing of one's neighbor), which culminates in the notion of a free autonomous self. Correspondingly, the present chapter will now examine how the division between the human (i.e., as subject) and nature (i.e., as object) is embodied in modern scientific "making" processes, which are represented as a break from natural limitations (or norms). In this scheme the human is displaced from and set over and against nature.

In order to extract the deeper implications behind Barfield's sweeping critiques, this chapter underscores the key scientific guideposts that inspire his harsh criticisms of modern science. To do so, the present section presents a brief genealogy of modern science by drawing upon various interlocutors who, like Barfield, share a deep concern for what they see as the abandon of modern science, and whose narratives trace the gradual separation of humanity and nature, its deleterious effects, and the various attempts to assuage this separation. This provides a context by which to approach Barfield's critique of science. In this narrative, as with the linguistic tendency to divide subjects and objects, as traced in Part I, and the rise of individualism traced in the previous chapter, the erosion of poetic making culminates in the aforesaid division between humanity and nature. According to Barfield, the evolutionary history of words yields a division between subject and object that is nowhere more evident than in the making practices of modern technology. Barfield believed it was the "prison wall" of "causality science" that had left the modern consciousness all but incapable of apprehending the real. His texts are fraught with criticisms of this anti-realist strategy. Indeed, quantum theorists' critiques of physics' own Cartesian legacy (e.g., "fields," "entanglement," and the "uncertainty principle") reinforced his overarching narrative that this poetic reality was never entirely lost and would soon reemerge in the age of the consciousness soul, yielding to a future epoch of final participation.

In Part I, it was argued that Barfield's poetic philosophy represents an alternative to the passive voice by situating the subject in a middle realm. The close of the present part will suggest how his poetic philosophy also resists the notion of a purely active subject. Poetic making, which constitutes a participation of humanity in the natural processes, represents an alternative

article-34598?l=english.

4. This section is indebted to Professor Michael Northcott for his list of resources and to Professor Simon Oliver for his work and many lectures on Platonic, Aristotelian, Newtonian, and Mechanistic cosmologies. See, Oliver, *Philosophy, God and Motion.*

to a conception of human making that pits the active subject over a passive nature. This form of making grants the subject a genuine participatory, mediated role in natural creative processes, which is further explored in Part III.

Art as *Technê* and Nature as *Phýsis*

For Aristotle, *technê* is a bringing forth of what is already within the natural order, or *phýsis*.[5] (There is here an analogous relation between poetic making as *technê* and speaking or living as poetic, in that these conceptions of subjectivity are opposed to the dominative imposition of the will upon objects.) In this way, human making could not exceed the natural order, because to the Greeks *technê*, that which is *art*ificial (i.e., human-made), is inferior to nature (*phýsis*), whose form or purpose is teleologically ordered.[6] Aristotle explicitly distinguishes between *phýsis* and *technê*, identifying *phýsis* as that which has an intrinsic form, whereas with *technê* (i.e., the *art*ificial or human-made) form is externally imposed.

Another distinction made by Aristotle was that natural forms have an intrinsic principle of motion and rest (both quantitative *and* qualitative, or rather, efficient and formal-teleological) and an ability to recreate, whereas artifacts do not.[7] Human-made artifacts lack this intrinsic teleology. Moreover, this intrinsic form represented the stability ("original wholeness") of the natural world in the flux between potentiality and actuality in the move towards each "thing's" particular teleological end.[8] While Aristotle maintained this clear distinction between natural and human making, he does not deny that there is a relation between *technê*, as in the idea of craftsman who imbues form upon matter,[9] and his "Unmoved Mover," who imbues teleological forms in nature. Nonetheless, what he makes clear, is that human making is subordinate to the natural because that which is artificial lacks an inherent teleology. Hans Jonas remarks that in this way, "the artificial thing is an image of the natural, not also the natural an image of the

---

5. Northcott, "Concept Art, Clones, and Co-creators," 225–26.

6. Szerszynski, *Nature, Technology and the Sacred*, 52–55.

7. Oliver, *Philosophy, God and Motion*, 30–31.

8. Walker, "'Original Wholeness,'" 156. For Aristotle, "original wholeness of the natural body consists in its maintaining itself, as such, through some kind of internally generated motion." See also, 157–58, For Aristotle, the cosmos is moved by the divine, which is the *telos* of all things.

9. Dupré, *Passage to Modernity*, 75.

artificial."[10] Again, the natural world (*phýsis*) has an internal principle of motion and rest. With this distinction in mind, *technê* could, at best, imitate nature (*phýsis*).[11]

The idea that *technê* ought to imitate nature was common parlance for the pre-modern theologian, and as far along as the medieval period it was generally understood that human making imitated the natural world (i.e., divine craftsmanship), it could not conceivably exceed it.[12] For example, in his commentary on Aristotle's *Physics*, Aquinas succinctly illustrates the distinction between human and divine making (as evident in the natural or created order). Using an analogy to distinguish divine and human making, Aquinas writes, "it is clear that nature is nothing but a certain kind of art, i.e., the divine art, impressed upon things, by which these things are moved to a determinate end. It is as if the shipbuilder were able to give to timbers that by which they would move themselves to take the form of a ship."[13] This follows Aquinas's two-tier participatory causation structure, which resists the autonomy of human power and self-sufficiency.[14] This distinction also indicates that God's making is ontologically continuous, whereas human making is not (e.g., the human making of the ship is complete when the human withdraws his hand. Nature, however, is in constant change. The ship's form is imposed externally, while the plant's is inherent). So, "humans do not create in the strict sense, but they are not denied a role in the temporal achievement or realization of the idea."[15] Aquinas properly distinguishes between divine and human making while granting the creature an analo-

10. Jonas, *The Phenomenon of Life*, 159. See also, 172. Herein, Jonas refers to this distinction as the "ontological incompleteness" of "likeness" that also attends the artificial imitative work of man. In making, a human can either render a "likeness" to the natural order or choose to depart from it.

11. Walker, "Original Wholeness," 162. Walker writes, "the original wholeness of living *phýsis* is something that *technê* ('art' taken in the broadest sense) cannot replace, but can only imitate."

12. Miner, *Truth in the Making*, 9. Miner suggests that Aquinas maintains an analogical relation between divine and human making. Tiptoeing the limits of language, Aquinas is careful to avoid a univocal construal. In so doing, Aquinas portrays human actions as subject to God, yet free. See also, 34. Humans, then, work in a way that mirrors the divine creative power without usurping it.

13. Aquinas, *Commentary on Aristotle's Metaphysics*, II.14.268.

14. Tanner, *God and Creation in Christian Theology*, 152–53. Tanner also maintains that the Thomistic account of causality respects a proper participatory relation between humanity and nature. In Thomistic language, humans share a role in sustaining nature and remain careful not to dominate it.

15. Miner, *Truth in the Making*, 2–9. See also, 126. Miner notes we should "think of human beings as making the truth, in a sense which affirms that human making is more creative than the imitation of nature, yet is not cut off from the divine logos, because its creativity is fundamentally a finite participation in the infinite *Verbum*."

gous role in the creative process.[16] As Adrian Walker puts it, "just as living nature is an original imitation of God, so, too, art is an original imitation of (living) nature."[17] So to summarize, until the medieval period philosophers and theologians distinguished between natural (and/or divine making) and human making by rendering human *technê* subordinate to *phýsis*, but with the rise of modern science this hierarchy is collapsed, as *phýsis* is envisaged as subordinate to *technê*, and the once co-operative poetic understanding of *technê* becomes exploitative.[18]

Nature Interrupted: Mechanism, Machines, and the New *Technê*

The aforementioned distinction between natural and human making placed limits on *technê*. Within these limits human making is most natural.[19] While modern science purports to have freed culture from these natural limitations, ecological issues raise questions regarding the toppling of this hierarchical distinction. While there is no single factor that precipitated the collapsing of this hierarchical distinction, there are subtle epistemological

16. Indeed, Aquinas goes further than the Greek philosophers. Distinct from Plato's *Timeaus* or Aristotle's eternal order sustained by the Unmoved Mover, God as Creator *ex nihilo* is other than human making precisely because divine making involves no distinction between matter and form, between means and end, and between raw material and finished product, because in God there is no temporal succession. See also, Walker, "'Original Wholeness,'" 161. See note 30. Walker describes the subtle difference between Aristotle's God and the Christian God who creates *ex nihilo*. See also, Cunningham, *Darwin's Pious Idea*, 286. Cunningham offers a proper theological understanding of divine causation as distinct from common modernist notions. See also, 298–99, for Cunningham's explanation of the doctrine of creation *ex nihilo*.

Another way of distinguishing divine and human making might simply be to say that human making always involves pre-existent material whereas God's making does not. See, for example, Northcott, "Concept Art, Clones, and Co-creators," 222–25. Northcott refers to "Dolly," the sheep conceived in a laboratory, as an example of the confusion of what it means to create. Northcott points out that the scientist is still working with pre-existent materials already created, but Dolly gives the illusion that humans have somehow become creators in the divine sense. See also, Berry, *The Unsettling of America*, 55. Berry notes, that when the great chain of being is dismantled humanity conceives itself as both creature and creator.

17. Walker, "'Original Wholeness,'" 162. For more on Aquinas's view of the co-operative causality of creatures see, Kerr, *After Aquinas*, 143.

18. Northcott, "Concept Art, Clones, and Co-creators," 227–28.

19. Again, here the reader is reminded that negative freedom removes social responsibilities crafting an ostensibly autonomous subject. This coincides with modern science's removal of natural limits, as both are based on a turn to subjectivity and the denial of participation that Barfield warned against.

moves made that coincide with the rise of modern science.[20] This subsection offers a critical analysis of the rise of modern science in order to contextualize Barfield's own critique that follows.

As already alluded to in chapter 3, Isaac Newton's *Principia* (1687) was a watershed in the emergence of the modern scientific worldview. Neil Postman, in his *Technopoly*, remarks that, "Copernicus, Kepler, and Galileo put in place the dynamite that would blow up the theology and metaphysics of the medieval world. Newton lit the fuse."[21] In the *General Scholium* Newton's admitted rejection of Aristotelian metaphysics rendered human and natural (and divine) making indistinguishable. In removing what he deemed "occult" qualities Newton effectively evacuated all form, teleology, quality, life,[22] etc., from the cosmos, leaving a dead passive matter that is acted upon by God's laws.[23] Gary Deason deems Newton's worldview mechanistic be-

20. For an excellent theological and philosophical genealogy of the rise of modern science and the usurpation of art over nature and its mechanization as seen in the inconsistencies of (ultra)Darwinism, see Hanby, *No God, No Science?* chapter 9, "Saving the Appearances."

21. Postman, *Technopoly*, 34. See also, Cunningham, *Darwin's Pious Idea*, 2.

22. Jonas, *The Phenomenon of Life*, 15. As mentioned in chapter 3, Jonas argues that materialism became the triumph of death over the experience of life. The mechanistic worldview is an ontology of death that envisages the world as an "empty tomb." See also, 27. Jonas notes that mechanism's, "dualistic antithesis leads not to a heightening of the features of life through their concentration on one side [materialism], but to a deadening of both sides through their separation from the living middle." See also, 74. See also, Bishop, *The Anticipatory Corpse*. Bishop's main thrust is that modern medicine, which originates in experimental procedures on the dead corpse, necessarily denies the form and *telos* that are inherent in life when dealing with the suffering patient. In this way, modern medicine errantly defines life as "nonliving matter in motion." Bishop argues that by reducing the flux of life to its efficient mechanistic function (i.e., treating the living body as a corpse and manipulating it to get a functional effect), medicine does violence by denying the suffering patient the dignity of various other alternatives that are more conducive to the more formal and teleological aspects of the lived experience. Bishop emphasizes that the Newtonian reduction of Aristotle's four causes to material and efficient deeply affected modern medicine in ways that it has only now begun to recognize. In response to this, Bishop locates his subtle phenomenological panacea in the call of the other, the very purpose (i.e., *telos*) that first "drew" the medical practitioner to her work; the same purpose and meaning that exists within each patient. The response to this "call" should not simply be reduced to correcting the mechanical functionality of the suffering (as good as that may be), but to the entirety of the person that can only be assuaged by the "being-there," the gift of self, of the practitioner in the presence of the "other" who suffers. Ultimately, Bishop intimates a theological reconstruction of medicine. See also, Cunningham, *Darwin's Pious Idea*, 316–19. Cunningham points out the philosophical absurdities of materialism by suggesting that it must conclude that life is dead, or at least that life does not exist. In a world of pure matter, "no one ever dies because no one is ever born."

23. Harrison, *The Bible, Protestantism, and the Rise of Natural Science*, 264. Harrison

cause it rests on the single assumption that *"matter is passive".*[24] Newton's voluntarist "Lord God *Pantokrator*" externally manipulates passive matter via active laws of motion.[25] Deason continues, "Unlike the world conceived by Aristotle by which inherent mindlike principles imbued matter with purposive development, the Newtonian world possessed no inherent activity and no inherent direction."[26] Now, only God could move matter, it could not move itself.[27] Mechanistic philosophy excludes all reference to vital forces or final causes.[28] It is a move from the internal of form and teleology to the external of efficient causation. Indeed mechanics assumes that nature is not the manifestation of a living principle but is a system of matter moved by the external application of laws. Although these laws could be demonstrated mathematically, they say nothing about the nature or the essence of the object. Objects are only understood by their effects that can be predicted mathematically. Here, causes replace meaning.[29] Hans Jonas shows that what happens with the mathematicization of the universe is that the

writes, "In the physics of Descartes and Newton, simple natural objects are denuded of all but basic quantitative properties." See also, Deason, "Reformation Theology and the Mechanistic Conception of Nature," 184. See also, Rossi, *The Birth of Modern Science*, 127. See also, Jonas, *The Phenomenon of Life*, 9.

24. Deason, "Reformation Theology and the Mechanistic Conception of Nature," 168. Now, it would be naïve to simply reduce Newtonian physics to a purely mechanistic philosophy. This will be more closely examined in section 2 of this chapter. For an excellent account of the distinction between a purely mechanistic worldview and Newtonian physics see, Freudenthal, *Atom and Individual in the Age of Newton*. Freudenthal argues that Newton himself did not believe in a mechanistic cosmos, but this was rather a misreading of Newton based upon the atomic philosophy, which dominated the social theory of his time. It was perhaps instead Descartes's notion of external force that played a significant role in forging the mechanistic trajectory of modern social science. Nonetheless, Newton's work does mark a significant break from the pre-modern conception of causality.

25. Latour, *We Have Never Been Modern*, 33. Latour states the mechanics "crossed-out God" from nature in order to keep him from interfering with Natural Law. See also, Schindler, *Beyond Mechanism*, 14–15. With mechanism all relations are external.

26. Deason, "Reformation Theology and the Mechanistic Conception of Nature," 185.

27. Ibid., 182–83.

28. Rossi, *The Birth of Modern Science*, 125. For a critique of the modern scientific rejection of teleology see, Jonas, *The Phenomenon of Life*, "Appendix 2: Note on Anthropomorphism," 33–37. Jonas states that *telos* is the most basic experience of human life. Ironically, because modern science views the mind (the bearer of *telos*) as separate from nature, humans are actually unable to project this into the natural world or into matter. This way Jonas links anthropomorphism to the rejection of teleology. Only man and his mind hold the "purposes." Once the mind is rendered separate from the world, to actually acknowledge any real purpose in the world is to anthropomorphize the world.

29. Szerszynski, *Nature, Technology and the Sacred*, 47.

things that were once thought most intelligible (forms and teleology) become subordinate to modern reductive quantitative materiality. "The least intelligible has become the most, nay only, intelligible."[30] By denying inherent qualities and stripping nature of any intrinsic meaning Newton paved the way to a new univocal relation between natural and human making.[31] He espoused that, like God, lesser beings have a univocal, although lesser, power, dominion, and rule over the world.[32] This move has a way of devaluing the natural world[33] and subjecting it to an arbitrary will (either God or man). This was one of the main reasons why Barfield was so critical of what he called "causality science."

In mechanistic cosmology, where *phýsis* and *technê* are conceived univocally, the Aristotelian hierarchy is collapsed[34] and God becomes increasingly distant.[35] One may now recall Aquinas's shipbuilder analogy used to articulate the difference between *phýsis* and *technê*. Aquinas, following

30. Jonas, *The Phenomenon of Life*, 66–70.

31. Szerszynski, *Nature, Technology and the Sacred*, 56. All of this begs the question: in a materialistic universe of pure substance, how can there be any recognizable causality? There is no way of apprehending movement in a purely material world bereft of form. If there is no form, there are no apprehensible objects. And if there is no teleology there is no apprehensible space in which these objects move. See, Jonas, *The Phenomenon of Life*, "Appendix 1: Causality and Perception," 26. See also, "Sixth Essay—The Nobility of Sight: A Study in the Phenomenology of the Senses," and "Appendix—Sight and Movement," 135–56. For the connection between movement and teleology see, 153–56. See also, Cunningham, *Darwin's Pious Idea*, 267. Cunningham says something similar when he notes, "To account for real difference, surely we must appeal to something other than matter—yet any such appeal is prohibited in what amounts to a monistic philosophy (the notion that existence is composed of only one type of substance, which we call 'matter'). . . . Consequently, the materialist must admit that his description is metaphysical; it tacitly invokes something that transcends what is basic at the level of immanence, or the merely physical. The only other option is to deny all change, just as one must, it seems, deny objects themselves." See also, 319–32, for Cunningham's critique of materialism.

32. Oliver, *Philosophy, God and Motion*, 160.

33. Schindler, *Beyond Mechanism*, 10.

34. Deason, "Reformation Theology and the Mechanistic Conception of Nature," 169. See also, Miner, *Truth in the Making*, 39. Miner notes that making is only via participation, which is precisely what later cosmologies deny.

35. Dupré, *Passage to Modernity*, 68. Dupré notes, "the main issue was causality. . . . The communication of motion, which had played such an important role in the ancient worldview and on which major arguments for the existence of God had rested, lost its significance in a mechanistic order where bodies, once they moved, would continue to do so until stopped by an external cause. It needed no further assistance after it had received its initial impulse. The new science of mechanics did not dispense with a Creator who would initiate motion, but it appeared to withdraw God from nature after his creative act."

Aristotle, spoke of an analogical relation between natural and human making. Although related, human making was subordinate to natural making because a human cannot imbue inherent principles of motion and rest upon that which he or she creates. By ignoring this distinction, mechanism univocally relates natural and human making by construing making as a mere efficient act of volition upon the passive other. As such, both God and humans make by an external imposition of the will upon nature. Further, when this analogous relation is made univocal a rupture between humanity and nature commences that can be located in the maladaptation of *technê*. Once *technê* meant to be in harmony with nature, to remain within the limits of the natural order, but in a mechanistic cosmology *technê* dominates nature under the assumption that the human can transform and improve the natural world.[36] In this scheme, nature (*phýsis*), once a source of norms and morals suffused with meaning and purpose, is gradually transformed by the imposition of human will.[37]

This transformation can also be linked to the emergence of Cartesian philosophy. Descartes's mechanistic philosophy assumes a dualism of matter and mind (*res extensa* and *res cogitans*).[38] By removing inert qualities (i.e., relegating them to the *res cogitans*) mechanics reduced the natural world to the *res extensa*.[39] This new frontier is a world bereft of meaning that is subject to man's volition.[40] Bereft of value, *phýsis* becomes a product of mere human intention.[41] This scheme necessarily jettisons poetic making

36. Szerszynski, *Nature, Technology and the Sacred*, 52–55 and 93.

37. Northcott, *The Environment and Christian Ethics*, 243. Several have noted a direct connection to errant theology. The loss of the Aristotelian worldview meant that absolute sovereignty fell from God into the hands of man, placing the will in charge of self and universe. See, Berry, *The Unsettling of America*, 55. Berry writes, "having placed ourselves in charge of Creation, we began to mechanize both the Creation itself and our conception of it." See also, Jonas, *The Phenomenon of Life*, 195.

38. See, Jonas, *The Phenomenon of Life*, 53–58. See also, Dupré, *Passage to Modernity*, 77. Dupré writes that, "the restriction of scientific knowledge of nature to extension and motion (in Newton also mass), separates this particular kind of being in an irreducible way from *res cogitans*."

39. See also, Rossi, *The Birth of Modern Science*, 135–38. Leibniz accused Descartes's mechanics of the reduction of physics to pure mechanism.

40. Northcott, *The Environment and Christian Ethics*, 52. Northcott notes that once nature is deprived of divine ordinance it becomes subject to human appetite.

41. Jonas, *The Phenomenon of Life*, 13. Jonas notes that this dualism left a world bereft of the spiritual and denude of arresting attributes. See also, xiv–xvi. Against the Cartesian divide, in the forward, Lawrence Vogel shows that for Jonas value is not something the human simply projects onto nature, but is something essential to all of life; thus, one must think of nature as a source of value if one is to place any limits on technological advancement. See also, Ingold, *The Perception of the Environment*,

in which one remains within the formal limits of the natural order. In so doing, it supposedly frees the subject from these constraints who can then impose his own will on to nature.[42] This Cartesian subject no longer imitates nature, but masters it.[43] Man no longer co-operates, but commands;[44] he no longer lives in the world, but "intervenes";[45] he no longer "works with," but "does to."[46] Indeed the new modern construal of *technê* frees man to make *phýsis* in his own image.[47] Here the shift is completed: in the mechanistic cosmology *technê* no longer imitates *phýsis*, but *phýsis* is forced to accommodate modern *technê*.

The following interlocutors, like Barfield, contend that the machine is a noteworthy progeny of the mechanistic worldview outlined above. The machine exemplifies the redefining of *technê*, and as such, it is a powerful symbol of the separation of humanity and nature. Humanity creates the

---

294–95. Ingold links technology with a radical shift in the cosmology of Galileo and Newton and Descartes's idea that the universe is a vast machine that can be harnessed to serve human interest and purposes by applying mechanics to nature. See also, 25, where Ingold writes, "the sovereign perspective of abstract reason, upon which Western science lays its claim to authority, is practically unattainable: an intelligence completely detached from the conditions of life in the world could not think the thoughts it does." See also, Guardini, *Letters from Lake Como*, 6. Guardini paints a picture of a nature reshaped by the mind. See also, 45–46. While modern chemistry and physics exemplifies this disengaged mastery of materials, such rational mastery is not natural.

42. Northcott, *The Environment and Christian Ethics*, 63.

43. Miner, *Truth in the Making*, 64. See also, Pieper, *Leisure, the Basis of Culture*, 106. According to Descartes, in his *Discours de la method*, man is "master and owner of nature." Marx notes that up to the present philosophy has been concerned with man's interplay with nature, but now he alters it. See also, Jonas, *The Phenomenon of Life*, 152. According to Jonas, with Francis Bacon this new understanding of nature takes the form of "power."

44. Szerszynski, *Nature, Technology and the Sacred*, 50.

45. Ingold, *The Perception of the Environment*, 215.

46. Ingold, *Being Alive*, 10.

47. See, Sennett, *The Craftsman*, 65–67 and 70–73. This turn is evident in the perspective of art as Sennett shows that by the time of the Renaissance, artists began to claim subjective creativity of their own, thinking they are their own maker. The medieval craftsman, who looked outwards towards his guild, is reversed by the subjective turn inward in the Renaissance artist. See also, Northcott, "Concept Art, Clones, and Co-creators," 225–26. Similarly, Northcott argues that even the postmodern artist repeats this radical subjectivity. See also, Rossi, *The Birth of Modern Science*, 126 and 129–32. See also, Postman, *Technopoly*, 117. See also, Jonas, *The Phenomenon of Life*, 110–11. Jonas describes how over time "servomechanisms" replace human functions and even humans begin to be described using mechanical language. This is similar to Bishop's critique of modern medicine that views the body as a functioning mechanism. See, Bishop, *The Anticipatory Corpse*, 293. See also, Cunningham, *Darwin's Pious Idea*, 219–20.

machine through the manipulation of natural materials and then ironically projects machine-like qualities back upon nature and mankind.[48]

The machine represents a marked break from the use of pre-industrial hand tools. Like the machine, primitive cultures used hand tools to create by drawing upon resources within the natural world. But unlike the machine, hand tools demand participation between the artisan and his or her medium, wherein the form and material of each particular medium limits the artist's capacity. The true artist is one with the tool in the act of artistic expression. Tim Ingold provides a beautiful picture of the cellist and his or her instrument whose boundaries collapse in the musical expression.[49] One might also think of the sculptor who uses a chisel to form a shapeless mass of marble into a stunning representation of the natural world. In this creative act there is a harmony between human and tool, human and medium. Here understanding and practice are inseparable as, "both the image of the projected form and the material artifact in which it subsequently comes to be embodied are independently generated and 'caught' within their respected intentional movements of imagination and practice."[50] The tool-using culture promotes harmony between humanity and nature.[51] Because they enrich the environment, hand tools constitute what Ivan Illich called, a "convivial society."[52] One finds a strong correlation between human participation with the natural world and notions of creativity.[53] Making (techné) is here conceived as nature creatively transforming itself, not as an unnatural or artificial human transformation of nature.[54] Over time man begins to slowly turn away from this harmonious union with nature. The "skill" of the craftsman is replaced by the "force" of the machine.[55] In this process these

48. See, Rossi, *The Birth of Modern Science,* 126. Rossi notes that humans are described as early as Descartes as machines. See also, Guardini, *Letters from Lake Como,* 110.

49. Ingold, *The Perception of the Environment,* 414.

50. Ibid., 418.

51. Guardini, *Letters from Lake Como,* 67–68.

52. Illich, *Tools for Conviviality,* 21–23 and 26. See also, Guardini, *Letters from Lake Como,* 78. Likewise Guardini notes that the pre-modern world "was sustained by human beings and in turn sustained them."

53. Northcott, *The Environment and Christian Ethics,* 270.

54. Ingold, *The Perception of the Environment,* 215. Illich, *Tools for Conviviality,* 21–23. Illich notes that hand tools enrich the environment whereas power tools externally manipulate it.

55. Ibid., 290–91. See also, 303 and 306. He describes the difference between tools as "skilled" and machines as "determining" systems. See also, Ingold, *Being Alive,* 6. The tool-using culture represents what Ingold calls the "intransitive relation" between image and object, as opposed to the "transitive" machine.

"convivial"[56] tools are slowly replaced by machines that harness the forces of nature directing it towards new ends.[57] With machines human thought is active, while action is passive.[58] External abstract concepts in the minds of men are applied to nature through the practical action of machines.[59] The integral relation of theory and practice maintained by tool using cultures is effectively sundered by the machine. As theory and practice begin to unravel, humans move away from a direct encounter with the natural world.[60] The modern machine operates outside of human control, thereby replacing the hand tools that were once merely an extension of the craftsman, connecting him or her to the medium. Ingold writes, "The image of the artisan, immersed with the whole of his being in a sensuous engagement with the material, was gradually supplanted by that of the operative whose job it is to set in motion an exterior system of productive forces, according to principles of mechanistic functions that are entirely indifferent to particular human aptitudes and sensibilities."[61] The human withdraws to the periphery of the productive process.[62] The machine literally sunders man and nature (think of the farmer sitting atop a massive harvesting mechanism). As the dichotomy between concept and execution widens (e.g., between architects and builders) true creativity is lost.[63]

In his, *Letters from Lake Como*, Romano Guardini illustrates the peril of life and culture in Northern Italy with the invasion of the machine,[64] which occurs when work is no longer done with direct participation as with hand

56. Illich, *Tools for Conviviality*, 107. Illich uses the metaphor of convivial tools being "crushed" by machines.

57. Guardini, *Letters from Lake Como*, 46, 48, and 71–72.

58. Ingold, *The Perception of the Environment*, 415. See also, 295 and 316. Ingold notes that modern technology divides knowledge and practice. Technology is concerned only with the external; it manipulates rationally. Whereas hand tools work with, internally, machines manipulate, externally.

59. Guardini, *Letters from Lake Como*, 20–23.

60. Illich, *Tools for Conviviality*, 51. For another example see, Ingold, *The Perception of the Environment*, 153–54. See also, Ingold, *Being Alive*, 10. Ingold compares what he calls the "poetic dwelling" perspective to that of "building." The dweller's world continually comes into being around him through incorporation into regular patterns of life as forms develop through the course of activities (e.g., the sculptor), while the builder constructs a world in consciousness before acting in it. Additionally, the building perspective sets the maker, "as the bearer of prior intention, over against the material world." The building perspective views the earth to be occupied not inhabited. An example of Ingold's building perspective is the machine.

61. Ingold, *The Perception of the Environment*, 295.

62. Ibid., 289.

63. Ibid., 295 and 316. See also, Guardini, *Letters from Lake Como*, 53.

64. Guardini, *Letters from Lake Como*, 5.

tools.[65] Guardini argues that the machine is neither human, nor natural, and thus, destroys both nature and human.[66] Richard Sennett's *The Craftsman* reflects upon his close interaction with a Greek bakery in Boston whose pride in baking is stripped by the mechanization of the baking process. No longer making physical contact with the bread, the bakers no longer know how to actually make bread. The computerized ovens distance its user from the product. Sennett argues that as craftsmanship and knowledge decrease today's bakers lose dignity in their craft.[67]

According to some the machine effectively displaces humanity.[68] Strong and Higgs note that, by reducing "ties to nature, culture, the household setting, a network of social relations, mental and bodily engagement, is taken over by the machinery . . . destroying most or all the relationships we once had in the world of things, devices completely change our lives."[69] Ivan Illich warns that in this way, a "tool can grow out of man's control, first to become his master and finally to become his executioner."[70] With the conquest of the machine, humans have withdrawn from nature and as such, the modern culture is now alien to nature, as things become more and more artificial and less and less human.[71]

All of this paints a picture of what Heidegger meant[72] when he warned of the "violence" of a new *technê* that interrogates and tortures nature

65. Ibid., 101.

66. Ibid., 73.

67. Sennett, *The Craftsman*, 64–75.

68. Fukuyama, *The Great Disruption*, 282.

69. Higgs, *Technology and the Good Life?*, 29–30.

70. Illich, *Tools for Conviviality*, 84. See also, Jonas, *The Phenomenon of Life*, 208. Jonas declares that, "if ever we entrust or resign ourselves wholly to the self-correcting machines of the interplay of science and technology, we shall have lost the battle for man."

71. Illich, *Tools for Conviviality*, 11–12.

72. Dreyfus, "Heidegger on Gaining a Free Relation to Technology," 97–107. Dreyfus argues that Heidegger's stance towards technology is ambiguous. Regardless of whether one can make a clear case for Heidegger's stance for or against modern technology, it is difficult to draw out anything positive he said about it. In light of Charles Taylor's contention that Heidegger's metaphysic lacked morals this is not a surprise. Good or bad, even Dreyfus agrees that Heidegger saw technology as an entirely new way of perceiving the world. As he writes, "the difficulty in locating just where Heidegger stands on technology is no accident. Heidegger has not always been clear about what distinguishes his approach from a romantic reaction to the domination of nature, and when he does finally arrive at a clear formulation of his own original view, it is so radical that everyone is tempted to translate it into conventional platitudes about the evils of technology. Thus Heidegger's ontological concerns are mistakenly assimilated into humanistic worries about the devastation of nature." Dreyfus concludes, that

(although for him, machines were morally neutral).[73] Heidegger, like Barfield, felt that the technological manipulation of nature was brought on by a unique epoch that was framed by a particular way of thinking (i.e., *Dasein*'s "temporality"). Heidegger talked of this "deprived time" of technological "obstruction" in terms of the subject's "enframing" or "*Gestell.*"[74] He argued that *technê* is not truth, but simply an appearance, another way of apprehending phenomena.[75] But, Heidegger, as previously suggested, went too far, as there must be some human culpability beyond mere passivity.[76] Nonetheless his reason for overcoming technology is of a piece with more recent critiques that regard technology as a "form" of making driven by a way of thinking.[77] In a similar vein, some linked the rise of this new form of *technê* with changes to ordinary language.[78] This ideology has been referred to as "pure idolatry"[79] and elsewhere a cultural "blindness" that only sees what the human wills.[80] According to Postman this ideology eventually took the form of a metaphysic[81] subsuming all forms of culture in its wake.[82] The

---

Heidegger's concern is not so much with the destruction of nature and culture, but the narrow-mindedness of the technological worldview. Heidegger saw technology as just another historical understanding that *Dasein* would eventually break free from, ushering in a new understanding of being, although he is unclear as to what kind.

73. Heidegger, *Introduction to Metaphysics*, 176 and 207. Heidegger refers to *technê* as "violence doing" or "knowing." See also, Northcott, "Concept Art, Clones, and Co-creators," 225–26.

74. Heidegger, *Poetry, Language, Thought*, xiii–xv. See also, Heidegger, *On the Way to Language*, 162.

75. Heidegger, *Poetry, Language, Thought*, 57.

76. Milbank, "The Thing That Is Given," 523–54. Milbank contends that Heidegger's concern with *technê* was that it represents a reduction of *poiēsis*; that is, making becomes merely the product of the subject's intentions. So, as with his theory of language traced in chapter 1, his response to technological "*Gestell*" is passive. As Milbank avers, "For once again the supreme poetic meaning is always the unconcealment of Being in beings—the arrival of a new epoch which is the work of a fate indifferent to human will, and which is only profound and resonant if it also discloses the nullity of Being as such." Against such passivity, again, a truly poetic making is by participation, which achieves harmony between human activity and passivity. See also, 530. Milbank notes that even though for Heidegger *technê* is bad, it is nonetheless, "fated and true."

77. O'Donovan, *Begotten Or Made?*, 3.

78. Illich, *Tools for Conviviality*, 85. See also, 89. Like Barfield, Illich locates this "corruption" in the linguistic shift from verbs to nouns.

79. Postman, *Technopoly*, 123–24. This idolatry may have an ideological agenda hidden from view, but it remains an expression of who we are. See also, 194. Postman wants to correct this by teaching on the relationship between language and reality.

80. O'Donovan, *Begotten or Made?*, 3

81. Ibid., 87.

82. Postman, *Technopoly*, 172. See also 52. Postman calls this a "technopoly," "the

new *technê* is a form of making that is entirely unnatural.[83] Accordingly the genealogy of modern science is a history of humanity's increasing confrontation with nature.[84]

These one-sided and rather critical interlocutors argue that the advance of the technological culture is promulgated by myths of "progress" and "freedom," which are integrally connected. As technology progresses freedom (from natural limitations) will increase.[85] Wendell Berry, in his *The Unsettling of America*, avers that the modern obsession with the future is based on a hope that science will gratify all of one's desires and solve all of one's problems.[86] Similarly, Strong and Higgs note that "people believe that technology has removed and can remove much, if not all, of the misery and toil that have plagued the human condition. Technology can reduce or eliminate darkness, cold, heat, hunger, confinement, and so on by bringing these harsh conditions of nature under control. Freedom from these conditions thus entails the conquest of nature."[87] Finally, Bruno Latour writes, "the natural sciences at last defined what Nature was, and each new emerging scientific discipline was experienced as a total revolution by means of which it was finally liberated from its prescientific past, from its Old Regime. No one who has not felt the beauty of this dawn and thrilled to its promises is modern."[88] This hope in the progress of science oftentimes carries eerily eschatological undertones. Such myths of salvation and progress deify the scientist.[89] Berry contends that these futurists desire that we might, "abandon ourselves to machines as people of faith abandon themselves to

submission of all forms of cultural life to the sovereignty of technique and technology." See also, 27, wherein he writes that in a technopoly, technology "attacks" culture. See also, 70–71. See also, Illich, *Tools for Conviviality*, 44. Illich notes that the illusion of technological progress subsumes all culture.

83. Northcott, "Concept Art, Clones, and Co-creators," 229. See also, Postman, *Technopoly*, 184–85. Postman notes that the one thing technology should never be understood as is natural. See also, Ingold, *The Perception of the Environment*, 289, 314, and 319. Ingold says that history is not one of complexification, but of externalization or objectification. See also, O'Donovan, *Begotten or Made?*, 8. O'Donovan describes the technological revolution as an attempt to escape or be free of natural limitations.

84. Postman, *Technopoly*, 198.

85. Postman, *Technopoly*, 35–36, and 117. Postman indicates that Francis Bacon linked scientific invention with "advancement" and "progress" and viewed science as a means to the improvement of the human condition and the happiness of man. See also, Guardini, *Letters from Lake Como*, 111.

86. Berry, *The Unsettling of America*, 57.

87. Strong and Higgs, "Borgmann's Philosophy of Technology," in Higgs, *Technology and the Good Life?* 27.

88. Latour, *We Have Never Been Modern*, 35.

89. Northcott, *The Environment and Christian Ethics*, 66–67.

God."[90] They see "the future as an earthly Heaven in which, by the miracles of technology, humans will usurp the role of God . . . ."[91] One author goes as far as to say that this view of progress is nothing more than a secularization of the Christian salvation story.[92] Promises of progress and freedom are the mythical waves upon which the technological culture rides.

To summarize, pre-modern making sought to imitate nature. Slowly a mechanical cosmos wherein nature is moved passively by some external forced supplanted the Aristotelian worldview. This new passive nature has no purpose of its own. As with gravity, an arbitrary human intention (or mechanical force) now moves nature, but unlike gravity this new human intention is driven by a desire for freedom and progress that alters the very nature (or purpose) of things. But has such altering of nature truly offered freedom? Like Barfield, the following interlocutors are keen to underscore the deleterious effects of technological manipulation.

Denatured Nature: Social Order, Morals, and Ecology

This subsection draws upon various interlocutors with views similar to Barfield in order to analyze the impact of modern technology upon society, morals, and the environment. As they see it, technology represents not an historical progress, but a "regress."[93]

These interlocutors believe that the negative effects of technology elude the modern consciousness.[94] One of the reasons for this is that technological advancement often exceeds the rate at which society is capable of adjusting to such demands.[95] Societies rarely display calculated resistance to technological advancement (e.g., the Amish). Technology adversely affects social relations in cultures that do not express such calculated resistance.[96] Some claim that the slide away from collectivism towards individualism traced in the previous chapter is indicative of a society's technological prowess. Statistics indicate that the more advance the technology, the more atomized the society. This indicates a strong link between negative freedom from social responsibility (as seen, e.g., in chapter 3) and the technological

90. Berry, *The Unsettling of America*, 78.

91. Ibid., 76–77.

92. Szerszynski, *Nature, Technology and the Sacred*, 146.

93. Northcott, *The Environment and Christian Ethics*, 50.

94. Illich, *Tools for Conviviality*, 30.

95. Fukuyama, *The Great Disruption*, 282.

96. For example, see, Ingold, *The Perception of the Environment*, 31 and 321. See also, Fukuyama, *The Great Disruption*, 6 and 12.

break from natural limitations. One is free to do as one pleases to fellow humans and nature.[97] Strong and Higgs note that the "irony of technology" is that while it claims to enrich one's life through consumption, it destroys the very engagement man once enjoyed with what they call "focal" things. Focal things (e.g., a fireplace) unify, while devices (e.g., "central" heating, ironically) divide and scatter.[98] Another author notes that technology contributes to "modern ills, including loneliness, narcissism, disempowerment, insecurity, stress, and alienation . . . ,"[99] while in a similar vein, Berry notes that modern man,

> assumes . . . that as a member of the human race he is sovereign in the universe. He assumes that there is nothing that he *can* do that he should not do, nothing that he *can* use that he should not use. His "success"—which at present is indisputable—is that he has escaped any order that might imply restraints or impose limits. He has, like the heroes of fantasy, left home—left behind all domestic ties and restraints—and gone out into the world to seek his fortune.[100]

In his *The Great Disruption* Francis Fukuyama links several statistics to the rise of technology and argues that

> as people were liberated from their traditional ties to spouses, families, neighborhoods, work places, or churches, they thought they could have social connectedness at the same time, this time the connections being those they chose for themselves. But they began to realize that such elective affinities, which they could slide into and out of at will, left them feeling lonely and disoriented, longing for deeper and more permanent relationships with other people.[101]

Due to the simple fact that one's individual freedom always conflicts with that of others, these societies find themselves "increasingly disorganized, atomized, isolated, and incapable of carrying out common goals and tasks."[102] Others aver that a world of free and autonomous individuals with conflicting morals (e.g., pluralism) does not in fact secure peace, but

97. Berry, *The Unsettling of America*, 79.
98. Strong and Higgs, "Borgmann's Philosophy of Technology," in Higgs, *Technology and the Good Life?*, 32.
99. Sclove, *Democracy and Technology*, 7.
100. Berry, *The Unsettling of America*, 53–54.
101. Fukuyama, *The Great Disruption*, 15.
102. Ibid.

actually destroys cultural coherence.[103] Additionally, political and spiritual traditions that unite cultures are cast aside by the myth of historical progress.[104] Hence, the irony of multiculturalism is that it ends up subjecting every culture to the "withering hegemony of cultural relativism and individual choice."[105] In this way technology seems to limit one's freedom rather than expand it.[106] It may be that this addiction to progress does not free, but actually enslaves people.[107] According to these critics, the unlimited sovereignty of modern science may provide a particular (negative) form of freedom to the individual, but this form of freedom necessarily alters the very relations that shape one's own individuality and the greater society. This also impacts man's relation to his environment. For the modern consumer "more" and surplus takes the place of the common good.[108] The logic is circular: such over-consumption creates scarcity, while this scarcity drives over-consumption. As more is produced, more is consumed, which creates the myth of scarcity, a world that is not naturally abundant. Driven by over-consumption, scarcity creates impoverishment and a widened gap of rich and poor. Complicating matters is the assumption that minorities should then be brought up to rich levels of consumption.[109] As Cavanaugh writes, "it is not simply the hunger of those who lack sufficient food to keep their bodies in good health. Scarcity is the more general hunger of those who

103. Postman, *Technopoly*, xii.

104. Ibid., 45 and 179.

105. Cavanaugh, *Being Consumed*, 67–68.

106. Sclove, *Democracy and Technology*, 3–4.

107. Illich, *Tools for Conviviality*, 84. See also, 9–10. Illich warned that either man controls technology, or it "enslaves" him.

108. Ibid., 94 and 98. See also, 74–75. In the modern world the "new" becomes the "better" and the "better" displaces the "good."

109. Ibid., 53, 60, and 68–73. For examples of modern overconsumption, excess waste, and environmental consequences see, Braungart and McDonough, *Cradle to Cradle*, chapter 4, "Waste Equals Food." The authors juxtapose natural making (from cradle back to cradle—where there is no waste) to unnatural making (from cradle to grave—where the earth becomes a graveyard full of unnatural waste).

want more, without reference to what they already have."[110] Not to mention the obvious ecological implications of over-consumption.[111]

Others have noted a connection between the ontological materialism of modern technology and the destruction of moral life.[112] Technological objectivity rejects morals precisely because they are not quantifiable.[113] When quality is evacuated from the cosmos even humans fall prey to objectification.[114] Modern injustices are a by-product of this materialist idolatry.[115] Fukuyama cites a range of statistics from "urban poverty to teenage pregnancy, child abuse, racism, the continued subordination of women, militarism, the marginalization of the elderly, high crime rates, and drug abuse."[116] Several have indicated a link between moral decline and the materialist denial of a transcendent narrative that binds things together.[117] One author describes this as the triumph of technology over cosmology.[118] Postman notes that when there is no transcendent sense of purpose or meaning uniting people there is no cultural coherence.[119] Northcott says that technology corrodes

110. Cavanaugh, *Being Consumed*, 90. For an excellent critique of the modern market's dependence upon the myth of scarcity see, chapter 4, "Scarcity and Abundance." Cavanaugh show that the assumption that through free-market competition one's consumption will feed another's is not true. In fact, the consumer's pursuit of low prices means lower wages for someone else. This individual consumerism breeds injustices. Against the idea of a consumerism based on scarcity, Cavanaugh offers the consummation of the Eucharist in terms of abundance. Cavanaugh remarks that a Eucharistic incorporation into the body of Christ overcomes individualism and passive consumerism, as individuals become food for others. The Eucharistic celebration breaks down social class and economic barriers and overcomes the fleeting eschatological hope of the free market by announcing the real presence of the kingdom. For Cavanaugh, one should not seek to gratify individualistic desires through consuming material goods, but rather, one's choices and ways of consumption should be directed by the *telos* of the human or common good.

111. Northcott, *The Environment and Christian Ethics*, 41.

112. Ibid., 36.

113. Postman, *Technopoly*, 90.

114. Northcott, *The Environment and Christian Ethics*, 110. See also, 254, where Northcott notes that materialism removes human value (e.g., abortion, sex trafficking, and child slavery).

115. Ibid., 190. See also, 258. Northcott avers that idolatry occurs when worship of consumer artifacts replaces the worship of God. See also, Postman, *Technopoly*, 13. See also, Berry, *The Unsettling of America*, 54. Berry notes that new world settlers saw creation not as something to respect, but "natural resources" to be used for purposes exterior to them, even human beings (i.e., slave trade).

116. Fukuyama, *The Great Disruption*, 15.

117. Postman, *Technopoly*, 83.

118. Ingold, *The Perception of the Environment*, 216.

119. Postman, *Technopoly*, 63.

religion, which is the very thing that nourishes society and nature.[120] He writes, "the scientific imposition of order on matter becomes the characteristically modern form of redemption, of transcendence. Radical disrespect, distrust and denial of any intrinsic beauty, goodness or truth in the original ordering of life itself is inherent in these technical procedures . . . there is no prior order which is deserving of ultimate respect."[121] Ultimately Guardini says, "technology . . . achieves an autonomy from divine command, from human community and from the natural order, eliminating moral value and spiritual significance along with natural necessity."[122] This sort of ontological materialism and consumerism destroy the religious life.[123]

In addition to its eschatological undertones, these interlocutors have argued that technological mastery is a secular enterprise that actually involves religious ways of thinking that are radically conditioned by Western society.[124] Szerszynski, in his *Nature, Technology and the Sacred*, refers to technology as the desacralization of nature,[125] or rather a reorganizing of the sacred[126] that was deeply influenced by theology.[127] Secularization is evident in the scientific transition from the superempirical to the empirical[128] that was modeled upon a Kantian paradigm that radicalized transcendence beyond this world,[129] wherein God is displaced and the cosmos is left to human agency.[130] This descralization endows science with the freedom to exercise power over nature. Man is now in charge of a nature that he externally re-orders.[131] Jonas summarizes this well:

> the indifference of nature also means that nature has no reference to ends. With the ejection of teleology from the system of natural causes, nature, itself purposeless, ceased to provide any sanction to possible human purposes. A universe without

120. Northcott, *The Environment and Christian Ethics*, 257.
121. Northcott, "Concept Art, Clones, and Co-creators," 230.
122. Northcott, *The Environment and Christian Ethics*, 257.
123. Guardini, *Letters from Lake Como*, 111.
124. Szerszynski, *Nature, Technology and the Sacred*, 7.
125. Ibid., 5 and 172.
126. Ibid., 26.
127. Ibid., 48.
128. Ibid., 12.
129. Ibid., 7.
130. Northcott, *The Environment and Christian Ethics*, 59.
131. Ibid., 218. See also, 57–58 and 71. See also, Szerszynski, *Nature, Technology and the Sacred*, 43. Nominalist and voluntarist ideologies lead to the modern scientific view of nature.

an intrinsic hierarchy of being, as the Copernican universe is, leaves values ontologically unsupported, and the self is thrown back entirely upon itself in its quest for meaning and value. Meaning is no longer found, but "conferred." Values are no longer beheld in the vision of objective reality, but are solely my own creation. Will replaces vision; temporality of the act outs the eternity of the good in itself.[132]

Jonas continues: in the mechanistic worldview

the universe does not reveal the creator's purpose by the pattern of its order, nor his goodness by the abundance of created things, nor his wisdom by their fitness, nor his perfection by the beauty of the whole—but reveals solely his power by its magnitude, its spatial and temporal immensity. For extension, or the quantitative, is the one essential attribute left to the world, and therefore, if the world has anything at all to tell of the divine, it does so through this property: and what magnitude can tell of is power. But a world reduced to a mere manifestation of power also admits toward itself—once transcendent reference has fallen away and man is left with it and himself alone—nothing but the relation of power, that is, of mastery . . . the will for power, the will to will.[133]

For these critics scientific worldviews are not free from theological prejudices. Worldviews such as materialism are a by-product of deism, which subordinates nature to supernature (or matter to mind), leaving a nature separated from God's purposes that is left for humans to master.[134] Indeed, the Protestant espousal of a predestined creation ruled by a transcendent sovereign Deity shares similarities with this vision.[135] The doctrine of the radical sovereignty of God aligns with the argument for the passivity of nature or matter. Deason notes that the Protestant, "understanding of natural things as passive recipients of divine power was entirely consistent with the mechanical philosophy."[136] Newton's physics were "consistent with the early Protestant and mechanist view that nature is completely passive

132. Jonas, *The Phenomenon of Life*, 214–15.

133. Ibid., 216.

134. Szerszynski, *Nature, Technology and the Sacred*, 17–18.

135. Ibid., 64. See also, 168. Szerszynski notes that such reformed deism pushes God out of the picture. See also, Northcott, *The Environment and Christian Ethics*, 259. See also, Rossi, *The Birth of Modern Science*, 133–35. Rossi links materialism and mechanism to deism and atheism.

136. Deason, "Reformation Theology and the Mechanistic Conception of Nature," 170–75.

and that God is the exclusive source of activity in the world."[137] Today these versions of God are still present, guised in various dogmas such as Intelligent Design and ultra-Darwinism.[138]

These strong points of convergence have led some, such as Lynn White Jr., to argue that the propagation of a Christian cosmology is responsible for the destruction of nature.[139] White argued that the concept of human "dominion" over the natural order grants freedom to humanity to rule over nature. Others have noted that the natural theology of the late eighteenth and early nineteenth centuries is predicated on the assumption that the fallen world is in need of physical transformation.[140] These theologians read the fall narrative quite literally. For them, dominion over nature is to be understood as the attempt to externally restore nature to a pre-lapsarian state of perfection.[141] From this perspective human labor is a negative repercussion of the fall. Man must now work by the sweat of his brow to restore creation. Work becomes a form of penance. Thus, the machine and technology are a blessing that not only works to physically restore creation, but also takes away literal "labor" pains.[142]

Although White may have been correct in his critique of particular Protestant proclivities, one must evoke the larger tradition to correct his theological misunderstandings. For example, White's claim against Christian dominion does not account for numerous biblical texts that speak of partnership with creation.[143] Willis Jenkins clarifies, yes, "human sin does introduce a kind of unruliness to the natural order, but not so pervasively as to undermine the integrity of creation or produce a cataclysmic change in the natures of other creatures,"[144] because even after the fall the integrity of creation still manifests the goodness of God. Jenkins renders a Thomistic ecology of "share" over that of dominion. "Not as coercive rule but as a sanctifying share in the pleasant labor of enjoying God from creation." In this view, "not only does God perfect humans through their special relation to

137. Ibid., 182.

138. Cunningham, *Darwin's Pious Idea*, 275–80.

139. Szerszynski, *Nature, Technology and the Sacred*, 31–32.

140. See, Szerszynski, *Nature, Technology and the Sacred*. See also, Northcott, *The Environment and Christian Ethics*, 219–21. Fallen nature with no sacred significance is exploited by outward transformation.

141. Harrison, *The Bible, Protestantism, and the Rise of Natural Science*, 230–35 and 249. See also, Berry, *The Unsettling of America*, 55.

142. Ovitt, "The Cultural Context of Western Technology," 490. See also, Gill, *Christianity and the Machine Age*, chapter 9, "The Leisure State."

143. Ovitt, *The Restoration Of Perfection*, 70.

144. Jenkins, *Ecologies of Grace*, 146–47.

creation; God perfects creation through its special relation to humanity."[145] Aquinas's idea of grace perfecting nature, brilliantly suspended between anthropocentrism and ecocentrism, refuses rivalry between humanity and natural world.[146] For Aquinas, argues Jenkins, perfecting the virtues is perfecting one's vulnerability to the world, one's intimacy with creatures.[147] Ecological harmony results when the human good does not threaten the good of other creatures.[148] Rather than enmity, communion between creature and Creator is what restores the original created order.[149] Aquinas sees that God invites "humans into a friendship shaped by their intimacy with all creation."[150] Jenkins concludes, "against the usual presupposition that grace threatens environmental concern, notice how a theological ('supernatural') virtue, contemplative charity, helps transform the rivalrous valence of the more mundane virtues into ecological friendship."[151] For Christian theology, humans are graced with a co-operative, participatory stewardship, not dominion.[152] The incarnation and resurrection are indicative of creation's goodness, which renders materiality as fundamentally good, a union of corporeal and incorporeal. The redemption of humanity coincides with the redemption of nature.[153] Similarly, Cavanaugh notes that in the Christian tradition, centered on the incarnation, "the material world is sanctified and charged with spiritual significance. The Christian is not meant to choose between God and the creation, because all of creation sings to the glory of God. In the catholic tradition especially, the sacraments show us how we encounter God in everyday material elements."[154]

The proper theological understanding of humanity's relation to nature is thus one of share and co-operation, not of dominion. This transforms the notion of labor as a form of penance. Theologically speaking, to regard work as a necessary repercussion of the fall is a form of Gnosticism, which denies

145. Ibid., 141.

146. Ibid., 148–49. For more on Aquinas's view of a co-operation between God and creatures see, Kerr, *After Aquinas*, 143.

147. Jenkins, *Ecologies of Grace*, 134–36. See also, 140. Jenkins speaks of a "liturgical intimacy with creation."

148. Ibid., 142.

149. Northcott, "Concept Art, Clones, and Co-creators," 231.

150. Jenkins, *Ecologies of Grace*, 150.

151. Ibid., 138.

152. Northcott, *The Environment and Christian Ethics*, 180.

153. Ibid., 208. See also, 202–3. Thus, restoration based on resurrection as sacrifice restores the created order. See also, 236, wherein, Northcott cites Hooker's cosmic incarnation, which changes the created order.

154. Cavanaugh, *Being Consumed*, 36.

the goodness of material labor. Because Adam worked before the fall one repercussion of sin is estrangement from the natural world and from human nature (a casting out of the garden). So from this perspective dominion is rather a consequence of sin, while stewardship a means of restoration.[155] In addition, the idea of the machine as an escape from labor actually reverses the "early Church doctrine [which] generally viewed free time as a temptation, leisure as an invitation to sloth."[156] As it turns out, the idea of the machine saving man from labor actually goes against the Christian view of labor as good, as a gift from God. It also denies the spiritual beneficence of manual labor, wherein work is not penance, but a way of controlling the flesh. For this reason, "[m]anual labor was esteemed by early Christians as a source of both material and spiritual sustenance."[157] The monastics used labor to purify, understanding it as beneficial, both spiritually and materially. John Paul II says, "Work is a good thing for man—a good thing for his humanity—because through work man not only transforms nature adapting it to his own needs, but he also achieves fulfillment as a human being and indeed, in a sense, is more a human being."[158] And according to Ovitt, "The legacy, then, of the first ascetics and the first monastic theorists favored manual labor, but always as a means to a spiritual end. Work was worship, but it was also a material precondition to prayer and a distraction easily surrendered."[159] Here sin is linked to materialism; the idolatry of believing one's life can be improved simply by material means.[160] From this perspective technology does not free man, but rather, it hinders the religious experience.[161] Northcott concludes that "it is not then simply a question of religious special pleading to suggest that the spiritual vacuum and the ecological crisis of modern civilization are closely related."[162] This

155. Ovitt, "The Cultural Context of Western Technology," 486–89.

156. Sennett, The Craftsman, 57.

157. Ovitt, "The Cultural Context of Western Technology," 490. See also, 492. Ovitt cites Augustine, "only those who labor and produce an excess of goods can be in a position to practice charity rather than to receive it." De opere monachorum, in PL 40, cols. 549–50.

158. Pope John Paul II, On Human Work [Laborem Exercens], 9.

159. Ovitt, The Restoration Of Perfection, 106. See, chapter 3, "Labor and the Foundations of Monasticism," for more examples of the monastic conception of labor. For further examples see, Venarde, The Rule of Saint Benedict, chapters, 35, 47, and 48.

160. Ovitt, "The Cultural Context of Western Technology," 493. See also, Northcott, The Environment and Christian Ethics, iii. Northcott outlines a biblical relation between the loss of morals and its adverse environmental effects.

161. Guardini, Letters from Lake Como, 111.

162. Northcott, The Environment and Christian Ethics, 37. See also, 316–17. Northcott calls the ecological crisis a moral crisis.

raises serious questions as to whether science alone is capable of addressing the ecological crisis.[163]

Overcoming Mechanism

How then must humanity overcome what Max Weber described as the "disenchantment" of the world?[164] The present interlocutors suggest that humanity must reconsider its relation to the natural order. This means to re-envisage the subject/object dualism that dominates modern culture. To overcome the present crisis requires a new way of thinking about humanity's stance toward nature.

Perhaps reaffirming the reality of natural forms may redirect the sort of radical subjectivity that gave rise to ecological issues.[165] Jonas recommends an ontology that relocates the ethical obligation not in the ego, but in the nature of being in general.[166] He states, "Only an ethics which is grounded in the breadth of being, not merely in the singularity or oddness of man, can have significance in the scheme of things."[167] Such a change may involve a theological re-orientation.[168] It is of utmost importance to remember that original abundance is a gift "not of our own making but that of the primordial maker."[169] This indicates that nature has a way it ought to be treated, which limits the scope of human making.[170] Man must learn to live "genuinely incarnational."[171]

More practically some have turned to primitive models in order to correct this paradigm. In his *The Perception of the Environment*, Tim Ingold

163. Fukuyama, *The Great Disruption*, 87–88. See also, Northcott, *The Environment and Christian Ethics*, 75. Northcott avers that Tocqueville found that materialism collapses society. See also, 37. Scientific narratives that fundamentally assume human behavior is above nature are incapable of changing human behavior toward nature. See also, Illich, *Tools for Conviviality*, 9. Illich has warned, "The attempt to overwhelm present problems by the production of more science is the ultimate attempt to solve a crisis by escalation."

164. Gerth and Mills, eds., *Max Weber*, 11.

165. Northcott, *The Environment and Christian Ethics*, 93.

166. Jonas, *The Phenomenon of Life*, 283. Jonas notes that originally ethics was always grounded in ontology. Accordingly, it was the divorce of ethics and ontology that revised the idea of nature.

167. Jonas, *The Phenomenon of Life*, 284.

168. Northcott, *The Environment and Christian Ethics*, 105.

169. Northcott, "Concept Art, Clones, and Co-creators," 234.

170. O'Donovan, *Begotten or Made?*, 12–13.

171. Northcott, *The Environment and Christian Ethics*, 319–21.

constructs a contemporary model of poetic dwelling by analyzing primitive practices.[172] Such a "perspective situates the weaver in amongst a world of materials, which he literally draws out in bringing forth the work."[173] In this paradigm the human is not set over against nature but poetically engages the world.[174] The human is attentive to nature. The maker does not impose his will but listens and sees the limits of each unique medium that ought not to be usurped.[175] Here, there is no sharp distinction between the natural and artificial. Again, the artificial is not a product of the domination of nature, but of its imitation.[176] Ignold notes that

> in the past there has been a tendency to write off such poetics as the outpourings of a primitive mentality that has been super-seded by the rise of the modern scientific worldview. My con-clusion, to the contrary, is that the scientific activity is always, and necessarily, grounded in a poetics of dwelling. Rather than sweeping it under the carpet, as an embarrassment, I believe this is something worth celebrating, and that doing so will also help us do better science.[177]

For Ingold there should be no sharp distinction between humans and na-ture.[178] Poetic making engages nature and is not detach from it.[179] Ingold critiques the notion of history as humans rising above nature (relations be-come one of "domination") and seeks to assuage this distance by offering a more primitive model.[180] He hopes to prevent humanity's further withdrawal

172. Ingold, *The Perception of the Environment*, 252. Ingold notes that research shows that the relationship between humans and nature is one of co-operation. See also, 189. He credits his theory to Heidegger's 1971 article, "Building, Dwelling, Think-ing." For more of Heidegger's influence on Ingold see, Ingold, *Being Alive*, 9–12. See also, 12 and 14. Ingold states that Maurice Merleau-Ponty influenced his idea of the body being weaved into the fabric of the world. This process is the creative trajectory of becoming, a self-surpassing "intwining," which constitutes the texture of the world. For an example of this in Heidegger see, Heidegger, *Poetry, Language, Thought*, xiii–xv.

173. Ingold, *Being Alive*, 10.

174. Ingold, *The Perception of the Environment*, 416.

175. Szerszynski, *Nature, Technology and the Sacred*, 177. Szerszynski remarks that in this view nature is not understood as an object, but a participant in dialogue.

176. Ibid., 153–54.

177. Ibid., 110.

178. Ibid., 314.

179. Ingold, *The Perception of the Environment*, 11 and 26. Ingold argues that in this view, there is no separation of mind and nature. See also, 15–16. Ingold states his desire, "to replace the stale dichotomy of nature and culture with dynamic of organism and environment, in order to regain a genuine ecology of life."

180. Ibid., 10.

from nature by engaging in an active participation with the environment.[181] Ingold's work is a particular example of a more general contemporary senti- ment among cultural critics who, like Barfield, have drawn upon primitive practices in their critique and questioning of the mechanistic worldview, which sets humans over and against nature.

This section began by showing how in the past human making (*technê*) was understood as subordinate to the natural order, albeit analogous. Over time natural forms, which limit the ends to which nature ought be utilized, migrate to the minds of men. Nature, now bereft of norms, is subject to the arbitrary imposition of the human will. A new mechanical cosmos emerges wherein passive matter is moved by external forces such as gravity. Man is now free to make what he wishes of a passive inert nature. Tools that once enriched the environment through an exchange of natural form and human ends gave way to machines that deny altogether natural form for the sake arbitrary human ends. Now *technê* no longer imitates *phýsis*, but alters its form promising to improve it. Such promises, at the cost of natural norms, echo eschatological undertones, which anesthetize the modern culture. Cultural critics have questioned the irony of such freedom by indicating a resultant slavery to technology that is evident in a social, moral, cultural, and ecological regress. In response, these critics want to re-envisage hu- manity's dominative stance toward nature by reexamining the philosophical and theological assumptions that drive this tendency. The opinions of these interlocutors provide a general context from which to approach Barfield's biases towards modern science and an impetus for rediscovering human- ity's proper poetic relation to nature.

Owen Barfield's Critique of Modern Science[182]

A Ubiquitous Disavowal of Materialism

To rehearse briefly, in the evolutionary history of consciousness Barfield identified a marked shift in sense perception. A large portion of his work explored the extent to which the participatory aesthetic is evident in past and present consciousness.[183] The evolution of consciousness is marked

181. Ibid., 218.

182. An earlier and abbreviated version of this section was presented in Kraków, Poland at the *Centre of Theology and Philosophy*'s "What is Life?" Conference in June of 2011.

183. Barfield, *Saving the Appearances*. His most popular work is entirely devoted to the evolution of the participatory worldview.

by the gradual decline of the participatory aesthetic, which he found evidence for in the evolutionary history of language. Past language is always metaphorical while literal or prosaic language (distinct from poetry) is only a late arrival in linguistic history. Barfield contends that over time the participatory aesthetic yields to a representational model that presupposes a division between subject and object. But Barfield wants to say that this evolution is not an ontological change, but more about a shift in epistemology, a reinterpreting of the aesthetic encounter through the lens of representation. As Barfield saw it, the modern social and physical sciences went awry by adopting this representational model. In doing so, these sciences presupposed a division between subject and object that jettisoned the real. As a result, the real is only today subconsciously known. Barfield believed that poetic diction, because it best represents reality, could invoke the modern consciousness to apprehend the phenomenal world as it actually is. This is coupled with a philosophical polemic against modern science for its explicit rejection of the participatory aesthetic.[184]

The present section begins with an overview of Barfield's polemic against modern science, which he argued, coincided with recent developments in quantum physics (examined in the close of the chapter). It is important to note that although Barfield constantly critiqued modern science, he was not opposed to science *tout court*, but only those methodologies that jettisoned the subjective (and therefore imaginative) element in the observational process (i.e., those that assume a purely objective gaze).[185] His work sought to underscore the adverse effects of this methodology.

Throughout Barfield's work one finds a sustained attack against the many "isms" used to describe the modern scientific worldview. His work is replete with pejoratives that he employs interchangeably such as mechanism, scientism, positivism, materialism, empiricism, and reduction; all of which denied the reality of inherent qualities, or what he, borrowing from Steiner, called "occult qualities."[186] As he saw it, this method was based on an erroneous subject/object dualism that sloughs off the participation aes-

184. Barfield, *Saving the Appearances*, 40. Barfield, *Romanticism Comes of Age*, 29. Barfield writes that modern science perceives, "everything included under the term Religion, Art, Culture and the like, [as] no more than an 'ideology'—a pale flickering reflection of purely physical and economic processes." See also, Barfield, *History, Guilt, and Habit*, 34, wherein he says, "the Scientific Revolution has played a prominent part . . . in strengthening and ingraining our present habit of perception . . . ." See also, Barfield, *Saving the Appearances*, 43, wherein he states that the attempt to exclude participation (what he refers to as "alpha-thinking") is embodied in the modern scientific endeavor to render phenomena more predictable and calculable.

185. Fulweiler, "The Other Missing Link."

186. Sugerman, *Evolution of Consciousness*, 23.

thetic. Although the modern worldview had been affected deeply by the scientific consciousness,[187] one must keep in mind that it is merely an epoch in the evolution of consciousness.[188] So regardless of its present supposed veracity, scientism is a "fallacy" that will neither work in the future nor relate to the past.[189] This is why Barfield claims he came to care less and less about whether science verified things or not.[190]

For Barfield, as with the previous interlocutors, science was trapped in the Cartesian mind, which posits a division between the *res extensa* and the *res cogitans*.[191] In his "Either: Or," Barfield argues that this is the fundamental principle upon which modern science rests.[192] Man is envisaged as detached from his surroundings[193] and set over and against a nature[194] with which he mixes as little as possible.[195] He sees this Cartesian dualism surfacing everywhere. He links it to positivism.[196] He coined the acronym "RUP" ("Residue of Unresolved Positivism"),[197] which he applied to any methodology that jettisoned what he held to be real qualities in the world.[198] In a similar vein, Barfield spoke out against materialism.[199] He called the materialism of "causality science" a "prison wall," a sad "mental habit" that cannot account for life, objects, people, facts, thinking, perception, etc.[200] He critiqued Francis Bacon who, by refusing to acknowledge the reality of

187. Barfield, *Saving the Appearances*, 53.

188. De Lange, *Owen Barfield*, 117. See also, Barfield, *Worlds Apart*, 182.

189. Barfield, *Worlds Apart*, 134.

190. Barfield, *Romanticism Comes of Age*, 7.

191. Barfield, "The Coming Trauma of Materialism," 117. Barfield explicitly blames Descartes's division of matter and mind for causing materialism.

192. Barfield, "Either: Or," 35.

193. Sugerman, *Evolution of Consciousness*, 78.

194. Barfield, *History, Guilt, and Habit*, 5. Also Barfield, *Saving the Appearances*, 55.

195. Barfield, *Poetic Diction*, 32. See also, Barfield, *Saving the Appearances*, 12. See also, Barfield, *History, Guilt, and Habit*, 5.

196. Sugerman, *Evolution of Consciousness*, 13.

197. De Lange, *Owen Barfield*, 92. De Lange notes that Barfield employed the term in a 1980 lecture at California State University.

198. Barfield, *Worlds Apart*, 206. Therein, Barfield says positivism is incompatible with religion in general, and more specifically, with Christianity, precisely because it denies incarnation. See also, Barfield, *Poetic Diction*, 194. Barfield indicates that mechanical "determinism" denies the theological. See also, De Lange, *Owen Barfield*, 250–51.

199. Barfield, "The Coming Trauma of Materialism." He argued that positivism was anti-theological. See also, De Lange, *Owen Barfield*, 20–21. De Lange mentions that Barfield was "miserable" for "being caged in the materialism of the age." He sought to cure his depression by finding beauty in nature.

200. Barfield, *History, Guilt, and Habit*, 73–74 and 82.

anything but matter, did not understanding Aristotle.[201] On several occasions he speaks out against reductive science and Humean empiricism for assuming that if a microscope were powerful enough one could see what was really there.[202] Against this he argued that microscopes are incapable of seeing form, shape, or anything qualitative.[203] Better technology is not the answer, what is required is the creative imagination.[204] His stance against RUP and his critique of such reductive methodologies indicate why the work of those such as Steiner, Coleridge, and Lévy-Bruhl were so important to him.[205] One might say that his entire literary endeavor was aimed at ridding the world of RUP by overcoming the passive intellect by way of an invocation of the imagination.

Barfield often critiqued the mechanical consciousness. As he saw it, over time the pre-modern priority of determining the sense world from the inner is reversed.[206] The inner (if it is now ever acknowledged) is now determined from the outer.[207] As a result, a modern person sees only that which is "external."[208] In this vein, he described Newtonian physics as, "one lifeless body acting on another from a distance."[209] He argued that as this new cosmos emerged (which elsewhere he refers to as a "detached" system of matter and forces that proceeds mechanically)[210] modern man began to view the universe as a mechanism governed by a sort of abstract causality.[211] This

201. Barfield, *Romanticism Comes of Age*, 72–74. See also, Barfield, *History, Guilt, and Habit*, 5 and 33.

202. Barfield, *Poetic Diction*, 18–19.

203. Barfield, *Worlds Apart*, 143. See also, Barfield, *History, Guilt, and Habit*, 12–13 and 16.

204. Barfield, *Poetic Diction*, 28.

205. Sugerman, *Evolution of Consciousness*, 16–17. I have here added Lévy-Bruhl.

206. Gerson, *Aristotle and Other Platonists*, 32–33. Barfield's observation is supported by Gerson who argues that both Plato and Aristotle agree that materialists and atomists are their true opponents. For the Greeks the essence of a physical phenomenon is not found in its elementary particulars, because for them it is an ontological reality that the intelligible whole (essence) always precedes the sensible particulars.

207. Barfield, *Poetic Diction*, 189–90. See also, Barfield, *What Coleridge Thought*, 139. This is why Barfield was attracted to Coleridge's polarity, because it rejects mere "outness."

208. Barfield, *Poetic Diction*, 164.

209. Barfield, *History in English Words*, 142–43. See also, 160. See also, Barfield, *Poetic Diction*, 137. Barfield was similarly critical of Bacon for applying mechanistic principles to nature.

210. Barfield, *History in English Words*, 191–92. See also, Barfield, *Romanticism*, 37. See also, Barfield, *Saving the Appearances*, 94.

211. Barfield, *History in English Words*, 188.

occurs when causality, which was once linked with God, becomes abstract and reduced to laws.[212] Once this move is complete what one is left with is a science that simply observes the natural law only in its effects, a science that deals exclusively with the external, "static part of nature—the mineral, the inorganic, the dead."[213]

He also spoke out against the rapid advance of technology and of how modern man's technological stance is oblivious to the teleological ordering proposed by Aristotle.[214] In his *History in English Words* he clearly distinguishes between divine and human making (*ex nihilo*, versus merely human making that works with pre-existent matter), which he describes in terms of "the imitation of 'creatures.'"[215] Once man begins to impart his own meaning into the cosmos[216] human art begins to dominate the natural world.[217] Modern man, tempted by technological materialism,[218] attempts to "save the appearances"[219] by making idols of ostensibly "material" static objects.[220] In this technological world nature does man's bidding.[221] He shows an awareness that human detachment from the world was driven by the technological promises of freedom.[222] Indeed, at least one author has used Barfield to critique Information Technology; an extension and furthering of the division between man and world inaugurated years ago by the scientific consciousness.[223] In his *Worlds Apart*, Burgeon (a character said to represent Barfield) describes the rapid advance of technology as a man "monkeying" from without rather than striving from within. He attributes this "cosmic masturbation" to modern physics.[224] Barfield maintained that while this obsession with materiality can increase "understanding" and "increase

212. Ibid., 187–88.

213. Ibid., 44.

214. Barfield, *Saving the Appearances*, 143.

215. Barfield, *History in English Words*, 202.

216. Barfield, *Saving the Appearances*, 127.

217. Ibid., 129.

218. Adey, *C. S. Lewis' Great War*, 29.

219. Barfield, *Saving the Appearances*, 49 and 51. Barfield says that scientists concoct false propositions or hypotheses to "save the appearances" and then presume their theories to be identical with the truth.

220. Ibid., 142. See also, Barfield, *Poetic Diction*, 18. Barfield accused the empirical sciences of "manipulating" matter and "carting it to and fro" treating its ever-changing functions as "given."

221. Barfield, *Saving the Appearances*, 56.

222. Barfield, *History in English Words*, 193.

223. Talbott, *The Future Does Not Compute*.

224. De Lange, *Owen Barfield*, 253–54.

true opinion," it can never increase true "knowledge."[225] Science works fine for purely technological purposes, but it can say nothing about the living or the qualitative.[226] In two telling analogies Barfield accuses modern science of obtaining what he calls "dashboard knowledge,"[227] wherein he likens the universe to a motorcar, whose driver, by "pushing and pulling" levers, discovers an "operative knowledge" of the universe, but fails to realize higher principles that cannot be discovered by tangible experiments. He laments,

> the physicists and all those concerned with the development of our technological civilization . . . are continually (because it is their business) tampering with, interfering with, investigating with a kind of curiosity—and of which they have no real control; which is indeed in danger of getting out of control, as we know all too well.[228]

He depicts the uninhibited advance of science in *The Silver Trumpet*, wherein the heroine "Princess Violet," who represents the affective and aesthetic side of life, is literally scared to death by her cynical sister, "Princess Gamboy," who coerces her naïve servant to enter Violet's room disguised as a large "mechanical" toad.

225. Barfield, *Poetic Diction*, 144. Herein, he also states, regarding this obsession with materiality, that "in no sense can it be said to expand consciousness." See also, Barfield, *What Coleridge Thought*, 24. Barfield criticizes science of knowing nothing of nature due to abstraction.

226. Barfield, *Worlds Apart*, 89.

227. Barfield, *Saving the Appearances*, 55. To summarize Barfield's motorcar analogy: if a clever boy was placed inside a car and asked to push and pull the levers he would eventually be able to drive the car, but he does not *know* the car. He simply has what Barfield calls an "operative knowledge" of the car based on his "empirical acquaintance" with the dashboard and pedals. This is an entirely different from the type of knowledge attained by someone who has studied internal combustion or has studied mechanics. "It seems that, if the first view of the nature of scientific theory is accepted, the kind of knowledge aimed at by science must be, in effect, what I will call 'dashboard-knowledge.'" See also, Barfield, *Poetic Diction*, 23–24, for his parable of the motorcar. Therein he likens the Universe to a motorcar in which humanity travels. In the attempt to understand how the car worked two groups emerged: those who were interested in invisible things like internal combustion, and those who push and pull the tangible levers on the dashboard. Because they are unable to be pushed or pulled, the latter group finds concepts like "internal combustion" meaningless. This same group eventually comes to believe that "pushing and pulling" is not simply a means to knowledge, but knowledge itself. They push and pull the big levers, then the small, and eventually all the effects seemed to act as accelerators. This causes things to advance at dangerously high speeds, while the second group sits back thinking that perhaps their knowledge might become useful after the crash.

228. Barfield, "The 'Son of God' and the 'Son of Man,'" 260.

Barfield also issued harsh warnings about the ecological consequences of modern science. At a July 1985 BDAA conference he spoke out against deforestation, pollution, chemical sprays, and factory farming, linking them to positivism. His work is riddled with genealogies of the technological destruction of nature. In *Poetic Diction* he goes as far as to say that Hiroshima is a result of an atomic tinkering with the world.[229] His *Romanticism Comes of Age* is dedicated to assisting England in evoking the imaginative soul to overcome the destruction of the scientific spirit.[230] De Lange notes that Barfield "leads a person in our modern times to stand against the pervading trend of scientific reductionism or materialism, against a non-spiritual view of the world, and of man's place in it."[231] Barfield sternly warned,

> It is no longer enough that the occasional artist here and there should see his parcel of truth and speak it out, while the actual direction taken by civilization continues to be wholly determined by a *soi-distant* scientific method of knowledge. Science must itself become an art, and art a science; either they must mingle, or Western civilization, as we know it, must perish, to make room for one that may have spirit enough to learn how to know God's earth as He actually made it.[232]

What's more, nearly all of his fiction narratives vividly display what he refers to as the technological "rape of nature." This is nowhere more clear than in his *Eager Spring: One Story, Two Tales*, written when he was nearly ninety, which conveys that "there is something profoundly wrong about man's present destruction and parasitic relationship to the earth . . . ."[233] The protagonist, Virginia, is deeply concerned with the advance of technology (i.e., "technological assault"—e.g., pesticides, antibiotics, chemicals in food, factory farming, hormones, genetic engineering, herbicides, packed food, pollution, the exporting of trash to third world countries, etc.). In her attempt to stop the devastation Virginia falls ill when she inhales a "toxic agent" and leaves behind only a *märchen*, which is depicted as a prophetic warning of the devastation to come. Her tale traces the rise of the Iron Age and the increasing loss of humanity's ability to see the "inside" world. The ironsmiths are eager to subsume a land still unindustrialized, but their twisted plan to obtain the land is eventually thwarted only when the dam containing the "Eager Spring" collapses, extinguishing the fires of the indus-

229. Barfield, *Poetic Diction*, 36.
230. Barfield, *Romanticism Comes of Age*, 63–64.
231. De Lange, *Owen Barfield*, 77.
232. Owen Barfield, *Romanticism*, 50.
233. De Lange, *Owen Barfield*, 105–7.

trial age. The Eager Spring represents Barfield's hope that the romantic spirit (the imagination) would overcome the deleterious effects of alpha thinking.

In a similar vein, his *The Rose on the Ash-Heap*, a short story also written in the *märchen* genre, traces the westward journey of the protagonist "Sultan" into the land of "Abdol." Sultan's journey west is one into further and further "solitude" in his search for "Lady," who represents the spirit of romanticism Sultan once lost. When he arrives in the west he discovers the "ash-heap," a symbol of the antagonist Abdol's dominion, whose penchant for materialism has entirely disenchanted the world. All that is left in Abdol's wake is dark sexual perversion, carnivals ("fairs"), market economies[234] in which only money has value, commerce, slavery, monopolies, machines that displace manual labor, ecological disaster, trash heaps, factories bellowing smoke and soot, and humans entirely bereft of love, knowledge, and imagination who are only capable of analytic discourse. But on the ash-heap glimmers the "rose," a symbol of the romantic spirit. Lying below the ash-heap Sultan discovers the "Ringmaster" whose realm cannot be purchased by Abdol. Here Sultan, reunited to the romantic spirit and friends, the Philosopher and the Poet, overcomes the abysmal reign of Abdol.

Finally, in his *Night Operation*, Barfield depicts a morally deprived future where humans, who now live in sewers, are only defined in terms of their biological function. Humans, completely cut off from the "Aboveground" of nature, live in a world dominated by what Barfield calls the "3E's of excretion": "ejaculation," "defecation," and "eructation." The story, remarks Jane Hipolito, is a "profoundly informed, lucid, and forceful critique of the main trends in contemporary culture."[235] "If the continuity of Western civilization is to be preserved, we need fresh creative thinking, the power to create fresh forms out of life itself, that is to say, out of the part of Nature which is still coming into being, the Spiritual World."[236]

It should now be obvious that Barfield believed this particular gaze had seriously endangered the planet.[237] The habit of projecting upon nature what it ought to be must change. One should not stand above nature (as with mechanism), nor be passively determined by it (e.g., Heidegger's agnostic stance toward the technological epoch), but rather one should stand in poetic harmony with nature. "It is only by the pursuit and application of knowledge [of the participatory aesthetic] that man can hope to live in

---

234. For his critique of modern economics see, Barfield, *Romanticism Comes of Age*, 49–50.

235. Barfield, *Night Operation*, ix. See the "Introduction."

236. Barfield, *Romanticism Comes of Age*, 45.

237. Barfield, *History, Guilt, and Habit*, 83–92.

harmony with nature, . . . to live in harmony with the unconscious depth of his own being."[238] This is why Barfield insists that a change of the outer world requires a change of consciousness (i.e., the presupposed aesthetic by which one lives). Such an approach does not "tinker" with the outside world, but changes it from within.[239] In this vein he often employed Goethe as an exemplar who saw quality as well as quantity.[240] He challenged scientists to become artists. The scientist must learn to seen the inner as well out the outer, to see the inner presuppositions which drive his outer ambitions.

Barfield's metaphysical realism is roughly Platonic and/or Aristotelian.[241] His admiration of Plato is evident in his own words and his scrupulous notes.[242] He says that the Platonic desire for sensual temporal objects initiates a "gradual metamorphosis" into a love for that which lies beyond the material, to the immaterial and eternal.[243] For Plato, universals are not abstract. It was the followers of Aristotle's categories that would first concentrate on the abstract qualities of universals.[244] Barfield called nominalism an "inveterate habit of thought which makes it so extraordinarily hard for Western man to grasp the nature of inspiration,"[245] which is not just about "classifying abstractions in the minds of men,"[246] but denying the reality of being.[247] This is a marked shift from the Greeks, who viewed nature as really

238. Barfield, *Poetic Diction*, 33.

239. Barfield, *History, Guilt, and Habit*, 92.

240. De Lange, *Owen Barfield*, 114.

241. In Barfield's, *Worlds Apart*, the dialogue takes the form of a Platonic dialogue as Burgeon (the interlocutor—who represents Barfield) plays the role of Socrates. See also, Barfield, *History in English Words*, 102, wherein Barfield calls Plato the consummate Greek philosopher.

242. See, "Owen Barfield Papers," "*Herclitus, Plato, Aristotle*," *Notes on Classical and Modern Philosophers*, 1950s–60s, Dep. D, 946. Barfield had a large notebook wherein he wrote detailed notes on several Platonic dialogues (*The Republic, Theaetetus, Gorgias, Protagoras, Sophist, Philebus*, and *Timaeus*) and some of the works of Aristotle (*De Anima* and *Ethics*), all of which were hand-written in Greek.

243. Barfield, *History in English*, 103.

244. Barfield, *Poetic Diction*, 95. See also, 105–9. Barfield says that with Aristotle the idea of inner and outer world developed. This coincided with the development of logic and analytic thought, which ultimately resulted in the separation of science and theology. See also, Barfield, *History in English Words*, 103–9 and 131.

245. Barfield, *Poetic Diction*, 204.

246. Ibid., 94–95.

247. Barfield, *Saving the Appearances*, 33–34. Barfield draws upon Lévy-Bruhl's "mystic" participation, "in which 'mystic' implies belief in forces and influences and actions, which though imperceptible to sense, are nevertheless, real." See also, Barfield, *History in English Words*, 103. Barfield remarks on the Greek conception of matter as an imperfect type of "ideas." These are not mere abstractions but the only real beings; that

living in a sort of becoming, a flux, or a blossoming. Those that accepted nominalism were the "forerunners" of the scientific revolution.[248] In failing to ask how perhaps spirit (or form) relates to nature and by reducing these real relations to abstract "laws of nature," the "flux" of nature is reduced to a static, motionless, and dead or rather pure nature.[249] Nature's inherent freshness is lost.[250] Eventually, modern man begins to conceive unity only as an "idea."[251] The nominalist denial of unity prompted Barfield to accuse natural science of what he called "that terribly obsessive, and terribly contemporary, fallacy which supposes that we must only distinguish things that we are also able to divide."[252] According to Barfield, this mental habit is the direction taken by modern science, which concentrates attention on smaller and smaller units of hormones, neurons, genes, molecules, atoms, etc., assuming reduction to be the only direction in which knowledge may advance.[253] Barfield remarks that, "however impressive may be the practical justification for this atomic obsession, there is no evidential justification whatever for the conclusion, or rather the assumption, to which it so often leads, namely that the parts precede the wholes . . . ."[254] Barfield argued that modern science "is losing its grip on any principle of unity pervading nature as a whole and the knowledge of nature."[255] In a disenchanted,[256] "dis-godded"[257] age of representation, "mere perception . . . is the sword thrust between spirit and matter."[258] Nominalism is a lack of the imagination that jettisons the "concrete experience," which demands unity.[259] The fatal flaw of science, then, is that it actually *eliminates its object*, for without the imagination one cannot apprehend *the whole*, the unity of the object. One is left only to perpetually reduce phenomena to their constituent parts.

---

is, they are eternal, both existing before, and remaining after, matter.

248. Barfield, *Saving the Appearances*, 91.

249. Barfield, *Romanticism Comes of Age*, 38–44. See also, 156–57, wherein Barfield cites Coleridge's critique of atomic philosophy as a "philosophy of death." By denying the fundamental unity of all things, atomism beholds only a dead nature.

250. Barfield, *Poetic Diction*, 174. See also, Barfield, *Romanticism Comes of Age*, 71.

251. Barfield, *Romanticism Comes of Age*, 86.

252. Barfield, *History, Guilt, and Habit*, 12.

253. Ibid., 12–13.

254. Ibid., 13.

255. Barfield, *Saving the Appearances*, 145.

256. Ibid., 51.

257. Ibid., 130.

258. Barfield, "Matter, Imagination, and Spirit," 149.

259. Barfield, *Poetic Diction*, 25.

The mind can never see the object without the imagination.[260] In order to perceive an object the imagination must first combine *disjecta membra* (scattered members) of unrelated percepts into the unity that constitutes the object.[261] Nominalism simultaneously fails to bracket the external and ignore the internal, because they are not mutually exclusive. The result is that ontologically, "science can give nothing; it can only classify what is there already and re-arrange somewhat its component parts,"[262] while real being is left unaccounted for.[263] For Barfield the poetic element is of vital importance precisely because it holds in tension the aspects of the physical sciences (matter) as well as those things often ignored by the sciences (spirit).[264] In light of this, Barfield desired to re-appropriate a worldview whereby man envisioned himself participating as part of the whole spiritual and physical world.[265] He discovered that as far back as one could know, human consciousness did not simply perceive material. The mind actually perceives an immaterial expressed by, or within, the material.[266]

260. Ibid., 25–27. See also, 35. He calls this an "objectified nothing," which scientism assumes is the base of the phenomenal world.

261. Ibid., 27–28. Herein Barfield seeks to resolve the subject/object duality in hopes of enriching modern man's conception of the world.

262. Barfield, *Romanticism Comes of Age*, 44.

263. Ibid., 47. Here, the reader is reminded of the motor-car analogy where the scientist, by pushing and pulling levers, "can understand what is at rest and what has become and [he] can deal with it as never before; but when [he tries] to grasp what is in motion or alive, [he] merely gibbers fantasies in a vacuum hermetically sealed from the truth." See also, Ardley, *Aquinas and Kant*. In an interview found here: https://www.youtube.com/watch?v=oedVDN1xOWM Barfield claims that it was Ardley's book from which he first learned the phrase "saving the appearances"—for Ardley this is to deny the real (231)—and by which his "mental world seemed to crystalize" resulting in what would eventually become *Saving the Appearances*. Ardley's critique of modern physics is based on a strong metaphysical realism that he gleans from Plato, Aristotle, and Aquinas. Ardley argues that modern "physics does not deal with the real world at all" (45). It belongs to the "categorical" and not the "real" (53).

264. See, Barfield, "Either: Or" and Barfield, "Matter, Imagination, and Spirit," 150. Science must not deal with mere perception if it is ever to move beyond matter. Herein Barfield also indicates that it is not so much what we see, but the manner in which we look.

265. Barfield, *History, Guilt, and Habit*, 60. Barfield's vision is similar to that of Jonas. See, Jonas, *The Phenomenon of Life*, xxiii. In the "Preface" Jonas writes, "scientific biology, by its rules confined to the physical, outward facts, must ignore the dimension of inwardness that belongs to life: in so doing, it submerges the distinction of 'animate' and 'inanimate.' A new reading of the biological record may recover the inner dimension—that which we know best—for the understanding of things organic and so reclaim for the psychophysical unity of life that place in the theoretical scheme which it had lost through the divorce of the material and mental since Descartes."

266. Barfield, *History, Guilt, and Habit*, 46. See also, 44. Barfield indicates that all

Barfield's polemic accentuates his want to re-appropriate his realist metaphysic in an epoch saturated by representational epistemology. What Barfield shares with the various interlocutors is a deep conviction that to treat nature as an objective means to a subjective end is fraught with adverse consequences. According to Barfield, modern science alone is incapable of reversing this trend so long as it continues to follow the representational model. As it turned out, later developments in physics revealed that it was not entirely correct.[267] These discoveries gave Barfield hope that science itself had begun to unveil its own inadequacies by calling into question its claims to objectivity.[268] Accordingly, Barfield questioned the very language of objectivity employed by science, asking if it is not the poetic element, the employment of metaphors that made conscious space for new discoveries in science?[269] He believed that even scientific language was inherently poetic. What's more, Barfield found an ally in the physical sciences. Quantum theorist David Bohm was busy re-envisaging the subject/object dualism and mechanistic cosmology that Barfield was fighting to overturn.

An Ally in the Enemy's Camp: Quantum Theorist David Bohm

In light of the aforesaid, it seems rather ironic that an advocate would emerge from the very field of which Barfield was so critical. But, as Barfield saw it, quantum theorists were allies inside the enemy's camp subtly disintegrating the very foundations upon which modern science stood.[270] In fact, quantum theorist David Bohm (1917–92),[271] an acquaintance[272] of Barfield's, a

words have an immaterial and material reference. See also, 46–47. Wherein, he states, "The outer and material is always, and of its own accord, the expression or representation of an inward and immaterial" reality.

267. Barfield, *History, Guilt, and Habit*, 89.

268. Ibid., 82. To do this of course, scientists would have to employ the imagination.

269. Barfield, *Speaker's Meaning*, 44–47. Barfield explicitly cites Newton's metaphorical use of "gravity," who in so doing, "succeed[ed] in making a word mean 'more than it is as yet recognized' to mean," by breaking from the aforementioned Aristotelian cosmology.

270. For example, "action-at-a-distance" undermined mechanistic assumptions, the discovery of quantum "fields" or "entanglement" challenged atomism, and the "uncertainty principle" compromised modern science's claims to materialism and objectivity.

271. See Bohm, "Interview with Physicist David Bohm."

272. Bohm contributed an article in a tribute to Barfield's seventy-fifth birthday. See, Bohm, "Imagination, Fancy, Insight, and Reason in the Process of Thought." See also, De Lange, *Owen Barfield*, 132. Therein, De Lange indicates that Barfield and Bohm corresponded from 1971 to 1976, and there is some evidence this continued

past student of Oppenheimer, and a colleague of Einstein, questioned the orthodox stance of modern physics. According to Bohm, positivist and empiricist attitudes hindered the progress of quantum theory by creating students with closed minds.[273] Eerily similar to Barfield, Bohm argued that because of this, "modern science (at least as this is now commonly defined) cannot address itself directly to the deepest dimensions of human reality. . . . [M]odern science, with its instrumentalist and positivist bias, tends at least tacitly to devalue these dimensions, by denying them any reality except in some abstract, insubstantial and therefore implicitly unimportant kind of mental or spiritual domain."[274] The following highlights the significance of Bohm's contributions to modern physics as they relate to Barfield's poetic philosophy.

Until the 1920s Newtonian[275] physics taught that the universe was a self-equilibrating mechanism whose reductive parts are determined by external laws of nature.[276] However, in the 1920s and 1930s, the work of various theoretical physicists, particularly Niels Bohr, questioned the validity of solid objects that are governed by mechanistic laws of nature.[277] As it turned out, quantum observations revealed an underlying "wholeness" or "entanglement" such that the world could no longer be reduced to a collection of independent objects that only act upon one another externally.[278] Following this development, years later David Bohm published *Quantum Theory* (1951), a book that was well received by Einstein and had much in common with the work of Bohr. But over time Bohm became dissatisfied

---

until 1982. See also, Barfield's mention of Bohm in the "Acknowledgements" of Barfield, *What Coleridge Thought*, xi.

273. Schindler, *Beyond Mechanism*, 150–51.

274. Ibid., 132.

275. The use of "Newtonian" is meant to maintain a distinction between Newton and Newtonians who associate Newton with a purely mechanical worldview. Newton himself was not a staunch mechanist, as implied by later Newtonians. For example, with gravity the relationship between two planets simply cannot be reduced to efficient causality or mechanism. Newton's theory of gravity proved "action at a distance" (which he admittedly overlooked) was a real force, which posed serious doubts to the mechanistic cosmology. Barfield is also well aware of this, as addressed in Barfield, *Worlds Apart*, 128–29. For further reading see, Bechler, *Newton's Physics* and Freudenthal, *Atom and Individual in the Age of Newton*.

276. Schindler, *Beyond Mechanism*, 21. David Bohm himself points out that the essential point of mechanism is that objects are understood as externally related.

277. Böhm, "Unremitting Contest," 10.

278. For a concise summary of the history of the demise of the reductive approaches following the discoveries of quantum physics see, Polkinghorne, "The Demise of Democritus," 1–14. For the Einstein-Bohr debate over quantum mechanics see, Bub, "The Entangled World," 15–31.

with a particular aspect of the classical quantum theory which he makes clear in his final posthumous publication in 1995 titled, *The Undivided Universe: An Ontological Interpretation of Quantum Theory.*[279]

What distinguished Bohm's theory from that of Einstein and Bohr was that Bohm attempted to overcome what he deemed a residual mechanism left in the wake of Newtonian physics, which he argued was still being subtly employed in quantum mechanics.[280] In classical quantum mechanical theory the quantum force carries energy or intensity that pushes particles around.[281] Bohm argued that these prior theories were incomplete because they ignored the obvious "non-locality" of particles[282] (e.g., experiments revealed that when one particle is disturbed this force is somehow instantaneously—beyond space/time[283]—transmitted to another non-local particle).[284] For Bohm, this went far to indicate that there was more than simple external force and relative space governing causality. Thus, in every observed phenomena or measured object there is an obvious connection that was being ignored, despite experimental results. Indeed, the most renowned physicists were aware of this. Newton referred to non-locality as "philosophical absurdity," while Einstein referred to it as "spooky."[285] According to Bohm, this intentional ignorance—inaugurated by Newton's admitted rejection of formal causality—represents a paradigm that developed in modern science that sought to overcome primitive superstitions in which

279. Bohm and Hiley, *The Undivided Universe.*

280. Schindler, *Beyond Mechanism,* 16–18. Bohm notes that Einstein's "fields" (and relativity) theory did not entirely shed mechanism as overall the cosmos was still viewed mechanically. "Nevertheless, the field approach was still an important step away from the mechanistic worldview, even though it remained within the general framework of this kind of view."

281. Schindler, *Beyond Mechanism,* 19 and 149. Bohm notes that quantum theory overcomes mechanism much better than the theory of relativity because it identifies the dual nature of particles manifesting as wave or particle. Depending on how they are observed, they behave "interchangeably." This is precisely not mechanical and much more like a living organism. Accordingly, quantum wholeness is much closer to the organic unity of living being than that of putting together parts of a machine.

282. Schindler, *Beyond Mechanism,* 19. Action at a distance goes against locality of connection of mechanism.

283. Bohm and Hiley, *The Undivided Universe,* xi.

284. Ibid., 136 and 352. See also, 203. "The essential point is that in an independent disturbance of one of the particles, the field acting on the other particle . . . responds instantaneously even when the particles are far apart. It is as if the two particles were in instantaneous two-way communication exchanging active information that enables each particle to 'know' what has happened to the other and respond accordingly."

285. Ibid., 157.

non-locality played a part.[286] Bohm argued that this obvious non-locality was continually being ignored in order to "save the appearances"[287] in the name of objectivity. For Bohm, this methodology was predicated on an errant epistemology that intentionally ignored a richer underlying reality implicit in the observed phenomena.[288] So instead of writing off this obvious inconsistency in quantum theory, Bohm attempted to incorporate an ontological level of reality (what he referred to as "wholeness") into his theory by reintroducing Aristotle's formal causality; the very causality that Newtonian physics had explicitly written off.[289]

Bohm's move from an efficient to a formal cause is what distinguished his view from the classical quantum theories of Einstein and Bohr. In the attempt to absorb non-locality into his theory, Bohm claimed that the quantum field has no efficient causal effect upon particles, but rather, that it provides simply form (beyond space/time), which he explicitly linked with Aristotle's formal cause.[290] This was meant to account for the crucial element ignored by classical quantum theory. He was adamant that the effect of the quantum field was in its form, not in its intensity or force. Accordingly, the quantum field does not push or pull the particles mechanically any more than a radio wave pushes or pulls a ship.[291] Rather than being pushed from the outside (as with classical quantum theory), the electron moves under its own energy (i.e., *inertia*),[292] while the field provides the form (e.g., the radio wave does not provide the energy to move the ship, but only the form, data or "information" that directs its path). In another analogy, Bohm likens quantum phenomena to a radio receiver that provides the energy that, when combined with radio waves, produces the unified phenomena of music.[293] Bohm also used the example of DNA, which provides the form, while the energy is provided by the rest of the cell.[294] Bohm is here roughly holding to a sort of Aristotelian ontology where the electrons (i.e., matter) are actual-

---

286. Ibid., 158. See also, Cobb Jr., "Bohm's Contribution to Faith in Our Time," 42. Cobb Jr. accuses Einstein of being a quasi-materialist for ignoring action at a distance. Cobb argues that there can be no action at a distance if the world is purely material.

287. Bohm and Hiley, *The Undivided Universe*, 145.

288. Ibid., 97.

289. Whittaker, "Aristotle, Newton, Einstein. I & II." Bohm is not alone in his return to Aristotelian causality, as Whittaker shows this is a dominant theme that emerges in quantum physics.

290. Bohm, "Interview with Physicist David Bohm."

291. Bohm and Hiley, *The Undivided Universe*, 37.

292. Ibid., 32 and 78–79.

293. Bohm, "Interview with Physicist David Bohm."

294. Bohm and Hiley, *The Undivided Universe*, 36.

ized not merely in terms of efficient causation, but by their participation in the quantum field (i.e., form). It is in this way that the field and electron, like form and matter, are inseparable, as together they constitute all phenomena. Bohm plays on the term "in-form" (i.e., "information") to develop his quantum ontology. He writes, "We are appealing to the notion that a particle has a rich and complex inner structure which can respond to information and direct it's self-motion accordingly."[295] For Bohm the quantum field carries "in-formation," it in-forms[296] the particles, thus, contributing fundamentally to, yet not ultimately determining, the properties and qualities of each particular substance.

From this, Bohm proposed what he called the "implicate order." The implicate order is the underlying wave movement (roughly the form) that becomes manifest to the viewer in the "explicate order" (i.e., phenomena).[297] Bohm writes, "All things found in the explicate order emerge from the [implicate order] and ultimately fall back into it. They endure only for some time, and while they last, their existence is sustained in a constant process of unfoldment and refoldment, which gives rise to their relatively stable and independent forms in the explicate order."[298] Viewed this way, "whatever persists with a constant form is sustained as the unfoldment of a recurrent and stable pattern that is constantly being renewed by enfoldment and dissolved by unfoldment. When the renewal ceases the form vanishes."[299] Seemingly then, the form actualizes the implicate order resulting in the explicate phenomena.

Bohm's work also revealed an integral relation between the wave and particle ("duality").[300] This means that quantum processes are irreducibly participatory as properties only have meaning in relation to the whole context. The universe appears to have an entangled nature.[301] More importantly, the wave-particle duality suggests that phenomena appear based on the way they are observed. Physics' objective third person gaze does not account for the first person subjective encounter of consciousness (or mind).[302] Indeed

295. Ibid., 39 and 200.

296. Ibid., 35. Bohm clarifies this literal definition: "to in-form, which is actively to put form into something or to imbue something with form."

297. Ibid., 354.

298. Ibid., 382. See also, 354, wherein this is described in terms of "enfoldment" and "unfoldment," whereby the implicate whole is enfolded in each part and is made explicit (manifest) through unfoldment.

299. Ibid., 357.

300. David Bohm, "Hidden Variables," 148.

301. Bohm and Hiley, *The Undivided Universe*, 108.

302. Cunningham, *Darwin's Pious Idea*, 365–70. Cunningham remarks that only a

Heisenberg's uncertainty principle indicates that objects "know" they are being observed. This is why for Bohm it was essential that the role of the observing subject be included in the overall view of the universe. As such, Bohm believed that in the long-run accounting for the subject was as important as the mathematical formulations.[303] The subject must be afforded a role in the formulations of quantum theory. Like Barfield, Bohm argued that the mind is not simply a passive recipient. Humans have active information. The observer participates in the observed. So as long as this continues, the scientific endeavor will never come to an end.[304]

Barfield found much in common with Bohm's contributions to quantum theory. Most importantly, Bohm sought to maintain an integral relationship between the subject and object (i.e., observer and observed) that was being ignored by physics (Barfield explicitly critiques this as well).[305] He found that the Cartesian descriptive order, which worked for classical physics, breaks down when applied to the constitutive order of quantum phenomena. Thus, the subject/object division becomes invalid at the quantum level, which desires instead what Bohm called "complementarity." This is again, precisely why human knowledge is never totalizable.[306] This affirmed Barfield's larger project that recognized the importance of accounting for the subject and the imagination in the otherwise objective sciences. As Bohm contends,

> In quantum theory the observer is an intrinsic part of the whole, and thus when an observation is made the subject and object are not distinct because they participate in each other so one's *a priori* assumptions mustn't be reduced to a reductive ontology or epistemology if true knowledge is to grow. Like two friends in relationship who participate together so that one is affected by

---

subject can actually carry out an objective analysis. Consciousness is the very possibility of the experience. See also, 328. Cunningham rightly avers that what quantum physics admits is, "although laws of physics are crucial, they offer an incomplete description of the world, one that requires the vital supplement of mental activity."

303. Bohm and Hiley, *The Undivided Universe*, 4 and 323.

304. Ibid., 323.

305. Barfield, *Speaker's Meaning*, 106–7. See also, the references to *Unancestral Voice* below.

306. Hiley, "David Joseph Bohm." Bohm held that because groups of particles have properties that go beyond the sum of their parts, it is not possible to display all aspects of the whole quantum process at one time. To prove this, Bohm used the analogy of a hologram. A hologram can be broken down into parts, but when a laser is projected onto the part the whole is still visible. The whole is contained within each part, but the part is concomitantly determined by the whole. The parts and the whole are thus correlative concepts.

the other and vice versa . . . that is exactly the sort of thing that happens in quantum [observations].[307]

Bohm maintained that the subject plays and integral role in the quantum processes and, in so doing, confirmed what Barfield had espoused in his critiques of physical science.

Equally akin to Barfield, was Bohm's belief that quantum theory provides a more coherent account of the actual experience of the mind, which constantly unifies phenomena. Bohm attempted to provide a more robust account of causality in order to overcome the residual "push and pull" causality of quantum mechanics.[308] By reintegrating formal causality into the physical processes, Bohm pointed out that the basic quality of the mind is that it responds to form and not materiality. This emphasis on wholeness and form counteracted the reductive tendency to know objects by reducing them to parts.

As with Barfield, perhaps the most legitimizing feature of Bohm's work was how effortlessly he applied quantum theory, and his desire for unity over-against atomism, to the world of everyday relations and experiences. Like Barfield, he often remarked on the social implications of the reductive or "fragmented" thought that he sought to overcome. He was deeply concerned with the direction of society as it relates to the nature of thought.[309] As with Barfield, Bohm believed it was not the political condition, but the failure to understand the nature of thought that was behind the problems in society.[310] Bohm stated that, "the way we see, depends on the way we think."[311] He believed that what was needed for the survival of mankind was a transition from viewing the world as parts to viewing it as a whole.[312] Similar to the premise of Barfield's *Worlds Apart*,[313] Bohm was deeply concerned with what he called the "fragmentation" of Western society that led

---

307. Bohm, "Interview with Physicist David Bohm."

308. Hiley, "David Joseph Bohm," 111. Hiley notes that, "This unbroken wholeness implied that it was no longer possible to explain quantum phenomena in terms of mechanistic philosophy."

309. Ibid., 123.

310. Ibid.

311. Bohm, "Interview with Physicist David Bohm."

312. Ibid.

313. *Worlds Apart* is a work of fiction that represents the stark divisions in academia. "Fragmentation" is a word frequently employed by both Barfield and Bohm that represents the division or exclusivity of academic disciplines. This fragmentation leads to a state of affairs in which fewer and fewer representations will be collective (unified), but rather become more and more private. See also, Barfield, *Saving the Appearances*, 145.

to separate fields such as sociology, psychology, philosophy, science, theology, etc., which he claimed confuse themselves as independent wholes.[314] When people act as if they have their own exclusive information they cut themselves off from the outside world, which results in the incoherence of human relationships and in society as a whole, leading to violence. Regardless of the assumptions of the last few centuries, it is not causal pushing and pulling, but observation, exchange, and dialogue that best capture the experience of life. Humanity can no longer go on behaving as if these respective fields are independent. For Bohm, as with Barfield, a fundamental change of consciousness is needed to solve this dilemma.[315] As Bohm saw it, a new worldview was emerging with more of a focus on wholeness rather than analysis into parts and static constituents.[316] Bohm, like Barfield, envisaged dialogue between disciplines as an attempt to "de-fragment" the pool of knowledge. Bohm hoped that from the interaction of scientists with scientists, scientists with non-scientists, or even religious thinkers a common pool of knowledge might emerge which guides society.[317]

Finally, what is perhaps most significant is that in 1965, thirty years before Bohm published *The Undivided Universe*, Barfield published his *Unancestral Voice*, which some have argued to be his most "profound and original contribution" to the intellectual development of his age.[318] The book represents a sustained attack on modern science's external take on biological evolution, which Barfield supplements with his insistence on the internal evolution of consciousness. Throughout the work, Barfield continually reminds the reader of the pitfalls of materialism and the scientific ignorance of the *logos*, the sustaining interior agent of transformation. Its main character is Burgeon (who represents Barfield), whose spiritual and intellectual journey is guided by "Meggid," the "Unancestral Voice." What is most pertinent to the present discussion is that his *Unancestral Voice* not only displays Barfield's knowledge of the latest developments in quantum theory, but it also makes several direct references commending the work of

---

314. Bohm, "Interview with Physicist David Bohm." See also, Hiley, "David Joseph Bohm," 119. Bohm was intrigued by the work of Spinoza, Schelling, and Hegel who regarded the world as an undivided whole. See also, Briggs and Peat, *Looking Glass Universe*. Bohm thought that, "unless we understand the subtleties of wholeness, we will not only divide what we can't divide, we'll try to unite what can't be united. Real differences and similarities will become hopelessly mixed up."

315. Bohm, "Interview with Physicist David Bohm."

316. Ibid.

317. Ibid.

318. De Lange, *Owen Barfield*, 255.

David Bohm, whose intuitions are afforded a seemingly prophetic status, although mixed with a few of Barfield's Steinerian proclivities.

In the third and final part of the work, Burgeon attends a conference of the *Physical Society*, at which an address is given by a young lecturer named Kenneth Flume,[319] who works under David Bohm. Flume's address is titled, "The Crisis in Microscopic Physics," which focuses on the fundamental dilemma in modern physics; that is, that the behaviors of the sub-atomic realm simply do not fit with the laws of classical physics. According to Flume, this discrepancy led to the substitution of probability for causality. Thus, when the atom failed, physicists dug deeper to the electron, when the electron failed they searched for smaller components leading to the development of mathematics and quantum mechanics, which only deals with pure abstractions. This leaves physics with experimentally nothing. Ultimately, quantum mechanics is entirely mathematical, it simply calculates an average outcome rendering sub-atomic or sub-phenomenal levels completely devoid of any meaning. Thus, in his address to the audience Flume states, "the limits imposed by quantum mechanics on our whole technique of observation actually prevented us from giving any *meaning*—in terms of physical observations—to statements *about* these supposed sub-quantum events."[320] He goes on to distinguish between the error of thinking in terms of models as opposed to the real scientific *spirit* of "open-mindedness," which he claimed, "had been impressed on him many times . . . by the distinguished physicist with whom he had had the privilege of working . . . ."[321] He ends the address by challenging his fellow physicists to avoid "subconscious reservations" and instead listen "without prejudice" to the "unexpected," and even the "apparently self-contradictory" "great voice."[322] History, he remarks, reveals that such open-mindedness will lead to new advances in physics. Flume mentions a need for the aid of other disciplines to assist in this endeavor. He notes the integral role of imagination and perception in the observational process, and talks of the replacement of the specified forces of Newtonian physics with fields without mass that are "*continuously* distributed throughout the whole of space."[323]

In response to the questions following the address, Flume references Bohm's suggestion that space and time are not Cartesian, but topological

---

319. Flume appears to be a fictional character developed by Barfield who embodies the thought of David Bohm.

320. Barfield, *Unancestral Voice*, 122.

321. Ibid., 123.

322. Ibid., 124.

323. Ibid., 129.

(i.e., inherently relational). He reminds his audience that the "zero size" of elementary particles is a clear indication of this. Therefore, objects should not necessarily be measured by their external significance of size and space, but internally defined. This suggestion roused the crowd of scientists prompting one to admit that they are scientists, not philosophers. In the close of the questioning Flume is overtaken by the "Meggid," who emboldens his response to his adversaries. He implores them,

> What is physics at all, if it is not the study of those processes by which some one thing comes from other things in the past and gives rise in its turn to yet other things in the future? . . . We find a thing in being . . . our vocation as physicists is to enquire what other things it comes from, and how; and to what other things it will give rise. . . . And chance? Do we simply shrug our shoulders when we come across it? That was not the gesture of our predecessors. For them the phenomenon of the random, the fortuitous, the unexplained, was a challenge to seek out its causes in some new, hitherto unexplored domain.[324]

Flume continues,

> What *kind* of source can there be for the complex interacting rhythms of energy, of which we now find that the physical universe consists? What other can it be than a system of non-spatial relationships between hierarchies of energetic beings? And how can we obtain access to their realm, unless we learn somehow to think of them without the help of models, without constructive models, without nature-models, yes, and also without the poetic and the theological models of a bygone age?[325]

Following the lecture, the work indicates that Flume is the nephew of an old friend of Burgeon's (quite possibly a reference to Bohm). Burgeon finds himself "strangely and strongly drawn to the speaker."[326] Their conversations continue in the closing chapters of the book illumining the need for the continual conversation between physics, philosophy, and theology. Flume, trained under Bohm, represents that open-minded scientist whom Barfield believed would lead the imminent advance of physics by uniting the scientific and imaginative consciousness.

In fact, in a typescript called "Concept of Causality," written in 1990, Barfield writes of "a dream" set in the twenty-third century wherein he

---

324. Ibid., 141–42.
325. Ibid., 143.
326. Ibid., 124.

meets a Professor of History and the Philosophy of Science. The Professor indicates that it was Bacon's denial of the Platonic and Aristotelian forms that led to such reductive accounts of causality. When Barfield asks him if he is going to publish his work the Professor responds, "Nobody would be interested. It's such a long time now since the scientific establishment saw through its own over-emphasis on causality, and gave up trying to apply it everywhere, instead of keeping it in its proper place." Barfield responds, "What place is that?" to which the professor answers,

> Any sense-perceptible subject matter that doesn't involve birth, development, metamorphosis, growth, evolution. Science has its own separate domain for all that now. Inquiry into causes is one thing, inquiring into sources another. It's one of the first things every student is taught. The frantic hunt after more and more minimal units to feed the causality concept has become a thing of the past.[327]

To conclude, Bohm's quantum theory affirmed Barfield's poetic philosophy in three ways:

1. Bohm's re-introduction of formal cause sought to overcome mechanism and reductive physical accounts. This granted validity to the qualitative dimension of reality and shifted the emphasis away from parts to wholeness as that which is most fundamental in the act of perception.

2. This emphasis on wholeness was practically applicable. Bohm believed reductive thought had fragmented knowledge.

3. Most importantly, Bohm argued that the subject played a role in determining the outcomes of ostensibly objective processes. This undermined the Cartesian dualism of modern physics, which sets the subject over/against his or her object, as well as notions of the subject as a passive onlooker.

Bohm's work, however, did not come without criticism from both inside and outside the sciences.

Physics, Philosophy, and Theology

Critics of Bohm point to a particular source of ambiguity in his quantum ontology. As previously mentioned, Bohm spoke of in-formation that exists

---

327. "Owen Barfield Papers," *Typescript Articles, Essays, Introductions, and Reviews,* 1980–91, Dep. C, 1156.

beyond space-time that emerges from an underlying implicate order, which thereby constitutes or actualizes observed phenomena (i.e., the explicate order). In this way Bohm spoke of two ontic layers and tried to link them by introducing formal cause (i.e., in-formation). This vision is reminiscent of a sort of Heideggerian or Bergsonian ontology of dual ontic layers, as Bohm's forms appear to oscillate between immanence and transcendence.[328] What critics question is the origin of this in-formation. In-formation for Bohm, as with other quantum theories, emerges from an immanent sub-realm that is ostensibly whole or complete even if it is unknowable. In response, Bohm remarked, rather insufficiently, that it might be built in, or there may be hidden connections of which science is yet unaware. Hence, Bohm rightly shies away from identifying the origin of in-formation, recognizing that such talk is beyond even the scope of quantum physics.

How then should one proceed? The discrepancies in Bohm's quantum ontology prompt the age-old question of the relationship between physics, philosophy, and theology first spelled out by Aristotle.[329] At the very least, Bohm has shown that physical accounts are not necessarily opposed to philosophy (or religious discourse), but rather, should be repeatedly subjected to such scrutiny in order to stave off closed-mindedness (i.e., fragmentation).[330] Bohm shows that physical science is limited to the metaphysical consciousness it chooses to adopt. Physical accounts of the universe that are based upon a philosophy that brackets out metaphysical phenomena (i.e., non-locality, action at a distance, uncertainty principle) are not then free to speculate about this same phenomena. As Michael Hanby has well illustrated, those methodologies that ignore this simple logic reveal their own obvious metaphysical and theological prejudices (e.g., the "new atheists").[331] In questioning the underlying assumptions of classical physics, Bohm revealed the importance of examining the philosophical presupposi-

328. Bohm, "Interview with Physicist David Bohm." See also, Talbot, *The Holographic Universe*, 271. Bohm would go as far as to suggest that the implicate domain, "could equally well be called Idealism, Spirit, Consciousness. The separation of the two—matter and spirit—is an abstraction. The ground is always one."

329. Aristotle, *The Complete Works of Aristotle*. In *Metaphysics*, Book *Epsilon* 1, Aristotle defines this relationship as follows: "So if there is no other substance besides those that exist by nature, natural science would be first science. If there is some immovable substance, this would be prior, and the science of it would be first philosophy, and first philosophy would be universal, in this way, because it is first. And it would be the concern of this science to study being *qua* being, both what it is and what belongs to it *qua* being."

330. For an explanation of the cordiality between science and religion see, Cunningham, *Darwin's Pious Idea*, 269–72.

331. Hanby, *No God, No Science?*, chapter 1, "Discourse on Method."

tions of science. This is what leads to Bohm's ontological interpretation of the physical world, which is laudable precisely because he clearly recognized the limits of such an attempt. Such limits ensure that the scientific quest for certainly remains endlessly evasive and open. Examining a few theological responses to Bohm's quantum ontology serves as a transition to the final part of the essay.

More recently, Wolfgang Smith's *Quantum Enigma* suggests that quantum phenomena can no longer be explained without metaphysics,[332] because as he boldly states, "no one has ever observed a physical object, and no one ever will."[333] Physicists tend to reify the objects, which the wave-particle dualism prohibits.[334] It is, rather, the very nature of an object to manifest itself only in part. This is not simply on account of the relative observer; it is because the object itself does not show its wholeness.[335] This is because for Smith neither the subject nor the object is wholly immanent. Thus, one perceives only an image, which is only an aspect of the object that always already transcends the image. Thus, when one observes the real external object one perceives a "resemblance," but not the fullness of it.[336] The crux of Smith's work is his contention that there will always be a gap be-tween the physical (the measurement) and the corporeal (what is measured) ontological planes. For Smith, the corporeal plain remains in potency and is actualized as the physical domain. He writes, "the transition from po-tency to actuality requires invariably a creative act—a creative fiat one could say—which nothing in the domain of potency can explain,"[337] and "such a transition can only be effected by the creative or 'form-bestowing' principle" that is operative here and now.[338] This is not far from Bohm's theory, but he begins to see beyond Bohm when he maintains that this actually intro-duces an ontological stratum more fundamental than the prior plane.[339] He is clear that this is not metaphysical speculation, but is made apparent by the discoveries of physics.[340] Smith is here incidentally touching upon the

332. Smith, *The Quantum Enigma*, 2.

333. Ibid., 33. Herein, Smith states that a "physical object cannot be reduced to its observable effects."

334. Ibid., 46–49.

335. Ibid., 10.

336. Ibid., 21–23. See also, 40, wherein, Smith speaks of the connection between the physical object and its representation as having something in common. He refers to this as "resemblance." This is very similar to Barfield's sacramental worldview.

337. Ibid., 68.

338. Ibid., 107–9.

339. Ibid., 78.

340. Ibid.

aforementioned discrepancy in Bohm's account (i.e., the dual ontic layers). Accordingly, "There is not only a space-time continuum containing various entities, but also—on a more fundamental level—an as yet undifferentiated potency, which is neither in space nor in time, and about which nothing specific can be affirmed."[341] As mentioned above, and affirmed by Smith, the closest physics has come to this is the discovery of non-locality. To address this "more fundamental level," Smith speaks of moving beyond immanent accounts of "horizontal" causation by challenging science to seek a "vertical" causation by which a transcendent higher order causality emerges that is distinct from temporal efficient causality.[342] Beyond Bohm, for Smith, the bestowal of form is a vertical act of causation.[343] The source of phenomena does not lie in a further ontic layer, but is rather transcendent, as seen in his description of the object as symbol (i.e., resemblance). The mind is able to access the vertical in the simple act of sense perception and in doing so the intellect "transcends the bounds of space and time."[344] Phenomena, thus, are not static objects whose appearances in space-time can be saved once and for all, but instead they are symbols temporarily sustained by transcendence. Paradoxically, one does indeed apprehend an exhaustible reality. This is why Smith concludes that neither science nor modern philosophy can move forward unless they are grounded in the traditional metaphysics that modernity has deemed "primitive, pre-scientific, and puerile."[345]

Smith's "vertical" causation moves beyond Bohm's immanent ontology by positing a transcendent cause that lies outside of any conceivable immanence. This move, which like Bohm reintroduces Aristotle's formal cause, goes further suggesting that theology's transcendent cause is the most fundamental of all the sciences. Aquinas, in baptizing the work of Aristotle, completes this move. Like Aristotle, Aquinas also distinguished between the physical and metaphysical; the physical being those things that depend on matter for existence and the metaphysical those things that do not depend upon matter in order to exist.[346] Thus, physics does not study the whole of being, but only a particular aspect of being, while metaphysics is a universal science (*sciencia communis*) of which knowledge of God (the First Being)

341. Ibid., 81.

342. Ibid., 110–13.

343. Ibid., 115.

344. Ibid., 114.

345. Ibid., 125.

346. Te Velde, *Aquinas on God*, 52. See also, Aquinas, *Summa Theologica*, Ia. q. 1 a. 5. "It was necessary for man's salvation that there should be a knowledge revealed by God besides philosophical science built up by human reason. It is only from metaphysics that one can arrive at the knowledge of the First Being."

is its goal.[347] This is precisely why Aquinas deemed theology the divine science.

> This science surpasses other speculative sciences; in point of greater certitude, because other sciences derive their certitude from the natural light of human reason, which can err; whereas this derives its certitude from the light of divine knowledge, which cannot be misled: in point of the higher worth of its subject-matter because this science treats chiefly of those things which by their sublimity transcend human reason; while other sciences consider only those things which are within reason's grasp.[348]

To be clear, proper theology does not posit a "god of the gaps" who simply fills an ontic void left unaccounted for by quantum physics.[349] "But in sacred science, all things are treated of under the aspect of God: either because they are God Himself or because they refer to God as their beginning and end."[350] When Aquinas addresses causation in the *Summa Theologica* he states that, "God has immediate providence over everything, because He has in His intellect the types of everything, even the smallest."[351] It turns out that proper theology, according to Kathryn Tanner, "talks of an ordered nexus of created causes and effects in a relation of total and immediate dependence upon divine agency. Two different orders of efficacy become evident: along a 'horizontal' plane, an order of created causes and effects; along a 'vertical' plane, the order whereby God founds the former."[352] What Aquinas and others are pointing to is a sort of sacramental sensibility that maintains God as transcendent, as both in-and-beyond the immanent realm; the sort of reality that physical theories always-already intimate in the infinite regress of immanent accounts (i.e., ontic layers).

Fortunately, Bohm remained committed to the "de-fragmentation" of knowledge. In 1986 he "kindly" accepted an invitation from David L. Schindler[353] to participate in a conference on Catholic theology and quan-

347. Te Velde, *Aquinas on God*, 53. This first principle must be a metaphysical object because it exists independently of motion and matter.

348. Aquinas, *Summa Theologica.*, Ia. q. 1 a. 5.

349. Cunningham, *Darwin's Pious Idea*, 275–80. Instead of the immanent world of science (e.g., Intelligent Design and/or Ultra-Darwinism) theology intimates traces of transcendence that are not merely gaps to be filled.

350. Aquinas, *Summa Theologica*. Ia. q. 1 a. 7.

351. Ibid. Ia. q. 22 a. 3.

352. Tanner, *God and Creation in Christian Theology*, 89–90.

353. I had the privilege of meeting David L. Schindler at the "What is Life?" Conference in Krakow, Poland in the summer of 2011 where I presented portions of the

tum physics at the University of Notre Dame. The results of the conference were compiled in a collection of essays responding to the work of Bohm titled, *Beyond Mechanism: The Universe in Recent Physics and Catholic Thought*. This compilation of essays sheds further light on the relation between quantum and theological ontologies.

In his response to Bohm's ontology, John B. Cobb Jr. notes that the positive insight one gleans from Bohm is that his is a religious move, because religion always sees the whole, while secularity fragments.[354] However, for theology, form is not strictly in the world as Bohm would have it.[355] For this reason, Cobb Jr. argues that Bohm still remains positivistic and empiricistic because he is still glancing upon the phenomena level.[356] To simply prioritize the whole does not work theologically.[357] The importance being that this misconstrues proper transcendence. It grants the "in" of immanence as "wholeness" in itself, but denies the "beyond" of proper transcendence. In this scheme, wholeness inevitably functions as a god of the gaps, so to speak, by collapsing transcendence into immanence (an example of this is the recent, albeit tentative, discovery of the Higgs boson particle, or the "God-particle").[358] In his essay, John H. Wright notes that the Christian view maintains that God not only contains the universe, but He is also distinct from it.[359] For theology the temporal participates in the eternal, the finite in the infinite, the immanent in the transcendent. Aquinas spoke of the transcendent God who is both wholly other and intimately present

---

present chapter. Schindler spoke very highly of David Bohm and mentioned that Bohm was very hospitable to the suggestions and criticisms of theologians.

354. Cobb Jr., "Bohm's Contribution to Faith in Our Time," 47.

355. Hill, "The Implicate World," 78–79.

356. Cobb Jr., "Bohm's Contribution to Faith in Our Time," 39.

357. Ibid., 49.

358. The discovery of the Higgs boson particle, an incredible feat indeed, marks another step for science. However, the media's talk of a "God-particle" is guilty of positing a god of the gaps. According to theology, if God were, in fact, discovered, if he were indeed an object among others (i.e., a "particle"), whether theoretical or actual, He would not be God, because properly speaking God transcends objectivity. Theology suggests that all discoveries, whether philosophical or those of the hard or social sciences, are a share in, or a partial grasping of, a truth that infinitely exceeds finitude. In this way, no knowledge is absolute, but a partial yet real grasping of an absolute reality. Thus, for science, the discovery of the Higgs boson marks an advance, but surely science's ephemerality will show its hand with each future discovery. This is why Barfield criticized science for claiming objectivity, yet continually saying, "we now know" (see, Barfield, *Saving the Appearances*, 54). This theological concept is further articulated in chapter 5.

359. Wright, "Cosmic and Human Evolution," 75. See also, Szerszynski, *Nature, Technology and the Sacred*, 38.

within everything,[360] because transcendence for Aquinas, "does not exclude God's positive fellowship with the world or presence within it."[361] "According to [this] position . . . God is [also] intimately present to creatures as the self-communicating principle of their very being."[362]

Even if one grants that Bohm reintroduced Aristotle's formal cause, his notion of form is one bereft of teleology (as mentioned earlier in the present chapter, for Aristotle form and teleology are inseparable).[363] This circles back to the opening of the present chapter, which held that the uniqueness of the natural order lies in its teleological nature (*phýsis*). In the same volume, William Hill's essay indicates, "the Christian philosopher or theologian has no way of integrating such a theory into a worldview that grounds creativity ultimately in matter itself, or in consciousness, or in the universe as a whole."[364] For theology, unity does not emerge, but participates in God, who unites by directing all things toward their teleological end. For the theologian it is precisely this teleological form that participates in its transcendent cause who endows all of creation with purpose and meaning.

In the end, Bohm's work indicates that the scientific attempt to ascertain the exact nature of the universe remains ephemeral. As the subject changes, so too will the objective truths of scientific observation. It is for this reason that the subject must be accounted for in the observation. On

360. Aquinas, *Summa Theologica*. Ia. q. 8 a. 1.

361. Tanner, *God and Creation in Christian Theology*, 79.

362. De Nys, "God, Creatures, and Relations," 613.

363. Additionally here, it might be helpful here to recall the pre-modern distinction between natural and artificial making; one in which teleology becomes the distinguishing feature. Recall Bohm's description of the wave particle duality using the radio transmitter as an example. The radio wave carries information, while the radio provides the power, which together produce sound. Bohm also used the analogy of a ship and its rudder. The ship provides the power, while the rudder provides the form. The problem with both of these pictures is that from a mechanistic worldview physics cannot account for teleology, which following the critique above indicates that Bohm is still a pseudo-materialist. Even if one wants to grant a formal cause to Bohm's ontology, it is a form bereft of teleology, and in the end not entirely compatible with Aristotelian metaphysics as outlined in section 1 of the present chapter. So, although Bohm explicitly draws upon Aristotle, he fails to account for the integral relation between form and *telos* expounded by Aristotle. For example see, Jonas, *The Phenomenon of Life*, 110–24. Jonas uses the term "servomechanism" to describe man-made objects that often are said to function in the same way as humans. He uses the example of a radar-guided torpedo (much like that of Bohm's ship) to show the difference between the natural and artificial. The torpedo, he says, is not actually teleological because it is not attracted but steered towards the target. The main point being that no part of the torpedo's mechanism embodies its "purpose." The torpedo can only be said to "serve a purpose" or "carry out a purpose," but it does not have a purpose of its own.

364. Hill, "The Implicate World," 95.

the positive side, it is this evolving tension between subject and object that allows science to talk of progress in its quest to unearth how the universe works.

In this vein, Barfield tried to show that the language employed by scientists is never merely figurative or object but is actually metaphorical.[365] He believed scientific knowledge could only expand through the employment of metaphor.[366] Metaphor instills fresh insight that shatters clichés: the outdated methods and errant presuppositions that were once groundbreaking metaphors themselves. Barfield writes, "without the continued existence of poetry, without a steady influx of new meaning into language, even the knowledge and wisdom which poetry herself has given in the past must wither away into a species of mechanical calculation."[367] It is paradoxically the mystery of the unknown that draws the scientist forward in his or her quest for knowledge. It was Goethe (Barfield's exemplar poetic scientist) who said, "marvel is my *raison d'etre*." As Josef Pieper says, the "very summit of man's attainment is the capacity to marvel."[368] Pieper indicates that the narrow-minded bourgeois man sees nature as an end to fulfill needs, he cannot wonder at the natural world needing the unusual to surprise him, while the receptive person finds wonder in the ordinary things of everyday life. The pursuit of knowledge is not to be understood as the attempt to possess an exhaustible knowledge of a thing (which brings an end to wonder), but rather a journey on the way to an inexhaustible truth.[369] As he states, "To enter into that infinite realm is to enter on a path along which one can continue forever without coming to an end."[370] Therefore, "only a spiritual capacity for knowledge that does not know once and perfectly is capable of becoming gradually aware of the deeper and more essential world behind the sensual, physical world . . . ."[371]

To rehearse, akin to Barfield's theory regarding the evolutionary history of language, Part I suggested that Barfield's poetic philosophy situates the subject in a middle realm between active and passive. For Barfield the truly creative subject is not passive, but reaches beyond immanence intimating a vertical inspiration that affirms the real. Yet, this realist aesthetic is presently overshadowed by the dominative epistemological theory of representation and the nominalist denial of constitutive universals from which it develops.

365. Barfield, *Poetic Diction*, 135–37.

366. Ibid., 141.

367. Ibid., 180.

368. Pieper, *Leisure, the Basis of Culture*, 130–32.

369. Ibid., 136 and 140.

370. Ibid., 160.

371. Ibid., 138.

The present part then sought to examine Barfield's belief that this same theory had captivated the social and physical sciences. The previous chapter showed how primitives embody (sociologically) something like Barfield's poetic aesthetic, while over time the subject grows increasingly autonomous under the guise of the representational model, which pits subjects (individuals) over/against the other. The present chapter then addressed what Barfield believed to be the culmination of this subjective autonomy, modern science. It opened by connecting the concepts of Barfield's poetic philosophy (covered in Part I) with the concept of *technê* and indicated that there is an analogous relation between Barfield's want to position the subject in a medial realm, and the Aristotelian practice of art (i.e., human making) as participation in the natural order (*phýsis*). But, the rise of the autonomous subject created a caesura that stifled such creative practice, wherein purposeless objects became subject to the will of humanity. When the analogous relation between *phýsis* and *technê* is rendered univocal, humanity takes on a dominative posture over nature. For Barfield, this is most vividly portrayed in the modern scientific purview, which operates on the premise that subject and object are irrevocably separate. However, according to the evolution of consciousness, modern science did not altogether do away with the participatory aesthetic, it had simply become less conscious of it. More and more science itself was proving that the mechanistic conception of the universe, predicated on the Cartesian scheme, could no longer go on ignoring those observable phenomena that were clearly undermining its own presumptions. As it turned out, quantum theorist David Bohm, an acquaintance of Barfield, had much in common with his (Barfield's) critique of the modern scientific worldview. Among his most relevant contributions, Bohm sought to overturn any residual mechanism in quantum theory by re-introducing Aristotle's formal cause. He suggested that particles are not dead objects moved by forces, but rather, had their own qualities (i.e., inertia). Additionally, these forms actually constituted the real. Most significantly, Bohm sought to redefine the notion of scientific objectivity by indicating that the subject must be included in the observational system. Indeed, if Heisenberg's "uncertainty principle" is correct, if objects "know" they are being observed, then the subject plays an integral role in shaping the outcome of an experiment, which meant that science could never claim a purely objective or totalizing gaze. Instead, because consciousness evolves (i.e., the subject always brings with him or her a variety of presuppositions that shape outcomes) so too does scientific truth. Ultimately, for Barfield, this indicates that the subject plays a role in unearthing fresh meaning, reinvigorating an otherwise banal science. To press on, scientists should be inspired, creative artists. Indeed this is the only way science can talk of progress. The sciences, too, are inherently poetic, intimating his poetic philosophy. A fitting quote from Barfield wonderfully illustrates the connection here made. Following Blake, he states that were it not for the poetic or prophetic, "the philosophic and experimental would soon be at the ratio of all things, and stand still, unable to do other than repeat the same dull round."[372] And it is in this way, that Parts I and II (aesthetic and sociological participation) come together. Whether philosophical or scientific, the inherent nature of poetic inspiration is above all necessary in overcoming prosaic or mimetic discourse. It is only by such a poetic philosophy that one can speak of progress. The poetic subject, suspended between passivity (Part I) and activity (Part II), indeed represents a formidable alternative to those otherwise mimetic discourses hitherto discussed. It is this "theological" middle that affirms the very opening that philosophies of immanence and the sciences that presuppose them have failed to close.

372. Barfield, *Poetic Diction*, 144.

PART III

THEOLOGICAL PARTICIPATION

Part I proffered Barfield's poetic aesthetic as a robust alternative to the division between poetic and prosaic language situating philosophical discourse. By placing the subject and object in polar tension, Barfield's poetic philosophy is more capable of expressing the true nature of being because it affirms the theological openness of being that philosophy presumed closed. Part II then showed how Barfield discovered a correlation between the loss of this poetic aesthetic and the rise of the autonomous subject. The poetic aesthetic gives way to epistemologies of representation that promulgate the objective, prosaic, mechanical, and/or technical language employed by the social and physical sciences. Yet the ephemerality of scientific proof revealed this to be ontologically untenable, incapable of accounting for the real, which intimated a return to this poetic aesthetic. In this vein, Parts I and II argued that representational epistemologies betrayed subsequent philosophical and scientific attempts to properly articulate the real. Moreover, by breaking from religious discourse the modern social sciences and the immanent philosophies upon which they are based, failed to secure a secular or totalized vision of reality, which ironically revealed an opening within immanence that they took to be closed. In so doing, philosophies that reject the poetic aesthetic exposed the very opening that Barfield's poetic philosophy affirms.

Part III will now complete the argument intimated in the conclusions of Parts I and II; namely, that to restructure the prosaic/poetic divide is to offer a participatory alternative that both affirms and outwits philosophy's feigned immanentized discourse. A final explication of Barfield's participatory philosophy is followed by a critique of its limitations which draws upon the theological tradition and some contemporary continental Catholic thinkers who employed a similar vocabulary to Barfield. Here, an attempt is made to construct *poiēsis* proper by employing proper theological language in the form of a metaphysic of analogy, which both baptizes and exceeds philosophies of immanence. This constructive portion of the essay is meant to be faithful to Barfield's poetic philosophy, albeit admittedly more properly theological. It is argued that language and being are inconceivable outside of a theological metaphysic of participation. Corresponding with the analogous nature of being, a theological language of non-identical repetition situates beings analogically, thereby rescuing language from the impossibilities of philosophy's supposed univocal identity and equivocal difference. It is not, therefore, a transcendental language that somehow saves theology, but a theology of transcendence that redeems language and being. Theological language is not meaningless talk about that which is unknown, but rather, all language and being is "no thing" without transcendence. In response to the implicit conclusions of Parts I and II (regarding the active/passive dialectic of modern/postmodern discourse) the final subsection suggests that a language capable of expressing the reality of creation's participation in God is one of middle voice. A theological rediscovery of the middle voice is consistent with a rich tradition of Christian theology and the New Testament consciousness of both Jesus and St. Paul. A middle voice, poetic, inspired, worshipful language stretches creation beyond the totality of its finite being. One's endless finite grasping is one's participation in, one's openness to, one's *epektasis* towards one's true identity that is found only in the Persons of the infinite God.

5

Poetic Theology

The poet only asks to get his head into the heavens. It is the logician who seeks to get the heavens into his head. And it is his head that splits.

—CHESTERTON[1]

. . . dialogicians, then, are philosophers who themselves need theology in order to develop their thoughts to completion.

—BALTHASAR[2]

Modern philosophy makes no movement; as a rule it makes only commotion, and if it makes any movement at all, it is always within immanence, whereas repetition is and remains a transcendence.

—KIERKEGAARD[3]

The Limits of Philosophy:
A Participatory Alternative

In the close of Parts I and II it was suggested that the significance of Barfield's work lies in his ability to utilizing language to expose the shortcomings of

1. Chesterton, *Orthodoxy*, 29.
2. Balthasar, *Theo-Logic*, vol. II, 49.
3. Kierkegaard, *Fear and Trembling/Repetition*, 186.

particular philosophies. According to Barfield, not only was the modern consciousness, with its representational epistemology, philosophically untenable, it became increasingly apparent that it could not account for those real qualities regularly associated with things in the world that constitute one's everyday experience.[4] Barfield resisted the Cartesian tendency to abstract subjective qualities from objects and instead argued that language and being are inherently poetic; that is, he maintained against such dualisms that life actually consists in a polar tension, where subjects and objects intermingle in what he called the "concrete experience" or "unity of apperception." Barfield did not believe it was right to assume that the subject was cut off from the objective world (as, e.g., with Cartesian mind/matter dualism), or to envisage an untraversable boundary between rational and poetic discourse where poetic language is relegated to subjective fancy (as, e.g., the Kantian "sublime")[5] and philosophical language is concerned with objective truth. Instead his poetic philosophy is based upon a realist metaphysic that sought to restore harmony to such divisions.

For a representational epistemology, subjectivity (e.g., the subject's relation to the object) can only be conceived of in either passive or active terms. In this dualist scheme the subject (as ground) can either project meaning or passively receive it. Crucially, there is no space for mediation. However, Barfield seemed to point to a middle realm that resists this dialectic. For this reason, each of the previous chapters concluded with the suggestion that by re-envisaging the subject as inherently poetic, or participatory, Barfield's work intimates a theological alternative that the present chapter now seeks to complete.

This essay now culminates by building upon Barfield's poetic philosophy, suggesting that if language is inherently poetic, and being is participatory, then perhaps the origin of modern philosophy was predicated on a naïve presumption of immanence; the same premise underlying modernity's search for indubitable "foundations," which, in turn, spawned postmodernity's anti-metaphysical gestures. What one can, however, glean from the efforts of such philosophies is that they prove inadequate, as the real seems to resist such simplistic resorts. Instead, it seems rather more faithful to say that the subject and object are held in an irresolvable tension, as neither is

4. See, "Preface to the Second Edition," in Barfield, *Poetic Diction*, 15. Therein, he critiques nominalist theories of language that divorce the "emotive" and "referential" and thereby, "write off . . . without veridical significance practically all the abstract words in our language (for at what particular point in their history did they acquire a referent?) including, naturally, such words as *meaning, verify, emotive and referential.*"

5. Adey, *C. S. Lewis' Great War*, 21. Adey notes that Barfield holds Kant responsible for saying that thought arises simply from neural activity.

the ground or "foundation" of itself, and nor is one's ground founded in the other. Yet, all phenomena remain irreducibly real. From the highest to the lowest realities, all really are apprehended; they really are referenced in and by language; they really desire to be known. This implies that their purpose or ground lies, as it were, in-and-beyond them, it is at once their own and not their own precisely because they are given.

If Barfield's theory of the evolution of consciousness is at all tenable, then perhaps this poetic aesthetic never truly died, and may even perhaps make a conscious return. Indeed, its vestiges live on, not only in one's subconscious, as Barfield would have it, but also in a tradition that Barfield himself largely ignored. In fact, this poetic aesthetic is becoming increasingly tenable as the search for truth (albeit speculatively) commences in the wake of postmodernity. In light of this, in the context in which it emerged, and in the contemporary discussion regarding the relationship between philosophy and theology, Barfield's poetic philosophy is significant because it turns philosophy away from an immanent trajectory and back towards its fulfillment in theological transcendence. For it will be argued that *only a theological language is capable of expressing philosophy's limits while paradoxically gesturing beyond them* (navigating between a totalizing grasp of being and relativism).[6] This inspired worshipful utterance, conceived as a perpetual finite grasping of the infinite, is the only possibility of becoming (i.e., forward movement).

From this perspective, it is not the case that theology's supposedly transcendental nature somehow quarantines theology from corrupting philosophical acuity, but rather, proper theological (analogical) language sustains philosophy from devolving into univocal repetition and/or equivocal non-identity.[7] For this reason, in closing, an attempt is made to construct such an inspired non-identical language in the middle voice[8] (i.e., situated between active and passive), which accounts for proper transcendence.

6. This is in response to those forms of philosophical theology that engage with metaphysics under the assumption that philosophy and theology are separate disciplines. Below, it is argued instead that Christian theology views philosophy as a handmaid. In this way, theology brings reason to its fulfillment and perfection in faith. Again, this means that no philosophical vision, nor theology, is totalizable. Instead, what is suggested is that philosophy points to an unanswerable mystery whose answer is paradoxically theological.

7. Theologically speaking, this is to suggest something like Kierkegaard's "nonidentical repetition" found in, Kierkegaard, *Fear and Trembling/Repetition*, 186. Kierkegaard writes, "Modern philosophy makes no movement; as a rule it makes only a commotion, and if it makes any movement at all, it is always within immanence, whereas repetition is and remains a transcendence."

8. Barfield, *Saving the Appearances*, 48–49. As already addressed in chapter 1,

To accomplish this, the present chapter begins by locating Barfield's participatory philosophy within the Christian tradition. It then critiques the limits of his work by surveying some Catholic contemporaries who were working within the same (continental) philosophical tradition and employing similar language. This first section will bring Barfield's poetic philosophy to its implicit conclusions, while the following section will supplement his work where it falls short by constructing a poetic metaphysics that is faithful to his work, but more thoroughly theological; that is, *poiēsis* proper.

Inspiration as Participation

Barfield writes specifically about Christian theology and was an eventual convert to the Church of England in 1949.[9] However, the extent to which Anthroposophy slanted Barfield's theology should not be overlooked (particularly his insistence on reincarnation).[10] With these concerns in mind,

---

Barfield juxtaposes the Greek middle voice use of phenomena (or appearances), to those objective sciences that attempt to "save the appearances" by concocting hypothesis.

9. Barfield and Tennyson, *A Barfield Reader*, xx.

10. For examples of Barfield's Anthroposophical reading of Christianity (particularly his theology of the incarnation) see, "Of the Intellectual Soul," in Barfield, *Romanticism Comes of Age*, 104–19 and 32–33. See also, Barfield, "The Psalms of David." This article was originally printed in 1945 in *Anthroposophic Movement*. Barfield indicates his Steinerian reading of the incarnation as follows: "I personally have long accepted Steiner's account of incarnation, according to which it was (inter alia) the event which made possible the complete 'descent' of any and every human ego into a physical body; it is thus the root of the increasing self-consciousness which, for good and ill, has marked the subsequent psychological history of mankind." See also, Barfield, "The 'Son of God' and the 'Son of Man,'" which was originally a lecture delivered in Zeist, Netherlands on August 31st 1958. Again, this essay shows his indebtedness to Steiner as he incorporates themes of the evolving consciousness and reincarnation. He writes, "I do not think myself that the mysterious and unclear relation between man and men will ever be understood without some understanding of the working of repeated Earth lives" (258). For more on Christianity and reincarnation see, chapter XXV, "The Mystery of the Kingdom" in Barfield, *Saving the Appearances*, 174–86. Like Steiner, Barfield views the incarnation as history's turning point towards final participation. As he sees it, the words of Christ recorded in the Scriptural parables intimate this reality. He refers to the incarnation as, "the mystery of the kingdom . . . that is to come on earth, as it is in heaven . . . ." He is also insistent upon reincarnation here. See also, "Afterword" in Barfield, *The Silver Trumpet*, 120. Even as late as his 1985 interview with Majorie Lamp Mead, Barfield notes that it was his study of the incarnation that led him to be a "convinced Christian." Herein he again notes his Anthroposophic tendencies indicating that his gradual conversion "culminated in his realization 'that the incarnation, and life, and death of Christ was at the center of the whole evolutionary process' of life itself." This insistence on reincarnation flies in the face of Christian theology, which maintains the immediate creation of the soul *ex nihilo*, and its continued presence with the body,

the following seeks to locate Barfield's participatory philosophy in light of the history of the Christian metaphysical tradition and to tarry with it to its conclusions.

To rehearse briefly, for Barfield, the participatory aesthetic served to overcome dualisms. By focusing on language, his unique approach absorbed many of the philosophical conundrums that he believed were caused by nominalism, which he saw as a denial of the constitutive real.[11] Barfield locates the origins of this beginning as far back as the interpreters of Aristotle who, he believed, denied reality to Plato's forms. He says, "In Aristotle's system—after Plato's death—the Ideas are dragged down from heaven into nature; then, in the Middle Ages, they move, as abstractions, out of nature into the classifying and 'naming' mind of man, where they are soon firmly entrenched by the increasing subjectivism of Descartes, Berkeley and Kant."[12] So as far back as Aristotle one can begin to trace the origins of the division between inner and outer, subject and object, poetic and prosaic,[13] science and theology,[14] that culminates in Descartes's *res extensa/res cogitans*, a philosophy of which he is highly critical.[15]

The reception of Plato and Aristotle (particularly in distinguishing their respective philosophies) is a source of contention amongst scholars,[16] but based upon his disavowal of Aristotle's "followers" in his earliest work,[17]

---

hence the resurrection. More on this to follow, but for a concise account of Catholic doctrine regarding the creation of the soul and body see, Clarke, *The Creative Retrieval of Saint Thomas Aquinas*, 175–77.

11. For his critique of nominalism see, Barfield, *History in English Words*, 131. See also, 171. He talks of a "scholastic progress" from realism to nominalism leading to the abandonment of the doctrine of the "real presence" in the Eucharist.

12. Barfield, "Greek Thought in English Words."

13. Adey, *C. S. Lewis' Great War*, 24.

14. Barfield, *History in English Words*, 109. He says theology follows Plato and science Aristotle.

15. Barfield, "Either: Or," 30. Herein, he critiques this type of dualism for being opaque to incarnation, Trinity, and sacrament.

16. For an exceptional work that reads Aristotle in line with Plato's realism see, Gerson, *Aristotle and Other Platonists*. Gerson contends that Aristotle is a Platonist precisely because he is not a nominalist (21–22). See also, Gadamer, *The Idea of the Good*, 8–9 and 177. Gadamer indicates that Aristotle never ceases to be a Platonist. For an approach to Aristotle more aligned with Barfield's critique see, Pabst, *Metaphysics*, 21–31. Pabst argues that it was Aristotle, who broke from Plato by prioritizing substance over relationality. Pabst's want to prioritize relation over substance aligns well with Adey's reading of Barfield's philosophy. See, Adey, *C. S. Lewis' Great War*, 101.

17. As previously mentioned, in his *Poetic Diction* and *History in English Words*, Barfield is critical of Aristotle for inaugurating the division between inner and outer worlds and the analytical methodology. Nonetheless, by 1968, in his *Saving the*

what one can ascertain is that throughout his work Barfield is indebted to a realist metaphysic (and, as such, Aristotelian—in the sense that he is not a nominalist).[18] So regardless of where one stands on Platonic-Aristotelian scholarship, Barfield's ubiquitous critique of nominalism maintained that the forms do not simply exist in one's mind, but are really in the world. Thus, he defines form as a unity that constitutes a "real being . . . a being, not an idea."[19] Contrary to the Cartesian vision the true nature of things exists, neither in a dualism of subject and object, nor in an either/or, but in a participation of subject and object.[20] He is particularly critical of those who project the modern consciousness back into Plato believing the forms to be abstract.[21] To correct this, Barfield argued that this realist metaphysic was more faithful to the way things actually are in the world. A telling example is found in his *Saving the Appearances* where, in his summarization of medieval thought, he explicitly aligns himself with the rich history of Christian Neo-Platonism (e.g., he cites Pseudo-Dionysius, Augustine, and Aquinas). To describe the medieval consciousness he utilizes Aquinas who he calls the "best choice."[22]

To clarify further his poetic philosophy, in *Saving the Appearances* Barfield constructs his aesthetic utilizing Aquinas. Therein, he evinces that prior to the Middle Ages humanity was understood to play a co-operative

---

Appearances, Barfield calls his version of participation Aristotelian. See also, Barfield, *Saving the Appearances*, 173. In *Saving the Appearances*, Barfield describes participation as most thoroughly Thomistic, calling him "specifically Aristotelian." See also, Adey, *C. S. Lewis' Great War*, 73. Adey notes a subtle distinction that Barfield tries to forged between his own philosophy that he calls "objective idealism" and Plato's idealism (which maintains that universals are more real than particulars), precisely because, for Barfield, the supersensible was equally as real as the sensible. However, it is hard to imagine why Barfield would distance himself from Plato. If anything, Plato is more of a realist than is Barfield. Nonetheless, if Adey is correct, then Barfield is guilty of his own "logomorphism" for suggesting Plato was an idealist.

18. See footnote 16, above.

19. Barfield, *Romanticism Comes of Age*, 86. See also, Barfield, *History in English Words*, 102–3.

20. See, Barfield, "Either: Or" and Barfield, "Matter, Imagination, and Spirit."

21. Sugerman, *Evolution of Consciousness*, 10.

22. Barfield, *Saving the Appearances*, 90–91. He summarizes medieval thought as follows: "At the one end of the scale the subject participates its predicate; at the other end, a formal or hierarchical participation *per similitudinem* was the foundation of the whole structure of the universe; for all creatures were in a greater or lesser degree images or representations, or 'names' of God, and their likeness or unlikeness did not merely measure, but *was* the nearer or more distant emanation of His Being and Goodness in them. It was a spiritual structure, and much of it lay beyond the world of appearances altogether." See also, 173, wherein, Barfield suggests that Aquinas already intimates final participation in the medieval period.

role in the act of creating or "naming." Unlike the present consciousness, this form of medieval naming (and here he draws on Pseudo-Dionysius) was not merely concerned "with philology but with epistemology and metaphysics."[23] He says that in the medieval world words had an ontological gravitas; they reflected the actual nature of the being to which they referred.[24] Referencing Augustine, Pseudo-Dionysius, and Aquinas, Barfield shows that in the human act of naming the phenomenon achieves its full reality (is brought from potentiality to actuality),[25] as that in nature unites with that in humanity which the name represents.[26] He here intimates the Delphic Oracle that to name being is to "know thyself." The path to knowledge is the actualization of the soul's potentiality to become what it contemplates on the journey back to God.[27] As Barfield saw it, such medieval naming—which is neither actively applying an arbitrary transcendental category to an object, nor passively receiving a copy or representation of the object—is a blending of the active and passive, a real participation in the divine creative act.[28] This medial subject as a co-creator is consistent with the poetic subject underscored in Parts I and II; as proper "language," "philosophy," "living," and "making" are, in this way, participatory.

Furthermore, the overarching premise of *Saving the Appearances* suggests that to go against such a view, to assume a representational paradigm, a totalized objective vision (which ironically leads to a total skepticism regarding the trustworthiness of the representation), is idolatry. Thus, to turn from such idolatry is to understand humanity's participatory role in the creative process.[29] Again his translation of phenomenon in the middle voice is here key (see, chapter 1). Instead of Heidegger's radical passivity, which delivers the subject over to the mystery of the *logos*, Barfield's poet (or subject) has a share (via participation) in the naming or knowing of his or her object; the poet is both passive and active. In this way, Barfield writes, humanity stands "in a directionally creator relation" to phenomena.[30] Directly

23. Barfield, *Saving the Appearances*, 84.

24. Ibid., 75. The medieval world is one of "symbols" and their inseparability from that which is "symbolized."

25. Ibid., 89. Barfield shows a strong understanding of Aristotle's prioritization of the actual over the potential crucial to proper theological reflection. He writes, "Indeed, it was only by virtue of participation that he [man] could claim to have any being." Finite being is brought from potency to act, by a prior actuality.

26. Ibid., 84–86.

27. Ibid., 88–89.

28. This should become clearer below.

29. Barfield, *Saving the Appearances*, 160 and 181.

30. Ibid., 156.

following this, in his chapter XXIII, "Religion," Barfield implicitly hints at the perils of a univocal ontology and its theological ramifications; when he, "dared to think of him as an existence parallel with [his] own. Herein lays the idolatry which infects contemporary religion."[31] When such an aesthetic is forfeited a bifurcation emerges between an "ever-increasing experience of the inwardness" of the divine presence and an "ever-increasing" idolatry where everything, even God, simply becomes an object.[32]

The only way to solve this is to see humans as co-creators. He asks, "Is God's creation less awe-inspiring because I know that the light, for instance, out of which its visual substance is woven, streams forth from my own eyes?" To which he responds, "no," because, "I did not create my eyes" (note the subtle distinction between divine and human making).[33] The phenomenal world is not free from human volition (surely he is drawing on Coleridge's notion of the active imagination as volitional; that is, morally culpable) nor is it entirely subject to it. Also, as co-creators humans are morally responsible for the direction of society (they are not doomed to the discretion of history as, e.g., with Hegel or Heidegger) and ought to tend to the purposes of the natural order. The co-creator stance is exemplified in the philosophical statement he continually borrows from Coleridge: "a repetition in the finite mind of the eternal act of creation in the infinite I AM." For Barfield, inspiration is participation and/or co-operation with the divine.

This means that if one is attentive to the Barfieldian corpus one discovers that all meaning is derived by participation in the divine. In his earliest work *History in English Words,* Barfield defines the Greek notion of *logos,* or "reason," as meaning "word," which is the creative faculty in humans. The *logos* was identified with the divine mind that pervaded the visible universe.[34] In his *Romanticism Comes of Age* he writes that reason, for Coleridge, "is not something to be found manifesting in human beings; it is something *in* which human beings—and the whole of nature—are

31. Ibid., 157. He also notes that if one views God as an object it leads to anthropomorphism and idolatry. See also, 147, wherein he explicitly renounces pantheism and occultism.

32. In the same chapter, he notes that the incommensurability of these two poles is a dilemma that plagues Protestant thought; that is, on the one hand, the inwardness of God (often associated with Schleiermacher's liberal Protestantism), and on the other, the resultant fundamentalism of biblical literalism (often associated with the conservative Protestantism of the Princeton school and later evangelicals). See also, 165–66. He continues, "Not to realize to the uttermost the otherness of God from ourselves is to deny the Father. But equally, not to strive to realize the sameness—to renege from the Supreme Identity—is to deny the Holy Spirit."

33. Barfield, *Saving the Appearances,* 159.

34. Barfield, *History in English Words,* 113.

manifest."[35] Reason has an ontological, even theological, nature.[36] Similarly, in *Saving the Appearances* one finds that for Plato and Aristotle and up until the medieval period "true" knowledge, as opposed to the "mutability" of empirical observation was a participation in the divine "Mind" or "Word."[37] He says that just as all things came into being through the creative Word (the source of the phenomenal world), the body was, as it were, "spoken even while it was speaking."[38] It is in this way that "Man's Creator speaks from within man himself . . . ."[39] The Creator speaks "with the voice and through the throat of a man."[40] Much later, in his "Meaning, Revelation and Tradition in Language and Religion,"[41] Barfield declares that all he wrote on language was an attempt to discover the relationship between human language and John's prologue. Utilizing Aquinas he articulates this relation in terms of a Trinitarian theology; that is, as a word going out yet remaining where it originated. He uses Trinitarian imagery to overcome Cartesian and Kantian subjectivity. The difference, he tells us, is that for Aquinas meaning is not merely a subjective process. In the aesthetic encounter the forms of the outer world that constitute the object make possible the naming of the active intelligence. In this way one can be sure that the form of the active intelligence is identical to the form that constitutes the object. He likens this to the Trinitarian procession of the Word, who proceeds from the Father, but does not leave Him. According to Barfield, this is precisely what happens when a human word is spoken. Meaning goes outside the subject, providing communication and revelation to the hearer, yet remains with the speaker.

In this same article Barfield then is careful to distinguish between the divine and human word. Namely, the divine word is self-generating. God, he says, is the "primary symbol-maker" whose symbols, which are given in nature, become potential human words. But, because finite memory is the origin of the human word, meaning fades over time (hence the slide

35. Barfield, *Romanticism Comes of Age*, 152.

36. Ibid., 153. Citing Coleridge, he writes of reason, it "is that *in* which I exist, the ocean of being by which my soul is upborn." See also, 157. He writes, "The Logos is the Word, but it is also that through which all things that are have come into being." See also, 153. For Coleridge, the act of thinking is the ground of being itself, of the being of all things, and in thinking we feel the presence of the *logos*. See also, 152. Reason is not a part or function of the individual mind, it is a "spiritual whole in which the individual mind—all individual minds—subsist."

37. Barfield, *Saving the Appearances*, 46–47 and 55.

38. Ibid., 125.

39. Ibid., 170.

40. Ibid., 171 and 182.

41. Barfield, "Meaning, Revelation and Tradition in Language and Religion."

from metaphorical to literal). He notes, these "fossilized metaphors, can be revivified, so that meaning again shines through them, so that language once again begins to reveal something behind or beyond its merely sensuous references. And that something is, precisely, the act of using language and the faculty of apprehending it as a tissue of symbols."[42] Such revelation occurs by the breaking in of the supernatural into the sensible world reminding the subject of the object's more original meaning, as in liturgical re-enactment. Stressing the importance of the typological, he intimates that the incarnation is the very possibility of historical progress.[43] Hence, he elsewhere writes, "the meaning of nature is today potential only. In the act of becoming aware of it we restore to nature the inwardness of which we have gradually and, I think, unlawfully deprived her. Nature today is, so to speak, hungry for myth or its equivalent, a fact of which some of the poets have had an inkling. She is tired of being experimented with and longs to be known."[44]

Time and time again Barfield references Coleridge's "active imagination" reiterating this scheme. It is the imagination that drinks from the primal source of meaning (the *logos*)[45] when actively participating in God's creative activity.[46] It is the creative imagination that assists in crafting forms in nature,[47] as humans "half perceive" and "half create" using the imagination.[48] Elsewhere he puts it another way: the poetic genius is given to the poet who does not possess it in oneself, but receives it as a gift from God.[49] A "genius," he notes, accompanies the poet, it is what he *has,* not what he *is.*[50] It is in some sense his own but not himself.[51] For Coleridge, the inspired poet was not *possessed by* the spirit, but *possessed* the spirit.[52] To articulate poetic inspiration Barfield readily drew upon Coleridge, who likened the inspired poet to an "Aeolian Harp"[53] whose strings are blown by the wind. Such language is intended to carefully distinguish the poet from the source

---

42. Ibid.
43. See also, Barfield, "The Concept of Revelation."
44. Barfield, "The Nature of Meaning."
45. Barfield, *Poetic Diction*, 151.
46. Barfield, *Saving the Appearances*, 160.
47. Barfield, *History in English Words*, 213.
48. Barfield, *Poetic Diction*, 27.
49. Barfield, *History in English Words*, 203–4.
50. Barfield, *Speaker's Meaning*, 78.
51. Ibid., 82.
52. Barfield, "Imagination and Inspiration," 121.
53. Barfield, "The Harp and the Camera," 67–73 and 77.

of inspiration. His description of inspiration by participation upholds the integrity (i.e., the co-operation) of the subject,[54] as he comments that the more active the thought of the subject the more the integrity of the subject is upheld.[55] And he could not be clearer when he critiques pantheism for dissolving the self, calling those who wish to do so, "extremists."[56]

At times, however, Barfield's description of inspiration sounds somewhat theurgic (e.g., when he moves away from his description of medieval Christendom or when he is not citing Coleridge). In these instances he describes the subject in increasingly passive terms. As discussed in Part I, he does explicitly say in one of his earliest works, *Poetic Diction*, that "in the moment of knowing, which is also the real moment of poetic diction, the knower ceases to exist as subject at all."[57] Similarly, in his work of fiction, *Night Operation*, he says "Men call themselves 'creative' and fill a Library with books and pictures, and the world with things they have made. But in the end, for good or ill, they can only do what the gods are doing *in* them."[58] And, as seen in chapter 4, in his *Unancestral Voice* the speaker gives himself over to the spirit of the "Meggid" to deliver his poignant lecture, which opens the eyes of his hard-hearted audience. All of this perhaps indicates what one finds direct evidence for in the "Preface to the Second Addition" of his *Poetic Diction*; that over time his view on the nature of inspiration changes.

Initially, in developing his theory of poetic inspiration Barfield frequently employed the proper noun, "Nature," to indicate the origin of inspiration (this certainly has similarities with Schelling's *Naturphilosophie*—revealing perhaps his earlier idealist and even pantheistic or immanentist tendencies). However, in the "Preface to the Second Addition" of *Poetic Diction*, written in February of 1951 (twenty-three years after the initial publication), he remarks that, "a certain unconscious, daemonic element now seems to me indispensable."[59] He is here referencing the conclusion of chapter VI, "The Poet," where he indicates a gradual "progress" away from passivity (he cites Plato's poet who is taken over by or "remains *in* the

---

54. Barfield, "Science and Quality," 180. Citing the work of Coleridge he says, "an idea is on the one hand a constitutive antecedent unity in some natural process; but on the other hand, howsoever objective it is, howsoever super*individual*, it is also the act of an individual thinker."

55. Barfield, "Self and Reality," 163–64.

56. Barfield, *Speaker's Meaning*, 84.

57. Barfield, *Poetic Diction*, 209.

58. Barfield, *Night Operation*, 57.

59. See, "Preface to the Second Addition" in Barfield, *Poetic Diction*, 26.

inspiration")[60] and towards a time when "The Poet" would find inspiration "in his own consciousness," which he indicates is a move from passivity to activity.[61] He notes that up until the seventeenth or eighteenth century, inspiration meant that poet was the direct mouthpiece of the divine, but this eventually becomes understood as something that comes from within, rather than arriving from without. Finally inspiration comes to be understood as subjective or internal. Here the word "inspiration" becomes associated with the "unreal," "romantic," "unnatural," "fanatical," "enthusiastic," and "superstitious."[62] In a later piece Barfield suggests that the modern spatialized (i.e., internal vs. external) vision of reality clouds our ability to come to grips with the true nature of revelation, which comes from what he calls a "transpersonal" or "metapersonal" source.[63]

Although his viewpoint regarding inspiration changed (varying between activity and passivity) and at times sounds rather theurgic, the onus of his entire corpus is to accentuate a co-operative vision; a participation in the divine *logos* that attempts to uphold the integrity of the subject in the moment of poetic inspiration without lapsing into a pure passivity or activity.

Barfieldian Philosophy:
Prosaic Mimesis and Poetic Repetition

In *Poetic Diction* and *Speaker's Meaning* one finds Barfield's most concise and cogent accounts of the nature of inspiration. Therein he encompasses nearly all of the concepts traced throughout the present work in his description of inspiration, which he develops through a detailed focus on the relationship between prosaic and poetic language. When articulating his account of inspiration, he continually employs language that suspends these two terms, indicating that they mutually intermingle, which of course, follows Coleridge's philosophy of polarity; that is, although they are distinguishable, prosaic and poetic remain inseparable. Recall that for Barfield all language begins as poetic or metaphorical and over time becomes prosaic. When words lose this poetic or "other-saying" element they become prosaic or "fossilized."[64] He found this mutation to be evident in the etymology of

60. Ibid., 169–70.
61. Ibid., 109–10.
62. Barfield, *History in English Words*, 202–3.
63. Barfield, "The Concept of Revelation."
64. Barfield, "The Nature of Meaning."

particular words.[65] Once a word becomes prosaic its meaning fades, it becomes a dead objectified tautology. Accordingly, when this occurs discourse becomes prosaic or mimetic; at worst, a passive identically repeated representation of the same, and at best, an active poetic (i.e., what one nowadays thinks of as poetic or mythical) *a priori* categorization of an otherwise banal object. Barfield insists that meaning simply cannot be reduced to this sort of analytic logic that shuttles between sameness and difference. He writes, "You cannot shuffle off the mystery of predication merely by inserting the word 'like' after the copula; nor of course by substituting a quasi-transitive verb, to 'resemble,' for both."[66] There must be something more, something inspired. Barfield asks, is it not certain combinations of words by which one encounters a deeper meaning that intimates a rupture of such mimetic discourse? Is it not this unveiling that affects a "felt change of consciousness" that invites the subject to see the world afresh? Indeed without it, how can one speak of forward movement and/or progress? This rupture, this opening, this revelation is the moment of inspiration whereby the poet joins with history (within language)[67] by passively receiving (in memory) the dead prosaic word and actively creating a fresh poetic utterance (for which paradoxically the poet must lend a certain passivity of the will to be active). In this scheme the minor poet imitates, the great inspired poet gives new meaning.[68] The poet must strive to overcome lazy univocal or mimetic discourse, for the poet's work is to create afresh.[69]

His description of inspiration accords with his poetic philosophy. For example, in *Poetic Diction* he states that poetic language is a both a product of language itself and of the poet.[70] Because the poet stands inside language, he can never be the creator of all meaning.[71] He stresses the inspired utterance is not merely the same thing said in a different way, but the realization

65. Barfield, *Speaker's Meaning*, 49–50. He writes, "the outstanding feature of language in its semantic aspect turns out to be the fact that words which were once figurative have ceased to be so and words that are still figurative are ceasing to be so. . . . Look for example at the phenomenon of the cliché."

66. Barfield, "The Nature of Meaning."

67. Barfield has a strong want to account for history in the story of salvation. He repeatedly notes that he was so attached to the evolution of consciousness precisely because of the value it placed on history. He is critical of talk of prehistory for similar reasons. See, Barfield, *Saving the Appearances*, 36–39 and chapter XXIV, "The Incarnation of the Word." See also, Barfield, "The 'Son of God' and the 'Son of Man,'" 259.

68. Barfield, *Poetic Diction*, 158–60.

69. Ibid., 131.

70. Ibid., 29–30 and 107.

71. Ibid., 50.

of a *"slightly different thing that is said."*[72] Shortly after, he states that in the poetic act repetition overlaps with "strangeness" but does not coincide.[73] The prosaic and poetic are thus held in tension as reason is joined with the imagination. Years later he espoused this same theory in his *Speaker's Meaning* where he metes out the passive and active elements in language. Therein, he separates word meanings into what he calls the "lexical" and "speaker's" meaning. The lexical (or prosaic) meaning is given (passively), while the speaker's (poetic) meaning is achieved by actively employing this given lexical meaning.[74] This is indicated by the polarity found in language between "expression" and "communication" that suspends "perfect communication," which he states would only

> occur if all words had and retained identical meanings every time they were uttered and heard. . . . [I]t is not much use having a perfect means of communication if you have nothing to communicate except the relative positions of bodies in space—or if you will never again have anything *new* to communicate.[75]

Again, he affords this active element to the imagination. Of a piece with the conclusions of chapter 2, this indicates that the proper poetic utterance is not one that is divorced from reason, but rather (remaining within language; that is, within history) the poetic endows the otherwise prosaic with deeper meaning.

One can here surmise that if the poet is within history, yet creates afresh, then language cannot be conceived of solely in terms of immanence because it would devolve into an endless banal mimesis (i.e., univocity). Oppositely, language does not arrive from an entirely ahistorical (i.e., totalized or transcendental) gaze; otherwise it could no longer refer to history (i.e., equivocity). Indeed, neither account can speak of movement (i.e., the becoming of finitude). However, if one is to talk at all of movement, it appears that reason and imagination, lexical and speaker's meaning, prosaic and poetic, and history and revelation remain in polar tension; they are indeed distinguishable yet inseparable.

Here the attempt to summarize Barfield's poetic philosophy culminates in the following definition: *reality is suspended in a polar tension between the*

---

72. Ibid., 172.

73. Ibid., 177.

74. Barfield, *Speaker's Meaning*, 85.

75. Ibid., 37. See also, 115. He goes on to say that in the history of consciousness what one finds is "a progression from one type of subject-object relation towards another; from the state of active object, correlative to passive subject, to the state of passive object, correlative to active subject."

prosaic and poetic poles. The terms prosaic and poetic are suitable because they are Barfield's own, and because their polar relation can be analogously applied to all of the dualisms he critiques throughout his corpus (e.g., object/subject, matter/spirit, scientist/artist, reason/imagination, passive/active, lexical and speaker's meaning, etc., as well as those brought forth for the sake of theological emphases, immanent/transcendent, univocal/equivocal, sameness/difference, and philosophy/theology).

More to the point, these terms serve as a reminder of how Barfield utilized language to mete out the integral relation between being and language. Accordingly, if one's language is to properly refer to the real (as symbolic or meaningful), it should be poetic; that is, it should affirm the inseparability of the physical and metaphysical. So not only do these terms refer to words and their usage, but also they are indicative of a fundamental metaphysical structure meant to overcome the aforesaid *aporias* that representational (or Cartesian) epistemologies forced upon the modern consciousness.

Finally, such polarity intimates a theological opening that is brought into relief in the aforesaid description of inspiration and further expounded below. Although Barfield's poetic philosophy necessitates a theological move beyond the bounds of immanence, he can proffer nothing further, for he lacked the necessary theological resources to do so. It was perhaps the limits of his own language that kept him from fully articulating his poetic aesthetic in a way that Christian theology has for centuries done.

What follows builds upon the work of Barfield in order to develop a theory of *poiēsis* proper. It has hitherto been argued that pure philosophy, a form of prosaic language (particularly found in analytical philosophy and theology), issues forth from an immanentized ontology. Such an ontology presupposes a representational epistemology because once the real is reduced to a flattened space objects can only be "saved" by their representation (or appearance) within the mind of the subject. No longer known (or participated) as they are, essentially, reality's meaning is reduced to measurable and calculable human ends. This leads to a radical metaphysical skepticism.[76] The continental tradition is also indebted to this immanentized vision. While it recognizes the untenable nature of representation in Nietzsche's subjective Will to Power, it shuttles between an equally untenable passivity,[77] which altogether abandons subjectivity. This is the inevitable

76. Taylor, *Philosophical Arguments*. See, "Overcoming Epistemology."

77. See, for example, Wall, *Radical Passivity*. Wall specifically indicates that such notions of passivity are products of the modern era. See also, Schrag, *The Self after Postmodernity*. Schrag critiques both modern and postmodern accounts of the self for being couched as either purely active or purely passive.

consequence of a flattened ontology, a philosophy tripped of the theological, the *forsaking of* transcendence *for the sake of* immanence.[78]

Philosophy's divorce from theology left centuries of philosophers ill-equipped to address its own glaring dialectic whose origins are shrouded for the sake of "progress" and whose solution remains guised under trendy pejoratives such as "classical theism," "onto-theology," "Platonism for the people," and/or "substance metaphysics." So not only was this form of philosophy unable to account for subjectivity, it also struggled to account for its endless heralding of progress or history (the irony of modern secular liberalism). For it will be argued that without transcendence, philosophical discourse, as well as the social and physical sciences, devolves into an endless identical (mimetic) repetition of the same (following Kierkegaard)[79] wherein meaning dissolves. But if there is indeed forward movement, and one can truly talk of inspiration, creativity, and progress, one can only conceive of this in terms of a transcendence that constantly breaks in, as the very sustenance of immanence, a non-identical repetition seen in the oscillation between prosaic and poetic language, by a subject suspended between active and passive.[80] This form of transcendence (the "transcendence" here evoked is a concept of which Barfield appears unaware) represents an alternative to a flattened discourse, and as such, moves beyond Barfield's poetic philosophy, culminating in a Trinitarian theology. It is a speculative

---

78. See, for example, Hoff, "The Rise and Fall of the Kantian Paradigm." Hoff tells the story of modern theology's indebtedness to the philosophy of Kant traced in chapter 2, which he argues led to a division between faith and reason, revelation and knowledge, theology and philosophy, and the natural and supernatural. This formed a purely immanentized vision that no longer acknowledges anything but what appears. For Kant, "Everything we know is not God; and anything that transcends this knowledge evaporates into an empty concept" (186). This leads to Hegel's "Absolute" where, according to Hoff, "it becomes increasingly difficult to draw a clear distinction between the mystery of the Trinity and its traces or images in the history of salvation (i.e., the 'economic Trinity')" (189). Against this paradigm, Hoff reads Cusa to indicate that there are traces of the invisible in the visible. See also, Hoff, *The Analogical Turn*.

79. See footnote 3, above.

80. Barfield, *Poetic Diction*, 179–80. Kierkegaard's non-identical repetition is similar to Barfield's "slightly different thing that is said." He does not however articulate the divine in terms of transcendence. Nor does he employ the terms "immanence" and "transcendence," although it is quite clear (as has been continually reiterated) that he believed that those things that are transcendent (or subjective) are actually in the objective world (i.e., the world participates in them). The forms are what unify the matter one apprehends as objects. See also, Sugerman, *Evolution of Consciousness*, 22. Barfield mentions that Lewis was unable to conceive of polarity because he thought of God as completely transcendent. But this critique of Lewis is more about the relation of spirit and matter than it is about the proper theological distinction between the creature and Creator.

metaphysic of theological participation whereby the subject is not a ground in him- or herself (e.g., a raw representational epistemology of the onto-logically given), but paradoxically is drawn forth in his or her encounter with the symbolic nature of the real, a gift that continually arrives and is sustained in transcendence. In this striving forth (*epektasis*), this oscillation between subjectivity and objectivity, the subject constantly unearths deeper unforeseen realities hitherto unimagined, a revelation within history that is both in-and-beyond immanence. Barfield's philosophy points to this open-ness, but because he wed himself to a pagan philosophy, he was truly unable to think the difference of being. What follows proposes *poiēsis* proper in terms of a theology as poetic metaphysics that is faithful to Barfield's poetic philosophy, although more thoroughly theological.

Poiēsis Proper: Theology as Poetic Metaphysics

A Real Distinction

This subsection addresses how Christianity decisively broke from pagan thought by moving beyond the distinction between the ideal and the real to that between the creature and Creator. The following serves as a correc-tion to those elements of Barfield's thought that fail to address this crucial theological distinction, and also serves to clarify the relationship between the poet and his or her inspiration.

At bottom Barfield's poetic philosophy functions as a way of articu-lating the reality of a supersensible world that constitutes the sensible (in his words the relation between spirit and matter).[81] This philosophy, which followed Steiner's Anthroposophy (which seeks to train individuals to use their imagination in order to see the spiritual qualities in the world), formed the basis of his criticisms against the various dualisms hitherto mentioned. But, Barfield is never able to articulate an ontological origin outside of sim-ply stating that spirit creates matter. Because of this, his poetic subject seems at times to mimic the immanent dialect of active and passive and often car-ried pantheistic undertones. This is because theologically speaking he failed to think properly the difference between the creature and Creator,[82] because he never really considers the transcendence of being even in Platonic terms.

81. He most explicitly lays this out in Barfield, "Either: Or." See also, Barfield, "Matter, Imagination, and Spirit."

82. This is seen most clearly in his failure to properly distinguish the economic and immanent Trinity. For some examples see, Adey, *C. S. Lewis' Great War*, 113. Adey sum-marizes this univocal relation as from words to the Word, the "very self-consciousness traced by Barfield utilizing philology, literary theory, and philosophy is evidence of the

There is, after all, an overarching narrative that straddles this essay that suggests that nominalism's supposedly closed space—of flattened ontologies and the representational epistemologies they yield—remains irresolvably open. This is a narrative not unlike those of some theologians who have linked the origins of the separation of philosophy and theology with the denial of the constituency of universals, which they argue begins in the Middle Ages.[83] Later philosophy, even theology, in failing to ask the

---

eternal act of creation of the great 'I AM.'" See also, Barfield, *What Coleridge Thought*, 146. Therein, Barfield links imaginative perception with perception of the Trinity stating that understanding alone (without the imagination) always fails to recognize tri-unity. See also, 101. Barfield writes, "through imagination and the gift of reason we realize, in polarity, that very culmination as the possibility of a different and higher order of attachment." See also, 35. He writes, "In the duality of the opposite forces is the *manifestation* of a prior unity; and that unity is a 'power'; a 'productive' unity." See also, 111. He writes, "only that which itself transcends two contradictories can have produced them." It is the most basic act of perception, the unity of all phenomena, which bears witness to this claim. See also, Barfield, *Romanticism Comes of Age*, 143. Barfield notes that Coleridge's notion of "seminal identity" purportedly allowed him, "to carry the problem of the One and the Many on to another plane." See also, Barfield, "Either: Or," 28. "Polar opposites are generative of each other—and together they generate a new product." See also, 29–30. Barfield writes, what is generally conceived as duality is, in fact, tri-unity. See also, 31. He notes, the doctrine of the Trinity for Coleridge was "the one substantive truth, which is the form, manner, and involvement of all truths." See also, De Lange, *Owen Barfield*, 177. De Lange indicates that this "tri-unity" or "Trinity" is Coleridge's "dynamic polarity," which Barfield claimed to be so unique.

83. A few noteworthy texts are, De Lubac, *Corpus Mysticum*. De Lubac's work traced the advent of nominalism as far back as the eighth and ninth centuries, which he identifies with the nuanced changes that the term *corpus mysticum* underwent. For de Lubac, these subtle changes defined the future of theology up until the present day. De Lubac adamantly opposes what he identifies as the division of the body of Christ (i.e., between the eucharistic and church body). Instead, following the church fathers he argues for a "mystical" understanding of the body of Christ stating, that "there is virtually no need to search for formulations or expressions to distinguish one 'body' from the other" (23). Hence the very meaning of mystical or "sacramental" suggests that it would be difficult to make firm distinctions between varying aspects of the body of Christ (23). The church fathers would have simply understood the *corpus mysticum* as a sacrament; the Eucharist as a visible sign pointing to that which it signifies. In the eighth and ninth centuries, however, the body of the church comes to be designated as the "mystical body" in opposition to the eucharistic body (74). With the loss of its mystical element, the ecclesial body is no longer a sign or a sacrament of the body of Christ, it becomes merely corporeal (87). As de Lubac writes, "The adjective 'mystical' passed from being the signifier to the signified, from the Eucharist, to the Church" (101). In fact, "it would become quite common to speak of the 'mystical body' with no reference to the Eucharist" (114). Ultimately, the disintegration of this ontological symbolism leads to a division between the corporeal, objective, sensible body of Christ and the spiritual and subjective body. For de Lubac, the new rationalism of the eleventh century marks the beginning of modern theology, which gave birth to the Renaissance. Within this new way of thinking dialectic emerges (228–29). Mystic and reason are opposed (232).

question of creation's transcendent origins failed to see that it was Christian theology that, for the first time, conceived of being in a way that outwitted pagan philosophy.

In the early years of Christendom there lurked a residual idealism that was eventually sloughed off. For pagan thought this meant that the real (or material) in some way diminished the ideal (immaterial).[84] For Christianity

---

On the heels of the opening of the chasm between faith and reason (236) Christian rationalism is founded (238) and "theology would never look back" (218).

See also, De Certeau, *The Mystic Fable*. De Certeau locates a loss of symbolic language in the Middle Ages. Mystical language, the "deontologization" of language (123), occurs when language is detached from its original function and is instead modeled on the passions of the speaking subjects (141). The "mystic adjective" applied to a noun causes the symbol to become "opaque," which in turn symbolizes only that which the mystic subject demands (145). In other words, words are not things; they are *signs* pointing to that which they signify. When a word becomes opaque it ceases to live, and can no longer be called into question or reinterpreted. It becomes hidden, and only the one who makes it opaque holds the "secret" to its meaning. De Certeau calls mystical language Nietzschean because internalized language has no reference to delineate truth from lie (175–76). Reference therefore, can only come from an authority that ironically turns out to be the doctrines of mystics. Mystic discourse operates within an immanent frame wherein experience becomes the foundation of faith (183). De Certeau writes, "The world is no longer perceived as spoken by God . . . it has become opacified, objectified, and detached from its supposed speaker . . ." (188). The ontological necessity of being is replaced by the will or disposition of the subject, which relegates the object (God) (247). See also, Pickstock, *After Writing*. See, specifically, "The Language of Modernity," 88–100.

84. Schindler, "What's the Difference?" Schindler indicates that Platonic participation, "explains how the many can, in fact, be one, but it does not account for the *fact* of multiplicity" (7). Plato overcomes dualism, but is unable to account for multiplicity (8). Schindler then turns to the Neo-Platonist Plotinus who asserts that to give being the one must be beyond being, thereby linking transcendence and generosity of productivity, which, out of abundance, makes something other than itself. Thus, Plotinus not only accounts for the way things are, but also that they are, their otherness is "produced" (9–10). Schindler concludes, "Plotinus affirms the *goodness* of difference, but he seems to do so *insofar* as it serves to 'multiply' unity, and not because difference is simply good *as such*" (14). In this way, even Neo-Platonic versions of emanation still lack a positive construal of the sensible world of difference. "Our only way out would be to affirm a first principle that, while absolutely simple, is not *mere* unity" (14); hence, later Trinitarian formulations.

See also, Milbank, "Christianity and Platonism in East and West." Similarly, in his response to Bradshaw, Milbank argues that for this reason one must reject the Eastern notion of emanations. Milbank argues against David Bradshaw's synergistic participation in divine energies, because, even though they are distinct from God's essence, they are still divine and therefore cannot avoid the idolatry of the univocity of being. Instead, Milbank makes a case for what he calls the "mediated" or "paradoxical" nature of participation in Aquinas. According to Milbank, Aquinas does not make the mediating term of participation the "Good" (as for the Neo-Platonists), but *esse*, which paradoxically indicates what is shared in by the creature and Creator. What is shared in is "to be."

this emerges in the various forms of subordinationism that the Councils of Nicaea and Chalcedon sought to correct. By bringing together the doctrinal formulations of these councils with the doctrine of creation *ex nihilo*, Christian theology broke from this residual idealism by asserting that the *kenotic* emptying that is creation was not a diminishing of the divine (hence, the Nicene Trinitarian formulations aimed at correcting subordination) but rather an expression of what it means to be most fully divine (as developed in Chalcedonian Christology). Christianity thus sought a way to account for the difference between Creator and creation without positing a dualism. For theology, finite being was no longer conceived of as a diminishing of the ideal or divine, but as an overflow of God's infinite being (*esse*).

So it was Christianity with its Trinitarian and Christological formulations that first remarked upon the totalization or closure of being by conceiving of God as a transcendent Creator *ex nihilo* who is utterly distinct from his creation and a created order whose very sustenance is, concomitantly, entirely in God; a God whose transcendent *esse* is not univocally shared by creation nor equivocally different from creation, but analogously both in-and-beyond creation. Doctrinally speaking, this vision maintained that the economic and immanent Trinity, while distinct, remain inseparably bound in the incarnation (the hypostatic union—one person [i.e., hypostasis] who consists of both human and divine natures that coincide but do not "mix"). Thus for creation to be "in" God, and he "beyond" it, is precisely what it means to be most fully God. This enabled theologians to affirm the ontological dependence of an otherwise immanentized cosmos without collapsing the distinction between that which participates in God and God Himself; what in theology would come to be known as the "real distinction" of creaturely existence. This scheme envisages a hierarchy of causal connections wherein the subject is free while God is concomitantly sovereign.

Various forms of Platonic idealism tend to grant transcendence to the form (or unity), but not the image itself.[85] This view leads to a discounted view of finitude because it conceives of the unity of form as more real than the diversity of its images. Instead, the particular metaphysic of participation employed by Christian theologians sought to avoid the two extremes of pantheism and the various forms of idealisms or Gnosticisms that envis-

---

As opposed to emanation, the participation is not *in* the similitude, but rather *is itself* the similitude, which, according to Milbank, avoids a *tertium quid* between God and creature. Milbank claims that, "This amounts to the strongest possible doctrine of both creation and grace as involving the presence of God himself to creatures, while in no way compromising the divine reserve of transcendence." This paradoxical or analogous participation is "[t]he only logic that can spell out the doctrine of creation *ex nihilo*."

85. Schindler, "What's the Difference?" 3–4.

aged the finite world as a sort of lack of infinite or of the divine, which subtly denigrates the body and ultimately downplays the resurrection. This is why Christian theology adopts, or rather adapts, a particular reading of Plato that not only conceives of the forms as transcendent (in-and-beyond matter),[86] but also conceives of the "Good" as the arch-form; the source of all being. In this way, the Good is not somewhere beyond, existing only in itself, but exists in everything one recognizes as good.[87] Accordingly, while the finite points to the infinite, it is paradoxically only by looking *through* the finite that one apprehends the infinite.[88] This sacramental gaze recognizes the goodness of materiality spoken of in the Genesis narrative and affirmed in the resurrection of Christ. Most crucially, the transcendent nature of the Platonic Good conceives of being beyond a mere totality, beyond those contemporary philosophical renditions of a metaphysic of "substance" or "presence" or "onto-theology," which misunderstand the crucial difference between Christian theology and Platonic metaphysics. Further, to conceive of metaphysics in such a way would be to misread even Plato. For already in Plato the forms and matter existed by a participation in the transcendent Good. Plato already hints that existence is mysteriously suspended between being and nothing. It is in this way that Plato's conception of the Good as beyond being denied any totality or closure to finite being; and, as will be seen, it is this particular form of Platonic metaphysics that Christian theol-

86. See, Perl, "The Presence of the Paradigm." Perl's main thesis regarding Platonic metaphysics is "that immanence and transcendence are not opposed but that, on the contrary, the former implies the latter" (340). "The transcendence of the forms . . . is thus not a denial but rather a consequence of the immanence of the form . . . of their being universal characters which are present in many instances" (346). See also, Schindler, "What's the Difference?," 6–8. Sensibles exist, but are "*wholly derived* from the truly existent forms," which is what it actually means to refer to sensibles as participations, because they are not set over against the forms, as "they *add nothing* to" them. See also, Pickstock, "The Late Arrival of Language," 239. Pickstock argues that Plato has a more positive view of material things than is generally granted him precisely because it is the particulars that "play a vital mediating role in terms of ascent to the forms."

87. For an exemplary reading of the Platonic Good as transcendent in the manner here suggested see, Gadamer, *The Idea of the Good*, 115 and 124–25. See also, Schindler, *Plato's Critique of Impure Reason*, 1, 86, 104, 159, and 220.

88. For a thorough summary of the history of participation and its Christian reception see, Schindler, "What's the Difference?," 2–3. Schindler maintains that for the Christian tradition, "Creation is ultimately *good*, and we encounter that goodness not merely in looking *past* things to their source, but also in looking *at* them, in celebrating their intrinsic solidity and their irreducible uniqueness." See also, Milbank and Pickstock, *Truth in Aquinas*, 47. Because finite minds can only grasp finite things through the mediation of the senses, things in themselves must be read as signs of God. "The metaphysics of participation in Aquinas is immediately and implicitly a phenomenology of seeing more than one sees, of recognizing the invisible in the visible."

ogy absorbs as a way of distinguishing between God and creation. Barfield nowhere articulates this notion of transcendence. Indeed, his Anthroposophic proclivities coupled with his own idealist tendencies led him to espouse reincarnation.[89] It is in this way that his poetic philosophy failed to realize how Christianity broke from pagan thought by envisaging proper transcendence in terms of a real distinction in the difference between creation and the Creator.[90]

Christian theology is predicated on an ontology that is understood, not in terms of recollection of a pre-existent past (as with Barfield's theory of reincarnation), but an immanent existence that arrives as a gift. Accordingly, knowing and being are, in the words of Gregory of Nyssa, an *epiktasis*; that is, a forward movement towards God. Creation, thus conceived, is an endless overflow or donation of being in beings, not a static presence that is merely recollected (by an incarnated eternal soul), but an arriving revelation from the divine. In light of this ontological realization it seemed, at least to Christian metaphysicians, that pagan ontology (based on the pre-existence or eternality of the soul) was no longer philosophically tenable. Because God does not lack in creating the finite, but rather, creation is an overflow of God's infinite love and Goodness, there should be no turning back, but a present forward gaze in hope and love. Plato seemed at least to glimpse beyond the totality of finitude by positioning the Good as transcendent, and in this sense as a sort of arrival from an infinite plenitude,[91] yet for all of his genius, he does not conceive of being as created *ex nihilo*. Christianity, in its formulation of the doctrine of creation *ex nihilo*, not only conceived of

89. Barfield, "Self and Reality," 171–75. The Platonic concept of anamnesis is here crucial for understanding Barfield's poetic philosophy. In this way, the creative mind participates in the ultimate creative act. Barfield often amalgamates the concepts of rediscovery, creativity, reincarnation, and anamnesis. See also, Barfield, "The Rediscovery of Allegory (II)." He sees that allegory is a sort of mimesis or anamnesis, a participatory activity. See also, Barfield, "Why Reincarnation?" Barfield admits that his view is incompatible with Christianity, but seeks to justify belief in reincarnation on the basis of the societal changes (e.g., class distinctions) that it might bring about.

90. Barfield, *Saving the Appearances*, 165–66. It should be noted that Barfield does indicate that within time humanity will never be in a direct relation to the eternal Trinity. See also, Barfield, *Poetic Diction*, 191. He denies "synthesis," calling it discursive and not poetic, because it puts together subjective ideas. Even if Barfield is guilty of a latent idealism, in both cases here, he seems to be against absolutizing God or, theologically speaking, collapsing the distinction between economic and immanent Trinity.

91. Milbank, "The Thing That Is Given," 525. In his critique of Heidegger, who's reading of Plato and subsequent rejection of metaphysics he calls "fancy," Milbank, like Hart (see next note, below), contends that Plato already sees beyond a metaphysical totality. This means that Plato's recollection is not of a given past or an already present, because the *eidos* lies beyond space and time arriving repeatedly as a gift, "reencountered as we advance towards the future . . . ."

being (and hence knowing) beyond any conceivable metaphysical totality,[92] but in so doing spoke of being as a gift that is ceaselessly given.

Also distinct from Barfield is that Christianity affirms that God creates the soul and body concomitantly.[93] Christianity does not speak of reincarnation or a created, yet pre-existent soul, because to do so would imply some form of idealism (i.e., a separation of body and soul), which the incarnation and resurrection simply do not leave open.[94] And this, again, regards the Trinitarian and Christological formulations that assert that God's taking upon flesh was not in any way a diminishing of who God is, but rather a fulfillment ("For in him all the fullness of deity dwells in bodily form")[95] or overflow ("He is the image of the invisible God, the firstborn over all creation. For by him all things were created, both in the heavens and on earth, visible and invisible, whether thrones or dominions or rulers or authorities—all things have been created through him and for Him. He is before all things, and in him all things hold together")[96] of who God is, and points to the eschatological redemption of all creation (Jesus, "whom heaven must receive until the period of restoration of all things about which God spoke by the mouth of his holy prophets from ancient time").[97] In this way, creation is not a static given, but always arrives as a gift, as an outpouring of God's transcendence from a God who freely creates all that is.

Christianity, distinct from Barfield's idealism, speaks of the forward repetition (as there is no need of recollecting a pre-existent soul) of a created (existent) soul and body that participates in the divine life ("For You formed my inward parts; You wove me in my mother's womb").[98] The soul (in becoming) does not look back, but reaches beyond its own otherwise immanentized selfhood to know God. In her *After Writing*, Catherine Pickstock reminds one that for Christianity, "what is recollected is not sought by a retrospective repetition, (for there is no question of recalling the experi-

---

92. Hart, "The Offering of Names," 275. Hart writes, "it was only when Christian thought arrived, and with it the doctrine of creation, that the totality was broken open and, for the first time ever, philosophy was granted a glimpse of being's splendid strangeness within its very immediacy and gratuity."

93. Clarke, *The Creative Retrieval of Saint Thomas Aquinas*, 175–78.

94. Gregory of Nyssa, *On the Making of Man*, 419 and 420–22 and *On the Soul and the Resurrection*, 433, 437, and 445, in Schaff and Wace, *A Select Library of Nicene and Post-Nicene Fathers*. Gregory goes so far as to affirm that the soul and body are inseparable from their inception, through death (even in death, in the disintegration of matter, the soul persists with the body), and through to the resurrection.

95. Col 2:9.

96. Col 1:15–17.

97. Acts 3:21.

98. Ps 139:13.

ence of the pre-existent soul) but a non-identical repetition in the inhabited present. This is not a retreat into an inviolable self, but rather an opening of the self to receive the mediation of the transcendent in and through the immanent."[99] Elsewhere she says, if Christianity is to talk of recollection, it is not a retrieval of the *a priori* via introspection but rather moves forward by, in a way, forgetting the past driven by the desire to know something in the world.[100]

An example of how Christian epistemology reflects this ontological paradigm is found in D. C. Schindler's critique of immanentized epistemologies.[101] Schindler juxtaposes immanent (representational) epistemologies ("the mind can receive only what it is in some sense already prepared to receive") with Balthasar's[102] "dramatic" (or analogical)[103] epistemology where, "anticipation is fulfilled by what it cannot have expected. . . . The form does not become less intelligible by the disruption, but, in fact, it becomes far more intelligible than one could have anticipated at the outset or along the way."[104] In this way, the most basic act of cognition is recast in the language of an encounter, not an immanent arrival *a priori* known, but a surprise that shatters the soul's immanent capacities.[105] In Christian epistemology there is always a correspondence between reason and revelation. Reason is always anticipating to be unsettled by an encounter, by the very fact that it is "recognized" as an encounter yet still corresponds to the nature of reason.[106]

99. Pickstock, *After Writing*, 25.

100. Pickstock, "The Late Arrival of Language." See, endnote 120, where Pickstock cites Chrétien's, *The Unforgettable and the Unhoped For*. I agree with Pickstock's reading here, although perhaps Chrétien ultimately fails to envisage Plato's vision of the Good as "beyond being" in a way truly distinct from Kant (i.e., he does not articulate being in terms of proper transcendence, as with Plato, and fails altogether to envisage being analogically, ultimately revealing his indebtedness to the Kantian paradigm).

101. Schindler, "Surprised by Truth."

102. Schindler sets up Balthasar's epistemology as follows: (1) It begins with the beauty of the form which beckons the subject. (2) The subject actively responds. (3) Truth is unfolded, "which is both anticipated and beyond all expectations" (606). For Schindler, this is what opens up the analogy between every act of cognition (as an act of faith) within philosophy and theology (607).

103. Schindler, "Surprised by Truth," 607. Schindler defines drama as "the simultaneity of continuity and discontinuity." See also, note 40 on the same page, wherein he calls this the very "essence of analogy" defined by Lateran IV as "similarity within a greater dissimilarity." He states, "The doctrine of analogy reveals the inadequacy of the view that insists on 'clarifying concepts' philosophically, and then applying them within theology."

104. Ibid., 604–5.

105. Ibid., 605.

106. Ibid., 607–8.

This cognitive act, a non-identical repetition, always points to transcendence in immanence and this is why, according to Schindler, "Christianity can lay claim to the assent of reason, can lay claim, in fact, to the very roots of reason, while at the same time claiming it arrives as a sheer gift of grace."[107] "Thus, the gratuity of revelation is intrinsic to, constitutive of, the integrity of reason, whether it be the revelation of being in its natural self-disclosure or the revelation of the triune God in history."[108] According to Schindler, revelation does not collapse the limits of humanity (into a sort of theo-pan-ism), but honors them, so that revelation remains a surprise as an inbreaking of transcendence.[109] Similarly, Milbank and Pickstock, in their *Truth in Aquinas*, indicate that the mind is endowed with an intimation of a desire to know something, and as such, the will is not entirely subjective but is drawn towards the object that is first disclosed, drawing the subject from potency to act.[110] This indicates that truth is never a direct representation, but rather, an analogous relation between the mind and the way things manifest themselves as one comes to know them.[111] Conor Cunningham also shows how closely Christian epistemology is allied with its ontology.[112] Following the tradition of Christian metaphysics, he suggests that because being does not belong to creatures essentially (i.e., only by participation), it is nothing but shear gratuity. It arrives as a gift. To talk of recollection, thus, "is not a denigration of creatures, but quite the reverse."[113] In this scheme, "Immanence is itself the recollection of transcendence."[114] Coincidently, one's life is not about a collecting, but of recollecting that which one does

107. Ibid., 608.

108. Ibid., 609.

109. Ibid., 611.

110. Milbank and Pickstock, *Truth in Aquinas*, 39.

111. Ibid., 9–11 and 17. Aquinas's ability to hold the tension between concepts exhibits a "profound obscurity which resists easy interpretation or analysis" (21). If there is no Kantian pure reason (*a priori*) then how can one be sure to know of God? If there is no pure experience (*a posteriori*), how can one know that experience or phenomenon is not tainted? To deny both the *a priori* and the *a posteriori*, there must be a disclosure of God to the intellect via participation (36). In utilizing analogy, Aquinas has already overcome Kantian epistemological categories by insisting on the ontological nature of knowing. Like Plato's Sun, God is known, or makes himself known, through the forms (28–29) or the good found in surrounding objects that participate in God. Hence, "The invisible things of God in Romans always made visible everywhere, suggested precisely a manifestation of the divine essence, which can only be made available by grace" (39).

112. Cunningham, "Being Recalled."

113. Ibid., 60.

114. Ibid., 73.

not and as such one's life is a gift of borrowed existence.[115] As mediated, all knowledge is one from potency to act, requiring a prior actuality to be potential. As such, all knowledge, like being, is a non-identical repetition of divine knowledge.[116]

So for Christianity the discussion was no longer how one might distinguish between the ideal and the real, the forms and material, beings and being, but about the distinction between the Creator (who is being) and his creation (that which participates in his being). Just how this distinction is articulated is detailed below. But, to briefly rehearse, the concept of being as gifted (*ex nihilo*), as constantly arriving from an infinite plenitude, breaks from any metaphysic or onto-theology that strives to conceive of being as a totality. More to the point, the affirmation of the doctrine of creation *ex nihilo* meant that Christian theologians would now have to think not of the difference between the ideal and the real, but between Creator and creation. This difference was not simply a dogmatic assertion, but was developed through years of metaphysical speculation regarding the nature of existence. Since it seemed philosophically untenable to claim that existence was pre-existent (an effect without a cause) or rather immanent, theologians developed the doctrine of creation *ex nihilo*, which sought (by faith) to clarify the relation between things that "have existence" and the "Creator of existence" or "existence itself." Following this, theology maintains that all finite "existents" (*ens commune*) have their origin in, and are therefore related to, an infinite divine act (*esse*). Just how one speaks of this relationship determines literally every thing.

Generally, the difficulty lies in articulating how to grant autonomy to creation, while at the same time insisting that the very being of creation is sustained by participation in God. More specifically, for Christianity this would have to be articulated in a way that outwitted various forms of agonistic philosophy; that is, in a way that envisaged the creation of being not as an original strife (between God and creation), a diminishing of the ideal, the forms, or of God, but rather, a peaceful overflow of divine transcendence, which, in turn, indicates that the participation of creation in God affirms what it is to be most fully God (Christological). And, regarding the present project, this is analogous to the question: how can one grant the subject creative freedom as a creature (active), while admitting the subject is in some way determined (passively)? To put it more bluntly, how can one define a relationship between the subject and his or her inspiration, without

115. Ibid., 59–60.
116. Ibid., 76.

collapsing one into the other (e.g., a Spinozistic pantheism or Hegelian "theo-pan-ism")?[117]

For theology, neither of these formulations proved adequate because they failed to account for what theologians saw as a distinction between "being" and those things that "have being." In this way, God (whose essence is to exist) is utterly distinct from his finite creation (whose essence and existence remain in tension). Another way of articulating this distinction is to say that creation is in "flux" or "becoming"; it is never a ground in itself, but always striving forth to resolve this tension (i.e., between essence and existence) in a God whose essence and existence are identical. This is how Christianity maintained the difference between Creator and creature.[118] The sharing of creation in God is thus neither univocal nor equivocal. Theology, instead, employs analogy as the only feasible way to describe the paradoxical relation established in this difference. The analogy is not meant to be a share in some common being between God and creatures (i.e., univocity), but rather the analogy is *in the difference* between God (whose essence is his existence) and the creature who participates in an existence that is never its own (i.e., its essence). This is further elaborated below.

But for now, this way of analogy formed the basis of how one must talk about God.[119] This creaturely tension points towards the inadequacy of finite language; that is, of created being's finitude. Thus, following the *apophatic* theology of the Neo-Platonists, this language of analogy was formally adopted at the Fourth Lateran Council in 1215, eventually taking on the title of *analogia entis*.[120] This analogical formulation, which blends both

117. Przywara, *Analogia Entis*. See, section 4, "Philosophical and Theological Metaphysics."

118. For a great summary of the relationship between theology and pagan thought, particularly regarding the development of the doctrine of creation *ex nihilo* see, Soskice, "Naming God," 247–54.

119. Ibid., 254. What was articulated was a two-way relation between God and creation. The theologian could say that because God acts freely in the creative event, being an uncreated Creator, he is in no way dependent on creation, whereas creation is entirely dependent on Him. This meant that not only did God create from nothing, but that Creation is continually sustained by God's free act of gratuity. Soskice notes that this breaks most decisively from the Aristotelian cosmology, which restricted the prime mover to the same laws governing the cosmos, and similarly from the Neo-Platonic One who emanates, and as such, is "metaphysically continuous with the world."

120. For a concise summary of the *analogia entis* see, Hart, *The Beauty of the Infinite*, 241–8. Hart notes that the development of the *analogia entis*, "succeeded in uniting a metaphysics of participation to the Biblical doctrine of creation, within the framework of trinitarian dogma, and in so doing, made it possible for the first time in Western thought to contemplate the utter difference of being from beings and the nature of true transcendence" (241). See also, Hart, "The Offering of Names," 285–91.

cataphatic and *apophatic* language, maintains that "whatever similarity there may be between the creature and God, the dissimilarity is always greater." This formulation, which serves as a model for theological discourse, is thus meant to coincide with a fundamental metaphysical structure, and for some, it was understood as buttressing the theological doctrine espoused at the Councils of Nicaea and Chalcedon, which enabled theologians to affirm the three persons of the Trinity as coeval, while allowing that Christ's taking on of flesh in no way diminished God. In this way, the creative act, the *kenotic* emptying of divine transcendence (i.e., the economic Trinity), in no way compromised God in Himself (i.e., the immanent Trinity), thus indicating that transcendence, is not opposed to immanence, but rather, in-and-beyond, as is detailed in the following subsection.

But as the "passage to modernity"[121] unfolds this type of language became increasingly obscure in light of modernity's univocal discourse and its penchant for objectivity. For, if proper theological discourse holds that God is not an object within creation, nor a transcendental unknown deity, modern discourse, by forgetting the aforesaid analogical difference between being and beings (i.e., that beings cannot account for being—one's essence is never its existence), divorced itself from theology and proceeded only after bracketing God out (e.g., phenomenology's "it appears" ignores that "it is"). Being, thus, is only conceived of in terms of what appears, in the form of representation.[122] One cannot ask "what" something is, while forgetting "that" something is. On the one hand, Barfield failed to think this crucial theological difference, yet on the other, his participatory philosophy serves as a reminder that any attempt to erect a totalizing philosophy is idolatrous, a "Tower of Babel" (to borrow a phrase of David Hart).[123] It is in this way that Barfield's poetic philosophy points towards its own theological culmination.

Analogy: Transcendence "in-and-beyond" Immanence

To clarify further this theological difference the following examines the theological relationship between transcendence and immanence prior to their supposed division. Here to conceive of transcendence, not as juxtaposed to, but in-and-beyond immanence indicates what the labors of modern and

121. Dupré, *Passage to Modernity*. Dupré outlines the "passage to modernity" as the turn to the subject as the sole source of meaning. Once transcendence is relegated to a supernatural realm the subject must turn in upon himself to find meaning. See also, Latour, *We Have Never Been Modern*.

122. See, Hart, "The Offering of Names," 262–63.

123. Hart, *The Beauty of the Infinite*, 248.

postmodern discourse have pointed to all along; that subjectivity is not tenable in purely active or passive terms, but instead as suspended in tension, analogically. Any lack in this proper *poiēsis* can only be conceived in terms of a momentary caesura of the peaceful donation of being from God. In this scheme the tension between subject and object remains irresolvable (in agreement with Barfield), precisely because, theologically speaking (beyond Barfield), creation itself is suspended in a tension, yet paradoxically it is this very tension "in" immanence by which God remains infinitely "beyond" his creation. Aquinas articulates this creaturely tension using the terms "essence" and "existence," as they differ in their relation within creation and in God, as will be further explicated. This is followed by an examination of some twentieth-century Catholic theologians who, building upon this Thomistic scheme, employed similar language to Barfield (e.g., likening the subject/object relation to the essence/existence polarity in creation) to articulate this tension (i.e., "creaturely metaphysic") within immanence.

In light of modern misconstruals of "classical theism,"[124] the discussion regarding the relationship between philosophy and theology, and the

124. For example see, Tanner, *God and Creation in Christian Theology*. Some relevant points are Tanner's critique of Kant's transcendentalism (21). She notes that the denial of proper transcendence (i.e., God who transcends the world and is intimately involved as Creator) has plagued modern theology leading to rivalrous accounts of God (122). She argues one must unsettle "the complacent self-evidence of modern assumptions used to interpret traditional Christian language" (6). She believes that it is the theologian's job to overcome the inadequacies of language (20) and to articulate this relation in a "non-contrastive way" (46–7) that prohibits univocity (59). Tanner states that when theology fails to account for these inadequacies, "Christian behaviors and attitudes may be skewed" (19). She suggests a helpful plumb-line is to ensure Aquinas's two causal orders be maintained (152–53). See also, Placher, *The Domestication of Transcendence*.

Evidences of such confusion are replete in those recent discussions that, proceeding under Cartesian or Kantian premises, have entirely misconstrued classical theism as a kind of "onto-theology." As such, classical theism has become a pejorative amongst pop-culture Christian sects (e.g., "open theism") who are unaware of their anachronistic prejudices. Ironically, such trends cannot conceive of a theology outside of the strictures of the same modern philosophy they claim to be rejecting. For a text that clarifies such errant views, see De Nys, "God, Creatures, and Relations." De Nys seeks to correct modern misinterpretations of classical theism, which insist that God cannot be transcendent (or "wholly other") and immanent ("intimately present in everything"). Against this misinterpretation, de Nys correctly argues that the God who is both "wholly other" and "intimate" is none other than the Thomistic God of classical theism: "It belongs to classical theism on account of the position about God, creatures, and the status of relations between them. According to that position God's transcendence is such that there is no connection with creatures that God requires in order to be or to be understood. At the same time God is intimately present to creatures as the self-communicating principle of their very being" (613). While in modern thought transcendence and immanence are juxtaposed, for Aquinas, who de Nys calls "a principle defining

debate between Catholics and Protestants regarding the *analogia entis*,[125] the twentieth century has seen an increase in Thomistic scholarship regarding just how Aquinas and his commentators couched the relationship between God and creation (whether successfully or unsuccessfully). For this reason, it is important to at least draw upon a few of those Thomists[126] to articulate this distinction.

Before proceeding, and in order to be faithful to Aquinas's notion of reason as the natural desire for the supernatural[127] one must always begin asserting that while theology demands the most rigorous of metaphysical speculation, God remains a mystery. Thus, to make a doctrine of analogy or the subjective middle here proposed would be to do precisely what theology intends to guard against, collapsing the being of God into a totalized or onto-theological gaze. For this reason all of the commentators here agree that Aquinas's notion transcendence is not opposed to immanence, but *in-and-beyond* immanence. In this scheme, one might say that metaphysical speculation is envisaged as something akin to Schlegel's phrase, "a finite longing for the infinite."

Aquinas's God is both transcendent and immanent in the modern conception of the words. Kathryn Tanner notes, that "Transcendence" for Aquinas "does not exclude God's positive fellowship with the world or presence within it."[128] Louis Dupré notes that, "the paradox of divine transcendence is that it can be consistently maintained only as long as God is conceived as fully immanent . . . ."[129] And, when D. C. Schindler distinguishes the Christian notion of participation from the pagan notion underscored above he notes that Aquinas's notion of participation is "an affirmation of the difference of

---

figure in classical theism" (595), as well as other classical theists, a transcendent God means that he is also immanent. It is obvious that, "Aquinas, and along with him classical theism, does not conceive of God as removed, remote, withdrawn, isolated from, or uninvolved with creatures" (604). See also, Dodds, *The Unchanging God of Love.*

125. There is of course Barth's famous charge against Przywara's *analogia entis* as the invention of the "anti-Christ." See, Barth, *Church Dogmatics*, vol. 1.1, xiii.

126. For an introduction on the present scholarship regarding Aquinas see, Kerr, *After Aquinas* and Jordan, *Rewritten Theology.* See also, Jordan, *Ordering Wisdom*; Clarke, *Explorations in Metaphysics*; Te Velde, *Participation and Substantiality*; Te Velde, *Aquinas on God*; Burrell, *Aquinas: God and Action*; and Schindler, "What's the Difference?"

127. For work regarding Aquinas's vision as stated above see, Dupré, "On the Natural Desire of Seeing God"; De Lubac, *The Mystery of the Supernatural*; and Milbank, *The Suspended Middle.*

128. Tanner, *God and Creation in Christian Theology*, 79.

129. Dupré, "Transcendence and Immanence," 9.

that which participates, and thus opens the world to its transcendent source without thereby making the world something 'insubstantial.'"[130]

As glossed above, Aquinas employed particular terms that aimed to articulate God's relation to creatures in a way that maintained this in-and-beyond paradigm. Because each particular "existent" (i.e., *"what"* something is) in creation cannot account for its own "existence" (i.e., *"that"* it is), Aquinas talks of a distinction between existence itself (*ipsum esse*) and created things that have existence by participation (*ens commune*). He indicates that no created existent can account for what being is in itself or being's essence (*essentia*),[131] because existents, by merely having existence (and therefore, not being existence in themselves), remain comprised of an incommensurable composite of essence ("what" it *is*) and existence ("that" it *is*). According to Aquinas, all finite existents (comprised of essence and existence) are always in a state of becoming what they are (from potency to act), whereas, purely actual being "is reserved for God alone, of whom it is said his essence it is to exist (*ipsum esse subsistens*)."[132] Aquinas here borrows from Aristotle to call God *actus purus*[133] in order to distinguish him from the creaturely realm of becoming.[134] It is in this way that the difference between God and creation is established.

For Aquinas, this incommensurable essence/existence distinction in creation is a transcendental intimation within finite creation of a transcendent infinite horizon wherein essence and existence perfectly coincide.[135] It is, thus, this absence of a distinction in God that separates God from the

130. Schindler, "What's the Difference?," 15.

131. Te Velde, *Participation and Substantiality*, 193.

132. Clarke, *Explorations in Metaphysics*, 94. Clarke notes, "For if [God's] essence were composed, [he] would necessarily have to be caused and therefore receive or participate the perfection in question from another instead of being its source."

133. Pieper, *Guide to Thomas Aquinas*, 137. Pieper also affirms that for Aquinas, God is the "Being of whom it may be said not only that existence is part of His nature, but that His nature consists in existing. . . . God is that Being whose whole nature it is to exist, that is to say, to be the *actus*. God is existence in itself, *actus purus*."

134. Clarke, *Explorations in Metaphysics*, 89. Clarke indicates that the decisive break from Aristotle made by Aquinas lies "at the very heart of the metaphysics of being, namely, in the radical shift of equilibrium operated by St. Thomas from form and essence to the act of existence or *esse* as the metaphysical core of every being and the basic unifying perfection of the universe."

135. Hart, "The Offering of Names," 284–85. Hart says, "One then sees that though the 'what it is' of a thing is never commensurate to the surprising truth 'that it is,' it is always good that this is *this*, and that this *is*. . . . This mysterious coherence of the wholly fitting and utterly gratuitous then urges reflection toward the proportion of their harmony, which is to say toward the infinity where essence and existence coincide as the ontological peace of both a primordial belonging-together and an original gift[;] . . . neither can be grasped according to the discrete properties of finite reality."

world, while at the same time it is this very difference that affirms the good-ness of the world.[136] Another way of putting it is to say that God, as self-subsistent (*ipsum esse subsistens*), is a "real identity" of essence (*essentia*) and existence (*esse*) (i.e., God's essence *is* His existence, or to exist *is* what He *is*—"I am who I am"), whereas creatures are constituted by a "real distinc-tion" between essence and existence.[137] One might say, God *is* existence, while the creature *has* its existence and essence by participation in God.[138]

At first glance it seems that *esse* is something that both God and cre-ation share univocally (indeed this assumption is what sparked Karl Barth's infamous rejection of Erich Przywara's formulation of the *analogia entis*). But, Aquinas is quite unique in his definition of the participation of *esse* by essences.[139] Commentators remark that unlike the creature, the *esse* of God is not *had* by God but *is* His essence.[140] Here it is important to note that for Aquinas, God (as *ipsum esse subsistens*) is the cause of *esse*.[141] To say that creatures participate in God's existence is not to say they share in the same *esse*, but rather, is a way of expressing the relation between creatures who depend on God for their origin and analogical imitation of the divine es-sence.[142] Ultimately then, the analogy is not *in* the *esse*, but *in the difference* between God (*ipsum esse*—whose essence is to exist) and creation (*ens com-mune*—whose essence and existence remain forever incommensurable). This allows Aquinas to say that the participation in *esse* is by the creature alone, for God (whose essence it is to exist) would not "share" in his own *esse*. Thus, God does not share in some common *esse* with the creature, but the creature shares his *esse*. Ultimately, the participation of creatures is not in God's being, precisely because the analogy is in the difference between God's being and the being of creation.[143]

136. Schindler, "What's the Difference?," 24.

137. See, Betz, "Beyond the Sublime (Part Two)," 13. See also, Clarke, *Explorations in Metaphysics*, 95–97. As Clarke puts it, all creatures (as composite) are distinct from their source, which is the sole cause of *esse* as such.

138. Te Velde, *Participation and Substantiality*, 193.

139. Clarke, *Explorations in Metaphysics*, 93.

140. Ibid., 94.

141. Jordan, *Ordering Wisdom*, 105. See also, Te Velde, *Aquinas on God*, 149.

142. Clarke, *Explorations in Metaphysics*, 93.

143. To further elaborate this distinction, in light of the aforementioned doctri-nal formulations it is helpful to summarize D. C. Schindler's reflections on Thomistic participation in his, "What's the Difference?" Schindler notes that if essence is merely a lack, limitation, or negation of existence (as with all pagan idealism, not excluding Barfield's work) it would seem the Creator/creature difference collapses (18). But for Aquinas *esse* is an act, not a form, essence, or a being (as such, forms alone do not account for the existence of things—as for Plato and Plotinus) (16). Schindler points

to the "extraordinarily paradoxical character of *esse*" in Aquinas (18). While *esse* is an act that makes all things be, it itself is not a thing, "but only inheres in *that which exists*" (19). For no thing, can be added to existence. In this way, *esse* becomes a "pure mediation" of "sheer generosity" (19). *Esse* is not that which is first created, but rather the multiplicity of beings proceeds from a perfect creative act found in their existence. *Esse*, thus, is not a third thing that is situated between God and creatures. Schindler notes, "The danger of conceiving of *esse* as super-added to essence (and vice versa) hovers over talk of the real distinction between essence and existence" (20). Instead, what Aquinas intimates is that creatures do not participate in God's being as *esse* (as if God were the "being" of things), but rather *esse* mediates the relation between God and creation, while insisting this is a pure mediation, and, as such, immediate, there is "no *thing* between God and creatures" (20–21). For Schindler this does two things. It ultimately overcomes any residual dualism (i.e., Platonic metaphysics) and ensures the goodness of creation (21). Essence is a positive principle, yet wholly subordinate to *esse*, the divine causality from which it is distinct (23). So how is this difference not negative? God's divine *esse* contains the perfection of both poles (essence and existence) without reducing one to the other, and as such, holds the difference which constitutes all difference in the world. In this way, difference can become a reflection of God himself (25). Because the Trinity is unity and difference, the difference of the created order can be seen to participate in God's image. As such, "the difference in God quite literally makes all the difference in the world," as otherness and difference is paradoxically a share in who God is (26). All of this upholds the rich doctrinal formulations that sought to articulate the difference between the economic and immanent Trinity, while affirming that God, in becoming man, is in no way a diminishing who he is in himself. As such, the diversity of the creative act declares a God whose essence is His existence. God's creative act is the actualization of all existents. The fact that God's essence is to exist confirms both the identity that is God and the difference that is creatures.

In a similar way, Te Velde, in his, *Participation and Substantiality*, asks how what seems to be an "addition" to *esse* should be understood (194). In Thomas, being is different in diverse things as man is distinct from dog. It is important that these differences subsist in being since nothing can be added to being. Te Velde writes, "Therefore things are not classified on account of their being, since being includes even their differences" (196). What this means is that being transcends all the categorical differences that make up the content of a thing (198). As potency is to act, form is to being, "each form still indeterminate, considered with its formal content, and therefore it requires the complement of *esse* in order to be in act" (198). Therefore, all particular forms relate to being as their common actuality (198). Te Velde notes that, "being is not common in the sense that it remains unaffected by the specific nature of a thing" (199). Therefore, "the unity of being is of a different nature from the abstract unity of a genus which signifies all particular things (essences) in what they have in common apart from their differences" (200). In Thomas, "being is something common precisely insofar as it is related as act to the whole of the particular essence according to which one thing differs from another. In their differences the many determinate acts of the essences relate to something common, the common actuality of all acts" (200). Te Velde then goes on to say that this is a Trinitarian formulation. To lose one's essential nature is to lose subsistence and existence altogether (203). In this way, essence cannot be said to have being unless is has subsistence (203). It appears, then, that substance and being are linked through essence, while essence and being come together in subsistence, because "only insofar as the essences subsists does it have being" (203). Additionally, essence subsists, "in and through the act of being" (203). Thus, being is a self-mediating whole

Now it would be an understatement to say that this relation is rather mysterious, as is evident in the complicated use of terms and the attempts to nail down the precise way of articulating such a distinction. But what is clear is that the irresolvable tension between essence and existence in creation points to the metaphysical limits of finitude and leads one into a theological mystery that always eludes a totalizing grasp. This coincides with the claim that creaturely "tension" is never resolved, and, therefore, remains open, following Aquinas's vision of reason perfected in faith.

Proleptically avoiding onto-theological speculation, Aquinas employed analogy to talk about God. For reasons expressed in the opening of this subsection his use of analogy has recently received a considerable amount of attention. This discussion concerns namely whether Aquinas simply employed analogy as a linguistic device,[144] or if it was something much more, a way of describing the fundamental metaphysical structure of creation as it relates to God. It is the latter that is here followed.

In his *Aquinas: God and Action*, David Burrell notes that Aquinas utilizes analogy in "practice." Of course, there is the oft-cited example of "health,"[145] but Burrell's crucial point should stand. While it is true that

---

wherein substance, essence, and being (or act) mutually penetrate and mediate each other (203). Substance has a specific nature, but also has being. Plurality is produced in that there is one difference, that between essence and existence. This remains true because in God substance is identical to essence and essence with being (204). The plurality of substances is identified in their essence, while the plurality of essences is identified in being (204). See also, Pabst, *Metaphysics*, 208–10.

144. See, for example, Quash, *Theology and the Drama of History*, 174. Quash argues that Aquinas's use of analogy is merely linguistic. To speak of the creature's actual "participation in God" "is not one that Aquinas's notions of analogy would have accommodated . . . ." See also Deely, "The Absence of Analogy," 527–28. Deely calls Aquinas's use of analogy a "strictly logical development" from experience (of being) to God. Accordingly, "we see the importance of Aquinas saying that we know the existence of God through the making of a proposition, not through direct experience." Deely says that the later development of the *analogia entis* in Przywara, Geiger, and Fabro occurs by reading Neo-Platonism into Aquinas. But one might want to ask, what's the other option? To instead read into Aquinas a form of Cartesianism or Kantianism that surfaces hundreds of years after Aquinas, which Deely seems to espouse in his conclusion? And further, how can one ignore Aquinas's ubiquitous references to Pseudo-Dionysius? Nevertheless, it is clear that Deely reads Aquinas's use of analogy as merely linguistic (548).

145. Aquinas, *Summa Theologica*, Ia. q. 16 a. 6. "So healthiness is predicated of animal, of urine, and of medicine, not that health is only in the animal; but from the health of the animal, medicine is called healthy, in so far as it is the cause of health, and urine is called healthy, in so far as it indicates health. And although health is neither in medicine nor in urine, yet in either there is something whereby the one causes, and the other indicates health." See also, Ia. IIae. q. 20 a. 3, wherein Aquinas later repeats the same analogy stating, "the healthiness which is in medicine or urine is derived from the

Aquinas does cite a "theory" of analogy,[146] he is careful to employ analogy "analogously."[147] What Burrell means is that Aquinas presents the reader with examples of analogy but never a specific treatment or treatise on analogy. However, later commentators, in attempting to create a doctrine out of his work, reduced the relationship to God and creatures to a share in a common being,[148] which is precisely what Aquinas's use of analogy intends to avoid.[149] It is instead for the sake of difference[150] that Aquinas employs analogy regarding creation's participation in God, as clearly evident in the opening questions of the *Summa Theologica*;

> Therefore if there is an agent not contained in any "genus," its effect will still more distantly reproduce the form of the agent, not, that is, so as to *participate* in the likeness of the agent's form

---

healthiness of the animal's body; nor is health as applied to urine and medicine, distinct from health as applied to the body of an animal, of which health medicine is the cause, and urine the sign."

146. Aquinas, "*Quaestiones disputatae de veritate*," q. 2 a. 11; B 3:16 c. "Whence it must be said that neither wholly univocally nor wholly equivocally is the name of knowledge predicated of the knowledge of God and of our knowledge, but according to analogy, which expresses no more than a relational similarity."

147. Thomists on either side of the debate are mostly in agreement here. Burrell, *Aquinas*, 55. See also, 57, wherein Burrell notes that Aquinas's discourse on God is everywhere analogical. See also, Deely, "The Absence of Analogy," 524. Deely remarks that although Aquinas's writings are fraught with analogy "he himself never pulled his various context of usage together into a unified treatise. Aquinas left the materials for a doctrine of analogy, but he did not explicitly formulate it as anything like a separate treatise."

148. Burrell, *Aquinas*, 56. Burrell notes that Cajetan's tendency to utilize mathematical formulae to speak of God as an analogous "ratio" presupposes univocal access to God, which is precisely what Thomistic language carefully avoids. See also, Marion, "The Essential Incoherence of Descartes' Definition of Divinity," 306. Marion refers to this as the "univocist drift that analogy undergoes with Suárez and others." For a critique of Cajetan's use of proportionality and its influence on subsequent Thomists see, Deely, "The Absence of Analogy," 540–46. For further clarification on Cajetan's and Suárez's Thomisms see, Placher, *The Domestication of Transcendence*, 74. See also, Miner, *Truth in the Making*, 13–14. Miner shows that, while in Cajetan being is a matter of proportion, Jesuit Francisco Suárez rejected this for analogy of attribution.

149. Throughout the *Summa Theologica* Thomas employs "attributive" analogy to avoid univocal and equivocal talk regarding causation (Ia. q. 44 a. 3), secondary causality (Ia. q. 45 a. 8), heavenly and corporeal bodies (Ia. q. 66 a. 2), man's likeness to God (Ia. q. 93 a. 1), in relating the goodness of an act of will to its exterior act (Ia. IIae. q. 20 a. 3), and in humanity's capacity to see God's essence (Suppl. q. 92 a. 1).

150. See, Milbank and Pickstock, *Truth in Aquinas*, 46–47. Milbank and Pickstock argue that one cannot separate the Thomistic use of analogy from metaphysics because it is predicated upon the metaphysics of participated being; that is, between univocal and equivocal. The very limits of language reflect the limits of the created order.

according to the same specific or generic formality, *but only according to some sort of analogy*; as existence is common to all. In this way all created things, so far as they are beings, are like God as the first and universal principle of all being.[151]

For Aquinas, analogy is way to speak about God precisely because finite beings will never entirely lay hold of God's infinite plenitude (whether ontologically or epistemologically).[152]

So when the use of analogy (i.e., *analogia entis*) is finally hammered out, it is not merely about God talk, but reflects a fundamental metaphysical structure that is indicative of, and informs, the very language Aquinas employs. This is why, in the *Summa Theologica*, just after the articles on God's existence, Aquinas introduces analogy to describe the relation between God and creation. Again, Aquinas does not have a doctrine on analogy, because to do so would defeat the purpose of analogy, to totalize metaphysics,[153] and ultimately wrest it from theology[154] (which is perhaps the product of

151. Aquinas, *Summa Theologica*, Ia. q. 4 a. 3 (emphasis added).

152. Placher, *The Domestication of Transcendence*, 31. Placher notes that Aquinas suspends modern categories with "*metalinguistic* rules that remind us of the limitations of our language about God and thereby make it clear that we cannot place God within the world we can understand."

153. See, for example, Pieper, *Leisure, the Basis of Culture*. Pieper indicates that for theology man is not pure spirit, he only sees the essences in part (119–21). Hegel's phenomenology of spirit contradicts this by making philosophy real knowledge and thereby denying transcendence (143–44). But, according to Pieper, a closed system of philosophy is not possible; "the claim to expound the world in a formula, or to have a formula with which to explain the world, is quite simply unphilosophic or pseudo-philosophy" (146 and 159). As such, "the nature of the philosophical act inevitably involves overstepping the frontier of 'pure' philosophy . . . " (157).

154. See also, Schindler, "Surprised by Truth." Schindler affirms that theology's *logos* is a rational discourse about God so it is, in some sense, a human activity, but distinct from philosophy, "theology has its ultimate foundation not in reason's own exigencies, nor in natural evidences, but in that which properly speaking comes from beyond the world itself: namely, in revelation" (587–88). To hold to utter transcendence is not to deny the rationality of theological discourse, but to reduce revelation to pure philosophy depriving it of its "revealed character" (588). This way, proper theological discourse affirms "both the discontinuity of revelation with respect to reason *as well as* a certain continuity" (589). Otherwise theology will fall prey to the idolatry of "mere history, fideism, biblical positivism, moralism, or a program of social justice and political action" (589). See also, Hart, *The Beauty of the Infinite*, 242. In his analysis of the *analogia entis* Hart writes, "apart from the *analogia entis*, the very concept of revelation is a contradiction: only insofar as creaturely being is analogous to divine being, and proper to God's nature, can God show himself; there would be no revelation otherwise, only legislation, emanating from an ontic god separated from us by an impossible distance, or perhaps the ghostly call of the gnostic's stranger god."

the medieval nominalists' systematization of Aquinas's use of analogy).[155]
Indeed any attempt to totalize being (i.e., Nietzsche's "Platonism for the
people," Heidegger's "onto-theology," or postmodernity's "substance metaphysics" and Kantian "sublime")[156] can only proceed by first ignoring (or
making an "identity" of)[157] the irresolvable metaphysical mystery within

155. McInerny, *The Logic of Analogy*, 32.

156. In the end, Heidegger absolutely immanentizes being revealing his incapability
to think the difference between being and beings. By associating being with non-existence (the *nihil*) he brings existence within the creaturely realm construing being and
non-being in terms of existence and non-existence, respectively (which is to prioritize
potentiality over actuality). But what he fails to realize is that *only* in the creaturely
realm does something *have* or not *have* existence, whereas, regardless of such creaturely
mutability, flux, becoming, or *Dasein*'s "temporality" being (existence) *is*. Heidegger's
ontology does not speak of existence *itself*, but only applies to the creaturely realm of
beings. To put it another way, to apply such creaturely categories to existence *itself* is utter nonsense; only a madman would attempt to talk of a non-existent existence (but he
would, in fact, have to *exist* to do so). Regardless of life, death, change, species evolving,
extinction, "un-concealment," etc., *existence exists*. Any such metaphysic that overlooks
this construes existence (or God) as an object, or a being. The failure to properly comprehend being as transcendent (in terms of analogy), yields to a totalitarian metaphysics of presence and its alternative abyss of non-existence (nihilism), as Nietzsche rightly
diagnosed. If the *nihil* really *is* then no-thing really *is*. Yet if being exists, it does so as
sheer gratuity, an overflow of being to beings. For an excellent critique of Heidegger
here followed see, Hart, "The Offering of Names," 255–91. See also, Aquinas, *Compendium of Theology*, 20–21.

Also, in a similar vein see Heidegger's student, Jonas, *The Phenomenon of Life*,
248–54. Jonas calls the "essential immanentism" of Heidegger's philosophy "pagan."
Jonas points out the irony in what he calls Heidegger's "ontic" "metaphysical" (not ontological) philosophy in that it does not escape his (Heidegger's) own critique of "onto-
theology." Still trapped in a post-Kantian metaphysics Heidegger's "being" is utterly
unknowable, and has no bearing upon the ontological difference between being and
beings. Jonas notes, "it must be clearly and unambiguously understood that the 'being'
of Heidegger is, *with* the 'ontological difference,' inside the bracket with which theology must bracket in the totality of the created world. . . . Against this, theology should
guard the radical transcendence of its God, whose voice comes not out of being but
breaks into the kingdom of being from without." See also, Betz, "Beyond the Sublime
(Part Two)," 15–16 and Betz, "Beyond the Sublime (Part One)," 391. Betz notes that
Heidegger's folly is to construe being as nothing while ignoring the "theological traces
of gift, revelation kenosis, etc. . . . ."

157. Milbank, "The Thing That Is Given," 517. See also, note 4 of same page. Milbank remarks that Heidegger's poetic account cannot overcome an ontology of original
strife (i.e., a "negative dialectic"); that is, truth as the primal conflict between clearing and unclearing), which even if it did would really only fulfill the law of identity.
Whereas, "By contrast analogy, or a thinking of mediation . . . thinks a blending beyond
identity and difference. Yet one can say that this transgression of identity alone ensures
that there are indeed identities and a law of identity that is always finitely observed."
See also, 525. By refusing analogical "fluidity, Heidegger promotes (without reason)
a *gnosis* of ontological rupture, instead of a faith in an ontological continuity from an

immanence (i.e., that beings cannot account for their being) and then try to establish the difference between being and beings, which is always to reduce analogy to pure metaphysics; the dialectic of univocity and equivocity, which has been continually reiterated.[158] Perhaps if this irresolvable tension was indeed resolved then the story of the separation of philosophy and theology is indeed one of the triumphs of secular reason over the irrationality of religious discourse. But, as it turns out, this ever-remaining tension indicates just how philosophy acts as a helpful handmaid to theology,[159] intimating reason's natural desire for supernatural grace.

It has been argued that with the rise of the representational paradigm this difference was largely forgotten. In forgetting creation's openness, philosophy and theology at best resorted back to various pagan forms of idealism (albeit a cruder subjectivized form that relegated the transcendentals to categories of the mind—i.e., Kant and later forms of idealism or the Transcendental Thomism of Maréchal), phenomenology's bracketing out *"that something is"* for the sake of *"what something is,"* or postmodernity's revision

---

inaccessible plentitudinous source."

158. Furthermore, this language of analogy is meant to establish a two-way relation that affirms that the creature is entirely dependent upon God, while God is in no way dependent on the creature. In affirming this metaphysical structure, analogical language thus declared that because there is only a real relation from the creature to Creator, no change is affected in the Creator. Aquinas, *Summa Theologica*, IIIa. q. 2 a. 7. De Nys, "God, Creatures, and Relations." De Nys maintains that Aquinas denies real relations of God to creatures, while affirming real relations of creatures to God (599 and 610). De Nys notes, if God was in any way dependent on creation, "it would follow that God's substance would depend on something extrinsic to it, so that He would not be, of himself, the necessary being. . . . Therefore such relations do not really exist in God" (597). He continues, "Because God surpasses the entire created order, real relations of creatures to God can be the ground that allows the predication of relative terms of God" (600). De Nys's most important point is that this paradigm is only possible if a "fundamental restructuring" of theological language be appropriated (606). In other words, because, metaphysically speaking, there are no real relations between God and creatures it is, in fact, totally necessary that Aquinas explicate his ontology analogically. As, "even the most basic categories that apply to creatures . . . apply only analogically to God" (613). Aquinas, "believes that the position that real relations obtain between creatures and God but not between God and creatures allows one to see how relative predications of God do and can have analogical significance" (607). This means that, "statements that predicate relative terms of God, like all analogical predications, must express an affirmation and then a negation that always preserves and supersedes that affirmation" (609). De Nys puts it another way, "in that dialectic analogical predication allows affirmation and negation to preserve each other, but only if each functions in determining the sense of the other, and only if the negation that preserves the sense of affirmation does that and at the same time exceeds that affirmation" (609).

159. Aquinas, *Summa Theologica*, Ia. q. 1 a. 5.

of ontological difference (the dialectic of univocity vs. equivocity).[160] At its worst, analytic philosophy sought to strip being of all quality, as evident in the Cartesian sundering of mind and body and the resultant materialism it provoked.[161] Such speculation presupposes an immanentized vision that fails to apprehend just how theology's participatory metaphysic both affirms and overcomes immanence. Indeed, as the search for truth commences in the wake of the modernity and postmodernity this vision long proffered by theology is gaining traction.[162]

And if it's any indication, twentieth-century theology has not seen a more lively debate amongst both Protestants and Catholics than that concerning the *analogia entis*.[163] In the twentieth century the *analogia entis* was revived by Erich Przywara and his pupil Hans Urs von Balthasar. In part due to Heidegger's attempt to couch Christian metaphysics as "onto-theology" and Barth's ironically similar criticism of analogy[164] (as the "invention of the

160. Betz, "Beyond the Sublime (Part One)," 400. For as Betz puts it in his critique of postmodernity's cry for difference and violence, "that nothing could be (or, in fact, is) more identical than a univocal 'plane of immanence' (the pure irony at the heart of the matter), this notion of difference is something that is shared by nearly all postmodern philosophers."

161. See, Dreyfus and Taylor, *Retrieving Realism*.

162. Pabst, *Metaphysics*, 437–38. This is in line with Pabst who argues, "if . . . the modern redefines metaphysics as the onto-theological sciences of transcendental ontology, then the post-modern marks not so much an alternative to this project as an aporetic extension of it. But there is an alternative modernity that builds on the metaphysical realism inaugurated by Plato and further developed by the Neo-Platonist Church Fathers and Doctors in both the Greek East and the Latin West. The triple current of participation, analogy and universalism flow through the work of Meister Eckhart, Nicolas of Cusa, the Cambridge Platonists, and the Neapolitan and the Scottish Enlightenment to the post-secular metaphysics in the work of J. G. Hamman, Jacobi, and Schelling, who reach back beyond Kant and Hegel to renew the tradition of metaphysical realism. *Common to these and other modern metaphysicians is a refusal to accept absolute finite limits on the cognoscibility of the infinite—without however returning to the transcendentalism of Cartesian innate ideas in the mind and the dualistic separation of knowing subject from known object*" (emphasis added).

163. For a collection of essays regarding the *analogia entis* and the debate between Catholics and Protestants see, White, *The Analogy of Being*. The summary that follows will here draw namely on the work of John R. Betz and David Bentley Hart, whose translation of Przywara's *Analogia Entis* and comments on Przywara's work have contributed to an increased recognition of Przywara. For an intro to Przywara's work on the *analogia entis* see, Betz, "After Barth" and Betz, "Beyond the Sublime (Part Two)." See also, Hart, *The Beauty of the Infinite*, 241–49.

164. Betz, "Beyond the Sublime (Part One)," 368–69. For both Heidegger and Barth, Christian metaphysics was understood as a totalizing will-to-power, the only alternative to which is a non-metaphysical theology. For Heidegger, the highest form of language is meaningless, for Barth a rupture, a divine revelation that shatters reasons capacities. In this scheme both can be seen to proffer reason against faith, the natural

Anti-Christ"),[165] the *analogia entis* and its most powerful proponent Erich
Przywara have been overlooked.[166] Here, latent within the Catholic tradition
remained a subtle yet profound gesture that exhibits a remarkable penchant
for absorbing modern and postmodern discourse. In haste to find modernity's progenitor, to cite Descartes's mind/body dualism is perhaps premature (e.g., in the analytical tradition various forms of realism are becoming
increasingly fashionable, even while still beholden to univocal certainty),[167]
for one can scarcely locate a modern or postmodern philosophical text that
considers being's analogical structure. If, in fact, it was this theological shift
away from analogy that inaugurated epistemologies of representation, then
in closing it is suggested, following Betz, that it is perhaps a return to analogy that can lead "theology out of the strictures of modern and postmodern
immanence . . . ."[168]

This insistence on analogy has much in common with Barfield's poetic
philosophy and reveals just how closely he aligned with the more profound
theological musings of his time. As with Barfield's poetic philosophy, analogy guards against idolatry by refusing totalization. Like Barfield, theological analogy suspends creaturely being between "two polarities" (essence
and existence or subject and object, as will be seen). Also, as previously
mentioned, the theological use of analogy suggests that human language
intimates creation's finitude. Analogy speaks of an opening within the immanent that allows for inspiration from "beyond the threshold," as Barfield
would describe it. It makes space for forward movement, for non-identical

---

against the supernatural and philosophy against theology.

165. See, Barth, *Church Dogmatics*, 1.1: viii. For an account of Barth's critique of the
analogia entis, see Betz, "Beyond the Sublime (Part Two)," 3–12. Most fundamentally
Barth believed that the *analogia entis* had supplanted Christ by theorizing the being of
God independent of Christ's revelation. Instead, for Barth, Christ should be the starting
point of a theological ontology (4). While Barth sees the *analogia entis* as an attempt to
overthrow God, the irony, according to Balthasar, is that Przywara utilizes it precisely to
avoid any such attempts to do so (11–12). For a concise account of Heidegger's critique
that renders the *analogia entis* a form of "onto-theology" see, 12–20. Betz summarizes,
"For not only is [the *analogia entis*] *not* what the early Barth makes it out to be, it
is also *not* what Heidegger makes it out to be: for it is neither a closed metaphysical
system, which subordinates the living God, who reveals himself in the sovereign event
of his self-revelation, to being, as Barth implies; nor is it a scheme in which God simply
grounds beings as the highest being (*ens supremum*) in a causal hierarchy as the *causa
prima*, which occludes the difference between being and beings (as Heidegger) would
lead one to believe). These are caricatures."

166. His most important work has only recently been translated to English. See,
Przywara, *Analogia Entis*.

167. Kimbriel, "Learning the Real."

168. Betz, "Beyond the Sublime (Part One)," 376.

repetition, as in the poet saying the same word in a slightly different way. The following is a short précis of Przywara's work on the *analogia entis*,[169] which underscores these similarities by elucidating what Przywara identifies as a "creaturely" metaphysic or tension within creation. This will set in relief the subsequent analysis of Balthasar's epistemology that follows.

As continually mentioned, the most fundamental question for theology was not the relationship between the ideal and the real, but rather, the difference between creature and Creator. In his defense against Barth's critique of the *analogia entis*, Przywara's *Polarity* opens (following the description of Thomistic analogy above) by distinguishing between the incommensurability of essence and existence in creation and the essence/existence identity in God. He does so as a critique of the various forms of modern philosophy that attempt to totalize subjectivity, or to ground being in the "I" (i.e., philosophies of "identity," "contradiction," "antithesis" or "synthesis"— he specifically cites Kant and Hegel).[170] He, instead, points to what he calls an irresolvable tension-in-unity of the creature that is not a ground in itself, but rather, suspended in an ontological tension between being and nothing. Since creation is an oscillation[171] (or becoming) of the "I" in the irresolvable tension between essence and existence, it is never a ground in itself, but only a tension-in-unity towards God (who is the unity or identity of essence and existence in which creation participates). He describes this movement as the in-and-beyond of God. The creature is, thus, an analogue of God (like Him through the tension of essence and existence, but unlike Him because He is the unity of essence and existence).[172] In this way, the creature is neither pure identity (absolute) nor a contradiction of God. Creation is thus open upwards in a "unity-in-tension" forever uncompleted in its becoming, whose unity is in that which it participates, which always remains infinitely above the creature. Thus, there is no way to absolutely ground the "ego," because in its tension of opposites it constantly strives beyond itself to an

169. The following draws upon two of Przywara's works: *Polarity* and an earlier manuscript of the now published translation of *Analogia Entis: Metaphysics*, while clarifying remarks draw upon Betz, "Beyond the Sublime (Parts One and Two)."

170. He indicates that once the subject is grounded dualisms abound; one has no way of dealing with activity ("I did it"—naturalism) and passivity ("God did it"— "supernaturalism") in these terms (e.g., he seems to hint that once this occurs, activity is conceived as a sort of immanence and passivity transcendence).

171. Erich Przywara, *Polarity*, 15. Przywara speaks of an, "oscillation . . . between the type of first activity (immanence) and that of the second activity (transcendence) [which] shows the inward necessity of a higher connexion [sic] between their opposites."

172. Ibid., 36. He writes, "the analogy between the tension-in-unity of the creaturely 'becoming' (between essence and existence) and the essential identity of the divine 'Is' (identity of essence and existence)."

absolute fixed point found only within God who is infinite (this infinite is
not opposed to the finite, but in-and-beyond it). Hence Przywara's statement, "the creaturely consciousness experiences the 'absolutely fixed point'
of its unity *beyond* itself."[173] Przywara declares that this is precisely what distinguishes the transcendent God of Catholicism from all other philosophies
of immanence. God is, thus, not confined to consciousness (a construct
of consciousness or of pure reason, etc.), but condescends, and in so doing, reveals himself within creation (i.e., the transcendentals—the true, the
beautiful, and the good). This allows for forward movement. Through that
which is comprehensible, one is continually drawn forward to that which is
incomprehensible. Following the above, in order not to altogether sunder
the economic and immanent Trinity, Przywara then speaks of the incarnation, as "the view *towards* God is already essentially the view *from God
hitherward* . . . ." It is not that God creates dialectically, because to become
God is not a negation of who He is, but an affirmation (a participation of
man in the divine nature is paradoxically a participation of God in human
nature). In this way, natural man is endowed with a supernatural end to
which he is constantly drawn. The incarnation is both, "the crowing point of
the supernatural creation . . . [and] an act of condescension due to original
sin." He talks of a rotation (and outgoing and return) of the divine life in
which creation participates. A synthesis of Augustine and Aquinas (respectively) reveals the true nature of Catholic thought that follows the doctrinal
formulation of the Fourth Lateran Council, "*That which lays stress upon the
relative likeness existing between Deity and creation* . . . [and] *That in which
the emphasis rests upon the relative unlikeness between Deity and creation.*"[174]
Following Aquinas, the analogy is, thus, in the difference between being
(God as the identity of essence and existence) and beings (creation as the
incommensurable tension of essence and existence that strives for unity in
its becoming).

Along with *Polarities*, Przywara penned his *Analogia Entis: Metaphysics: Original Structure and Universal Rhythm*. The entire text brought
together a 1932 work on the *Analogia Entis* (which constitutes Part I, "Original Structure") with the reflections gleaned prior to the 1962 publication
date (which constitutes Part II, "Universal Rhythm"). For brevity's sake the
following refers to Part I. This text glimpses the depth of Przywara's thought
on the *analogia entis*, which weaves Aquinas's use of analogy with his in-
and-beyond scheme.

---

173. Ibid., 46 and 52. Przywara states clearly that God is not part of creation. He is
not the "essence" of creation (52–53).

174. Ibid., 117.

Like Barfield, Przywara had a knack for pointing out philosophical dualisms. He opens the text introducing the dualism between being (ontic) and consciousness (noetic) (i.e., object and subject, *a posteriori* and *a priori*, or history and truth). He says, not unlike Barfield, that they exist in a "coinherence" or a "suspended tension." This coinherence or oscillation is indicative of the in-and-beyond that always points beyond itself ("becoming"—between what one is and what one will be). Any metaphysic must therefore affirm this fundamental law (i.e., accordingly Hegel is wrong to step outside of history and grasp the whole. The *a priori* and *a posteriori* do not form a closed circle but rather a constant rhythm, a back and forth motion, that is never complete, always renewed in the in-and-beyond of the creature).[175] Distinct from Hegel's "concept," Pryzwara's "dynamic antithetics" leads one "through and beyond," from a positive affirmation to a negative declaration, remaining incomplete. He refers to this as the "creaturely metaphysic" or the "intracreaturely problem." Importantly for Przywara, one must not mistake this creaturely metaphysic with God, or attempt to grasp the absolute within immanence (i.e., one must not grasp God *as* creature, but rather *in* the creature). He claims that the creaturely metaphysic, which he thus formulates as "essence in-and-beyond existence," is "vertically transcected" by God who is beyond-and-in the creature. Any failure to uphold this distinction necessarily construes finite existence as essence *as* existence, which is alone reserved for God. Creaturely becoming lies in God who is beyond and to whom creation is analogously related (whose essence and existence perfectly coincide in his simple act of being).[176] For analogy, there is no univocity between God and creature (God "is," the creature "becomes").[177]

For Przywara, metaphysics is made possible by the self-revelation of the divine in immanence. Philosophy projects itself into theology, while a pure philosophy attempts to only deal with the "creaturely metaphysic" (he calls this "methodological atheism") by ignoring the beyond within the immanent revealed in the incommensurability of philosophical discourse that fails to ask the difference between being and beings. But, likewise, if theology attempts to construe God in terms of philosophical purity it "degenerates" into philosophy (a theology that is a philosophy or a philosophy that is

---

175. Betz, "Beyond the Sublime (Part Two)," 18. This means that the analogy of being refuses an absolute identity to which this peaceful tension might be reduced.

176. Ibid., 11. The *analogia entis* admits that no creaturely being or knowing can be a ground in itself, but is instead suspended both ontically and noetically unable to secure any pure starting point.

177. Ibid., 13. To reiterate, the *analogia entis* does not subordinate God to being, because God does not *have* being as creature do, as Betz writes, "he *is* being; he is being itself (*ipsum esse subsistens*), whereas creatures have their 'being' from him."

a theology—e.g., Hegel). Whereas Catholic theology knows no extreme, as God is both in-and-beyond creation. In this way, the grace of faith (theology) perfects the nature of reason (philosophy).

The "ana" in "analogy" means that within the creaturely realm there is simply no way to totalize being. It means that the dialectic is never resolved immanently (or logically), but is instead indicative of the breakthrough of the *logos*, as the above that orders. Again, to absolutize the *logos* is to collapse the economic and immanent Trinity. Instead, an analogical dialectic is a dynamic (i.e., not a fixed middle, but a "suspended middle") that is ever renewed. It is not an identity of opposites, but a possibility towards a transcending analogy between God and creature (as activity and passivity have an analogical rhythm in the creaturely).[178] This middle of non-contradiction is directed towards identity, but not equated with it (as only God is true identity), always drawn from potentiality to actuality (an active potentiality).[179] Thus, whereas all other starting points attempt to be in themselves, the analogy is suspended in the middle. It is never absolute but always becoming. The forward movement is never complete, one must see through and beyond everything that seems to be finished towards what is always fresh. "The 'being'—*Sein*—which all philosophies take to be the primordial question and primordial datum with respect to everything else, does not (consequently) 'have' analogy as an attribute or as something derived from it; rather analogy *is* being, and thus thought *is* (noetically) analogy," a primordial dynamic rhythm (or music).[180]

Przywara remarks that creatures (beings) have nothing in themselves, but are only by an analogical participation in God. The "Is" of God is self-sufficient, and as such, is not related to the creature, while the "is" of the creature is entirely dependent on the "Is" of God. So whatever is said of the creature is not to say God has it in common, because there is always a greater dissimilarity. However, this dissimilarity is not a separation from God, for he is infinite and transcendent. Yet, any affirmation or move towards God (becoming) is always negated by the ever-greater dissimilarity of a God

178. Ibid., 25–28. All immanence is undergirded by transcendence. Within the immanent analogy there is a greater theological analogy (*vestigia*). This indicates that creaturely being is open to something beyond itself; that is, "fundamentally geared towards transcendence." "So that the tension of creaturely being in the immanent analogy ("essence in-and-beyond existence") points to and is *fulfilled by* the tension of the theological analogy—by a God who is himself 'in-and-beyond' creation, i.e., at once immanent to creation, yet excessively, abundantly beyond it."

179. Ibid., 40. Betz describes this creaturely "becoming" as "a moving image of infinite Being."

180. Przywara, *Analogia Entis*. See, Section Two, § 8, "The *Analogia Entis* as a Principle."

who is infinite (who is). The creature is, thus, suspended between being and nothingness. Like those aforementioned Christian Platonists, Przywara sees the in-and-beyond in Plato's paradigms and talks of a "middle" where by a "vertical breakthrough" to the "intracreaturely" eternity is born. One is reminded that God is not the being that none-greater can be thought, but rather he is unthinkably beyond comprehension. One's natural desire to see God is drawn forward by grace.[181] Przywara closes with a theological anthropology whereby the incommensurablity between essence and existence points to the incommensurablity between God and Creation, found in Christ.

Przywara's work blends Aquinas's language to indicate that immanence is at all times suspended or transected by transcendence. To do so, he employs a language of analogy that coincides with what he perceives as an original metaphysical structure that avoids closure. Przywara's talk of polar tension, his insistence on the relation between language and being, and creation's openness towards transcendence has much in common with Barfield's poetic philosophy. In turning to Przywara's pupil Hans Urs von Balthasar, whose creaturely logic followed the metaphysical rhythms of Przywara's *analogia entis*, one finds further similarities with Barfield's poetic philosophy. Balthasar's work also provides an impetus for the examination of the theological middle, which constitutes the final subsection.

In the first volume of his *Theo-Logic*, Balthasar utilizes Przywara's polar logic to speak of creativity in terms of active and passive. As with his teacher, Balthasar's logic moves forward as a critique of any attempt to totalize being, suggesting that while one does indeed grasp the truth, it always escapes one, urging one forward. The subject, for Balthasar, is not purely active, nor purely passive. While the active subject is creative, and truly does bring truth into being, this activity remains analogous, a participation in the divine, otherwise a rupture occurs between the creaturely and the divine whose result is a domineering subject that sees his own truth (i.e., a "fundamentalist").[182] Thus, truth "moves" in the balance (or "polarity") between active and passive. Here, "an indissoluble 'polarity' or reciprocity between subject and object" (comprehending each other reciprocally) is displayed in the tension ("coincidence" or "reciprocity") between active

181. Betz, "Beyond the Sublime (Part Two)," 2–3. The *analogia entis*, "points beyond the immanent tensions of creaturely being to a God who is beyond all analogy . . . ," which ultimately points to God's incomprehensibility. The *analogia entis* is constantly, "vigorously reinstating the distance of transcendence over against every immanentizing philosophy and theology that would compromise it . . . ." See also, 7 and 11.

182. Equally, he indicates that any form of idealism (without analogy) will have grave difficulty distinguishing between unique centers of consciousness.

and passive. The two poles exist for each other. For Balthasar, this affects one's aesthetic gaze, reminding one that God's truth is mediated through the world. Subjects must learn to see objects as a gift from God, not as a means to an end. But alternatively, apart from the active subject, the object becomes purely material, bereft of all quality. In this way, the object finds its completeness in the subject.[183] The creative subject gives definition to the object and thereby completes it, by seeing what it is and what it is meant to be. Objects are, thus, not a truth in themselves, but God is their measure. The creative subject analogically participates in God.[184] Truth remains as a finite openness to transcendence, which marks a true progress of knowledge. If this aesthetic is not guided by love, being loses all of its value, becoming simply a product of the uncreative subject (the will to power). This is what any turn to the subject (Kantianism or idealism) promotes, a mere "projection" of subjectivity that he calls "irredeemably hopeless." The universal is never, in fact, universal, because it is constantly in tension with the particular. As such, the universal is never graspable or totalizable. Similar to Barfield's logic and his stance against idolatry, Balthasar notes that truth (revelation) comes through a language of images and signs, but when these signs are reinterpreted as immanent or a permanent property, the truth is turned into a lie.[185] As Balthasar puts it, "The object already contains its complete ontological truth, while the truth of knowledge consists solely in the subject's conformity to this already establish fact."[186] This harks back to the Genesis account of creation that speaks of man as a co-creator who names the being of the world.

He then turns to articulate an ontology (following Przywara) in terms of essence and existence to which his epistemology corresponds. The "polarity" of "creatureliness" reveals something of creation's dissimilarity to God, which paradoxically reveals something of the divine truth, whose existence is most revealed, yet most veiled. God's essence, as with the essences of creation, is elusive and never graspable, it is in the world, but its essence always escapes us. This mystery as truth is both in-and-beyond the immanent. Existence is an unfathomable gift; it is not a property among others. Again, something's essence is never commensurable with its existence. As such, "These relations remain irreducible to each other, and their mysterious dual

183. Balthasar, *Theo-Logic*, vol. I, 65. The object has an "ontological truth" that the subject conforms to. See also, 73. Balthasar shows that one does not bestow meaning upon objects but recognizes what the object has had all along.

184. Ibid., 78.

185. Ibid., 236.

186. Ibid., 65.

unity is the eternal mystery of every ontology of the created world."[187] For this reason the truth must be continually sought. Immanence is ontologically dependent; it is held in suspense, never whole; it is groundless, having nothing in itself; it is a finite participation in the infinite. The "unity-intension" of essence and existence is the worldly ontological structure, whose existence and essence depend on God. There is then an analogy between God and creature. The search for unity of the creature is the endless search for God.

At bottom, Barfield's poetic philosophy, his tension of polarities, which coincides with his ceaseless critique of idolatry, had much in common with the metaphysical schema of these Catholic thinkers. Their polar logic served as a warning against idolatry by reserving finite being's openness. In affirming meaning in the world, the subject's quest for truth was conceived as a forward movement (an oscillation) towards the inexhaustible truth. Their insistence on the polar relation between subject and object resituates the subject as a co-creator in a medial or participatory realm. But, in the end, it is Barfield who lacked the theological language to speculate further regarding philosophy's shortcomings. Unlike these Catholic theologians, Barfield was unable to think the analogical difference. So, in some ways, Barfield's poetic philosophy does not escape Przywara's critique regarding attempts to ground subjectivity in the "I" or "I AM."[188] For Przywara the created "I" never purely *is*, but *is becoming* by participation in God. The *analogia entis* serves as a correction to those who fail to comprehend this subtle yet crucial difference. Ultimately, when this difference is not properly articulated (i.e., any totalizing metaphysic that attempts to analogize God and creation under the general category of being) it yields what Przywara called either pantheism or "theo-pan-ism" (e.g., Hegelianism).[189] Alas, in failing to articulate the difference of being theologically (analogically, i.e., the difference between being and beings) Barfield remained a poetic philosopher. Nonetheless, his

187. Ibid., 194. Balthasar describes this as an analogical movement between two poles.

188. Even in his attempts to locate the source of inspiration as in his 1951 preface to *Poetic Diction* (as something like Plato's *deamonio*), and in his later attempts found in "Meaning, Revelation and Tradition in Language and Religion," "The Concept of Revelation," and "The Nature of Meaning" Barfield never seems to work this out. Additionally, are the comments where he seemingly blurs the distinction addressed above (see, footnote 82).

189. Betz, "Beyond the Sublime (Part Two)," 5. "Theopanism" was coined by Przywara to indicate an unmediated revelation that Betz here defines as a form of Hegelianism where, "any knowledge of God on the part of the creature is necessarily a moment of God's self-interpretation, and the creature is absorbed without remainder into the Trinitarian process of revelation."

theory of poetic inspiration, which implicitly resituates the subject in a theological "middle," reveals just how philosophy is irretrievably theological. It is in this way that his poetic philosophy represents a formidable alternative to philosophies of immanence. As with all such philosophies, even where he falls short, his work inevitably demands the theological complement hitherto remarked upon. In light of the contemporary discussion regarding the relationship between philosophy and theology, the relevance of Barfield's poetic philosophy cannot be overstated. Before concluding, the following subsection remarks on just one more of its theological implications.

Explicit in Barfield's work is his insistence on the polar relation of subject and object, which that coincides with a more implicit move that situates the subject in a tension between the passive and active voice; these were the underlying themes of Parts I and II, respectively. It is this subtle gesture— only expressed explicitly in his translation of the Greek word "phenomenon" in the middle voice (see chapter 1)—perhaps more than any other facet of his corpus that not only distinguished Barfield from his philosophical contemporaries, but may also prove fruitful for further theological discussion. Therefore, the close of the essay proposes a rediscovery of the middle voice as a properly theological language that is both faithful to Barfield's poetic philosophy yet thoroughly theological.[190]

Rediscovering the Middle Voice

The following briefly proposes a potentially fruitful way of articulating theology in the present context that implicitly accords with the breadth of Barfield's work as presented in this essay. Simply put, a creaturely language that is consistent with a creaturely metaphysic of theology may be found in a recovery of the middle voice. This subsection opens by surveying the recent discussion regarding the middle voice and then suggests that to conceive of the middle voice theologically (i.e., in terms of proper transcendence) would be to offer a necessary correction to these contemporary anachronistic analyses. Finally, an attempt is made to construct *poiēsis* proper utilizing the middle voice in a way that is faithful to both the Christian metaphysical tradition hitherto discussed and the New Testament witness.

190. Milbank, "The Thing That Is Given," 538. The attempt to construct a poetic ontology builds upon Milbank's critique of Heidegger's immanent account of poetry to which he asks, "Perhaps this insight can be elaborated in more truly poetic terms, involving a metaphysic and a theology of transcendence?"; hence, *poiēsis* proper: theology as poetic metaphysics.

In 1993, Suzanne Kemmer opened her seminal *The Middle Voice* stating, "At present there is no generally accepted definition or characterization
of the middle voice, let alone a satisfactory account of the relations among
the various phenomena that have been given that name."[191] In her analysis,
Kemmer indicates that the middle voice generally regards the notion of what
she calls "subject-affectedness" and is often indicated by intransitive verbs
that have no direct object.[192] As such, it is difficult to identity "to whom" or
"to what" the verb is referring whether actively or passively. In other words,
the middle voice rarely identifies a causal agent. Indeed, in a more recently
published article that incorporates Kenner's analysis, Artemis Alexiadou
and Edit Doron[193] identify the middle as the voice in which a verb does not
indicate a causal agent. All other verb forms (active and non-active) always
indicate what they variously refer to as an "external argument," "agent," "ex-
periencer," or "cause." For this reason the middle voice is often interpreted
as reflexive, which if spoken literally always ends up sounding really odd,
as in, say, Austin Powers's, "allow myself to introduce myself." Derrida and
Sartre's explanations of the middle voice are not free from lapsing into such
reflexivity. For them the middle voice is the occasion when subject is both
the subject and the object, active and passive, both acted and acted upon.[194]

This reveals the inevitability of immanentized discourse traced
throughout this essay. In its inability to envisage a subject that is not a ground
in itself—a product of philosophy's constant attempt to close the irresolvable tension—secular discourse results in either a subject/object dualism

191. Kemmer, *The Middle Voice*, 1.

192. Kemmer's analysis focuses on languages that have what she calls "middle
markers," which indicate that the language has, or, at one time, had a middle voice.
She notes that the middle voice typically changes over time resulting in various passive
constructions. Kemmer points out that the middle voice tends to lack a certain clarity
in the sense that it is not transitive. In such cases there is a heightened emphasis on how
the subject is "affected."

Interestingly, Kemmer argues that the middle voice gradually surfaces in the development of languages. However, what one might suggest is that looking for markers to
identify the middle voice is anachronistic, as markers are always later developments
in language. As such, Kemmer's evolutionary proposal falls prey to Barfield's critique
of modern philology. What one might instead suggest is that contemporary linguistic
paradigms that remain within an immanent space will always yield the sort of active
and passive dialectic one sees in Kemmer. This is perhaps why the middle voice typically ends up in some sort of non-active or passive category (i.e., within immanence,
language is ostensibly grounded in either subject or object). Yet, when conceived
theologically (in terms of proper transcendence) the middle voice seems to resists this
immanentist shuttling.

193. Alexiadou and Doron, "The Syntactic Construction."

194. Martinot, *Forms in the Abyss*, 64–66. Martinot is here referring to Derrida,
Speech and Phenomena, 130, and Llewelyn, *Derrida on the Threshold of Sense*, 91.

(i.e., Cartesianism) or a subject and object resolved in the subject (i.e., a sort of "reflexivity" or Hegelian identity of, e.g., subject and object and/or active and passive). Within this paradigm, subjective agency is inconceivable outside of either active or passive terms (as, e.g., with mechanism).[195] Alas, interpretations of the middle voice inevitably migrate back towards a reflexive subject who actively subjects oneself (e.g. negative freedom). This may, in fact, be because contemporary interpretations of the middle voice are inhibited by a particularly modern (i.e., immanent or non-participatory) consciousness that lacks the theological insights hitherto remarked upon. As such, the loss of the middle voice may coincide with a misconstrual of the theological notion of transcendence. Perhaps the middle voice was, as it were, lost in translation.[196]

In fact, in his erudite, "Reflections on the Indo-European Medium" (I & II),[197] published in *Lingua* in 1961, Jan Gonda offers an alternative reading to those "inadequate and unsatisfactory observations" that occur when "translating ancient middle forms into modern languages," which typically resort to "purely reflexive" (denoting an "identity of subject and [unexpressed] object")[198] or intransitive[199] categorizations, and in so doing, remain "limited to the sphere of the subject with regard to whom it took place."[200] In addition to such categorizations, Gonda states that it

195. As implied in chapter 4, one of a variety of reasons that the classical Christian cosmology was lost is the advent of Newtonian physics. In a mechanistic cosmos linguistic emphases reflect efficient causality, as an object in rest or motion will remain in that state unless acted upon. Such empty objects are passively moved by an active external force. In a mechanistic Cartesian space objects are either active or passive and language reflects this.

196. There, is after all, an irony in those present linguistic analyses that attempt to locate the middle voice by identifying textual markers as mentioned above (see, footnote 192). If language is only secondarily written then the spoken consciousness of the past cannot be reduced to a set of linguistic markers. Reducing the middle voice to markers within a written text tells one nothing about the middle voice consciousness unless such analyses coincide with an understanding of differences between past and present consciousness. Notwithstanding their relevance, the aforementioned readings of the middle voice are perhaps guilty of what Barfield called "logomorphism"; that is, projecting one's consciousness backwards. Instead, if one truly wanted to make sense of the middle voice one might heed Barfield's suggestion to understand how a past consciousness might be different than a present consciousness. In this vein, Jan Gonda's work (as seen below), like Levi-Bruhl's studies of primitive consciousness, represented an anomaly in his own field.

197. Gonda, "Reflections on the Indo-European Medium I and II." Credit to Catherine Pickstock for her mention of Gonda's work.

198. Gonda, "Reflections on the Indo-European Medium I," 30–31 and 43.

199. Ibid., 45–46.

200. Ibid., 49.

seems to be plausible that a widespread use was already in pre-
historic times made of the middle forms to indicate that something comes or happens to a person (or object), befalls him,
takes place in the person of the subject so as to affect him etc.,
without any agens [sic] being mentioned, implied or known.
Very often the subject is a person or other living being and the
process may take place even contrary to his wishes, unintentionally, more or less automatically. . . . In the ancient periods of
the I-E languages this use was very frequent.[201]

He concludes,

On the strength of the preceding considerations the hypothesis seems therefore justified that the "original" or "essential"
function of the medial voice was not exactly to signify that the
subject "performs a process that is performed in himself," but to
denote that a process is taking place with regard to, or is affecting, happening to, a person or a thing; *this definition includes
also those cases in which we are under the impression that in the
eyes of those who once used this category in its original function
. . . some power or something powerful was at work in or through
the subject, or manifested itself in or by means of the subject . . .*
on the one hand are those cases, in which the process whilst
properly performed by, or originating with, the subject, obvi-
ously was limited to the "sphere" of the subject . . . .[202]

In Part II of his work, Gonda comes close to Barfield and Levi-Bruhl's
conclusions regarding primitive collective representations and the rise of
subjectivity traced in chapters 3 and 4, wherein he suggests,

Semi-primitive . . . and archaic man evidently felt a want to
avoid, for a variety of reasons, an active form, or preferred to
use a more or less "eventive" [sic] expression. Instead of attribut-
ing the performance of a process to a subject which in many
cases was not or only vaguely know to him, he made the person
(or object) which was the "seat" of the process the subject, connecting it with a middle verb. There is indeed no denying that

201. Ibid., 49. See also, 53 and 61–65. Gonda calls this a sort of "agentless passive"
where, "in the person of the subject a process takes place, by which the subject is, in
some way or other, affected." He notes that to the ancients, the distinction between past,
present, and future was not so clear, but over time (with the development of linear time)
this middle voice of wish, desire, emotion, hope, or will (i.e., subjunctive mood) here
invoked, evolves into a stable or "mechanized" time that secures the future tense. This,
he states, encouraged a move away from the middle to the future tense.

202. Ibid., 66–67 (emphasis added).

it is—even for us—in many cases a more easy and obvious procedure to assert something of the person who (or thing which)
undergoes a process and who is as a rule well known, than to
the power, being, entity or phenomenon which scientifically or
objectively speaking is the author or originator of the process.[203]

Such resistance to subjectivity is because ancient vocabulary often
attributes agency to influential powers, etc., that are often present within
objects, persons, and phenomena that are less personal or impersonal in
character. It is precisely this religious dimension that evades subjective
autonomy.[204] But, gradually Gonda notes that these impersonal verbs are
replaced by personal ones.[205] So not surprisingly he concludes,

that the former generation had preferred impersonal constructions must be due to factors of a cultural and psychological
character, of a change in "Weltanschauung" . . . and of the pene-
tration of a more rational, ego-, or rather, anthropocentric ideas,
of more pronounced feelings of human self-consciousness, of a
more complete realization of man's own position in the world
and of his power, influence and possibilities, of a decline of the
archaic belief in gods, demons and impersonal powers affecting
men and other begins with fear, panic, love, longing, sorrow,
pain, regret, hunger, thirst, of an increasing inclination to as-
cribe the manifestation of these feelings and sensations to internal processes rather than external powers.[206]

Following Gonda's appraisal, perhaps then the middle voice eludes
such simple explanations, which attempt to account for an agent in terms
of an immanent subjectivity, because at one time such phenomena were
conceived of in theurgic terms. This would be somewhat similar to Calvin Schrag's suggestion regarding human action, wherein the middle
voice, instead of destroying the subject (which he calls a postmodern
exaggeration),[207] or establishing identity as a "changeless substratum" (the
modern turn to the subject),[208] is meant to situate the subject in terms of

203. Gonda, "Reflections on the Indo-European Medium II," 180–81.

204. Ibid., 184–87.

205. Ibid., 189. He notes, "There is . . . an unmistakable tendency in many languages
to reduce, in the course of time, the number of impersonal verbs and to replace them by
personal expressions." See also, 192.

206. Ibid., 191–92.

207. Schrag, The Self after Postmodernity, 61.

208. Ibid., 53.

transcendence.[209] He notes, "The main challenge of sketching a portrait of the self after postmodernity is that of thinking our way through and beyond the protocols that divide the moderns and the postmoderns on the meaning and role of unity. A new perspective of transcendence can help us meet this challenge."[210] In Schrag's scheme the subject is

> neither a sovereign and autonomous self, whose self-constitu-
> tion remains impervious to any and all forces of alterity, nor a
> self caught within the constraints of heteronomy, determined by
> forces acting upon it. The self as the who of action lives between
> autonomy and heteronomy, active and reactive force, pure activ-
> ity and pure passivity. The grammatical voice of action is the
> middle voice, neither a sovereign active voice nor a subordinate
> passive voice.[211]

Schrag's "thought experiment"[212] is a step closer to this theological middle. Although, however successful his attempt to place the subject in the "middle" is, it still remains immanent or creaturely,[213] as his notion of

209. Ibid., 148.

210. Ibid., 127.

211. Ibid., 59.

212. Ibid., 110.

213. Ibid., 110–36. Schrag's description of transcendence is still immanent in that for Schrag transcendence occurs only within the realm of becoming (i.e., his is a sort of horizontal transcendence that moves forward within time). The self, at every moment, transcends what it is. He explicitly refers to this as "transcendence within immanence." But, then, he quite clearly goes on to explain that there is a mode of transcendence in classical theism that goes beyond the "intramundane" forms of transcendence (or tran-scendence in the weak sense), which he calls "metaphysical transcendence" (or tran-scendence in the strong sense), even if he is a bit too close to describing this in terms of Levinas's "radical exteriority." Nonetheless, in his reading of metaphysical transcen-dence, which he draws from the Christian Neo-Platonist tradition, transcendence "is understood as residing on the other side of the economies of human experience—and yet playing a role, and possibly a pivotal role, in the drama of self-constitution, in the attestation of the self as constituted in an through its relation to the radically transcen-dent" (114). He does not seem to be able to bring the two together (i.e., the in-and-beyond with strong transcendence), although he does clearly distinguish between the two in calling Sartre's account "purely horizontal" (117).

Schrag then goes on to make a case for strong transcendence following Kierkeg-aard's transcendence and repetition (117–18). He explicitly states the Kierkegaard does not oppose immanence and transcendence by referencing an incarnate transcendence, the absolute paradox (120–21 and 135–36). He writes, "The grammar of paradox, occa-sioned by the particularity of the incarnation of the divine in the human, the incursion of eternity into temporal and historical becoming, points beyond the economies of the culture-spheres, which remain beholden to the metaphors of production consumption, distribution and exchange. The semantics of self-understanding thus itself undergoes a

transcendence also tends to lapse into reflexivity.[214] Nonetheless, following Schrag, language should seek to avoid the two extremes of activity and passivity by eschewing finitude (i.e., without claiming an end, totality, identity, or synthesis).

More to the point and beyond Schrag, *poiēsis* proper is something not unlike that which Professor Robin Kirkpatrick constructs in his concluding remarks at a 2013 seminar in Jerusalem where he challenged theologians to be poets by evoking the middle voice.[215] The poem itself, he notes, is both active and passive. It must be passively received, while in its interpretation an active contribution is added to the life of the poem. Thus, according to Dante, it is more human to be understood, to be heard and sensed,

refiguration in the struggle of the self to understand itself in its moments of transcendence" (135). Overall, his use of Kierkegaard is accurate, although his own reason for employing Kierkegaard sounds too postmodern in the sense that he views Kierkegaard as trying to plunder an illegitimate classical theism. Without citing any classical theist whatsoever, Schrag states that the work of those indebted to Kierkegaard, "demonstrate[s] that the classical metaphysics of theism comes up lame in locating the source and dynamics of transcendence" (138). This sounds too Heideggarian. Instead, the way in which Schrag employs Kierkegaard to overcome modern and postmodern construals of the self is something that the theological tradition has always done, yet in a more profound way.

In the end, Schrag makes a case for gift exchange where he suggests that economic exchanges are indicative of a gift that arrives as "wholly other" in that it simply cannot be returned (utilizing Levinas's and Derrida's language), although it is mirrored in common economic practices. Love is to give and expect nothing in return. He then suggests that love is the hallmark of, and perhaps a way to unite, the diversity of religions. Again this talk of wholly other fails to think the true difference of being and beings as discussed. In this scheme immanence is seen as a lack of transcendence. This again is why Christianity conceives of creation as a gift that can be, and indeed is, reciprocated albeit asymmetrically by creation (most eminently in worship). For Christianity, since the original source from which the gift arrives is always already an economy of mutual exchange all of creation's asymmetrical immanent economic practices are analogously an asymmetrical return of this original gift. Regarding Schrag's pluralism, there is simply no other religion that talks of gift in these terms.

214. Ibid., 55–56. Ultimately, even his favorable reading of Kierkegaard does not suggest a notion of the self beyond couching the middle voice as a sort of self-action or reflexivity (e.g., 62–70). Against this, one might suggest that the subject is never the ground of its own immanent action. Theologically speaking, while one is morally responsible for one's own actions one simply cannot act without that which is fully actual. This aligns with something like Aquinas's notion of secondary causality as previously discussed.

215. Credit to Catherine Pickstock for pointing this out. Professor Kirkpatrick was generous enough to share his concluding remarks addressed to theologians at the Tantur Ecumenical Institute in Jerusalem held the 17th–28th June, 2013 at a seminar entitled "Dante's Theology." Most of the quotations that follow are drawn directly from his concluding remarks, while a few are from his cordial email exchange with the author: Robin Kirkpatrick, email message to author, "Middle Voice," August 7, 2013.

than to understand. Moreover, drawing on Dante, Kirkpatrick spoke of the middle voice in terms of the subjunctive mood, as a language of hope that is "simultaneously theological, liturgical, and imaginative." The middle voice "woos the mind towards an infinity of as yet unrealized possibilities." Such language, as Dante employed it, would teeter between the modern and post-modern constrains of univocal and equivocal language, remaining situated "at the boundary of the sayable and unsayable." Although, however alluring and mystifying such language may be, it would be "utterly reprehensible if a poet, when asked, could not say what he meant by the words he has employed." Explicitly remarking on the *cataphatic* and *apophatic* nature of such language Kirkpatrick reminds one that this type of language should arrive at no final conclusion. He follows de Lubac and wants to avoid totalization or dialectic and, instead, embrace paradox, which never arrives at idolatrous conclusions, but demands continued "patience" and attentiveness. If we were to relinquish the

> paradox and the absolute beyondness of our Creator we are likely to set out to breach those limits, on the crazy assumption that transcendence can be possessed and grasped in complete experience. In a word, we shall forget that limit actually is a condition of our particular existence, not as a restriction but as the shape and design of our particularity.[216]

For the poetic theologian, "truth," thus, remains open, it is seen not as a "conclusion" at which one arrives, but as an "event" that resists closure. The secular mind, he says, "seeks to possess the world—in the mentality of a kind of perpetual gap year—and thus gets caught in a double bind rather than a patient paradox. It imprisons itself in its own rather blurry photographs of nighttime [*sic*] in Khatmandu." Instead, "the purpose of theology . . . is to enrich the vocabulary in which we engage with other lives and enhance the communion of existence," an active and passive participation in the absolute gift of the I Am. He even refers to Coleridge's "Aeolian Harp" as an image of such inspired oration.

More than any other contemporary theologian, it is Catherine Pickstock to whom this final proposal is most indebted. While her *After Writing* at all times intimates such language, her work on Plato provides a unique reading of this middle or rather liturgical voice.[217] The "Socratic gaze," she

216. Ibid.

217. In her, "The Late Arrival of Language," Pickstock offers a reading of Plato's account of recollection that outflanks the Kantian innate ideas. For Plato, it is not so much about innate knowledge conceived in terms of mimesis. Pickstock reads Socrates as critiquing the represenationalist theory of language, what she calls a "dumb-show

states, "hovers between activity and passivity."[218] Regarding Plato, "one could say that for him speaking is fundamentally 'in the middle voice'; it is willed and active, volunteered and intended, and yet also passively received."[219] Like Gonda, her reading of the Greek middle voice indicates that "there is some evidence to suggest that its use was . . . to express the mediation of divine by human action."[220] Her theurgic appraisal points towards "a theological order genuinely spoken in the middle voice, an wholly other mode that authentically outwits the shuttling between the action and passion of the secular order."[221] Instead, one is driven by a desire that is both "intended and yet arrives, as it were, from without . . . language is both active and passive, and the very fabrication of language is something oracularly revealed. The existence of language must 'originally' have been the divine gift of the capacity to speak, the capacity to make up words."[222] Indeed, "all language," for

---

mimetic language." Language "is never a matter of mere representational copying or of theoretical labeling or classifying—which Socrates associates with the sophist . . . [but] like reality, is a matter of generation and non-identical repetition . . ." (246). On the other hand she notes that, "were a copy a perfect copy, it would no longer be a copy, since it would be identical with the original" (251). This she claims would be to overlook the religious and mysterious dimension (mediation) in Plato, who maintains "an obscure pre-understanding of the unknown . . . a philosophically irreducible *aporia* which can only be religiously resolved in terms of the myths of pre-existence of the soul and recollection of this estate" (240). Instead, Plato's theory of recollection is one of "desire" which she, not unlike Kirkpatrick, describes in terms of a "subjunctive emotional dimension for cognition" that makes possible objective knowledge. "Desire," she states, "mediates the cognitive tension between the unknown, which one seeks to know, and fully realised understanding" (238). In this way, knowledge somehow contains a pre-understanding in the desire to know (239).

218. Pickstock, *After Writing*, 32. She juxtaposes the philosophical gaze that is subordinate to its object to the sophistic gaze that manipulates its object.

219. Pickstock, "The Late Arrival of Language," 245.

220. Pickstock, *After Writing*, 35–42. Pickstock argues that in Plato there are intimations of a doxology in the form of poetry; that is, a certain liturgical poetry (39). Pickstock concludes that, "Socrates's indictment of the poets is therefore *not* a condemnation of poetry as such, but rather of the separation of language from doxology, of art from liturgy, resulting in a sophistic 'virtual reality,' or a realm of mere fiction which is manipulable, ironic, and uninhabited" (42).

For Pickstock's theological description of the middle voice see note 8 on page 105, wherein she writes, the middle voice is meant "to denote the way in which God can act in and through a subject but without denying the subject freedom, and to describe the way in which action under grace is neither active nor passive in voice." She also critiques Heidegger here for not actually having a middle voice, but always either active or passive, which is similar to the earlier critique of Heidegger in this essay.

221. Ibid., 112.

222. Pickstock, "The Late Arrival of Language," 254.

Plato, is "a kind of poetry, divinely inspired, which discloses being . . . ."[223] This is why naming for Plato must remain true to reality, always guided by the Good.[224] Each name points beyond itself to that which it intimates, and beyond that, to the highest realities.[225]

In analyzing the middle voice one always runs the danger of formalization, to bring it within philosophy's finite grasp. To do so would be to reduce it to something conceivable, which like analogy, is precisely what one should seek to avoid. As such, its mystery should remain just that, a mystery. Following Kirkpatrick, to conceptualize the middle voice should be to grasp, yet never completely comprehend it. There are also ethical questions that ought to be considered.[226]

Finally, while biblical scholarship on the middle voice is philosophically lacking, it is unquestionably biblical.[227] The middle voice is ubiquitous

223. Ibid., 249.

224. Ibid., 250.

225. Ibid., 255–56.

226. There are of course crucial ethical implications that required consideration. If action arrives in the middle, with whom does moral and/or ethical culpability lie? In brief, the middle voice still allows for culpability precisely because it wants to uphold the activity of the subject. In this way, it may serve to suspend the dialectic of a passive determinism and the arbitrary "choice" of the autonomous active subject.

227. Wallace, *The Basics of New Testament Syntax*, 182–86. Wallace defines the middle voice as when, "the subject *performs* or *experiences the action* expressed by the verb in such a way that *emphasizes the subject's participation*. It may be said the subject acts 'with a vested interest.'" He breaks down the NT usage of the middle voice into four categories: 1. Direct, which is essentially reflexive (where the verb indicates the self as a direct object). 2. Indirect, which is one of the more common usages, whereby the subject acts for or by himself or in his own interest. 3. Permissive, which is when the subject allows something to be done for or to himself, which tends to lapse into a passive translation. 4. Deponent, which is the most common usage of the middle voice regarded as a verb that "has no active *form* but is active in *meaning*." He states, "English (as well as other modern Indo-European languages) has few analogies, making analysis of this phenomenon particularly difficult."

Regarding (3) the Permissive category, it was suggested earlier in the essay why this might lapse into a passive translation. Regarding (4) the Deponent category, it was also suggested why one might assume that a verb, which "has no active form," could, according to an immanentized vision of language, only be described as being "active in meaning" or, as Wallace alternatively describes it, "evidently active." Again, this line of thinking demands that middle verbs like ἔρχομαι ("I go") in the Greek NT, which do not have a "force," must be understood as either as active or reflexive. But one only needs to revert to this when agency is immanentized as previously argued, whereas a participatory middle could perhaps better accommodate such biblical language (e.g., the middle form of ἔρχομαι ("I go") might indicate something like, "in being moved by God, I go." Such consciousness would be of a piece with Paul's participatory utterance to the Athenian philosophers, "for in him we live and move and exist . . ." (Acts 17:28). Herein, coincidentally, Luke moves from an active ("live"), to a passive ("move") and back

in New Testament literature. Indeed, even if it is not always located by textual markers the language of Jesus and Paul clearly represents a first-century Christian consciousness consumed by the middle voice. It is difficult to make since of New Testament discourse otherwise.

John's Gospel depicts Jesus's divine Sonship, his unity with the Father, and the unity of the ecclesial body, in a middle voice consciousness. Jesus's acts are those of the Father: "Therefore Jesus answered and was saying to them, 'Truly, truly, I say to you, the Son can do nothing of himself, unless it is something he sees the Father doing; for whatever the Father does, these things the Son also does in like manner'" (John 5:18). In his prayer in the presence of the disciples Jesus says to the father, "Glorify your Son, that your Son may glorify you" (John 17:1). He continues, "For I gave them the words you gave me . . . " (John 17:8), and he goes on to say, "All I have is yours, and all you have is mine" (John 17:10). "As you sent me into the world, I have sent them into the world. For them I sanctify myself, that they too may be truly sanctified" (John 17:18–9). And finally,

> . . . that all of them may be one, Father, just as you are in me and I am in you. May they also be in us so that the world may believe that you have sent me. I have given them the glory that you gave me, that they may be one as we are one—I in them and you in me—so that they may be brought to complete unity. Then the world will know that you sent me and have loved them even as you have loved me. Father, I want those you have given me to be with me where I am, and to see my glory, the glory you have given me because you loved me before the creation of the world. Righteous Father, though the world does not know you, I know you, and they know that you have sent me. I have made you known to them, and will continue to make you known in order that the love you have for me may be in them and that I myself may be in them (John 17:21–5).

One finds this same language employed by Paul who constantly describes union with Christ employing the preposition "in" (*en* in Greek). He says, "I have been crucified with Christ; and it is no longer I who live, but Christ lives in me; and the life which I now live in the flesh I live by faith in the Son of God, who loved me and gave himself up for me" (Gal 2:20). Elsewhere he states, "I can do all things through him who strengthens me" (Phil 4:13). He implores, "Or do you not know that your body is a temple of

---

to an active ("have our being"). One could argue here that Gonda's findings offer a compelling remedy to such middle voice confusion. To introduce differences in worldviews may be a welcomed supplement where linguistic analyses fall short.

the Holy Spirit who is in you, whom you have from God, and that you are not your own? For you have been bought with a price . . ." (1 Cor 6:19–20). He says, "for if we live, we live for the Lord, or if we die, we die for the Lord; therefore whether we live or die, we are the Lord's" (Rom 14:8). He writes, "To the church of God which is at Corinth, to those who have been sanctified in Christ Jesus" (1 Cor 1:2). In an additional letter to the Corinthians he tells them, "He made him who knew no sin, to be sin on our behalf, so that we might become the righteousness of God in him" (2 Cor 5:21). In his letter to the church at Philippi he urges them to "work out your salvation with fear and trembling; for it is God who is at work in you, both to will and to work for his good pleasure" (Phil 2:12–3). Paul also employs a language of middle voice to describe his own participatory relationship in Christ: "But by the grace of God I am what I am, and his grace toward me did not prove vain; but I labored even more than all of them, yet not I, but the grace of God with me" (1 Cor 15:10). Although there is evidence that in *Koine* Greek this ancient function of the middle voice may have partially disappeared,[228] one discovers that in the New Testament the middle voice is often use for verbs such as pray, fast, and prostrate, evoking the participatory nature of such actions.[229] Indeed, in the New Testament both Jesus and Paul's language is couched in the middle voice consciousness here suggested.

There is also more to be considered regarding the implications for modern hermeneutics, which, having sloughed off the middle voice leaving only the active and passive voice, may have altered the biblical worldview in order that it might align with later languages.[230] Some questions for further reflection might be: in failing to recognize the inherent middle voice consciousness of early Christendom, has modern biblical scholarship promoted unnecessary dualisms that dominate contemporary lay church and arm-chair theological rhetoric (e.g., nature/grace, free-will/predestination, faith/reason, God/creation, real/mystical, prosaic/poetic, secular/Christian, etc.)? Is this why Christianity has become so strange to a church culture whose pulpits are expunged of this middle realm? In such cases, has the mystery of kingdom of God been reduced to univocal dogmatic

228. Gonda, "Reflections on the Indo-European Medium I," 41.

229. Credit to Catherine Pickstock for pointing this out.

230. One significant work done on the hermeneutical implications of the middle voice is Eberhard, *The Middle Voice in Gadamer's Hermeneutics.* See, specifically, the section of chapter 5 titled, "The Mediality of Faith" and the "Conclusion," 204–21. Therein, Eberhard describes faith as a "medial experience." Faith is something that stretches one to understand. He states that faith works in the believer, while, paradoxically, it is faith that one works. Hermeneutically then, he argues that for Gadamer language is something like faith, as something one is born into yet is stretched and learned as one employs it.

assertions? How might a change in our understanding of divine action affect analogously the way we lead others (no longer as top-down or bureaucratic, but in terms of a secondary causality by which God paradoxically orders creation to order itself)?

Regardless, it seems that a middle-voice theology as poetic metaphysics is the only possibility of maintaining the real revelation of Christ while upholding the mystery, which Paul speaks of paradoxically as "revealed," having "insight into," and "given," yet "unfathomable" and "surpassing knowledge" (Eph 3:11–9). After all, it is Jesus who Matthew tells us, "spoke to the crowds in parables. . . . He did not speak to them without a parable" (Matt 13:34). Jesus's disciples are said to know the mystery of the kingdom, yet they continually ask Jesus for clarification, who responds in a parabolic utterance. His continued use of parabolic language coupled with the incessant questioning of the disciples (those to whom the mystery had been revealed) and those around him (to whom it was not revealed) suggests that this mystery is never final. Even in the real grasping of the gospel, its mystery remains.

In bringing this brief analysis of the middle voice to a close, it seems that theology has something substantial to say about the absence of a causal agent in contemporary analyses of the middle voice. Immanentized discourse always-already assumes the subject as a ground, either active or passive. But if being is finite, open, participatory, poetic, a tension between subject and object, active and passive—as theology would have it—then a language capable of both admitting the limits of finitude and affirming its openness is medial. Pure philosophy, as argued, can at best admit (literally) this tension and accept the analogical nature of being. If it is ignored, philosophy can only speak of the real in terms of pure activity or pure passivity, which appears untenable. But, if one can speak at all of truth, then it seems subject and object must be analogically mediated. In such a scheme, the subject is resituated as more or less in the middle; that is, via participation in a transcendent God who is both in-and-beyond creation. In this way, theology saves language from devolving into meaninglessness.

In sum, a theology as poetic metaphysics that is faithful to Barfield's poetic philosophy invokes Kierkegaard's concept of non-identical repetition. It indicates that if language is not open to proper transcendence then one is left simply repeating the same thing (univocally). Oppositely, if this form of transcendence is not conceived of in terms of analogy then it yields an equally untenable equivocity. In either case, language is unintelligible. By contrast, theological language (i.e., *poiēsis* proper), by maintaining analogical mediation, allows for a speculative "forward movement" or progress. For a theology of poetic metaphysics, the subject is not a ground in oneself, nor paradoxically is the subject absolutely determined, for one's speech is by participation, one's naming and acting is a share in God who in his infinite act is the source of all being and hence meaning. Language, like being, thus arrives analogically; it repeats, or shares in, something known, albeit in a new creative way; it is never merely mimetic, it is rather like Barfield's blending of prosaic and poetic, lexical and speaker's meaning, it is always a, "slightly different thing that is said." As non-identical one recognizes it, yet it arrives as a surprise in which one delights. Such a poetic language is capable of delving further into the infinite mystery of the kingdom of God that is revealed yet mysterious; and this is one's *epektasis*, the everlasting "way" into the infinite "truth" that is found in the "life" of God (John 14:6).

This chapter attempted to baptize the philosophical opening observed in the tension between subject and object in a theological narrative whose "creaturely metaphysic" relates analogously to its Creator. In this vein, *poiēsis* proper was posed as an alternative to modern/postmodern discourse that is faithful to Barfield's poetic philosophy yet more thoroughly theological.

This was followed by a brief examination of the middle voice as it relates to the theological notion of transcendence. The chapter began by defining Barfield's poetic philosophy as: *reality is suspended in a polar tension between the prosaic and poetic poles*, and indicated that nearly all of his thought either explicitly or implicitly iterates this tension. Most basically, this definition expresses how Barfield employed language to make a case for his metaphysical realism against nominalism. Coincidently, when qualities (once taken to be ontologically real) were evacuated or relegated to the mind, the subject became the sole arbiter of meaning. Once this move is made inner subjectivized qualities must either be projected onto objects by an active subject or the object's outer appearance is represented in the mind of the passive subject. If quality and quantity, outer and inner, and active and passive remain trapped in such dualism, then the only language capable of speaking of this presumed reality would be objective; that is, bereft of qualities, measured, calculated, quantified, and mimetically reproducible, language in its most prosaic of form. But if Barfield is correct to claim that the rise of nominalism coincides with the rise of representational epistemologies, then a rediscovery of this realist aesthetic may again affirm supersensible realities that had been relegated to the mind. Indeed, if a realist metaphysic is most faithful to the symbolic world of finite being, then a language most capable of articulating such a reality would be poetic (one that holds subject and object in polar tension).

It was then suggested that the use of analogy in theological discourse absorbs and completes Barfield's poetic philosophy. By moving the discussion from the ideal/real distinction to that between the Creator/creature, theologians—speaking of being analogously (and employing a realist meta-physic)—cogently articulated the difference between God and creation. In expounding this difference, twentieth-century Catholic thinkers, building upon the Augustinian and Thomistic traditions, maintained that all of creation exists in a creaturely tension. Remaining consistent with its Latin formulations, the *analogia entis* spoke of an incommensurable tension be-tween something's essence and its existence, and when contextualized in late modernity this formulation, not unlike Barfield, affirmed the irresolv-able creaturely tension between subject and object and active and passive. Like Barfield's critique of scientific objectivity, the *analogia entis* was meant to guard against idolatry, of thinking one could have a totalizable or abso-lutized vision; a vision that according to theologians is afforded solely to the infinite Creator, while the creature's finite tension forever remains one of oscillation in a striving forth (*epektasis*) towards its identity in God. In this way, analogical language is meant to be consistent with the very being in which creation shares. Because God is infinite, and the creature finite, theological language can indeed talk of God (*cataphatically*) (his good-ness, truth, and beauty), but because one is finite one must also speak in a language that acknowledges that because God is infinite, one paradoxically grasps nothing of Him (*apophatically*). Holding to the Fourth Lateran for-mulation, the task of theology is then to non-identically repeat "whatever similarity there may be between the creature and God, the dissimilarity is always greater." This affirms that God is paradoxically in-and-beyond His creation. In this way, theologians moved beyond Barfield by speaking of being analogously. Mediated analogically, one's participation in being is a constant reminder of one's finitude.

The final subsection of this chapter envisaged *poiēsis* in terms of a the-ology as poetic metaphysics, which was faithful to Barfield's work but more thoroughly theological, by conceiving of language in the middle voice. It was argued that when *poiēsis*, an inspired poetic language that combines the prosaic word with the imaginative poetic utterance, history and revelation, a non-identical repetition, is properly articulated it appears faithful to the biblical consciousness evident in Christ's words and in the Pauline language recorded in the New Testament. In this way, this chapter brings to close the overarching premise which sought to underscore that even in the attempt to wrest itself from theology, philosophy, in its failure to close being's openness (to secure a secular space), as seen in its passive and active dialectic, points all along to that "creaturely tension" which theology calls finitude. In light of this post-secular vision, it seems increasingly apparent that philosophy ought not to go on ignoring this crucial theological difference.

Concluding Remarks

To rehearse, this essay utilized the work of Owen Barfield to construct a notion of *poiēsis* that culminates in a theological vision. It presented Barfield's poetic philosophy (i.e., his attempt to wed poetic and philosophical language)—the central and most insightful theme in his thought—as a formidable alternative to those immanentized discourses predicated on nominalism (and representational epistemologies). To bring together poetry and philosophy, to hold the subject and object in polar tension, not only questions the presupposed integrity of immanence but also resituates accounts of subjectivity that bracket the theological. Barfield's subtle gesture outflanks both modern and postmodern attempts to ground the subject—which inevitably result in a dialectic between pure activity and pure passivity, respectively—because he envisages discourse as mediated, in terms of inspiration, and thereby absorbs the opening often ignored by supposed secular discourses. A theology as poetic metaphysics intends to baptize the irresolvability of this supposed immanence, of which Barfield is aware, in a Christian theology of transcendence; a proper *poiēsis* of non-identical repetition saves both language and being from philosophy's univocal repetition and non-identical equivocity. But beyond Barfield, such theological language is analogical; that is, it conceives of creation's participation in God as a gift that constantly arrives and surprises us in our encounter with it. As creation evokes worship and praise, all of creation is thus properly conceived as the "finite longing for the infinite" God. And it is here, beyond philosophy's immanent dialect of active and passive, that one discovers theology's inexhaustible middle voice; an alternative that saves us from the idolatrous gaze that Barfield warned against time and time again.

In a roundabout way this essay draws upon the work of Barfield to suggest that perhaps the solution to philosophy's irresolution lies in a redis-covery of (a "half-turn back to")[1] the rich theological tradition prior to the dawn of nominalism. Reflecting upon this tradition in our present context

---

1. Milbank, "Postmodern Critical Augustinianism." See, response 4.

is challenging, in part due to what has resulted in either the blurred relation-ship between philosophy and theology or the utter separation of the two (not to mention the various other resultant dualisms hitherto cited either implicitly or explicitly), a relationship that has, as of late, come to the fore of theological and philosophical dialogue, and for which this attempt to construct a theology as poetic metaphysics has hopefully proffered some helpful suggestions.

In the end, Barfield's prophetic emphasis on the participatory nature of language insists that one remains within language, and, as such, one will never have a totalizing gaze of reality.[2] His warnings against idolatry serve as a reminder of our finitude, while paradoxically his poetic philosophy ad-mits of our real, albeit co-operative participation in the divine life. Barfield's work not only unsettles our epistemological assumptions and aesthetic un-derstandings but also our practices. In a time when we have become less conscious of the gift of creation his poetic philosophy goes far to reshape our relationship to one another and to the natural world. He challenges us not just to think, but also to "live" and "make" poetically, to work with and not against one's neighbor and the natural environment. Lastly, what is most significant about his poetic philosophy is that it is genuinely post-secular; that is, it leads one to the theological conclusion that what we *know*, what we *say*, what we *do*, and who we *are* is always-already a gift, and, as such, we should do well to reciprocate it with the same generosity and love in which it "was, and is and is to" (Rev 1:8) be given, which is our "economic" participation in a transcendent love that is always-already "immanent" and inexhaustibly replete in the Trinitarian God who is the mutual sharing of Father, Son, and Spirit . . . .

2. In this way, Barfield's emphasis on language is reminiscent of Johann Georg Hamann. For a work on the theological implications of Hamman see, Betz, *After Enlightenment*.

Bibliography

Adey, Lionel. *C. S. Lewis' Great War with Owen Barfield*. Wellington, NZ: University of Victoria Press, 1979.

Ardley, Gavin. *Aquinas and Kant: the Foundations of the Modern Sciences*. London: Longmans, 1950.

Alexiadou, Artemis, and Edit Doron. "The Syntactic Construction of Two Non-Active Voices: Passive and Middle." *Journal of Linguistics* 48.1 (2012) 1–34.

Aquinas, Saint Thomas. *Commentary on Aristotle's Metaphysics*. Translated by J. R. Blackwell et al. New Haven: Yale University Press, 1963.

———. *Compendium of Theology*. Oxford: Oxford University Press, 2009.

———. *The Summa Theologica of Thomas Aquinas*. Literally translated by Fathers of the English Dominican Province. 2nd ed. 10 vols. London: Burns, Oates, and Washbourne, 1920–22.

Aristotle. *The Complete Works of Aristotle: The Revised Oxford Translation, vol. 2*. Princeton: Princeton University Press, 1984.

Ashton, Rosemary. *The German Idea: Four English Writers and the Reception of German Thought, 1800–1860*. Cambridge: Cambridge University Press, 1980.

Balthasar, Hans Urs von. *Theo-Logic: Theological Logical Theory, vol. I "Truth of the World."* San Francisco: Ignatius, 2000.

———. *Theo-Logic: Theological Logical Theory, vol. II "Truth of God."* San Francisco: Ignatius, 2000.

Barbeau, Jeffrey. *Coleridge's Assertion of Religion: Essays on the Opus Maximum*. Leuven: Peeters, 2006.

Barfield, Owen. "Coleridge Collected." *Encounter* 35 (1970) 74–83.

———. "The Coming Trauma of Materialism." In *The Rediscovery of Meaning and Other Essays*, 187–200. Middletown, CT: Wesleyan University Press, 1985.

———. "The Concept of Revelation." *Journal of the American Academy of Religion* 47.2 (1979) 221–33.

———. *Eager Spring*. Oxford: Barfield, 2008.

———. "Either: Or." In *Imagination and the Spirit: Essays in Literature and the Christian Faith Presented to Clyde S. Kilby*, 25–42. Grand Rapids: Eerdmans, 1971.

———. "Form in Art and Society." In *The Rediscovery of Meaning and Other Essays*, 217–27. Middletown, CT: Wesleyan University Press, 1985.

———. "A Giant in Those Days." *The Denver Quarterly* 11.1 (1976) 102–11.

———. "Giordano Bruno and the Survival of Learning." *The Drew Gateway: A Journal of Comment and Criticism* 42.3 (1972) 147–59.

———. "Goethe and Evolution." *The Listener* 42 (1949) 945–46.

———. "Greek Thought in English Words." In *Essays and Studies 1950*, collected for the English Association by G. Rostrevor Hamilton, vol. 3, 69–81. London: Murray, 1950.

———. "The Harp and the Camera." In *The Rediscovery of Meaning and Other Essays*, 65–78. Middletown, CT: Wesleyan University Press, 1985.

———. *History in English Words*. London: Faber and Faber, 1926.

———. *History, Guilt, and Habit*. Middletown, CT: Wesleyan University Press, 1979.

———. "Imagination and Inspiration." In *The Rediscovery of Meaning and Other Essays*, 111–29. Middletown, CT: Wesleyan University Press, 1985.

———. "Matter, Imagination, and Spirit." In *The Rediscovery of Meaning and Other Essays*, 143–54. Middletown, CT: Wesleyan University Press, 1985.

———. "The Meaning of 'Literal.'" In *The Rediscovery of Meaning and Other Essays*, 32–43. Middletown, CT: Wesleyan University Press, 1985.

———. "Meaning, Revelation and Tradition in Language and Religion." *The Missouri Review* 5.3 (1982) 117–28.

———. "The Nature of Meaning." *Seven: An Anglo-American Literary Review* 2 (1981) 32–43.

———. *Night Operation*. Oxford: Barfield, 2008.

———. "On C. S. Lewis and Anthroposophy." *The Golden Blade* (1976) 95–97.

———. *Owen Barfield on C. S. Lewis*. Middletown, CT: Wesleyan University Press, 1989.

———. Owen Barfield Papers. Department of Special Collections and Western Manuscripts, Bodleian Library, Oxford University.

———. "Participation and Isolation: A Fresh Light on Present Discontents." In *The Rediscovery of Meaning and Other Essays*, 201–16. Middletown, CT: Wesleyan University Press, 1985.

———. *Poetic Diction: A Study in Meaning*. London: Faber and Faber, 1968.

———. "The Psalms of David." In *The Rediscovery of Meaning and Other Essays*, 237–48. Middletown, CT: Wesleyan University Press, 1985.

———. "The Rediscovery of Allegory (II)." In *The Rediscovery of Meaning and Other Essays*, 101–10. Middletown, CT: Wesleyan University Press, 1985.

———. "The Rediscovery of Meaning." In *The Rediscovery of Meaning and Other Essays*, 11–21. Middletown, CT: Wesleyan University Press, 1985.

———. *The Rediscovery of Meaning, and Other Essays*. Middletown, CT: Wesleyan University Press, 1985.

———. "Review of *Coleridge as Philosopher* by John H. Muirhead." *The Criterion: A Quarterly Review* 10 (1931) 534–38.

———. "Romanticism and Anthroposophy." *Anthroposophy: A Quarterly Review of Spiritual Science* 1.1 (1926) 111–24.

———. *Romanticism Comes of Age*. London: Anthroposophical, 1944.

———. *The Rose on the Ash-Heap*. Oxford: Barfield, 2009.

———. *Saving the Appearances: A Study in Idolatry*. Middletown, CT: Wesleyan University Press, 1988.

———. "Science and Quality." In *The Rediscovery of Meaning and Other Essays*, 176–86. Middletown, CT: Wesleyan University Press, 1985.

———. "Self and Reality." In *The Rediscovery of Meaning and Other Essays*, 155–75. Middletown, CT: Wesleyan University Press, 1985.

———. *The Silver Trumpet*. Longmont, CO: Bookmakers Guild, 1986.

———. "The 'Son of God' and the 'Son of Man.'" In *The Rediscovery of Meaning and Other Essays*, 249–60. Middletown, CT: Wesleyan University Press, 1985.

———. *Speaker's Meaning*. Middletown, CT: Wesleyan University Press, 1967.

———. *Unancestral Voice*. London: Faber and Faber, 1965.

———. *What Coleridge Thought*. Oxford: Oxford University Press, 1972.

———. "Where Is Fancy Bread?" In *The Rediscovery of Meaning and Other Essays*, 79–92. Middletown, CT: Wesleyan University Press, 1985.

———. "Why Reincarnation?" *The Golden Blade* (1979) 33–43.

———. *Worlds Apart: A Dialogue of the 1960s*. London: Faber and Faber, 1963.

Barfield, Owen, et al. *A Barfield Sampler Poetry and Fiction*. Albany, NY: State University of New York, 1993.

Barfield, Owen, and G. B. Tennyson. *A Barfield Reader: Selections from the Writings of Owen Barfield*. Middletown, CT: Wesleyan University Press, 1999.

Barfield, Raymond. "Philosophy, Poetry, and Transcendence." PhD diss., Emory University, 2001.

Barth, Karl. *Church Dogmatics*, vol. 1.1. Edinburgh: T. & T. Clark, 1975.

Bechler, Zev. *Newton's Physics and the Conceptual Structure of the Scientific Revolution*, vol. 127, Boston Studies in the Philosophy of Science. Dordrecht: Kluwer Academic, 1991.

Berman, Morris. *The Reenchantment of the World*. Ithaca, NY: Cornell University Press, 1981.

Berry, Wendell. *The Unsettling of America: Culture & Agriculture*. Rev. ed. San Francisco: Sierra Club, 1996.

Betz, John R. "After Barth: A New Introduction to Erich Przywara's *Analogia Entis*." In *The Analogy of Being: Invention of the Antichrist Or the Wisdom of God?* 35–87. Grand Rapids: Eerdmans, 2010.

———. *After Enlightenment: The Post-Secular Vision of J. G. Hamann*. Oxford: Wiley-Blackwell, 2008.

———. "Beyond the Sublime: The Aesthetics of the Analogy of Being (Part One)." *Modern Theology* 21.3 (2005) 367–411.

———. "Beyond the Sublime: The Aesthetics of the Analogy of Being (Part Two)." *Modern Theology* 22.1 (2006) 1–50.

Bishop, Jeffrey P. *The Anticipatory Corpse: Medicine, Power, and the Care of the Dying*. Notre Dame, IN: University of Notre Dame Press, 2011.

Blake, William. *The Complete Poems*. London: Penguin, 1977.

Bode, Christoph. "Coleridge and Philosophy." In *The Oxford Handbook of Samuel Taylor Coleridge*, 588–619. Oxford: Oxford University Press, 2009.

Bohm, David. "Hidden Variables and the Implicate Order." In *Beyond Mechanism: The Universe in Recent Physics and Catholic Thought*, 144–56. Lanham, MD: University Press of America, 1986.

———. "Imagination, Fancy, Insight, and Reason in the Process of Thought." In *Evolution of Consciousness: Studies in Polarity*, edited by Shirley Sugerman, 51–68. Middletown, CT: Wesleyan University Press, 1976.

———. "Interview with Physicist David Bohm." (Parts 1–5) Film, 1989. Online: http://www.youtube.com/watch?v=SvyD2o7w24g.

Bohm, David, and Basil J. Hiley. *The Undivided Universe: An Ontological Interpretation of Quantum Theory*. London: Routledge, 1995.

Böhm, Ekkehard. "Unremitting Contest Between Physics and Philosophy." *The German Tribune,* June 12, 1988.

Bortoft, Henri. *The Wholeness of Nature: Goethe's Way of Science.* Edinburgh: Floris, 1996.

Braungart, Michael, and William McDonough. *Cradle to Cradle: Remaking the Way We Make Things.* New York: North Point, 2002.

Briggs, John C., and F. David Peat. *Looking Glass Universe: The Emerging Science of Wholeness.* London: Simon & Schuster, 1986.

Bub, Jeffrey. "The Entangled World: How Can It Be Like That?" In *Trinity and an Entangled World: Relationality in Physical Science and Theology,* 15–31. Grand Rapids: Eerdmans, 2010.

Burrell, David B. *Aquinas: God and Action.* London: Routledge and Kegan Paul, 1979.

Cavanaugh, William T. *Being Consumed: Economics and Christian Desire.* Grand Rapids: Eerdmans, 2008.

Cazeneuve, Jean. *Lucien Lévy-Bruhl.* Oxford: Blackwell & Mott, 1972.

Chesterton, G. K. *The Everlasting Man.* 1925. Reprint. Garden City, NY: Image, 1955.

———. *Orthodoxy.* London: Lane, 1908.

Clark, James Fulton. "The Sacred Word: An Introduction to Owen Barfield's Linguistic Epistemology." PhD diss., University of Denver, 1977.

Clarke, S. J. W. Norris. *The Creative Retrieval of Saint Thomas Aquinas: Essays in Thomistic Philosophy, New and Old.* 3rd ed. Bronx, NY: Fordham University Press, 2009.

———. *Explorations in Metaphysics: Being-God-Person.* 1st ed. Notre Dame, IN: University of Notre Dame Press, 1995.

Cobb Jr., John B. "Bohm's Contribution to Faith in Our Time." In *Beyond Mechanism: The Universe in Recent Physics and Catholic Thought,* 38–50. Lanham, MD: University Press of America, 1986.

Coleridge, Samuel Taylor. *Specimens of the Table Talk of the Late Samuel Taylor Coleridge.* New York: Harper & Brothers, 1835.

Cunningham, Conor. "Being Recalled: Life as Anamnesis." In *Transcendence and Immanence in the Work of Thomas Aquinas: A Collection of Studies Presented at the Third Conference of the Thomas Instituut te Utrecht,* edited by Harm Goris et al., 59–80. Leuven: Peeters, 2009.

———. *Darwin's Pious Idea: Why the Ultra-Darwinists and Creationists Both Get It Wrong.* Grand Rapids: Eerdmans, 2011.

De Certeau, Michel. *The Mystic Fable: Vol. 1: The Sixteenth and Seventeenth Centuries.* 2nd ed. Chicago: Chicago University Press, 1992.

De Laguna, Frederica. "Lévy-Bruhl's Contributions to the Study of Primitive Mentality." *The Philosophical Review* 49.5 (1940) 555–66.

De Lange, Simon Blaxland. *Owen Barfield: Romanticism Come of Age—A Biography.* Forest Row, UK: Temple Lodge, 2006.

De Lubac, Henri. *Corpus Mysticum: The Eucharist and the Church in the Middle Ages.* London, UK: SCM, 2006.

———. *The Mystery of the Supernatural.* New York: Crossroad, 1998.

De Nys, Martin J. "God, Creatures, and Relations: Revisiting Classical Theism." *The Journal of Religion* 81.4 (2001) 595–614.

Deason, Gary. "Reformation Theology and the Mechanistic Conception of Nature." In *God and Nature: Historical Essays on the Encounter Between Christianity and*

Science, edited by David C. Lindberg and Ronald L. Numbers, 167–91. Berkeley: University of California Press, 1986.

Deely, John. "The Absence of Analogy." *The Review of Metaphysics* 55.3 (2002) 521–50.

Deeny, Anna Christine. "Consciousness unto Itself: The Convergence of Poetry and Thought in Latin America and U.S. Literature." PhD diss., University of California, Berkeley, 2009.

Derrida, Jacques. *Speech and Phenomena: And Other Essays on Husserl's Theory of Signs.* Evanston, IL: Northwestern University Press, 1973.

Diener, Astrid. *The Role of Imagination in Culture and Society: Owen Barfield's Early Work.* Berlin: Galda & Wilch, 2002.

Dodds, Michael J. *The Unchanging God of Love: Thomas Aquinas and Contemporary Theology on Divine Immutability.* Washington, DC: Catholic University of America Press, 2008.

Dreyfus, Hubert L. "Heidegger on Gaining a Free Relation to Technology." In *Technology and the Politics of Knowledge*, edited by Andrew Feenberg and Alastair Hannay, 97–107. Bloomington, IN: Indiana University Press, 1995.

Dreyfus, Hubert L., and Mark A. Wrathall. *A Companion To Heidegger.* Oxford: Blackwell, 2005.

Dreyfus, Hubert L., and Charles Taylor. *Retrieving Realism.* Cambridge: Harvard University Press, 2015

Dupré, Louis. "On the Natural Desire of Seeing God." *Radical Orthodoxy: Theology, Philosophy, Politics* 1.1 & 2 (2012) 81–94.

———. *Passage to Modernity: An Essay in the Hermeneutics of Nature and Culture.* New Haven: Yale University Press, 1993.

———. "Transcendence and Immanence as Theological Categories." *Proceedings of the Catholic Theological Society* 31 (1976) 1–10.

Eberhard, Philippe. *The Middle Voice in Gadamer's Hermeneutics: A Basic Interpretation with Some Theological Implications.* Tübingen: Mohr Siebeck, 2004.

Engell, James. *The Collected Works of Samuel Taylor Coleridge, Vol. 7: Biographia Literaria.* Annotated ed. London: Routledge & Kegan Paul, 1983.

Evens, T. M. S. "On the Social Anthropology of Religion." *The Journal of Religion* 62.4 (1982) 376–91.

Feinendegen, Norbert, and Arend Smilde, eds. "The Great War of Owen Barfield and C. S. Lewis." *Inklings Studies Supplement* no 1. Oxford: C. S. Lewis Society, 2015.

Flieger, Verlyn. *Splintered Light: Logos and Language in Tolkien's World.* Kent, OH: Kent State University Press, 2002.

Frank, Manfred. *The Philosophical Foundations of Early German Romanticism.* Albany, NY: SUNY, 2004.

Freudenthal, Gideon. *Atom and Individual in the Age of Newton.* Boston Studies in the Philosophy of Science, vol. 88. Dordrecht: Reidel, 1986.

Fukuyama, Francis. *The Great Disruption: Human Nature and the Reconstitution of Social Order.* London: Profile, 1999.

Fulweiler, Howard W. "The Other Missing Link: Owen Barfield and the Scientific Imagination." *Renascence* 46.1 (1993) 39–54.

Funkenstein, Amos. *Theology and the Scientific Imagination from the Middle Ages to the Seventeenth Century.* Princeton: Princeton University Press, 1986.

Gadamer. *The Idea of the Good in Platonic-Aristotelian Philosophy.* New Haven: Yale University Press, 1986.

Gerson, Lloyd P. *Aristotle and Other Platonists*. New Edition. Ithaca, NY: Cornell University Press, 2006.

Gerth, H. H., and C. Wright Mills, eds. *Max Weber: Essays in Sociology*. New York: Oxford University Press, 1946.

Gill, Eric. *Christianity and the Machine Age*. London: The Sheldon, 1940.

Goethe, J. W. von. *Faust: Part I*. London: Penguin, 1988.

Gonda, J. "Reflections on the Indo-European Medium I." *Lingua* 9 (1961) 30–67.

———. "Reflections on the Indo-European Medium II." *Lingua* 9 (1961) 175–93.

Griffiths, Paul J., and Reinhard Hütter. *Reason and the Reasons of Faith*. London: T. & T. Clark, 2005.

Guardini, Romano. *Letters from Lake Como: Explorations in Technology and the Human Race*. Grand Rapids: Eerdmans, 1994.

Hanby, Michael. *No God, No Science?: Theology, Cosmology, Biology*. Oxford: Wiley-Blackwell, 2013.

Hannay, Alastair, and Gordon Daniel Marino. *The Cambridge Companion to Kierkegaard*. Cambridge: Cambridge University Press, 1998.

Harrison, Peter. *The Bible, Protestantism, and the Rise of Natural Science*. Cambridge: Cambridge University Press, 2001.

Hart, David Bentley. *The Beauty of the Infinite: The Aesthetics of Christian Truth*. Grand Rapids: Eerdmans, 2004.

———. *In the Aftermath: Provocations and Laments*. Grand Rapids: Eerdmans, 2009.

———. "The Offering of Names: Metaphysics, Nihilism, and Analogy." In *Reason and the Reasons of Faith*, edited by Paul J. Griffiths and Reinhard Hütter, 255–91. London: T. & T. Clark, 2005.

Harwood, A. C. *The Faithful Thinker*. London: Hodder & Stoughton, 1961.

Hedley, Douglas. "Coleridge as a Theologian." In *The Oxford Handbook of Samuel Taylor Coleridge*, 473–97. Oxford: Oxford University Press, 2012.

———. *Coleridge, Philosophy and Religion: Aids to Reflection and the Mirror of the Spirit*. Cambridge: Cambridge University Press, 2000.

Heidegger, Martin. *Being and Time*. Rev. ed. New York: Harper and Row, 1962.

———. *Introduction to Metaphysics*. New ed. New Haven: Yale University, 2000.

———. *On the Way to Language*. New York: Harper and Row, 1971.

———. *Poetry, Language, Thought*. New York: HarperCollins, 2001.

———. *The Question Concerning Technology, and Other Essays*. London: Garland, 1977.

Higgs, Eric. *Technology and the Good Life?* Chicago: University of Chicago Press, 2000.

Hiley, B. J. "David Joseph Bohm. 20 December 1917–27 October 1992." *Biographical Memoirs of Fellows of the Royal Society* 43 (1997) 107–31.

Hill, William J. "The Implicate World: God's Oneness with Mankind as Mediated Immediacy." In *Beyond Mechanism: The Universe in Recent Physics and Catholic Thought*, 78–98. Lanham, MD: University Press of America, 1986.

Hipolito, Terry A. "Owen Barfield's Poetic Diction." *Renascence* 46.1 (1993) 3–38.

Hocks, Richard A. "Novelty in Polarity to 'the Most Admitted Truths': Tradition and the Individual Talent in S. T. Coleridge and T. S. Eliot." In *Evolution of Consciousness: Studies in Polarity*, edited by Shirley Sugerman, 83–97. Middletown, CT: Wesleyan University Press, 1976.

———. "The 'Other' Postmodern Theorist: Owen Barfield's Concept of the Evolution of Consciousness." *Tradition and Discovery: The Polanyi Society Periodical* 18.1 (1992) 27–38.

Hoff, Johannes. *The Analogical Turn: Rethinking Modernity with Nicholas of Cusa.* Grand Rapids: Eerdmans, 2013.

———. "The Rise and Fall of the Kantian Paradigm of Modern Theology." In *The Grandeur of Reason*, edited by Conor Cunningham and Peter Candler, 167–96. London: SCM, 2009.

Illich, Ivan. *Tools for Conviviality.* London: Boyars, 1990.

Ingold, Tim. *Being Alive: Essays on Movement, Knowledge and Description.* London: Routledge, 2011.

———. *The Perception of the Environment: Essays on Livelihood, Dwelling and Skill.* London: Routledge, 2011.

Jenkins, Willis J. *Ecologies of Grace: Environmental Ethics and Christian Theology.* New York: Oxford University Press, 2008.

Jonas, Hans. *The Phenomenon of Life: Toward a Philosophical Biology.* Evanston, IL: Northwestern University Press, 2001.

Jordan, Mark D. *Rewritten Theology: Aquinas After His Readers.* Oxford: Blackwell, 2006.

———. *Ordering Wisdom: Hierarchy of Philosophical Discourses in Aquinas.* Notre Dame, IN: University of Notre Dame Press, 1987.

Kant, Immanuel. *Critique of Judgment.* Indianapolis: Hackett, 1987.

Kemmer, Suzanne. *The Middle Voice.* Amsterdam: Benjamins, 1993.

Kern, Raimund. "Tolkien's 'Essay on Man': A Look at *Mythopoeia*." *Inklings: Jahrbuch für Literatur und Asthetik* 10 (1992) 221–39.

Kerr, Fergus. *After Aquinas: Versions of Thomism.* Oxford: Blackwell, 2002.

Kierkegaard, Søren. *Fear and Trembling/Repetition: Kierkegaard's Writings, vol. 6.* Princeton: Princeton University Press, 1983.

———. *Philosophical Fragments/Johannes Climacus: Kierkegaard's Writings, vol. 7.* Princeton: Princeton University Press, 1985.

Kimbriel, Samuel C. "Learning the Real: Realism and the Pedagogy of Encounter." *Notes et Documents,* January 2013, 36–42.

Kirk, Alan. "Karl Polanyi, Marshall Sahlins, and the Study of Ancient Social Relations." *Journal of Biblical Literature* 126.1 (2007) 182–91.

Kirkpatrick, Robin. "Middle Voice." Email to the author, August 7, 2013.

Lachman, Gary. *A Secret History of Consciousness.* Herndon, VA: Steiner, 2003.

Lakoff, George, and Mark Johnson. *Metaphors We Live By.* Chicago: University of Chicago Press, 1980.

Latour, Bruno. *We Have Never Been Modern.* Translated by Catherine Porter. Cambridge: Harvard University Press, 1993.

Leask, Nigel. *The Politics of Imagination in Coleridge's Critical Thought.* New York: Macmillan, 1988.

Lefebvre, Henri. *The Production of Space.* Oxford: Wiley-Blackwell, 1992.

Lévy-Bruhl, Lucien. "A Letter to E. E. Evans-Pritchard." *The British Journal of Sociology* 3.2 (1952) 117–23.

———. *Les carnets de Lévy-Bruhl.* Paris: Presses Universitaires de France, 1949.

———. *L'expérience mystique et les symboles chez les primitifs.* Paris: Alcan, 1938.

———. *The "Soul" of the Primitive.* Chicago: Regnery, 1971.

———. *Le surnaturel et la nature dans la mentalité primitive.* Paris: Presses Universitaires de France, 1963.

Lévy-Bruhl, Lucien, and Lilian Ada Clare. *Primitive Mentality*. London: Allen & Unwin, 1923.

Lewis, C. S. *The Abolition of Man*. San Francisco: HarperCollins, 2001.

———. *All My Road Before Me: The Diary of C. S. Lewis, 1922–1927*. Edited by Walter Hooper. San Diego: Harcourt Brace Jovanovich, 1991.

———. *Surprised by Joy: The Shape of My Early Life*. San Diego: Harcourt Brace Jovanovich, 1966.

Llewelyn, John. *Derrida on the Threshold of Sense*. New York: St. Martin's, 1986.

Lorand, Ruth. "Bergson's Conception of Art." *British Journal of Aesthetics* 39.4 (1999) 400–415.

Lotz, Christian. "From Nature to Culture? Diogenes and Philosophical Anthropology." *Human Studies* 28.1 (2005) 41–56.

Marion, Jean-Luc. "The Essential Incoherence of Descartes' Definition of Divinity." In *Essays on Descartes' Meditations*, edited by Amélie Rorty, 297–338. Berkeley: University of California Press, 1986.

Martin, Tiffany Brooke. "'For the Future': Consciousness, Fantasy, and Imagination in Owen Barfield's Fiction." PhD diss., Idaho State University, 2013.

Martinot, Steve. *Forms in the Abyss: A Philosophical Bridge between Sartre and Derrida*. Philadelphia: Temple University Press, 2006.

Mauss, Marcel. *The Gift: The Form and Reason for Exchange in Archaic Societies*. London: Routledge, 2002.

Mauss, Marcel, and Robert Brain. *A General Theory of Magic*. London: Routledge, 2001.

McInerny, Ralph M. *The Logic of Analogy: An Interpretation of St. Thomas*. The Hague: Nijhoff, 1961.

Milbank, John. *Being Reconciled: Ontology and Pardon*. London: Routledge, 2003.

———. "Can a Gift Be Given? Prolegomena to a Future Trinitarian Metaphysic." *Modern Theology* 11.1 (1995) 119–61.

———. "Christianity and Platonism in East and West." In *Divine Essence and Divine Energies: Ecumenical Reflections on the Presence of God in Eastern Orthodoxy*, edited by Constantinos Athanasopoulos and Christoph Schneider, 158–209. Cambridge: James Clarke, 2013.

———. "'Postmodern Critical Augustinianism': A Short Summa in Forty Two Responses to Unasked Questions." *Modern Theology* 7.3 (1991) 225–37.

———. *The Suspended Middle: Henri De Lubac and the Debate concerning The Supernatural*. Grand Rapids: Eerdmans, 2005.

———. *Theology and Social Theory: Beyond Secular Reason*. 2nd ed. Oxford: Wiley-Blackwell, 2006.

———. "The Thing That Is Given." *Archivio Di Filosofia* LXXIV.1–3 (2006) 503–39.

———. "The Ungiveable." Forthcoming.

———. *The Word Made Strange: Theology, Language, Culture*. Oxford: Wiley-Blackwell, 1997.

Milbank, John, and Catherine Pickstock. *Truth in Aquinas*. London: Routledge, 2000.

Miner, Robert C. *Truth in the Making: Creative Knowledge in Theology and Philosophy*. London: Routledge, 2003.

Mounce, H. O. "Understanding a Primitive Society." *Philosophy* 48.186 (1973) 347–62.

Muirhead, John H. *Coleridge as Philosopher*. London: Allen & Unwin, 1930.

Newton, Isaac. *The Principia: Mathematical Principles of Natural Philosophy.* 1687. Edited by Bernard Cohen and Anne Whitman. Berkeley, CA: University of California Press, 1999.

Northcott, Michael S. "Concept Art, Clones, and Co-creators: The Theology of Making." *Modern Theology* 21.2 (2005) 219–36.

———. *The Environment and Christian Ethics.* Cambridge: Cambridge University Press, 1996.

O'Donovan, Oliver. *Begotten Or Made? Human Procreation and Medical Technique.* Oxford: Clarendon, 1984.

Oliver, Simon. *Philosophy, God and Motion.* London: Routledge, 2005.

Ovitt, George. "The Cultural Context of Western Technology: Early Christian Attitudes toward Manual Labor." *Technology and Culture* 27.3 (1986) 477–500.

———. *The Restoration of Perfection.* New Brunswick: Rutgers University Press, 1989.

Pabst, Adrian. *Metaphysics: The Creation of Hierarchy.* Grand Rapids: Eerdmans, 2012.

Patterson, Richard G. "Philosophical Hermeneutics and the Nightmare of History." MA thesis, California State University, 2006.

Perez, Eloise Stauffer. "Coleridgean Polarity in the Poetry of Gerard Manley Hopkins." PhD diss., University of Southwestern Louisiana, 1991.

Perl, Eric D. "The Presence of the Paradigm: Immanence and Transcendence in Plato's Theory of Forms." *The Review of Metaphysics* 53.2 (1999) 339–62.

Peters, Jason Randall. "Owen Barfield and the Heritage of Coleridge." PhD diss., Michigan State University, 1994.

Pickstock, Catherine. *After Writing: On the Liturgical Consummation of Philosophy.* Oxford: Blackwell, 1998.

———. "The Late Arrival of Language: Word, Nature and the Divine in Plato's Cratylus." *Modern Theology* 27.2 (2011) 238–62.

Pieper, Josef. *Guide to Thomas Aquinas.* San Francisco: Ignatius, 1991.

———. *Leisure, the Basis of Culture.* London: Faber and Faber, 1952.

Placher, William Carl. *The Domestication of Transcendence: How Modern Thinking about God Went Wrong.* Louisville: Westminster John Knox, 1996.

Plato. *Plato: Complete Works.* Edited by John M. Cooper. Indianapolis: Hackett, 1997.

Polkinghorne, John. "The Demise of Democritus." In *Trinity and an Entangled World: Relationality in Physical Science and Theology,* 1–14. Grand Rapids: Eerdmans, 2010.

Pope John Paul II. *On Human Work [Laborem Exercens].* Boston: St. Paul Editions, 1981.

Postman, Neil. *Technopoly: The Surrender of Culture to Technology.* New York: Vintage, 1993.

Potts, Donna Louise. "Howard Nemerov and Objective Idealism: A Study in the Relationship between the Poetry of Howard Nemerov and the Philosophy of Owen Barfield." PhD diss., University of Missouri, Columbia, 1992.

Przywara, Erich. *Analogia Entis: Metaphysics: Original Structure and Universal Rhythm.* Grand Rapids: Eerdmans, 2013. (All citations are drawn from an earlier working manuscript of the translation by John R. Betz and David Bentley Hart.)

———. *Polarity: A German Catholic's Interpretation of Religion.* 1st ed. Oxford: Oxford University Press, 1935.

Quash, Ben. *Theology and the Drama of History.* Cambridge: Cambridge University Press, 2008.

Reilly, Robert James. *Romantic Religion: A Study of Owen Barfield, C. S. Lewis, Charles Williams and J. R. R. Tolkien.* 2nd ed. Great Barrington, MA: Lindisfarne, 2007.

Rossi, Paolo. *The Birth of Modern Science.* 1st ed. Oxford: Wiley-Blackwell, 2001.

Sahlins, Marshall. "Other Times, Other Customs: The Anthropology of History." *American Anthropologist* 85.3 (1983) 517–44.

———. *Stone Age Economics.* 2nd ed. London: Routledge, 2003.

———. *The Western Illusion of Human Nature: With Reflections on the Long History of Hierarchy, Equality and the Sublimation of Anarchy in the West, and . . . on Other Conceptions of the Human Condition.* Chicago: Prickly Paradigm, 2008.

———. "What Is Anthropological Enlightenment? Some Lessons of the Twentieth Century." *Annual Review of Anthropology* 28 (1999) i–xxiii.

Sallis, John. *Logic of Imagination: The Expanse of the Elemental.* Bloomington, IN: Indiana University Press, 2012.

Schaff, Philip, and Henry Wace, eds. *A Select Library of Nicene and Post-Nicene Fathers of the Christian Church, vol. 5: Gregory of Nyssa: Domatic Treatises, Etc.* Grand Rapids: Eerdmans, 1988.

Schalow, Frank. "Language and the Social Roots of Conscience: Heidegger's Less Traveled Path." *Human Studies* 21.2 (1998) 141–56.

Schindler, D. C. *The Perfection of Freedom: Schiller, Schelling, and Hegel between the Ancients and the Moderns.* Veritas. Eugene, OR: Cascade, 2012.

———. *Plato's Critique of Impure Reason: On Goodness and Truth in the Republic.* Washington, DC: Catholic University of America Press, 2008.

———. "Surprised by Truth: The Drama of Reason in Fundamental Theology." *Communio* 31 (2004) 587–611.

———. "What's the Difference? On the Metaphysics of Participation in a Christian Context." *The Saint Anselm Journal* 3.1 (2005) 1–27.

Schindler, David L. *Beyond Mechanism: The Universe in Recent Physics and Catholic Thought.* Lanham. MD: University Press of America, 1986.

Schrag, Professor Calvin O. *The Self after Postmodernity.* New Haven: Yale University Press, 1999.

Sclove, Richard E. *Democracy and Technology.* New York: Guilford, 1995.

Sennett, Richard. *The Craftsman.* New Haven: Yale University Press, 2008.

Simons, Thomas R. "Coleridge Beyond Kant and Hegel: Transcendent Aesthetics and the Dialectic Pentad." *Studies in Romanticism* 45.3 (2006) 465–81.

Smith, Wolfgang. *The Quantum Enigma: Finding the Hidden Key.* 3rd ed. San Rafael, CA: Sophia Perennis, 2005.

Soskice, Janet Martin. "Naming God: A Study in Faith and Reason." In *Reason and the Reasons of Faith,* 241–54. London: T. & T. Clark, 2005.

Spurr, David. "Myths of Anthropology: Eliot, Joyce, Lévy-Bruhl." *PMLA* 109.2 (1994) 266–80.

Steiner, Rudolf. *Occult Science: An Outline.* Forest Row, UK: Rudolf Steiner, 2005.

Sugerman, Shirley. "An Essay on Coleridge on Imagination." In *Evolution of Consciousness: Studies in Polarity,* edited by Shirley Sugerman, 189–203. Middletown, CT: Wesleyan University Press, 1976.

———. *Evolution of Consciousness: Studies in Polarity.* Middletown, CT: Wesleyan University Press, 1976.

Szerszynski, Bronislaw. *Nature, Technology and the Sacred.* Oxford: Wiley-Blackwell, 2005.

Talbot, Michael. *The Holographic Universe*. New York: HarperCollins, 1991.

Talbott, Stephen. *The Future Does Not Compute: Transcending the Machines in Our Midst*. Sebastopol, CA: O'Reilly Media, 1995.

Tanner, Kathryn. *God and Creation in Christian Theology: Tyranny or Empowerment?* Oxford: Blackwell, 1988.

Taylor, Charles. "Heidegger on Language." In *A Companion to Heidegger*, edited by Hubert L. Dreyfus and Mark A. Wrathall, 433–55. Oxford: Blackwell, 2007.

———. *Philosophical Arguments*. Cambridge: Harvard University Press, 1995.

———. *A Secular Age*. Cambridge: Belknap, 2007.

Te Velde, Rudi A. *Aquinas on God: The "Divine Science" of the Summa Theologiae*. Farnham, UK: Ashgate, 2006.

———. *Participation and Substantiality in Thomas Aquinas*. Leiden: Brill Academic, 1995.

Tolkien, J. R. R. *The Fellowship of the Ring*. New York: HarperCollins, 2007.

Venarde, Bruce L. *The Rule of Saint Benedict*. Cambridge: Harvard University Press, 2011.

Vigus, James. *Platonic Coleridge*. London: Modern Humanities Research Association, 2009.

Walker, Adrian. "'Original Wholeness.' (Living) Nature Between God and *Technê*." *Radical Orthodoxy: Theology, Philosophy, Politics* 1.1 & 2 (2012) 152–66.

Wall, Thomas Carl. *Radical Passivity: Lévinas, Blanchot, and Agamben*. Albany, NY: SUNY, 1999.

Wallace, Daniel B. *The Basics of New Testament Syntax: An Intermediate Greek Grammar*. Grand Rapids: Zondervan, 2000.

Warner, Sharon. *Experiencing the Knowing of Faith: An Epistemology of Religious Formation*. Lanham, MD: University Press of America, 2000.

White, Thomas J. *The Analogy of Being: Invention of the Antichrist Or the Wisdom of God?* Grand Rapids: Eerdmans, 2010.

Whittaker, E. T. "Aristotle, Newton, Einstein. I & II," *Science* 98.2542–43, September 1943, 17–24.

Winch, Peter. "Understanding a Primitive Society." *American Philosophical Quarterly* 1.4 (1964) 307–24.

Winter, Gibson. "Society and Morality: The French Tradition." *Review of Religious Research* 5.1 (1963) 11–21.

Wright, John H. "Cosmic and Human Evolution in Theological Perspective." In *Beyond Mechanism: The Universe in Recent Physics and Catholic Thought*, edited by David L. Schindler, 65–77. Lanham, MD: University Press of America, 1986.

Name/Subject Index

soul, 3, 24n25, 25n32 and 34, 26,
    33n80, 35n88, 60, 74, 78, 81,
    131, 133, 164, 194–5n10,
    197, 199, 212–14, 246n217
space–time; *see* Kant, space–time in
spatialization, 91, 93
Spinoza, Baruch, 72, 78, 217
spirit, 5, 10n19, 14, 22, 30, 33n80,
    36n99, 60, 86, 88n209,
    92n225, 95, 104, 110, 115,
    132, 164–65, 167–68, 177,
    180n328, 200, 201, 205,
    206n80, 207, 226n153,
    as Holy, 198n32, 249, 254
spiritual, 19n3, 20n5, 21–27, 32,
    51n179, 52n186, 76n130, 77,
    102, 110, 115, 120, 125n111,
    140n41, 149, 151, 154,
    155, 164–65, 168, 170, 176,
    186, 196n22, 199n36, 207,
    208n83
Steiner, Rudolf, 32, 33, 35–6, 56, 81,
    96–97, 130, 159, 161, 177,
    207
    Anthroposophy in, 20–26, 194,
    207
    evolution of consciousness in,
    10–11, 19–27
    influence on Barfield; *see*
    Barfield, Owen, reception
    of Steiner's evolution of
    consciousness
    occult in, 22, 25, 159
subject(s), 2, 4–6, 8–9, 10n19–20,
    11–15, 17–18, 25n32, 30–31,
    33–34, 36n99, 37–38, 40–42,
    44, 47, 49–51, 53–56, 58,
    61n18, 72–73, 75n116, 77,
    79–80, 84, 86, 89n216, 93,
    94n235, 95–97, 99–100,
    103–4, 110, 116–18, 122,
    130–31, 133–34, 136n19,
    140–41, 145, 156, 159,
    168n261, 169, 174–75, 179,
    181, 185–89, 192, 195–97,
    199–203, 204n75, 205–7,
    209n83, 210, 214n102,
    215–16, 218n121, 219,

229n162, 230, 231n170, 233,
    235–43, 244n214, 246n220,
    247n226–27, 247, 250–53
subjective (or subjectivity), 2, 3–5,
    11–15, 18, 30–31, 34, 36n99,
    39–42, 44–47, 49n166,
    50, 51n179, 53, 55–56, 58,
    61n18, 76, 79, 80n165,
    82–83, 86, 94–96, 97n250,
    100, 103n10, 110, 117–18,
    122–23, 134, 136n19,
    141n47, 156, 159, 169, 173,
    187, 192, 195, 199, 202,
    205–7, 208n83, 212n90, 215,
    219–20, 228, 231, 236–37,
    240–42, 251, 253
sublime, 12, 18, 47n164, 58, 61, 76,
    95n243, 192, 227
Sugerman, Shirley, 7, 55
supernatural, 104, 114, 119–20, 154,
    200, 206n78, 218n121, 228,
    230n164, 231n170, 232
    natural desire for, 220, 228
supersensible(s), 14, 22n10, 23–27,
    33, 81, 93, 97, 99, 110, 113,
    196n17, 207, 251
symbol(s) (or symbolic), 3n, 14,
    24n25, 30n57, 31–35, 55, 58,
    76, 80, 82–84, 97, 131, 141,
    165, 182, 197n24, 199–200,
    205, 207, 208–9n83, 251
Szerszynski, Bronislaw, 151
Talbott, Stephen L., 8, 97
Tanner, Kathryn, 183, 220
Taylor, Charles, 4, 41–43, 51, 53
technology (or technological),
    6, 8, 42, 45, 121n94, 126,
    127n126, 133, 136–65
    as *technê*; *see* making, human
teleology, 44n139, 110, 134, 137–39,
    150n110, 151, 162, 185
telos; *see* teleology
tension, 56, 62, 168, 204, 215n111,
    233n175, 236, 238, 250–52
    as polar, 5, 15, 18, 54, 84, 87–88,
    89n216, 91–96, 189, 192,
    235, 253

tension (*continued*)
  between essence and existence,
    217, 219, 224, 228, 231–32,
    234n178, 237, 252
  between God and Creation, 219,
    235, 237, 252
  between subject and object,
    55n204, 86, 95, 186, 192,
    219, 233, 239, 250–52
  theology, 2, 6, 38, 47n164, 56, 58,
    77–80, 89n216, 116n67,
    118n80, 122n100, 125n111–
    12, 136n16, 137, 140n37,
    151–54, 156, 158, 160n198,
    166n244, 176, 178, 191
  as culmination of philosophy,
    2, 10n20, 13–14, 15, 18,
    55n204, 56, 90n219, 98, 100,
    189–238, 253–54
  as middle voice, 5, 9, 14, 188,
    190, 235, 238–53
  as poetic metaphysics; *see poiēsis*
    proper
  as related to physics, 179–86
  as separate from philosophy,
    17, 52n186, 205–6, 208n83,
    226–29, 233–34, 253–54
theurgy (or theurgic), 201–2, 242,
  246
Tolkien, J. R. R., 1–2, 101
transcendence, 6, 13–14, 18, 37,
  51n185, 60n12, 69–70,
  77–78, 89n216, 91n222,
  92, 151, 182, 183n349, 185,
  190–91, 193, 209n84, 210,
  212, 239n192, 240, 243–45,
  250–51, 253
  as in–and–beyond immanence,
    13, 15, 55n204, 92, 98, 184,
    193, 206–7, 213, 215–38
  as opposed to immanence, 15,
    36, 58n6, 59, 60n12, 61–62,
    65–67, 69, 72–74, 77, 92,
    111n43, 116n66, 151–52,
    180, 190, 193, 197, 204–6,

    211n86, 214n100, 218n121,
    219n124, 226n153, 228,
    229n162, 243–44n213
tri-unity, 55, 208n82
Trinity, 55n206, 77, 195n15, 199,
  206n78, 207n82, 208n82,
  210, 212n90, 223n143, 232,
  234
unity, 2, 51, 82n176, 87, 89n216,
  90n219, 94, 148, 167–68,
  171n281, 175, 185, 192, 196,
  206n80, 210n54, 208n82,
  209n84, 210, 223n143,
  231–32, 237, 243, 248
Vico, Giambattista, 121
Vigus, James, 62, 74–77
voice (linguistic)
  as active, 9, 14, 238, 243, 249
  as middle, 9, 10n20, 14, 15,
    48–49, 190, 193, 194n8, 197,
    235–52
  as passive, 9, 14–15, 133, 238,
    243, 249
Walker, Adrian, 136
Warner, Sharon, 7–8
wave-particle(s), 173, 181
Weber, Max, 156
White Jr., Lynn, 153
whole (or wholeness), 7, 10n19,
  86, 92n225, 120–21, 134,
  135n11, 152, 167, 170,
  171n281, 172, 175–76, 179,
  181–82, 184, 233, 237
  as related to part, 91n224, 113,
    116n65, 121, 161n206, 167,
    173n298, 174, 199n36
will to power, 11, 37, 39n106
  and 112, 42n129, 45, 53,
    125n113, 205, 229n164, 236
Winch, Peter, 118, 121–22
Winter, Gibson, 112–13
work; *see* labor
worship; *see* liturgy
Wright, John H., 184